The Polish Solidarity Movement

This book provides a groundbreaking analysis of democratization in Poland by placing Solidarity in the context of the major democratic upheavals of modernity: the French and American Revolutions. Departing from case studies of Solidarity that treat the movement in isolation, this study undertakes the first full historical comparison of the Polish movement with the ideals and institutions of democracy achieved in the last centuries.

Arista Maria Cirtautas explains that the institutionalization of a strong democracy in Poland will ultimately depend upon whether the similarities to the great tradition of democratic revolutions outweigh the differences. Providing the historical and theoretical groundwork for the future comparative study of contemporary democratic movements, *The Polish Solidarity Movement* addresses the most vital and pressing questions about the underlying meaning of one of the most important social revolutions of our time.

Arista Maria Cirtautas is Assistant Professor in the Department of Government at Claremont McKenna College.

Routledge Studies of Societies in Transition

1. **The Economics of Soviet Break-up**
   Bert van Selm
2. **Institutional Barriers to Economic Development: Poland's Incomplete Transition**
   Edited by Jan Winiecki
3. **The Polish Solidarity Movement: Revolution, Democracy and Natural Rights**
   Arista Maria Cirtautas

The Polish Solidarity Movement

Revolution, democracy and natural rights

Arista Maria Cirtautas

Routledge
Taylor & Francis Group
LONDON AND NEW YORK

First published 1997
by Routledge
2 Park Square, Milton Park, Abingdon, Oxon, OX14 4RN

Simultaneously published in the USA and Canada
by Routledge
605 Third Avenue, New York, NY 10017

Routledge is an imprint of the Taylor & Francis Group, an informa business

Typeset in Times by Routledge

British Library Cataloguing in Publication Data
A catalogue record for this book is available from the British Library

Library of Congress Cataloguing in Publication Data
Cirtautas, Arista Maria.
The Polish solidarity movement: revolution, democracy and natural rights/Arista Maria Cirtautas.
p. cm. – (Routledge studies of societies in transition)
Includes bibliographical references and index.
1. civil rights – Poland. 2. Natural law. 3. Democracy – Poland. 4. NSZZ "Solidarność" (Labour organiszation) 5. Poland – Politics and government – 1980–1989. I. Title. II. Series.
JC599.P6C57 1996
340'.112 – dc21 97 – 5239 CIP

ISBN 13: 978-0-415-16940-0 (hbk)

Publisher's Note
The publisher has gone to great lengths to ensure the quality of this reprint but points out that some imperfections in the original may be apparent

For my teachers—

most especially for my parents and Ken Jowitt

Contents

Preface ix

Introduction: revolution, democracy and Solidarity 1
A Weberian alternative 15

1 **The charismatic presentation of natural rights: a Weberian theory of democracy** 21
The spirit of modern democracy 21
The will to freedom: the legitimating power of natural law 31
Democracy and charisma: the charismatic presentation of natural law 36
Reason and the institutionalization of rights 41

2 **Formal natural rights and the American Revolution** 52
Natural rights and the charismatic creation of citizens 53
Antecedents 55
The natural rights doctrine 57
Charismatic communities 62
Institutional consequences 67

3 **Substantive natural rights and the French Revolution** 75
Antecedents 78
The natural rights doctrine 82
Charismatic communities 88
Institutional consequences 93

4 **Natural rights and liberal capitalist development: an overview** 105
Revolutionary conditions 105
Origins of the free market 109

5 **The Marxist–Leninist response to natural rights and liberal capitalism** 133
Marx's critique of natural rights 135
Lenin's creation of a charismatic party 143
The institutional domains of Leninism 146
Poland: antecedents 153

6 Solidarity's articulation of natural rights 165
The natural rights doctrine 166
Charismatic communities 192

7 Solidarity and liberal capitalism 206
Solidarity's weaknesses: the failure to construct institutional domains 209
Solidarity's strengths: the impact on the domains of liberal capitalism 231

Epilogue: the Polish Revolution in comparative context 256

Notes 263
Bibliography 301
Index 313

Preface

One summer, in June, Solidarity demonstrators marched through the streets of Warsaw in support of the Gdańsk shipyard workers and in protest against a government that arrogantly refused to meet with union representatives. Some vandalism occurred during the protest as red paint was thrown on government buildings. In response, the government refused absolutely to talk with people who could perpetrate such acts of disrespect against the state. The year of this demonstration was, however, not 1979 or 1980, but 1996, and the government in question, while headed by the communist successor party, was now a democratically elected one. At the time, this government stood on the verge of closing down the Gdańsk shipyards, the birthplace of Solidarity, as the cost of subsidizing these and other unprofitable enterprises still in state hands was mounting. So the June demonstrators were marching for jobs and a secure work place, not for freedom and an independent trade union.

As the environment has changed since 1989, so too has Solidarity. Once an all-encompassing opposition movement, with a broad membership base reaching throughout Polish society, Solidarity has been reduced to a pure trade union organization with a declining membership limited mainly to the large, obsolete Leninist enterprises. Moreover, Solidarity has faced stiff competition from other trade unions seeking to represent workers' interests in the new conditions of a marketizing economy. It would accordingly be natural to conclude that, after the events of 1989, Solidarity has served its purpose as a vehicle of protest against the communist party–state, and has become a casualty of the necessary and desired transformation of Poland into a liberal capitalist country. In this context, a new study of the movement might not be necessary or warranted. Such a conclusion would, however, be premature.

In spite of the movement's decline, the relationship between Solidarity and democracy remains one of the pivotal aspects of the post-communist transition in Poland.[1] For if democracy, as a set of ideas and institutions, is to be the outcome of the processes under way in Poland, then Solidarity will have been the means to that end. In the three phases of Solidarity's existence from social movement to underground resistance to elected political leadership, on the one hand, and trade union, on the other hand, it has set the agenda for transformation in Poland. The ethical values of human dignity and worth, freedom and equality that Solidarity espoused have, from the very beginning, been inseparably linked to democracy as the ultimate expression of these values.

The linkage between democracy and Solidarity has, of course, not gone unnoticed in analyses of the movement. Much has already been written about the "glory days" of the movement; excellent work has been done by journalistic observers and by scholarly analysts alike.[2] By and large, the major focus of these works has been on in-depth analyses and/or descriptions of Solidarity alone. Consequently, there is room for an approach that places the movement in comparative historical and theoretical context. What does Solidarity have in common with the democratic revolutions of the past? What sets Solidarity apart from these revolutions? What is the exact nature of the relationship between 1789 and 1989? These would appear to be interesting and fruitful questions to guide comparative research.

For the most part, however, such historically oriented comparative studies of countries undergoing democratization have been discouraged. The exceptional character of contemporary efforts to move toward liberal capitalism is thought to preclude historical reference points. For example, Schmitter and Karl point out that:

> The new and fragile democracies that have sprung up since 1974 must live in "compressed time." They will not resemble the European democracies of the nineteenth and early twentieth centuries, and they cannot expect to acquire the multiple channels of representation in gradual historical progression as did most of their predecessors. A bewildering array of parties, interests, and movements will all simultaneously seek political influence in them, creating challenges to the polity that did not exist in earlier processes of democratization.[3]

Yet in the absence of historical comparisons, this exceptionality is simply assumed and not demonstrated. Only a comparative framework that is historically grounded can distinguish analytically between what is indeed exceptional and what is generally shared in the processes of democratization regardless of time and space.

In particular, what such a framework can demonstrate is that the need to legitimate democracy is the most significant shared aspect of all efforts to found and institutionalize modern democratic polities. Some analysts such as Przeworski deny that legitimacy, in the form of a "normative commitment to democracy,"[4] is necessary for the establishment of a democratic political order. By focusing on the pay-off structures that can induce critical factions of a political elite to accept, on instrumental grounds, the "institutionalized uncertainty" that defines democracy, it is possible to conceive of "democracy without democrats."[5] However, this reduction of democracy to proceduralism is an extrapolation from the procedural character of contemporary democracies. Yet the history of these very democracies demonstrates that the adherence to procedures, rules and positive laws itself needed to be legitimated beyond purely instrumental grounds. Natural law provided this legitimation. As Weber points out:

> Natural law is the sum total of all those norms which are valid independently of, and superior to, any positive law and which owe their dignity not to arbitrary enactment but, on the contrary provide the very legitimation for the binding force of positive law.[6]

Without such legitimation, positive laws and proceduralism can be readily contested and overturned on both instrumental and value-rational grounds as the pay-off structures change.

Modern democracy, as manifested in the American and French Revolutions, was originally articulated, animated and legitimated in terms of the natural rights doctrine. As the language of rights came to be held in common by both gentry and artisans; by both radical nobles and sans-culottes, this doctrine facilitated the formation of broad social coalitions supporting revolutionary change. Indeed, in the case of the American Revolution, Staughton Lynd maintains that the colonists developed the diffuse and often contradictory conceptions of natural rights prevalent during the era into a "coalition ideology" that promoted and justified a "new social coalition" for change.[7] That this social coalition was successfully able to overcome the status distinctions of the time in putting forward the "Cause of the People"[8] against hierarchy, privilege and the divine right of kings, can be explained by the lasting impact the doctrine of natural rights had on people's beliefs and conduct. By and large, this impact was achieved in the context of the charismatic communities that emerged during the revolutions. Communities such as the Sons of Liberty and the Jacobin clubs became the organizational vehicles for an enduring transformation of identity. Briefly put, subjects of varied rank became equal citizens, not just in rhetoric but in reality, as they met and deliberated on common ground, in a common language for a shared purpose. Subsequently, the essential characteristics of liberal capitalist democracy—citizenship, representative government, proceduralism and the free market—would be institutionalized on the basis of this transformation and legitimated by continued reference to rights deemed natural and inalienable.

By comparing Solidarity to other cases of democratic development, specifically the American and French Revolutions, it will be possible to ascertain the extent to which Solidarity either replicates or deviates from the historical pattern of liberal capitalist development. Such a comparative point of reference will enable a more precise understanding of the particular nature of the problems faced by Poland as a latecomer to democratic ideas and institutions. Through Solidarity, Poland may well have experienced a natural rights articulation comparable to that of the past "great revolutions," but the content and the context of this articulation manifest certain differences which have affected the consequences and outcomes. A theoretically informed comparatively based study of Solidarity should help us to understand exactly what these consequences entail for the future of democracy in Poland.

This book could not have been undertaken without the support and critical input of friends and colleagues both in Poland and at the University of California, Berkeley. Most especially I would like to thank Stephen Hanson, Krzysztof Jasiewicz and Edmund Mokrzycki for their patient and careful scrutiny of the various drafts. Words alone are inadequate to express my thanks to Ken Jowitt and Michael Rogin for overseeing this project when it was in its dissertation phase. They made this work both a pleasure and a challenge. While I bear full responsibility for any failings and shortcomings, I have no doubt that the quality of the final product has been greatly enhanced by all of these contributions. Finally, I would like to acknowledge the financial support of the Alexander von Humboldt Foundation, the International Research and Exchanges Board, and of the American Council of Learned Societies.

Introduction

Revolution, democracy and Solidarity

Have not the prayers of the humiliated been heard?
The bereft of their possessions, the slandered, the
murdered, the tortured behind barbed wire?

He broke the teeth from the jaw that devoured the
humble.
He overthrew the strong one who was to rule for
centuries.

Monuments of boastful theory lie between nettles.
Darkness descended on the infallible empire.[1]
(Czesław Miłosz)

Although relatively little time has passed, much has already been written and said about the significance of 1989, the "*annus mirabilis*" when communism collapsed in Eastern Europe.[2] Poets, philosophers, politicians and social scientists have all addressed the consequential aspects of this decisive year as, in the words of Daniel Chirot, "decades of slow political and economic change and development culminated in a series of unexpected, dramatic events that suddenly redefined the world."[3] While debates have emerged as to what the contours, parameters, problems and opportunities of this newly redefined world will be, there is a general consensus that, at the very least, East Europeans can now finally embark on a "return to Europe" after decades spent behind the Iron Curtain, and that the Cold War can finally be declared over.

This consensus over the outcomes of 1989 is, however, not matched by a consensus over the nature of 1989 itself. Do the events of this year constitute a revolution or can they better be understood as negotiated transfers of power from communist to non-communist elites? Are the post-1989 changes in the political, economic and social realms best analyzed as revolutionary institutional breaks with the past or as continuous, albeit radical, reforms? Can 1989 rightfully be compared to the historical cases of great revolutions or are essential revolutionary elements missing?

As Kumar points out, for those who advocate placing 1989 in a revolutionary context:

> 1789—the Great French Revolution—is a natural reference point. It is the year most commonly referred to by most East European participants (including Russian reformers), and by many western commentators as well. 1789 is almost impossible to avoid. Rightly or wrongly it has long been regarded as the symbolic starting point of the whole modern revolutionary tradition. Since that tradition is about the struggle for democracy, and since the 1989 revolutions were in the first place about democracy and human rights, it has seemed well-nigh inevitable that homage should be paid to the revolution that issued the Declaration of the Rights of Man and the Citizen and carried out the first real experiments in democracy in the modern world.[4]

Seen in this light, 1789 and 1989 represent a continuum of revolutionary development culminating in a triumph of the Enlightenment project, a triumph of the free market and civil society over the command economy, a triumph of liberal democracy over communism. Modernity and modernization theory, with which one could predict that the "dynamics of modernization" would ultimately render the communist version of forced modernization obsolete, have emerged victorious.[5]

Seen in a different light, one articulated most forcefully by Zygmunt Bauman, 1989 should instead be interpreted as the revolutionary endpoint of the Enlightenment project; a project characterized by "grand designs, unlimited social engineering, huge and bulky technology, total transformation of nature."[6] As this project was carried out even more radically under communism than under capitalist auspices, the end of communism represents the end of the Enlightenment and modernity writ large. Accordingly, Bauman maintains that "the events of 1989 in the East-Central European belt of satellite communist regimes was a most fitting finale for the twentieth century, bound to be recorded in history as the age of revolutions."[7] Indeed, for Bauman the events of 1989 represent an opportunity for us to update "our orthodox views of how revolutions come about and how they are conducted in a new sociocultural context."[8] In this "new sociocultural context" of postmodernity, characterized by Bauman as a "narcissistic culture of self-enhancement, self-enjoyment, instant gratification and life defined in terms of consumer styles,"[9] communism was undone as East Europeans experienced an "overwhelming desire to share (and to share immediately) in the delights of the postmodern world."[10] Not modernity, but postmodernity has triumphed.

Interestingly, analysts who share the view that 1989 does indeed represent a revolution, differ radically in their interpretations of that revolution. Given that these interpretations are derived by locating the events of 1989 in the context of existing theories, either supportive or critical of the Enlightenment project, the differences are perhaps not surprising. In this process, however, a sense of the specificity of the East European events tends to be lost because they have been used largely as confirming evidence for two well-articulated, yet highly abstract theoretical approaches to the study of modern revolutions. For other observers, it is precisely the specificities of 1989 that render these events problematic in analytical terms. The fact that 1989 took place largely without the "multiple features of the past's great revolutions: the vindictive violence, the class base, the charismatic vision, the faith in politics as an instrument of constructive change and the resistance of old powerholders to removal,"[11] is an indication that revolution may not be an appropriate analytical metaphor. To this list one might add the lack of revolutionary élan and sense of purpose in the populations of Eastern Europe. The euphoria of 1989 was extremely short-lived, replaced almost immediately by widespread apathy and disengagement from public life. In this context, it is worth noting that Miłosz begins the poem cited above with the following question:

> Why hasn't it risen, the powerful hymn?
> Of thanksgiving, of eternal glory?[12]

The lack of thanksgiving is perhaps an inevitable corollary of the fact that, unlike past revolutions, the events of 1989 were apparently not guided by a "totalistic, utopian vision rooted in eschatological expectations of a new type of society."[13] In order to give thanks, one must have faith in the future. Yet without a utopian vision to ameliorate the problems of the post-communist present, such faith is difficult to obtain, let alone sustain.

In the absence of many of the defining attributes of the great revolutions, alternative ways of understanding the events of 1989 have been developed. For example, Garton Ash has proposed the concept of "refolution" as a way of capturing both the rapid, radical nature of the changes *and* their negotiated qualities. Accordingly, he perceives 1989 in terms of "a mixture of reform and revolution" as "there was a strong and essential element of change 'from above,' " matched by "a vital element of popular pressure 'from below.' "[14] The ensuing interaction between "change from above" and "change from below" was "largely mediated by negotiations between ruling and opposition elites."[15]

Tilly echoes this analysis of 1989 as a mixture of revolutionary and non-revolutionary features when he answers the question: "[D]o Eastern European events of 1989 qualify as revolutions?" by stating that "[T]he question is not so pressing as it first seemed, since in each country the events of 1989–92 obviously had something revolutionary about them; how much is a matter of degree rather than kind."[16] It follows then, that in the place of the rather abstract determinations of whether 1989, as a whole, does or does not constitute a revolution, it is preferable to analyze each country separately to see where it can be located on a continuum from reform to revolution. Such a case oriented research agenda would appear to offer a reasonable solution to the problem of how to define and analyze the events of 1989 in terms that capture both their particular, unique aspects, and the general features they might yet share with revolutions that have emerged elsewhere in place and time.

Given Poland's undoubtedly significant role in precipitating the collapse of communism in Eastern Europe, a close analysis of this country is clearly indicated. After all, Poland pioneered the Round Table negotiations that brought the regime and the opposition together in a peaceful transition of power. Subsequently, Poland held the first legitimately contested elections in Eastern Europe and established the first non-communist government. Yet, do these undoubtedly unprecedented tasks constitute a revolution? According to Tilly, Poland did indeed experience a revolution in 1989, but it can be classified as only a "marginal" revolution.[17]

Although Poland does manifest a majority of the crucial revolutionary outcomes outlined by Tilly ("defection of polity members; neutralization or defection of the regime's armed force; control of the state apparatus by members of a revolutionary coalition"), the "revolutionary situation" in 1989 (defined briefly as "the appearance of contenders, or coalitions of contenders, advancing exclusive competing claims to control of the state or some segment of it; commitment to those claims by a significant segment of the citizenry; incapacity or unwillingness of rulers to suppress the alternative coalition and/or commitment to its claims") is "marginal."[18] Since, in Tilly's opinion, the "depth of the revolutionary situation" is less extensive in Poland than in Czechoslovakia and in East Germany where a "forcible transfer of power over a state in the course of which at least two distinct blocs of contenders made incompatible claims to control the state" can be identified, he maintains that Poland represents a less revolutionary case than its neighbors.[19]

This position is, however, untenable if one extends Tilly's very useful definition of what constitutes a revolutionary situation to the decade before 1989. The emergence of Solidarity in 1980–81 can readily be analyzed in terms of "multiple sovereignty," the "identifying feature of revolutionary situations." As Tilly elaborates:

> A revolutionary situation begins when a government previously under the control of a single, sovereign polity becomes the object of effective, competing, mutually exclusive claims on the part of two or more distinct polities. It ends when a single sovereign polity regains control over the government.[20]

Although Solidarity was a "self-limiting" movement in that it refused to contest formally the Party's control over the government, the very existence of a free and independent mass-based organization in the context of a monopolistic communist party–state constituted a situation of "multiple sovereignty." Moreover, Solidarity's emphasis on human rights, human dignity and democratic procedures created a "distinct polity" that contrasted vividly with the Party's corruption, hypocrisy and authoritarian practices.

Within the context of the movement, people managed to translate the miseries and pointlessness of everyday existence in the Poland of the 1970s into a meaningful experience by creating a collective consciousness based on the pursuit of human rights, worth and dignity. This consciousness was put into practice on the shop floors and in union meetings as Solidarity attempted to ameliorate the conditions of life for average Poles. Again, although Solidarity did not directly contest the Party's authority, the movement did demand control over critical aspects of the Party's functions such as the distribution of goods and positions.

The idea that people could participate in public life both efficaciously and ethically in the midst of even a corrupt and decaying polity proved to be an immensely powerful one. Ultimately, Solidarity had almost ten million members. As Jowitt points out, Solidarity did not just represent an "effective, competing, mutually exclusive claim" on the commitments and loyalties of its members, Solidarity embodied an entirely different way of life:

> If part of a Leninist Party's uniqueness rests in its political conflation of the state and public realms; in its effort to have the cadre fuse the roles of state official and citizen, then Solidarity's challenge is immediately apparent. Solidarity was more than a threat to Party power. Solidarity offered an opposing definition of political leadership and membership. It confronted the Party cadre with the national citizen. As a politically "self-limiting" movement, Solidarity was an organized public whose membership consisted of voluntarily associated individual citizens opposed to a hierarchical, corporate Party polity. Solidarity and the Party were mutually exclusive *ways of life*.[21]

Commitment to this new way of life was demonstrated not just during the period of Solidarity's legal existence, but even afterward during the underground years when substantial numbers of Poles continued to support the movement. According to Tilly, under the conditions of "multiple sovereignty . . . previously acquiescent people obey the alternative body" as they "pay taxes, provide men to its armies, feed its functionaries, honor its symbols, give time to its service, or yield other resources despite the prohibitions of a still-existing government they formerly obeyed."[22] This description certainly applies to the case of Poland throughout the 1980s as Poles provided financial support to Solidarity, fed and housed its "functionaries" even when they were hunted by the police, honored its symbols (for example, the slogan "*nie ma wolności bez solidarności*"—"no freedom without solidarity"—was prevalent at almost all strikes and protests), and, most significantly, donated time and resources, especially to the activities of the underground press.

Thus, even martial law did not end the situation of "multiple sovereignty." Indeed, one can argue that in spite of the Party's efforts to suppress Solidarity, these efforts were ineffective and half-hearted enough to constitute an additional cause for the prevalence of "multiple sovereignty," namely an "incapacity or unwillingness of the agents of the government to suppress the alternative coalition and/or the commitment to its claims."[23] Ultimately, by 1988, reform-minded members of the Party and the military were willing to negotiate a power sharing agreement with Solidarity as a way out of the stalemate created by the two polities.

Consequently, in 1989, the Polish Party and opposition did not face off on the basis of "incompatible claims to control the state," as occurred in East Germany and Czechoslovakia. This face-off had already taken place in 1981 with indeterminate results. Martial law had weakened both Solidarity and the Party to the extent that the emergence of a consensus shared by certain "established members of the polity and mobilizing nonmembers"[24] on the value of negotiations was made possible. The fact that the ensuing Round Table negotiations led to a peaceful, rather than violent, "displacement of one set of members of the polity by another set"[25] should not obscure the revolutionary quality of the situation that led up to this "displacement," nor should it cast doubt on the revolutionary nature of the outcomes. In this context, it is important to note that, unlike most definitions of revolution which are based on the violent overthrow of an existing government, Tilly's framework does allow for a broader interpretation of what constitutes a revolution.

In short, even this cursory application of Tilly's conceptualization of the two constituent components of a revolution demonstrates the degree to which Poland experienced a substantial, not marginal, revolutionary situation which, in turn, led to substantive revolutionary outcomes. Moreover, Solidarity also manifests many of the other attributes found in the "great revolutions." The ethos of Solidarity can be understood in terms of a "charismatic vision"; its emergence is analyzable in class terms and its leadership can be seen as a mobilized and committed "vanguard."

According to Michael Walzer's definition, which is directly derived from an examination of the "great revolutions," revolutions constitute "conscious attempts to establish a new moral and material world and to impose, or evoke, radically new patterns of day-to-day conduct."[26] These attempts are based on "a revolutionary class whose discontent provides the energy and whose members supply the manpower, and an intellectual vanguard that provides ideology and leadership."[27] As noted above, the people of Solidarity did indeed consciously attempt to establish "new patterns of day-to-day conduct" based on open and honest dialogue, democratic procedures of accountability and associative practices. This conduct was validated by a moral vision that emphasized the equal rights, worth and dignity of all participants. That these participants were working toward the eventual creation of a "self-governing republic," which was not far removed from past revolutionary goals of creating a "holy commonwealth, republic of virtue, communist society,"[28] provides a further point of comparison with the "great revolutions."

In addition, Poland's "revolutionary class" encompassed the communist equivalent of an upwardly aspiring, but ultimately frustrated, middle-class—namely, skilled workers, professionals and intellectuals.[29] The "vanguard" leadership of Solidarity that emerged, in part, from the dissident organization KOR, was comprised of both skilled workers and intellectuals—again functionally equivalent to the social composition of the vanguard, "middling and professional groups," outlined by Walzer.[30] Solidarity leaders as diverse as Michnik, an intellectual, and Wałęsa, a worker, manifest a similar "vanguard consciousness" of being "cut loose from the constraints of the old order."[31] As Walzer elaborates, revolutionary leaders are people who "give up conventional modes of existence, conventional families and jobs; they choose marginality; they endure persecution; they go into exile."[32] With the exception of the last characteristic, this description fits the members of KOR and later the leaders of Solidarity who were certainly willing to endure persecution in order to give up a "conventional mode of existence" rooted in fear, dissimulation and accommodation in favor of the "marginality" of living a life without lies; living a life "as if" one were truly free.[33]

Just as the principal actors of Solidarity can be placed in a revolutionary light, so too can the structural causes and consequences of the movement. According to Skocpol, "social revolutions are rapid, basic transformations of a society's state and class structures; and they are accompanied and in part carried through by class-based revolts from below."[34] Solidarity certainly represented a "class-based revolt from below." The irony of a largely working-class revolt against a workers' state has, of course, not gone unnoticed in analyses of Solidarity.[35] Although Skocpol identifies the peasantry as the crucial initiator of the class-based revolts that accompanied the French, Russian and Chinese Revolutions, it can be argued that, in the case of Poland, workers constituted a "resistant social community" and that Solidarity, therefore, represents a "functional substitute" for a classic peasant uprising.[36] Moreover, workers were subsequently joined by peasants who formed their own version of Solidarity as a vehicle of protest. Since these revolts accompanied the "breakdown of the state organizations of the old regime," both domestically as the Polish Party lost its ability to rule effectively, and later internationally as the Soviet Union withdrew its control over Eastern Europe, "basic changes in social structure and in political structure" were made possible.[37]

Accordingly, within a ten-year period, Poland experienced the "coincidence of societal structural change with class upheaval, and the coincidence of political with social transformation" that characterized the social revolutions in France, Russia and China.[38] Indeed, in Poland we have seen multiple social transformations as the changes in social structure that gave rise to Solidarity are now being superseded by the socioeconomic changes initiated since 1989. By the late 1970s, industrialization and urbanization, combined with demographic changes, had produced a large number of young, self-confident, educated, skilled workers who were demanding greater control over production processes. These demands were ultimately expressed in the form of Solidarity. This class is, however, currently embattled as free market reforms and changes in property relations designed to produce a capitalist middle class threaten its socioeconomic standing. In yet another irony, the class that made the revolution is now seen as a threat to the viability of liberal capitalist socioeconomic and political transformation. Structurally, this situation corresponds to the fate of the Russian peasants after the Russian Revolution. As Skocpol points out:

> Indeed, the great irony—and poignancy—of the Russian Revolution lies in the role and fate of the peasantry. For the peasants made their own thoroughgoing social revolution in 1917—and as a result became a threat to the viability of Russia as a revolutionized nation-state in a world of militarily competing nation-states.[39]

The extent to which the very different definitions of revolution developed by Tilly, Walzer and Skocpol can successfully be applied to the case of Poland and Solidarity, leads to the conclusion that for Poland, at least, the year 1989 does mark the culmination of a revolution that began a decade earlier. The question then becomes: What kind of revolution was it? Was it a modern democratic revolution in keeping with the historical traditions of the American and French Revolutions, or was it a national liberation revolution more in keeping with the traditions of 1848? While most analyses of Solidarity give greater weight to its democratic features, there are interpretations that stress the nationalistic and populistic components of the movement.[40] Reality, however, is likely to be messier than a pure reliance on analytical distinctions would have us believe. Doubtless, Solidarity comprised both democratic and nationalistic features, both liberal and populistic aspects. This mixture of varied, and often conflicting, ideological and institutional attributes does not, however, automatically set Solidarity apart from the American and French Revolutions. Both of these "great revolutions" manifested similar mixtures and tensions between conflicting ideological and organizational imperatives. Both revolutions have also left behind conflicting legacies as, for example, the radical (or social) democratic efforts to preserve social equality have clashed continuously with liberal democratic efforts to maintain the scope for individual freedom and free market entrepreneurship. Accordingly, there is no a priori reason to reject a comparison between the Polish, American and French Revolutions.

Indeed, it is my assumption that these three countries represent distinctive cases in which modern democracy was introduced into public life in the context of an indigenous revolutionary upheaval encompassing the social, political and economic realms. In other words, democracy did not evolve slowly via institutional reform in these countries, allowing for measured accommodation between traditional and modern institutions, and between rising and falling social groups. Nor was democracy resisted institutionally and ideologically as a foreign invention designed to produce nothing but political chaos and social fragmentation. Nor was democracy forcefully imposed in the wake of military defeat. Instead, in the American, French and Polish Revolutions, democracy was experienced, not as a threat, nor as an imported or imposed form of political life, but as a powerful and unique "experience of being free."[41] As Arendt points out:

> what the [American and French] revolutions brought to the fore was this experience of being free . . . and this relatively new experience, new to those at any rate who made it, was at the same time the experience of man's faculty to begin something new. These two things together—a new experience which revealed man's capacity for novelty—are at the root of the enormous pathos which we find in both the American and French Revolutions.[42]

The case of Poland's Solidarity, as well, "revealed man's capacity for novelty" as the movement provided participants with the new experience of creating a free and independent space in which principled public action could take place.

This creation, this manifestation of man's ability "to begin something new," both institutionally and ideologically, led to the demise of communist absolutism just as the American and French Revolutions ended the era of monarchical absolutism. By experiencing freedom in new ways, these revolutions produced ideological and institutional alternatives to absolute rule. While oppressive conditions will tend to be endured in the absence of alternatives, once a sense of new possibilities arises oppression becomes intolerable. Solidarity provided such a sense of new possibilities, not just for Poles, but also for other East Europeans who either attempted to replicate the movement's features or set out to supersede the movement by improving on it. To a large extent, therefore, the specific features of 1989—the commitment to non-violence, to negotiated settlements, to human rights—are due to the example set by Poland. Certainly, Gorbachev's withdrawal from the region created the structural conditions and determined the context within which change could take place. Solidarity, however, generated the model that influenced the form and direction of that change. Consequently, the American, French and Polish Revolutions can all be seen as pivotal "core" cases (to borrow Wallerstein's terminology) of democratic development that had significant impact not just domestically but also internationally.

While the "core" status of the American and French Revolutions for democratic development has been well documented and researched, the validity of including Poland in this rather exclusive grouping clearly needs to be justified beyond the level of the assertions made so far. To this end, a careful comparative study of these three cases is best suited for illuminating the extent to which Solidarity and the Polish Revolution can indeed lay claim to "world historical" significance. As Hermassi explains, "the world-historical character of revolutions means that they exert a demonstration effect beyond the boundaries of their country of origin, with a potential for triggering waves of revolution and counterrevolution both within and between societies."[43] However, for a revolution to have such an international "demonstration effect," the internal content of the revolution itself must be novel, compelling and consequential. Any analysis of a revolution's character must, therefore, begin with its internal characteristics. Accordingly, if it can be determined that Solidarity does in fact share many of the crucial characteristics of the American and French Revolutions, then the inclusion of Poland in this category will make more analytical, as opposed to simply rhetorical, sense. Moreover, the linkage between 1989 and 1789 that observers have, to date, postulated in only the most abstract of terms, will be placed on firmer, theoretically and empirically tested ground.

Comparative studies of revolution have, for the most part, been rooted in historical sociology and this work is no exception. Within the overall tradition of historical sociology, there are, however, numerous approaches or analytical frameworks to choose from. These approaches can be categorized according to the significance they attribute to the role of structures, interests and ideas in promoting and explaining revolutions. For example, Skocpol's highly influential comparative study of social revolutions is based on an analysis of "states in relation to social structures and international circumstances."[44] From this perspective, the structural interplay between the state and critical social groups, especially the peasantry, is of primary importance to the study of revolution. According to Skocpol, without an analysis of the "conjunctures of administrative-military breakdown and popularly based radical revolts,"[45] we cannot understand how and why revolutions occur. While the study of additional factors such as ideology and culture may enrich our understanding, "such research would not necessarily change the basic picture of the causes of social revolutions that has already been developed by scholars who have focused primarily on states in relation to social structures and international interests."[46] Skocpol also rejects the notion that class interest alone can account for revolutionary outcomes:

> [N]o single acting group, whether a class or an ideological vanguard, deliberately shapes the complex and multiply determined conflicts that bring about revolutionary crises and outcomes. The French Revolution was not made by a rising capitalist bourgeoisie or by the Jacobins; the Russian Revolution was not made by the industrial proletariat or even by the Bolshevik party. . . . Rather than seeking to ground the causes of social revolutions and their outcomes in hypostatized interests or outlooks, *States and Social Revolutions* focused on "structures" or patterned relationships beyond the manipulative control of any single group or individual. Such social structures, understood in historically concrete ways, give us the key to the conflicts among groups that play themselves out in revolutions, producing results outside of the intentions of any single set of actors.[47]

Tilly's approach to the study of collective action and revolution does, however, place significant weight on the role played by group interests. While not neglecting "big structural changes" such as "urbanization, industrialization, state making, and the expansion of capitalism,"[48] Tilly's main concern is with how these changes affect group interests, specifically, "what kinds of groups gain or lose the capacity to act together effectively, and how the forms of action themselves change."[49] In his "mobilization model," Tilly explains that "collective interests are given a priori":

> We impute them from some general historical analysis (my preferred analysis being Marx's relation of different segments of the population to the prevailing means of production) or we determine them empirically (my preferred procedure being to pay attention to what people say are their grievances, aspirations and rights).[50]

Thus, Tilly's model attempts to explain revolutions by integrating not only the macro-structural processes listed above, but also micro-structural aspects such as a group's "internal organization, its relationship to other groups, and the current state of opportunities and threats in the world," with the "purposive" component inherent in collective action.[51] According to Tilly, one should "ultimately visualize the various groups involved as undertaking their action purposively: seeking to realize their interests with the means at their disposal within the limits set by their relationship to the world around them."[52]

Subsequently, Tilly identifies and analyzes the "political processes which lead from organized and conflicting interests to revolution."[53] As we have seen, these processes involve the appearance of "contenders or coalitions of contenders, advancing exclusive alternative claims to the control over the government."[54] It is at this point in his analysis that Tilly is open to the potential role played by ideas, not just interests, in mobilizing such contenders:

> Most likely the articulation of ideologies which capture and formulate the problems of such contenders in itself accelerates their mobilization and change of direction: how great an independent weight to attribute to ideological innovation is another recurrent puzzle in the analysis of revolution.
>
> The need for elaboration of ideologies is one of the chief reasons for the exceptional importance of intellectuals in revolutionary movements. . . . [A]s Barrington Moore suggests, an outpouring of new thought articulating objectives incompatible with the continuation of the existing polity is probably our single most reliable sign that the first condition [the appearance of contenders] of a revolutionary situation is being fulfilled.[55]

Other analysts go even further in the weight they attribute to ideas. Calvert, for example, states quite unequivocally that:

> Ideas are central to the notion of revolution, first because all political life is structured in terms of ideas, second because revolution, an essentially-contested concept, is a label attached to events or sequences of events which mean different things to different people, and third because the very concept of change, the yardstick which people use to determine whether or not a revolution has occurred, is itself culturally determined.[56]

Sewell echoes this assessment by concluding that:

> One of the most important ideological products of the [French] Revolution was the idea of revolution itself. . . . It was the events of 1789 to 1794 that introduced the modern notion of revolution to the world. Revolution came to mean not any sudden change in the affairs of the state, but something much more specific: the overthrow of one government by the people and its replacement by another government. Revolution was henceforth inseparable from the exercise of popular sovereignty.[57]

In his debate with Skocpol over the role of ideas, Sewell presents his "conception of ideology as an anonymous and collective, but transformable, structure." Accordingly,

> ideology must be seen neither as the mere reflex of material class relations nor as mere "ideas" which "intellectuals" hold about society. Rather, ideologies inform the structure of institutions, the nature of social cooperation and conflict, and the attitudes and predispositions of the population.[58]

This "structuralist" understanding of ideology as part of a "cultural system" was, interestingly enough, rejected by Skocpol who would

> prefer to reserve the term "ideology" for idea systems deployed as self-conscious political arguments by identifiable political actors. Ideologies in this sense are developed and deployed by particular groups or alliances engaged in temporally specific political conflicts or attempts to justify the use of state power.[59]

This more voluntaristic and intentionalistic definition of ideology is consistent with the analytical framework developed by Walzer. Yet, unlike Skocpol and Tilly, who see the role of ideology to be at most part of an "intervening causal process,"[60] Walzer sees ideology as integral, not incidental, to the revolutionary process. Indeed, as we have seen, his view of revolutions as "conscious attempts to establish a new moral and material world and to impose, or evoke, radically new patterns of day-to-day conduct"[61] assumes purposive action on the part of particular actors in the pursuit of ideologically determined objectives. In the research agenda underlying *The Revolution of the Saints*, Walzer focuses first on the social conditions that give rise to the "marginal elites" or "masterless men"[62] that are most susceptible to new moral visions. This is followed by an examination of the content of that vision and the actions taken by the committed vanguard in Puritan England, the "saints," to shape political, social and economic outcomes in ways that were consistent with their vision. In Walzer's framework, social conditions and the revolutionary actions of groups animated by a new ideology interact with one another in complex ways:

> In a sense, the saint is the cause rather than the product of that crisis [brought on by the modernizing process]; it occurs, in different countries at different times, whenever a group of men, hardened and disciplined by an ideology, decisively challenge the old order, offering their own vision as an alternative to traditionalism and their own persons as alternatives to the traditional rulers. But in another, equally important, sense, the saint is a product of his times: for men are open to ideological discipline only at certain moments in history.[63]

There are no simple unidirectional causal processes here. Instead, certain crisis environments give rise to disaffected social groups who are open to new visions and identities. As people commit to these new ideologies, revolutionary vanguards are formed which, in turn, seek to reshape their environment. Central to this complex process, however, is the role of ideology as the nature of the beliefs involved will determine the kind of alternatives that are offered to "traditionalism."

Walzer's approach dovetails well with the Weberian tradition in which "beliefs have their own logic and force."[64] As Tilly elaborates:

> In Max Weber's treatment, groups commit themselves to collective definitions of the world and of themselves. The definitions incorporate goals, entail standards of behavior, and include justifications for the power of authorities. Constituted authorities act on behalf of the groups. Sometimes the authorities act on the basis of their traditional roles, sometimes on the basis of their extraordinary personal character—their charisma. Which of these bases the group adopts strongly affects its organization and its fate. Whether in traditional, charismatic, or rational-legal form, however, the justifications all constrain the authorities' actions. In Weber's account, the structure and action of the group as a whole spring largely from the initial commitment to a particular kind of belief system.[65]

In regard to the analysis of revolutions, this approach provides a possible answer to the crucial question of "why and how . . . the group committed from the start to fundamental transformation of the structure of power—forms?"[66] From Weber's teachings, one can derive the answer "that such groups formed around charismatic individuals who offered alternative visions of the world, visions that made sense of the contemporary chaos."[67]

In what follows, a Weberian theory of democracy will be developed in order to answer the question of when and how groups form that are committed to a "fundamental transformation of the structure of power" in a *democratic* direction. The focus will clearly be on the nature of the ideas and beliefs that animated particular groups to contest existing political structures and to replace them with new institutional arrangements that conformed to their sense of what democracy should entail. Given the degree of compatibility, this Weberian theory will be augmented by the research agenda developed by Walzer in his study of the Puritan Revolution. Accordingly, the American, French and Polish Revolutions will be studied, first, in terms of the conditions that gave rise to disaffected social groups, and, second, in terms of the vanguard or revolutionary core elite that emerged to articulate an "alternative vision" of the way political life should be organized. How this vision legitimated democracy as the appropriate ideological basis for rejecting the old regime and for constructing a new form of government will represent the third principal focus of the study.

Seen from an historical perspective, it becomes clear that democracy is not self-legitimating. It is not a self-evident truth. Rather, democracy has always been justified and legitimated in the face of considerable and consistent opposition. As Arblaster indicates:

> An historical perspective reveals, in particular, one at first sight rather puzzling and paradoxical feature of the history of democracy. That is that, for most of its long history, from the classical Greeks to the present day, democracy was seen by the enlightened and educated as one of the worst types of government and society imaginable. It was more or less synonymous with the "rule of the mob," and that was, by definition, a threat to all the central values of a civilized and orderly society.[68]

How democracy is legitimated thereby becomes a critical variable in determining the ability of this form of political conduct to emerge and to entrench itself institutionally against all odds. Not only democracy, but revolutionary undertakings in general need to be legitimated. The ability of contenders to gain popular support and to provide a viable alternative to the old regime also depends on the extent to which the mobilizing ideology is considered valid and legitimate by critical actors. The "undivided commitment"[69] of revolutionaries to their cause is only possible if the aims pursued are believed to be just and morally sanctioned.

In this context, Skocpol, while firmly dismissing such a research agenda, does agree that "revolutionary ideologies and people committed to them were undoubtedly necessary ingredients in the great social revolutions" she investigated.[70] She goes on, however, to reject a simple causal arrow linking revolutionary ideologies to revolutionary outcomes: "any line of reasoning that treats revolutionary ideologies as blueprints for revolutionaries' activities and for revolutionary outcomes cannot sustain scrutiny in the light of historical evidence."[71] This is no doubt a valid observation. The relationship between ideas and revolutionary processes; between pre-revolutionary ideas and post-revolutionary institution building is certainly not an automatic one. Instead, the relationship is a tenuous one, mediated through structures and by interests. Accordingly, a Weberian alternative to the study of democracy and revolution must take these factors into account as well.

A WEBERIAN ALTERNATIVE

Although Weber himself never completed a theory of the legitimation of democracy, his work provides a compelling point of departure for the construction of such a theory. As is well known, much of Weber's theoretical work is focused on the question of legitimacy. At the base of Weber's theoretical interest in legitimacy, lies his belief that the need to justify the pervasive inequities and inequalities that characterize all societies is an inherent and unavoidable human trait:

> [T]he fates of human beings are not equal. Men differ in their states of health or wealth or social status or what not. Simple observation shows that in every such situation he who is more favored feels the never ceasing need to look upon his position as in some way "legitimate," upon his advantage as "deserved," and the other's disadvantage as being brought about by the latter's "fault." That the purely accidental causes of difference may be ever so obvious makes no difference.[72]

Consequently, a classification of the bases upon which legitimacy can be claimed and ascribed is a central theoretical concern for Weber. In his sociological framework, a social order (defined as a social relationship that is "oriented toward determinable maxims") can be called valid or legitimate "if the orientation toward these maxims occurs, among other reasons, also because it is in some appreciable way regarded by the actor as in some way obligatory or exemplary for him."[73] Such legitimacy may be ascribed by virtue of: tradition, affectual faith, value-rational faith or "positive enactment which is believed to be legal."[74] Of these four ways in which social action can be oriented, value-rationality (i.e. adherence to and faith in those values that have been rationally deduced as being absolutely binding) has received the most attention from Weberian scholars, since Weber himself used the concept inconsistently.[75] On the one hand, he ascribed a specific significance to the legitimating power of value-rationality by connecting it to the empirical example of natural law. He considered natural law to be the "purest type of legitimacy based on value-rationality," and went on to define natural law as "the sum total of all those norms which are valid independently of, and superior to, any positive law and which owe their dignity not to arbitrary enactment but, on the contrary, provide the very legitimation for the binding force of positive law."[76] On the other hand, neither value-rationality nor natural law appear subsequently in Weber's famous typology of legitimate domination (traditional, charismatic and legal-rational) even though they are apparently directly linked to the other three social action orientations. The legitimacy of tradition "rests on an established belief in the sanctity of immemorial traditions and the legitimacy of those exercising authority under them." The legitimacy of legal-rational domination is based on a "belief in the legality of enacted rules and the right of those elevated to authority under such rules to issue commands." Finally, legitimate domination based on charismatic grounds which rests "on devotion to the exceptional sanctity, heroism or exemplary character of an individual person, and of the normative patterns or order revealed or ordained by him," is clearly a rendition of affectual faith.[77] Weber goes on to state that charisma is the "specifically creative revolutionary force of history" because of its ability to effect a "central metanoia (change) of the followers' attitudes":

> Charisma . . . may effect a subjective or internal reorientation born out of suffering, conflicts, or enthusiasm. It may then result in a radical alteration of the central attitudes and directions of action with a completely new orientation of all attitudes toward the different problems of the world.[78]

While these ways in which domination can be legitimated obviously correspond to the ways of validating a social order, there is a crucial distinction. The types of legitimate domination apply best to an organization, i.e. a "social relationship which is either closed or limits the admission of outsiders," and which possesses regulations enforced by specific individuals such as a chief and an administrative staff.[79] In the case of a charismatic leader and his disciples, the ethos of the group will determine the kinds of collective and individual behavior that are consistent with the guiding beliefs of the group. Such behavior will then be sanctioned, while inappropriate behavior will be prohibited. To the extent that these sanctions work, the ethos thereby gains an "independent influence on the conduct of life"[80] that transcends the mere regulatory power of traditionally or legal-rationally oriented organizations.[81]

The types of social action orientations, on the other hand, are to be applied to the general behavior and motivation of individuals, and cannot therefore be applied automatically to the more tightly organized relationships of reciprocity that Weber conceived of under the concept of *Herrschaft* or domination. This appears to be the reason why Weber did not reintroduce value-rationality into his discussion of domination. Although value-rationality can be a potential source of motivation for individual action and belief, it cannot generate an integrative force capable of sustaining collective action to the extent that an organized relationship of domination occurs. Unlike the social action orientations of habit, instrumental rationality and affect, Weber believed that values, however rationally deduced, can only be binding for the individual. And because individuals can hold any number of conflicting and contradictory values, value-rationality can only become binding for a collective and capable of determining collective behavior within the context of a charismatically oriented organization. Value-rationality may then characterize the "normative pattern or order" or the ethos of a charismatic setting.

It is in this context that one must place Weber's enigmatic assertion that the "charismatic glorification of Reason, which found a characteristic expression in its apotheosis by Robespierre, is the last form that charisma has adopted in its fateful course."[82] This Enlightenment value, namely the belief in the individual's capacity for reason "which, if unimpeded, would result in the at least relatively best of all worlds, by virtue of Divine providence and because the individual is best qualified to know his own interests,"[83] could only be made binding for the collective, for society at large, under the charismatic impact of the French Revolution. Similarly, Weber mentions that the belief in the individual's right to the freedom of conscience was put into collective practice under the charismatic impact of the Protestant sects. "Thus the consistent sect gives rise to an inalienable personal right of the governed as against any power, whether political, hierocratic or patriarchal."[84] Since Weber points out that both of these beliefs were legitimated and enacted on the basis of natural law, it would appear that both value-rationality and charisma have played a significant role in the early history of modern democracy.[85]

Unfortunately, Weber did not systematically develop these insights which he presented in his essay "Sect, Church and Democracy." Whereas he does elaborate on the relationship between charisma and democracy (as the routinization or transformation of charisma in a legal-rational direction), and on the relationship between natural law and the evolution of democratic legal norms, he does not connect these two developments. A theory of democracy would, however, profit from a systematic integration of these two strands of Weber's work.

To develop such a theory is the first task of this work. Three central propositions, derived from Weber, will inform the theory. First, democracy as a set of ideas bases its claim to legitimacy on the principles of natural law, specifically on the natural rights doctrine. These principles may be interpreted in either a formal or in a substantive way. Second, since the doctrine of rights cannot, in and of itself, bind and place sanctions on collective behavior, a charismatic presentation of natural rights is necessary for democratic ideas to have an effective impact on collective behavior. Third, such a charismatic presentation may result in one of three possible outcomes which one can derive from the distinctions Weber makes between the two interpretations of natural law. Essentially, Weber distinguishes between formal natural law axioms "which guaranteed to the individual his rights vis-à-vis the political authorities," and the substantive axioms which emerged as rights "came to be tied up with the substantive economic (modes) rather than with the formal modes" of the acquisition and exercise of rights.[86] While Weber admits that this distinction "is not a clear-cut one, because there simply cannot exist a completely formal natural law; the reason is that such a natural law would consist entirely of general legal concepts devoid of any content," he maintains that the "distinction has great significance."[87] This significance becomes apparent when one examines the possible institutional expressions of these two axioms. If formal natural law principles predominate, then institutionalization on the basis of individually based, negatively understood rights is likely. In this case, rights are institutionalized as "protective devises for self-sufficient individuals,"[88] with the state limited to securing the realm of autonomous individual choice; a realm of non-intrusion and forbearance on the part of public authorities. The state may, for example, provide a level playing field by assuring a "basic equalization of opportunities,"[89] but it should not step beyond this role. If, however, substantive natural law principles prevail, then institutionalization on the basis of collectively oriented, positively understood rights will be likely. In this case, rights are seen as "enabling injunctions to assist a mutually dependent and cooperative individual"[90] who is embedded in the larger collectivity of social life. Accordingly, the state will develop an interventionist capacity in the course of determining and providing the "rights to positive assistance."[91]

Yet a third outcome is possible if the inevitable conflict between substantive and formal natural law principles is left unresolved. In this case, a successful institutionalization of either variant will be rendered highly problematic. The conflict will be most intense in the case of resource-poor latecomer societies as the demands of disadvantaged social groups for an expanded state role in guaranteeing positive rights, such as the right to subsistence, will clash with the desire of other groups to safeguard individual freedoms by limiting the role of the state.

The methodological approach underlying this theoretical endeavor is also derived from Weber's work, namely from his "interpretive sociology." The fundamental concern of Weber's sociology is how we, as intellectual observers, can understand the meaning individuals ascribe to their actions. He believed that only with such an "interpretive understanding" can one arrive at a causal explanation of the course and consequences of any given example of social action. His work, *Economy and Society*, begins with the following elaboration:

> Meaning may be of two kinds. The term may refer first to the actual existing meaning in the given concrete case of a particular actor, or to the average or approximate meaning attributable to a given plurality of actors; or secondly to the theoretically conceived pure type of subjective meaning attributed to the hypothetical actor or actors in a given type of action.[92]

Weber goes on to reject any notion of an objective truth or meaning. But in order to study the subjective meanings that orient behavior, a methodology is necessary that will remain faithful to that subjectivity without becoming trapped by it. Without, in other words, studying every actor's mindset as an unique and discrete construct. The pure type, what he later termed the ideal type, is Weber's answer to this dilemma. As an abstraction distilled from historically observable patterns, or in Weber's words, from the "generalized uniformities of the empirical process,"[93] the ideal types can guide research by providing a method of categorizing the subjective meanings actors will manifest under specific circumstances. This method of using ideal types to guide research facilitates comparisons of any given case or set of cases over time and across space by providing a way of measuring change and continuity. According to Weber:

> The more sharply and precisely the ideal type has been constructed, thus the more abstract and unrealistic in this sense it is, the better it is able to perform its functions in formulating terminology, classifications, and hypotheses.[94]

In short, my purpose is to create an ideal type of modern democracy, distilled from the historically observable pattern of democratic development, and then to apply it to the case of Solidarity. The Solidarity period of 1980–81 can best be conceptualized as a charismatic setting. Such a conceptualization could make theoretical sense of the ubiquitous descriptions of Solidarity's transformatory power. For it is not just Western observers who speak of Solidarity in terms of transcendence and transformation, average Poles caught up in the movement also describe the meaning they attribute to the Solidarity experience in this way. Weber's concept of charisma provides a theoretical basis for explaining how Solidarity shaped the new values and beliefs that enabled Poles to break the rules that had previously governed their conduct; to transform and transcend their environment. Indeed, it is striking how easily Solidarity can be viewed as a charismatic community with its fluid lines of authority, the lack of a functional hierarchy, the cavalier attitudes toward financial and personal security, the consistent need for Wałęsa to demonstrate his ability to perform "miracles," and finally the autonomy of the movement from all external sources of authority (be it the Catholic Church or the communist party). All claims were rendered secondary to the transcendent, moral authority vested in the movement. The extent to which this moral authority was legitimated by natural law principles will determine the extent to which the ethos of Solidarity represents a manifestation of the spirit of democracy. Chapter 1 will develop an ideal typical representation of the spirit of modern democracy, elaborating the distinctive and essential features of this type of political conduct. A theory derived from Weber's insights will then be presented to explain how this particular type of political conduct can be legitimated and institutionalized. As indicated above, the question of legitimation is a critical factor in explaining the revolutionary emergence of democracy. Chapters 2 and 3 will apply this theoretical framework to the historical examples of how democracy has been legitimated and institutionalized in the American and French traditions. In both cases, natural law mandated the establishment of new political orders. Moreover, natural law also legitimated the emerging institutions of the new capitalist economic order as Chapter 4 demonstrates. Whereas it has often been noted that capitalism can survive and even flourish without democracy, a modern democracy without some variant of the free market has yet to be developed. Consequently, liberalism and capitalism have been conjoined to such an extent that we now speak of "liberal capitalism." The common origins in natural law for these mutually reinforcing political and economic orders explain this enduring relationship.

Historically, of course, this relationship has not been uncontested nor have the principles and the institutions of liberal capitalism been left unchallenged. As outlined in Chapter 5, Marx provided a scathing critique of natural law principles and proposed an alternative basis for legitimating a different kind of social, political and economic order. The consequences of Marx's critique for the institutional development of Leninist regimes will be assessed, along with the declining ability of the Leninist regimes in general, and of the Polish regime in particular, to sustain and justify their existence in principled terms. It was in this environment of decay and corruption that Polish dissidents, be they workers or intellectuals, began to formulate new principles for ethical conduct in order to legitimate opposition to the regime. The extent to which these principles can be captured under the concept of natural law, and the impact of these principles as mediated through the charismatic setting of the social movement, will be analyzed and documented in Chapter 6.

By placing Solidarity in the comparative framework established in the previous chapters, it will be possible in Chapter 7 to ascertain the extent to which Solidarity either replicates or deviates from the ideal type of modern democracy and from the historical pattern of liberal capitalist development. Such a comparative point of reference will enable a more precise understanding of the particular nature of the Polish Revolution in both its positive and problematic aspects. Based on this understanding, the prospects for an institutionalization of liberal capitalism will then be outlined. As indicated by the theory, the conflict between substantive and formal natural law axioms, and the capacity to resolve that conflict, will play a central role in shaping the institutional forms of the new democratic political order. Moreover, the outcome of this conflict has ramifications for the ability to institutionalize a capitalist economic order. Weber's work clearly demonstrates the extent to which formal natural law axioms were essential for the development of the spirit of capitalism.[95] An analysis, therefore, of the conflict of these axioms within Solidarity and in the post-Solidarity political groups is crucial for understanding the post-Leninist environment in Poland. Like the United States and France, Poland is one of the few nations that has experienced an indigenous democratic revolution; an indigenous articulation of natural rights. As a consequence, Poland, unlike her Central European neighbors, must come to terms with a dual legacy: the legacy of the old regime and the legacy of Solidarity.

1 The charismatic presentation of natural rights

A Weberian theory of democracy

The belief that democracy represents a desirable goal or reality is so prevalent today that it is almost taken for granted. Throughout the world, a plethora of constitutions and battalions of politicians pay homage to the "will of the people" as the essential attribute of democracy. How this popular will is actually to be represented and articulated may be subject to various interpretations, but a commitment to the people's will as the leitmotif of government is universally acknowledged by those nations considering themselves to be democratically constituted. This commitment is, however, of relatively recent vintage. As David Held remarks, "the widespread adherence to democracy as a suitable form for organizing political life is less than a hundred years old."[1] While democracy itself has a long history dating back to the Greek city states, for most of that history it was considered a radical and dangerous form of organizing political life. At some point, however, a change in perception took place. A form of government that was once considered radical is now considered eminently rational and morally suitable. Yet what precisely is the nature of this rationality, and on what basis can it be legitimated? These are the central questions that will concern us in this chapter.

THE SPIRIT OF MODERN DEMOCRACY

When Weber conceived of his ideal typical representation of the spirit of capitalism in his famous work *The Protestant Ethic and the Spirit of Capitalism*, he did so on the basis of his methodological concept of the "historical individual," i.e. "a complex of elements associated in historical reality which we unite into a conceptual whole from the standpoint of their cultural significance."[2] Weber believed that one could only arrive at such a conceptual definition by understanding historical reality in terms of "concrete genetic sets of relations which are inevitably of a specifically unique and individual character," not in terms of "abstract general formulae."[3] In other words, the phenomenon under consideration must be observed from an historical perspective in order to distill the "complex of elements" or the "sets of relations" that make an essential contribution to the cultural significance of the phenomenon. Before generating such a conceptual or ideal-typical definition of capitalism, Weber provided a "provisional description" of the spirit of capitalism based on the texts of Benjamin Franklin. In what follows, by drawing on Thomas Paine's *The Rights of Man*, a similar description of the spirit of modern democracy will be presented. The intention here is not to present a fully elaborated review of major democratic thinkers. Rather, it is to provide some insight into the essential nature of democracy by drawing on the work of a representative author. Subsequently, a conceptual definition of democracy will be attempted. Both the description and the definition are intended to address two analytical levels. First, the nature of the ethos or the guiding beliefs that animate modern democracy will be illustrated. Second, the practical conduct and the form of political organization typical of modern democracy will be assessed. Taken together, these two analytical levels comprise the spirit or the "historical individuality" of modern democracy. At first glance, Paine might seem like an odd choice for the purpose of determining this "individuality" given the prevalent tendency in the literature on democracy to focus on the works of such undoubtedly important figures as Locke, Mill, Jefferson or Madison. In this company, Paine is not often seen as a particularly profound or original thinker. However, *The Rights of Man* warrants closer examination because of its powerful popular impact. In England, for example, Paine became an "instant hero" after its publication,

> not only to the intellectual radicals among whom he moved, such as Blake, Holcroft, Horne Tooke, Godwin and Wollstonecraft, but to hundreds of thousands of artisans and journeymen who bought *Rights of Man* for sixpence or read it reprinted by their provincial radical association.[4]

Written in the heat of battle, like the *Communist Manifesto*, it is a focused and concentrated work condensing the fundamental principles of democracy into an abbreviated format in order to win adherents to the cause of democratic revolution. Accordingly, whatever Paine's work might lack in intellectual depth is more than compensated for by its clarity and forcefulness. As Foot and Kramnick point out,

> Paine developed and was the first master of democratic prose, which is as important in explaining his appeal to a mass readership as is the content of his arguments. Jefferson, himself a master of political prose, saw the unique strength of Paine's prose, writing in 1821 that "No writer has exceeded Paine in ease and familiarity of style in perspicuity of expression, happiness of elucidation, and in simple and unassuming language."[5]

Moreover, "the content of his arguments" as well have considerable merit—to the extent that the historian A. J. P. Taylor deemed *The Rights of Man* to be "the best statement of democratic belief in any language."[6] Taken together, then, a democratic style of writing combined with the elaboration of democratic ideas made Paine a highly influential, some would argue *the* most influential, writer of the revolutionary era.

For Paine, the ethos and organization of democratic life were, first and foremost, the products of reason. Yet he found himself having to defend the reasonableness and the rationality of democracy from the attack launched by Edmund Burke against the democratic principles of the French Revolution. In response to Burke, Paine constructed a series of arguments in favor of the rights of man and the government best able to guarantee these rights, namely representation grafted onto simple democracy. The logic of these arguments represents a pivotal chapter in the transformation of democracy from a radical manifestation of the will of the feckless mob, or of the "swinish multitude," to a rational manifestation of the will of reasonable individuals endowed with natural rights. Paine attacked both the principles and the form of the traditional government of hereditary monarchy on the grounds that man, as a rational being with natural rights, could only be content with principles of government derived directly from these natural rights, and encased in a form of government consistent with these principles.

In the course of his debate with Burke, Paine elaborates on the two major themes that animate the spirit of modern democracy. First, the conviction that man has rights as an individual, not as the member of a family, a status group, a tribe or a race. Second, simply by virtue of being a man it is assumed that the capacity for reason and rational conduct follows. Provisionally, therefore, one can describe modern democracy as the rational political organization of free individuals.[7] For Paine, the foundation of individual freedom lies in the natural rights that endow man with the right to act as an individual:

> Natural rights are those which appertain to man in the right of his existence. Of this kind are all the intellectual rights, or rights of the mind, and also all those rights of acting as an individual for his own comfort and happiness, which are not injurious to the natural rights of others. Civil rights are those which appertain to man in right of his being a member of society. Every civil right has for its foundation some natural right pre-existing in the individual, but to the enjoyment of which his individual power is not, in all cases, sufficiently competent. Of this kind are all those which relate to security and protection.[8]

According to Paine, these natural rights derive their force and validity from the religiously defined origins of man.

> The illuminating and divine principle of the equal rights of man (for it has its origin from the Maker of man), relates not only to the living individuals, but to generations of men succeeding each other. Every generation is equal in rights to the generations which preceded it, by the same rule that every individual is born equal in rights with his contemporary. Every history of the Creation, and every traditionary account,

> whether from the lettered or unlettered world, however they may vary in their opinion or belief of certain particulars, all agree in establishing one point, the unity of man; by which I mean that men are all of one degree, and consequently that all men are born equal, and with equal natural rights, in the same manner as if posterity had been continued by creation instead of generation, the latter being only the mode by which the former is carried forward; and consequently, every child born into the world must be considered as deriving its existence from God. The world is as new to him as it was to the first man that existed, and his natural right in it is of the same kind.[9]

Because Paine believed that "man did not enter into society to become worse than he was before, nor to have fewer rights than he had before," the only reasonable form of government consistent with the natural rights of man was derived from the "social compact," wherein man "deposits his right in the common stock of society, and takes the arm of society, of which he is a part, in preference and in addition to his own. Society grants him nothing. Every man is proprietor in society, and draws on the capital as a matter of right."[10] Based on this logic, Paine drew three crucial conclusions about the principles that should animate government derived from the "social compact":

> First, that every civil right grows out of a natural right; or, in other words, is a natural right exchanged. Secondly, that civil power, properly considered as such, is made up of the aggregate of that class of the natural rights of man, which becomes defective in the individual in point of power, and answers not his purpose, but when collected to a focus, becomes competent to the purpose of every one. Thirdly, that the power produced from the aggregate of natural rights, imperfect in power in the individual, cannot be applied to invade the natural rights which are retained in the individual, and in which the power to execute is as perfect as the right itself.[11]

Subsequently, Paine applied these principles to the formation of governments:

> In casting our eyes over the world, it is extremely easy to distinguish the governments which have arisen out of society, or out of the social compact, from those which have not: but to place this in a clearer light than what a single glance may afford, it will be proper to take a review of the several sources from which the governments have arisen, and on which they may be founded. They may all be comprehended under three heads. Firstly, superstition. Secondly, power. Thirdly, the common interests of society, and the common rights of man. The first was a government of priestcraft, the second of conquerors, and the third of reason.[12]

Based on this definition of reason, Paine accorded the French Constitution and the American system of government the accolade of being rational in both form and principle:

> In contemplating the French Constitution, we see in it a rational order of things. The principles harmonize with the forms, and both with their origin. It may perhaps be said as an excuse for bad forms, that they are nothing more than forms; but this is a mistake. Forms grow out of principles, and operate to continue the principles they grow from. It is impossible to practice a bad form on anything but a bad principle. It cannot be ingrafted on a good one; and wherever the forms in any government are bad, it is a certain indication that the principles are bad also.[13]

By "ingrafting representation upon democracy" the American government has "fixed the form by a scale paralleled in all cases to the extent of the principle."[14] As Paine concluded unequivocally, "the representative system takes society and civilization for its basis; nature, reason and experience for its guide."[15] Moreover, such a system is eminently desirable for the beneficial effects it produces:

> As the republic of letters brings forward the best literary productions, by giving to genius a fair and universal chance; so the representative system of government is calculated to produce the wisest laws, by collecting wisdom where it can be found.[16]

To this system of wisdom and reason, Paine contrasted the fatuousness of hereditary monarchy:

> How irrational then is the hereditary system which establishes channels of power, in company with which wisdom refuses to flow! By continuing this absurdity, man is perpetually in contradiction with himself; he accepts, for a king, or a chief magistrate, or a legislator, a person whom he would not elect for a constable.[17]

Again and again, Paine argued against the world of custom and privilege and hereditary status on the basis that it is unnatural and therefore unreasonable. For example:

> We must shut our eyes against reason, we must basely degrade our understanding, not to see the folly of what is called monarchy. Nature is orderly in all her works; but this is a mode of government that counteracts nature. It turns the progress of the human faculties upside down. It subjects age to be governed by children, and wisdom by folly. On the contrary, the representative system is always parallel with the order and immutable laws of nature, and meets the reason of man in every part.[18]

In Paine's opinion, the "rational system of representative government" was the logical outcome of the capacity for rational conduct that he believed was inherent to man. Every individual is capable of defining and pursuing his interests:

> Every man is a proprietor in government and considers it a necessary part of his business to understand. It concerns his interest, because it affects his property. He examines the cost, and compares it with the advantages; and above all, he does not adopt the slavish custom of following what in other governments are called *leaders*.[19]

In contrast to such slavish customs which were buttressed by the traditional perception that "government is some wonderful mysterious thing,"[20] Paine maintained that "the government of a free country, properly speaking, is not in the persons, but in the laws. The enacting of those requires no great expense; and when they are administered, the whole of civil government is performed."[21] For Paine, the purpose of government could not be ascribed to tradition or superstition, rather government had to be the means to a particular set of ends:

> Government is nothing more than a national association; and the objective of this association is the good of all, as well individually as collectively. Every man wishes to pursue his occupation, and enjoy the fruits of his labors, and the produce of his property, in peace and safety, and with the least possible expense. When these things are accomplished, all the objects for which government ought to be established are answered.[22]

Similarly, the forming of a constitution also had to follow this logic:

> In forming a constitution, it is first necessary to consider what are the ends for which government is necessary: secondly, what are the best means, and the least expensive, for accomplishing those ends.[23]

Paine evidently considered the creation of the American Constitution to be exemplary in this regard:

> Here we see a regular process—a government issuing out of a constitution, formed by the people in their original character; and that constitution serving, not only as an authority, but as a law of control to the government. It was the political bible of the State.[24]

Yet even that constitution may be subject to revision in the future if the progress of reason were to determine a more appropriate and even more rational form. As Paine concluded:

> The best constitution that could now be devised, consistent with the condition of the present moment, may be far short of that excellence which a few years may afford. There is a morning of reason rising upon man, on the subject of government, that has not appeared before.[25]

Under the influence of this "morning of reason," Paine sought to discredit decisively the traditional forms and principles of government that stood in the way of what he believed was a more rational, reasonable and efficient organization of political life. The rational nature of modern democratic political organizations, so vividly exemplified by Paine's work, can be captured by Weber's concept of instrumental rationality. Paine's belief that democratic government, and the constitution it is founded upon, should be the product of a calculation of the best and least expensive means for accomplishing certain ends corresponds to Weber's statement that:

> Action is instrumentally rational when the end, the means, and the secondary results are all rationally taken into account and weighed. This involves rational consideration of alternative means to the end, of the relations of the end to the secondary consequences, and finally of the relative importance of different possible ends.[26]

Yet, as Paine's treatise also demonstrates, this rational form of organization was bound to the ethical norms provided by the natural rights doctrine. Such a form of political rule or government was thus both sanctioned and constrained by the "ethically colored maxims"[27] that comprise the ethos of modern democracy. This paradoxical relationship wherein reason is validated by the divinely informed principles of the ethos of natural rights is an essential attribute of the phenomenon of modern democracy. The conviction that man, as an individual, has both natural rights and a natural capacity for reason is derived from a religiously based interpretation of man and, therefore, constitutes the "irrational" element of the rationality characteristic of democratically organized political life. Indeed, the very belief that rational conduct is possible among all individuals, that discipline and self-control are universal attributes of reasoning individuals, arose from this ethical base. Paine could not have elaborated on the rational organization of political life, if he had not been convinced that all men were capable of rational conduct. Such disciplined behavior is needed if men are to respect each other's natural rights. For as Paine states:

> A Declaration of Rights is, by reciprocity, a Declaration of Duties also. Whatever is my right as a man, is also the right of another; and it becomes my duty to guarantee, as well as to possess.[28]

Consequently, the instrumental rationality of the means–ends form of democratically based government, and the instrumentally rational conduct of individual citizens, cannot be understood without reference to the value rationality of the natural law ethos.

Weber defines value rationally oriented social action as "determined by a conscious belief in the value for its own sake of some ethical, aesthetic, religious, or other form of behavior, independently of its prospects of success."[29] He goes on to elaborate:

> Examples of pure value-rational orientation would be the actions of

> persons who, regardless of possible cost to themselves, act to put into practice their convictions of what seems to them to be required by duty, honor, the pursuit of beauty, a religious call, personal loyalty, or the importance of some "cause" no matter in what it consists. In our terminology, value-rational action always involves "commands" or "demands" which, in the actor's opinion, are binding on him.[30]

In Paine's words one can clearly see a manifestation of such passionate conviction. The striking aspect of this conviction is that the "demands" Paine made to foster the cause of the rights of man were cast in instrumentally rational terms. It would be tempting to focus solely on this latter aspect of democratic development and to relegate the significance of natural rights to the status of providing the values toward which instrumental action is oriented. Since Weber states that "the orientation of action wholly to the rational achievement of ends without relation to fundamental values"[31] is rare, an orientation toward values is generally present even in instrumentally oriented social action.

Yet this would be a misleading assessment of modern democracy. For it is only because the individual endowed with natural rights and natural reason was elevated to the status of an absolute value that people, such as Paine, were willing to risk their lives and their security to implement the rational form of political organization that corresponded to their sense of what was ethically appropriate. The extent to which the spirit of modern democracy is consistent with the instrumental rationality predominant in present day liberal democratic governments or institutions should not overshadow the fact that the natural rights ethos provides the ethical basis for the development of this form of rational conduct and organization. An ideal-typical definition of modern democracy must, therefore, be able to encompass this historical relationship between ethical beliefs and rational conduct that resulted in the disaggregation of the "swinish multitude" into an aggregation of reasoning individuals considered capable of creating and sustaining democracy as a rational form of political organization.

We are now in a position to expand the provisional description of modern democracy, as the rational political organization of free individuals, by identifying the "sets of relations" that are essential to the phenomenon, in order to arrive at a conceptual definition of democracy. The crucial relationship inherent to the phenomenon of democracy is the interplay between the ethical nature of democratic beliefs and principles and the rational form of democratic organization and civic behavior. Conceptually, therefore, modern democracy can be defined as a particular synthesis of value-rationality and instrumental rationality. The belief in the freedom and equality of individuals as an absolute value, as a cause worth dying for, is exemplified by the natural rights ethos. Instrumental rationality then became the basis upon which these free individuals relate to each other and to the government, as well as the basis for government itself. Given the fact that individuals were believed to have freely chosen to belong to society, instrumental rationality is the logic according to which individuals weighed the costs and benefits of giving up some of their freedom in order to belong to society. As Paine illustrates:

> To understand the nature and quantity of government proper for man, it is necessary to attend to his character. As Nature created him for social life, she fitted him for the station she intended. In all cases she made his natural wants greater than his individual powers. No one man is capable, without the aid of society, of supplying his own wants; and those wants acting upon every individual, impel the whole of them into society, as naturally as gravitation acts to a center.[32]

Society, in other words, is the means to satisfy every individual's natural wants or ends. The existence of this calculated "mutual and reciprocal interest"[33] between individuals represents the fundamental principle underlying an instrumentally rational orientation toward social action. Once calculated interests are thought to govern men's conduct, a stable and predictable set of expectations about the behavior of others becomes possible that allows "these expectations to be used as 'conditions' or 'means' for the attainment of the actor's own rationally pursued and calculated ends."[34] Thus, the logical affinity between the rational organization of modern democracy and the "irrational" ethos of natural rights is what gives this form of political life its defining character.

This conceptual definition is more complex and, at first glance, no doubt more abstract than the minimalist, procedurally based definitions prevalent in the literature on democratization. Huntington, for example, defines democracy in the twentieth century as determined by the extent to which a political system elects its "most powerful collective decision makers" through "fair, honest, and periodic elections in which candidates freely compete for votes and in which virtually all the adult population is eligible to vote."[35] In this definition, political and civil freedoms or rights are implicit as being "necessary to political debate and the conduct of electoral campaigns."[36] Rights are accordingly reduced to the status of means which contribute to the ends of fair and meaningful elections.

Clearly, just as it is tempting to relegate rights to the status of simply providing the values toward which instrumental action is oriented, it is also tempting, in the interests of definitional clarity, to view rights as simply the means guaranteeing certain procedural outcomes—which are then emphasized as the primary indicators of democracy. As Huntington points out, such a "procedural definition of democracy provides a number of benchmarks . . . that make it possible to judge to what extent political systems are democratic, to compare systems, and to analyze whether systems are becoming more or less democratic."[37] While benchmarks such as voting participation and multi-party competition do allow for easy comparisons, these comparisons are relatively static in nature, telling us very little about the developmental prospects of any given case. Issues of legitimacy, stability and institutionalization are not readily encompassed by this minimalist definition.

As our task is to address precisely these issues in order to provide a richer analysis of the nature of democratic development in Poland, a more complex conceptual definition of democracy is necessary. By maintaining that *both* the value-rationality of the natural rights doctrine and the instrumental rationality of procedural government represent the crucial defining attributes of modern democracy, a clearer understanding of the factors involved in the creating and sustaining of democratic institutions is made possible. Simply put, electoral procedures are necessary but not sufficient indicators of democratic development, since without a value-rational commitment to rights on the part of critical members of the polity, these procedures will be subject to subversion and/or outright replacement as conditions change. Here, the example given by Huntington of Nigeria and New Zealand is instructive. While both countries could be classified as equally free and democratic in 1983, a military coup in Nigeria on New Year's Day 1984 "effectively ended Nigerian democracy," while New Zealand has obviously continued as a democratic state.[38] Clearly, democratic procedures alone are incapable of inspiring loyalty or compliance in the face of adverse circumstances. Only when democratic procedures are believed to serve the additional purpose of guaranteeing rights and freedoms will they be maintained over time.

This is not to say that the calculation of interests is insignificant for continued and consistent compliance with democratic procedures. Weber himself clearly stated that interests, not ideas, "directly govern men's conduct." Yet Weber also maintained that "very frequently the 'world images' that have been created by 'ideas' have, like switchmen, determined the tracks along which action has been pushed by the dynamic of interest."[39] In the case of democratic development, natural rights created a new "world image" that shaped people's perception of their interests and how these interests should most appropriately be pursued.

The conceptual definition offered above does, however, beg the question of how the ethos of natural rights can gain an independent influence on collective behavior so that the rational, procedural conduct characteristic of modern democracy can be articulated, institutionalized and sustained. Before addressing this question it would be useful to gain a sense of how the ethos itself originated, and of how it is legitimated. The natural rights ethos is a manifestation of natural law and derives its legitimacy from this source. In order to address the legitimating power of natural law, an overview of the attributes and evolution of this form of value-rationality will be presented. Subsequently, the relationship between charisma and democracy will be examined to generate a theoretical answer to the question of how the ethos of modern democracy can achieve a transformation of consciousness and conduct. Finally, the institutional outcomes of this transformation will be examined. As the history of the eighteenth-century democratic revolutions demonstrates, the ethos of natural rights did not remain an abstract doctrine. Instead, these rights were given concrete institutional form and expression which further served to consolidate this way of organizing political life.

THE WILL TO FREEDOM: THE LEGITIMATING POWER OF NATURAL LAW

> For a nation to love liberty, it is sufficient that she knows it; and to be free, it is sufficient that she wills it.[40]
>
> (Lafayette)

To such passionate advocates of democracy, like the Marquis de Lafayette, the will to freedom was both self-sustaining and self-sufficient. Even such dispassionate observers of democracy like Max Weber considered this will to be a significant factor in determining democratic outcomes:

> It is ridiculous to ascribe to present day advanced capitalism as it is currently being imported to Russia and as it exists in America—this inevitability of our economic development—an elective affinity with democracy or even with freedom, in any sense whatsoever. The question can only be posed: how are, under [capitalist] domination, these things even possible in the long run? They are actually only present where the determined will of a people not to be ruled like a herd of sheep persists. We are individualists and advocates of democratic institutions against the stream of material interests.[41]

Yet on what basis is this will to freedom articulated and on what basis is it validated or legitimated? For as Weber points out, freedom is not as self-sufficient and as self-evident as Lafayette assumed. Before and during the course of the American and French Revolutions freedom was defined in both positive and negative terms; freedom for and freedom from. As defined by Paine, freedom for the individual and for rational government, freedom from tyranny and the irrationality of traditional government. In this process of articulating the content of freedom, the advocates of democratic ideas drew on principles derived from natural law in order to legitimate their challenge to the existing order. Stable orders and stable institutions do not necessarily require conscious legitimation. Habit, or the pursuit of material interests, will determine most people's attitudes and behavior in such stable and secure environments. However, an individual or a group that seeks to oppose the existing state of affairs will generally be motivated by affect or value-rationality. To endure the risks of either entering a turbulent environment or of creating one, people need to legitimate their actions on the basis of social action orientations that provide a maximum degree of psychological security. Moreover, in the rapidly changing circumstances of a turbulent environment, habit and the calculation of material interests lose their ability to provide a consistent basis upon which to orient behavior. Certainly, people will continue to orient themselves according to these possibilities, but they will not be able to take the risks necessary to have an impact on such an environment.

Natural law, as a type of value-rationality, provides the legitimation necessary for individuals to risk the articulation and presentation of democratic ideas in opposition to an existing order. But why natural law? Why not some other form of value-rationality? Natural law manifests three characteristics that render it suitable for the task it has been called upon to fulfill.[42] First, natural law in its long history has managed to sustain, both philosophically and institutionally, two essentially democratic principles, namely the rights of personal autonomy and of equality. Second, the fact that natural law is inherently contradictory has left it open to continuous redefinition. Therefore, no order or hierarchy of power could sustain a lasting monopoly on the correct interpretation of natural law. Oppositional groups or individuals could always claim a more correct interpretation of the law. Third, natural law provides, by definition, a legally sanctioned code of conduct that can be employed to judge, restrain and regulate political authority. Natural law generates a standard of justice according to which an order can be judged and found wanting. Natural law can also provide the principles upon which a new order can be founded. These unique features enable natural law to endow modern democracy with the legitimating force it needs as a form of political conduct and organization articulated in opposition to existing orders.

Since the days of the Greek polis, people have referred to natural law as a reflection of the natural and, therefore, just order of life. While predominantly remembered as the purview of ancient philosophers such as Aristotle and Cicero, natural law was firmly established in the canons of Roman law and medieval Church doctrine before achieving its apotheosis in the revolutionary declarations of the rights of man in the United States and France. In these institutionalized forms, natural law has had an impact on the structures of legal, political and religious authority far beyond its ancient philosophical origins.

Natural law can be defined as a system of legal norms that is universally binding on all men judged capable of reason. These norms are binding without reference to, or even in conflict with, all positively established laws and declarations. Since natural law determines which conception of justice corresponds to man's ability to live in accordance with a higher natural order, and fulfill the divine purpose, it has priority over all positive law. Once man was defined as a creature capable of reason, the effort to use that reason to determine man's just and appropriate place in the universe has been remarkably tenacious throughout European history. Different historical periods have given rise to new definitions of how natural law is to be understood. The inherent conceptual contradiction between laws that are man-made and therefore profane, yet deduced from that which is considered natural, eternal, and therefore sacred, has meant that natural laws can be declared, proven and developed anew. The validity of a legal system proclaimed on such a basis can persistently be challenged on the grounds that either the true nature of the natural order has been misunderstood, or the deductions themselves are faulty. The validity, however, of the effort itself to determine what is the natural law appropriate for a given historical period was not questioned until Marx's era.

In spite of this long history, the distinguishing characteristics of natural law that make it a recognizable and coherent concept, regardless of time and context, were already developed in ancient Greece. In defining nature, the Greek philosophers defined man—what he is capable of, namely, reason and how he should live or could live. From this point on, human thought was introduced to the notion of deliberately defining the parameters of human existence, instead of unthinkingly accepting one's fate and one's existence. This, in turn, opened the question of either adapting to the existing order or of changing it. Man's life within the community became a matter for conscious reflection. On the basis of reason, it was deemed possible to deduce what constitutes a just and virtuous life, and what are the elementary needs, the natural rights, required for such a life. Those natural rights were then considered to be inalienable, man's birthright as a rational being made in the divine image and, therefore, distinct from the beasts.

Consequently, although one can trace the historical evolution of different conceptions of natural rights, two features have been consistent over time. First, the right to autonomy or freedom was defined on the basis of natural law. Autonomy defined as "having the right or power of self-government"[43] entails both a subjective and an objective component. By virtue of his ability to reason, man is capable of governing himself. But, should he delegate the authority to govern to others, natural law establishes that those with the power do not necessarily have the right to govern if they violate the maxims of natural law. Therefore, by virtue of his ability to reason, man is capable of passing judgment on those in power, and retains his right to autonomy. Second, the concept of equality (i.e. the right to equal public status within a community) was developed on this basis. Since natural law is binding on all men capable of reason and judgment, all have the right to the same status within the community. Moreover, the fact that natural law is universally binding places certain limits on what one is legitimately expected to endure in this lifetime from the hands of one's fellow men. If the ruled are equal in status to the rulers on some divine principle, then the former cannot be subjected to the unlimited power of the latter.

The central conflict in the history of natural law has revolved around the issue of how to determine who is capable of reason and, therefore, able to partake of life in the public community. During the Greek and Roman periods the public community was defined largely in political terms, and membership in that community meant having an equal say in the political affairs of the city or empire. Yet only those who were born into a certain station in life could lay claim to reason, and thereby to political membership. Under the influence of the Christian interpretation of natural law, the public community was redefined as a religious community of believers wherein members were equal in the eyes of God, but not in the eyes of secular authorities. The secular political community remained narrowly defined according to status relationships and hereditary hierarchies. Historically, then, the rights of autonomy and equality defined in political terms were narrowly applied. Under the impact of the natural rights doctrine of the French and American Revolutions, however, these rights were expanded and applied to all men regardless of birth or status. The rights and ideals maintained in the sacred community of free and equal Christian believers were transferred to the secular political community. As Paine stated, "every child born into the world must be considered as deriving its existence from God," and therefore the "divine principle of the equal rights of man"[44] must be applied to every child born into the world. Those who are created equal by God, and are equal before God, must have equal rights in the secular realm as well. As we shall see in the following chapter, the desire of eighteenth-century democrats to escape the confines of their non-aristocratic status led them to expand the scope of natural law. In their opinion, neither birth nor privilege nor royal authority could be allowed to impede the individual's ability to express his will freely and rationally. Indeed, such "unnatural" impediments had to be removed so that individuals could rise to the status they were entitled to on the basis of merit and talent.

Determining exactly what membership in this new secular community of free and equal individuals entails, however, has been problematic and contested since the eighteenth century. Based on the two conflicting approaches to reason embedded in the modern natural rights doctrine, two different assessments of the relationship between the individual and the community, and two different assessments of the scope of participation, are possible. According to the formal interpretation of the natural rights doctrine, the capacity to reason is enhanced by the degree of autonomous freedom an individual possesses. Consequently, the community cannot infringe upon this autonomy. The individual must be free of all unnecessary obligations and entanglements. Only if unencumbered, uninhibited and uninfluenced by the social forces around him, can the sovereign individual determine his own interests and decide on the best means to pursue them. While, in theory, every individual is capable of autonomous reason, in political and legal practice, however, a certain proof of autonomy is deemed necessary before any given individual can participate legitimately in public life. Criteria such as, for example, property ownership, independent employment, residency and/or age have all been considered proof of autonomy. To the extent that these criteria are "expressed in numerical, calculable terms,"[45] and are open, in theory at least, to all individuals regardless of any inherent qualities, such as those determined by heredity or character, they can be considered formal. Eventually, all restrictions on participation related to heredity, ethnicity, race, gender or virtue were undermined on the basis of this formal understanding of rights.

A substantive interpretation of natural law principles, in contrast, focuses on the imperfect autonomy of the individual's capacity for reason and the circumstances beyond the individual's control that inhibit his natural ability to reason. These inhibiting circumstances, such as a lack of education, must first be addressed and removed or mitigated in order for the individual to take his rightful place in the political community. According to the substantive understanding of rights, the removal of such impediments is considered a responsibility borne collectively by the community, rather than by the individual alone. The community is thereby obligated to assist individuals in attaining and retaining their status as equal members. In its role as guarantor of the ties of mutual obligation that bind individuals within the community, the state hereby assumes a critical role. Again, in theory every individual is capable of reason, and therefore has the right to participate in public life. In social, political and legal practice, however, since the individual must be assisted by the state to fulfill this potential, the state establishes the parameters of legitimate participation. The substantive goals or ultimate ends mandated by the doctrine, such as social justice and equality, serve as the absolute standard according to which participation should be structured.[46] If these goals are better served by restricting the scope of individual rights, the state may restrict even these rights and freedoms.

In short, regardless of how it has been defined and applied in the course of its history, natural law has been characterized by two distinguishing features: that man's fate and his environment are matters for conscious reflection, and that by virtue of this capacity for reflection and reason, man has certain natural rights that guarantee him a degree of autonomy and equality of membership in the public community. These features have provided a standard of justice on the basis of which political, social and economic orders could be judged. If these orders were found wanting, challenges could be mounted and legitimated with reference to the fact that man's natural rights were not being met. An alternative community could then be proposed that would be able to provide these rights. Consequently, the will to democratically defined freedom is dependent on the legitimating principles of natural law. Natural law provides a divinely sanctioned standard according to which freedom from what and for what can be defined and defended. For the will to freedom does not have to be expressed in democratic terms. Only when the principles of natural law inform the "determined will not to be ruled like a herd of sheep," can one speak of a will to freedom that is consistent with democracy.

DEMOCRACY AND CHARISMA: THE CHARISMATIC PRESENTATION OF NATURAL LAW

In *The Protestant Ethic and the Spirit of Capitalism* and in *The Sociology of Law*, Weber offers an historically informed analysis of the role played by natural law in the democratic development of England, France and the United States. The sacred and secular variants of natural law as presented by Protestant theologians and Enlightenment philosophers provided the "world images" according to which people could potentially define their interests and orient their actions. Implicit in Weber's analysis is, however, the realization that natural law was only rendered absolutely binding, and therefore capable of transforming the way in which people conduct their lives, within the context of a charismatic setting such as those prevailing within the Protestant sects and during the French Revolution.

Historically, the proclamation of natural law in terms of "natural rights" clearly has an affinity to the Protestant concept of "natural morality." This is highlighted by the definition of natural law provided by Peter Gay in his seminal work on the Enlightenment: "there are laws independent of, and superior to, human enactments; they are engraved in men's hearts, eternal, immutable, universal, and they impose moral obligations on the ruler and give moral rights to the ruled."[47] Both the doctrine of natural morality and the doctrine of natural rights represented revolutionary challenges to the existing order. During the Puritan Revolution of the seventeenth century these challenges coincided to produce the Levellers, members of Cromwell's army, who constituted perhaps the "world's first organized radical-democratic political party."[48] The Levellers justified their demands for broader political participation and representation with reference both to the moral principles of their religious beliefs, and to the rights of "freeborn Englishmen"; rights that were considered natural and self-evident. However, after the restoration of monarchical rule brought the Puritan Revolution to an end, the sects retreated from political life, effectively bringing to an end their efforts to establish a new political community on the basis of Protestant congregationalism. Private "questions of conduct and personal morality" subsequently tended to dominate the lives of the Protestant sects.[49] Consequently, Protestantism's most lasting impact has manifested itself in the realm of ethical conduct, as the doctrine changed the internal conditions of life for believers. Eventually, these internal reorientations resulted in the "spirit of capitalism" as analyzed by Weber. In contrast, Weber maintained that natural rights had a great impact on the formulation of the legal codes of the following century, thereby affecting the external conditions of life for all.

The significance of natural law on the formulation of these legal codes was the focus of Weber's interest in the *Sociology of Law*. According to Weber, the secularized conception of natural law is

> [The] sum total of all those norms which are valid independently of, and

> superior to, any positive law and which owe their dignity not to arbitrary enactment but, on the contrary, provide the very legitimation for the binding force of positive law. Natural law has thus been the collective term for those norms which owe their legitimacy not to their origin from a legitimate lawgiver, but to their immanent and teleological qualities. It is the specific and only consistent type of legitimacy of a legal order which can remain once religious revelation and the authoritarian sacredness of a tradition and its bearers have lost their force. Natural law has thus been the specific form of legitimacy of a revolutionarily created order. The invocation of natural law has repeatedly been the method by which classes in revolt against the existing order have legitimated their aspirations, in so far as they did not, or could not, base their claims upon positive religious norms or revelation.[50]

Weber characterizes such a revolutionary situation as a time when "practical legal life is materially affected by the conviction of the particular legitimacy of certain legal maxims, and of the directly binding force of certain principles which are not to be disrupted by any concessions to positive law imposed by mere power."[51] In Weber's opinion such situations had existed in England, during the French Revolution, and still existed in the United States of his day. Although it is quite clear from Weber's historical sociology that he ascribes a significant role to natural law, both in its sacred and secular variants, in the development of modern democracy, he does not pursue this insight theoretically. Oddly enough, there is no explicit theoretical linkage between charisma as the "specifically creative and revolutionary force in history"[52] and natural law as the "specific form of legitimacy of a revolutionarily created order."

In Weber's theoretical writings, charisma appears as the "specifically creative and revolutionary force in history." The direct and unmediated relationship between a leader who can articulate new values with unprecedented power and conviction, such as Cromwell or Robespierre, and his followers generates a situation in which people have the courage to act consistently on the basis of these new values and beliefs even in the face of tremendous opposition and turbulence. The abstract principles of natural law have to be presented in a charismatic context in order to achieve a revolutionary impact. For, as we have seen, Weber maintains that "not ideas, but material and ideal interests, directly govern men's conduct."[53] In order for these interests to be redefined according to an alternative world image, the intervening mechanism of charisma is necessary to give these ideas an organizational form and to provide a concrete locus of identity for people. In Weber's opinion, the transformatory power of the Protestant sects and of the French Revolution, which could only be understood in terms of charisma, resulted in a substantive adherence to the natural rights ethos and the impersonal rationality characteristic of modern democracy.[54]

However, since Weber does not include natural law or value-rationality as an ideal type in his famous discussion of the types of legitimate domination, the causal relationship between charisma and democracy is emphasized at the expense of minimizing the crucial role played by value-rationality in providing the democratic ethos, the world image, that both leaders and followers were inspired to implement and institutionalize within a charismatic context. In his historical sociology, Weber answered the question of how a democratic will evolves and persists "against the stream of material interests" by pointing to the value-rational principles that legitimated particular democratic outcomes. In his more conceptual work, however, Weber addressed the theoretical question of how democratic institutions can be created generally by emphasizing the role that charisma plays in leading to democratic outcomes. Here, Weber views value-rationality as a potential source of motivation for individual action and belief, but not as an integrative force capable of sustaining collective action to the extent that an organized relationship of domination ensues. Consequently, value-rationality, in and of itself, cannot generate and maintain "psychological sanctions" on the behavior of a group or a collective. Only if these sanctions are effective does an "ethic gain an independent influence on the conduct of life"[55] capable of transforming existing conditions. Such sanctions are generally only possible within a charismatic setting.

The transformatory power of the charismatic relationship between leader and followers is rooted in the creation of a new, albeit transitory, social order. All other ways of life are marginalized by the overriding imperatives of faith in the prophet and his mission. As Weber states:

> It is recognition on the part of those subject to authority which is decisive for the validity of charisma. This recognition is freely given and guaranteed by what is held to be a proof, originally always a miracle, and consists in devotion to the corresponding revelation, hero worship or absolute trust in the leader. But where charisma is genuine, it is not this which is the basis of the claim to legitimacy. This basis lies rather in the conception that it is the duty of those subject to charismatic authority to recognize its genuineness and to act accordingly. Psychologically this recognition is a matter of complete personal devotion to the possessor of the quality, arising out of enthusiasm, or of despair and hope.[56]

Based on this "complete personal devotion" a charismatic community may emerge that dissolves old ties and loyalties, and levels the hierarchies and status relationships that previously had governed people's lives. This emotional and organizational leveling may result in a "radical alteration of the central attitudes and directions of action with a completely new orientation of all attitudes toward the different problems of the 'world.' "[57] Because a charismatic community cannot sustain this degree of autonomy from the surrounding world over a long period of time, it must transform itself, or routinize into a more stable and secure environment capable of meeting the material needs and interests of the followers. In this process, democratic outcomes are possible:

> The basically authoritarian principle of charismatic legitimation may be subject to an anti-authoritarian interpretation, for the validity of charismatic authority rests entirely on recognition by the ruled, on "proof" before their eyes. To be sure, this recognition of a charismatically qualified, and hence legitimate, person is treated as a duty. But when the charismatic organization undergoes progressive rationalization, it is readily possible that, instead of recognition being treated as a consequence of legitimacy, it is treated as the basis of legitimacy: democratic legitimacy.[58]

Weber goes on to catalogue numerous types of democratic rule, such as direct democracy, plebiscitary leadership, the types of collegiality and the division of powers and, finally, representative administration. He concludes the section on democracy with the following observation:

> Genuine parliamentary representation with the voluntaristic play of interests in the political sphere, the resulting plebiscitary party organizations with its consequences, and the modern idea of rational representation by interest groups, are all peculiar to the Western World. None of these is understandable apart from the peculiar Western development of status groups and classes. Even in the Middle Ages the seeds of these phenomena were present in the Western World, and only there. It is only in the Western World that "cities" and "estates" (*rex et regnum*), "bourgeois" and "proletarians" have existed.[59]

By not taking theoretical account of the role value-rationality can play, Weber is unable to predict with any certainty when democratic outcomes are likely, and what kind of democracy will follow from any given manifestation of charisma. Throughout history, in times of turbulence and institutional breakdown, the charismatic relationship between a leader and his followers has played a critical role in establishing new patterns of conduct and new institutions. Weber's theoretical work as it stands cannot answer the question that interests us, namely, when do these charismatic eruptions lead to democratic outcomes? Based on a synthesis of Weber's historical sociology and his theoretical sociology, one can, however, hazard an answer to this question. Historically, the role played by a particular kind of value-rationality, natural law, in the development of modern democracy was amply demonstrated by Weber. By drawing the theoretical consequences from these historical insights, a new Weberian theory of democracy becomes possible.

The crucial role played by value-rationality in conjunction with charisma needs to be made explicitly part of the ideal type of charismatic domination. Once this is done, the institutional outcome of any given manifestation of charisma, its routinization in Weber's terms, will be rendered more predictable. For charismatic leaders rarely create new values. Rather, they articulate, in a novel and compelling way, values that are already part of the cultural milieu. Which values are chosen and the manner of their presentation will be critical determinants of institutional outcomes and should, therefore, become part of the ideal type. To say that an analysis of the values of a charismatic community is necessary, however, does not imply a normative judgment of these values. Therefore, Weber's methodological rule of value-neutrality will not be violated. Indeed, to connect value-rationality to charisma represents a methodological improvement and increases the explanatory power of the ideal type. For if value-rationality is studied without reference to charisma, it becomes simply a history of ideas unconnected to institutions. Similarly, the study of charisma without value-rationality easily lends itself to a "great men of history" reification. Seen from this perspective, a theoretical synthesis of Weber's work on democracy, charisma and natural law can reclaim the deep insight of his sociological method, and provide us with a fruitful point of departure for the problems faced by latecomers to democracy.

We have seen how modern democracy can be defined in ideal typical terms as a particular synthesis of value-rationality and instrumental rationality. If the rational conduct and organization characteristic of modern democracy can be captured under the concept of instrumental rationality, then the divinely inspired belief in the "free individuals" who comprise this form of political organization can be encompassed by the concept of value-rationality. Value-rationality cannot, however, simply be relegated to a secondary position in the constellation of characteristics that make up modern democracy. Its significance is twofold. First, the natural rights ethos provides the ethical norms, the "psychological sanctions" that predispose people to act in instrumentally rational ways. This is made evident by the affinity between the ethical belief in free individuals and the rational social and political organization that is considered logically appropriate for these free individuals. Second, the natural rights ethos and the natural law it is derived from provide the legitimation necessary for democratic ideas to be articulated in opposition to existing orders. Since value-rationality cannot by itself affect collective behavior, however, it must be presented in a charismatic context in order to achieve a transformation of consciousness and conduct on a broad scale. Generally, values, no matter how rationally deduced, are only binding for the individual who believes in them. An ethos derived from value-rationality may acquire an independent influence on the conduct of a charismatic community by virtue of the fact that devotion to the leader and/or his mission (if it is defined according to such an ethos) will affect the behavior of the followers. By integrating Weber's historical insights on the development of democracy and his theoretical insights on the nature of charisma, one can draw the following conclusion: a charismatic presentation of the value-rationality of natural rights has the potential of transforming both consciousness and conduct in a democratic direction. Charisma, as a type of domination, provides an organizational structure (characterized by the intense personal devotion between leader, disciples and followers) wherein value-rationality can become the predominant collective basis for ascribing legitimacy to the social order proclaimed or articulated by the leader. In such a situation, charisma and natural rights can combine their revolutionary potential to generate a breakthrough to modern democracy.

However, charismatic communities based on the value-rationality of natural rights will manifest particular features, as the absolute commitment to a single charismatic leader that is generally associated with this type of domination will be attenuated. Essentially, devotion to the values embodied by a leader will outweigh devotion to the person of the leader. Already, in the context of certain Protestant sects, for example, the idea that "God might be in every believer, or indeed in every man and woman, worked powerfully against traditional social deference, and for human equality," thereby leading to charismatic communities based on "discussion and participation by the congregation."[60] Similarly, the charismatic communities that took shape before and during the American and French Revolutions were characterized more by "discussion and participation," than by slavish devotion to a particular leader. In spite of this lack of absolutized leadership, charismatic authority was maintained on the basis of mutual devotion on the part of both leaders and followers to the natural rights doctrine. The power effectively to sanction the behavior of both leaders and followers was consequently invested in all members of the community, regardless of their standing. Weber himself provides indications that such an "anti-authoritarian interpretation" of charismatic legitimation is possible in his discussion of how charisma can be transformed in a democratic direction. In this case:

> the personally legitimated charismatic leader becomes leader by the grace of those who follow him since the latter are formally free to elect and even to depose him . . . now he is the freely elected leader. Correspondingly, the recognition of charismatic decrees and judicial decisions on the part of the community shifts to the belief that the group has a right to enact, recognize, or appeal laws, according to its own free will, both in general and for an individual case.[61]

In short, the fact that a given manifestation of value-rationality may mandate a non-authoritarian understanding of leadership should not blind us to the possibility that even this type of value-rationality may be combined with charismatic domination.

REASON AND THE INSTITUTIONALIZATION OF RIGHTS

In the event that the value-rationality of natural rights and charisma can successfully combine their revolutionary potential to generate a breakthrough to modern democracy, particular institutional arrangements will follow. Having defined modern democracy in ideal-typical terms as a particular synthesis of value-rationality and instrumental rationality, it is now incumbent upon us to examine what, specifically, was achieved institutionally in the wake of the democratic revolutions of the eighteenth century as this manifestation of charisma became routinized. To the extent that the principles of the natural rights doctrine were held in common by democrats throughout Western Europe and the United States, the central governing institutions founded on the basis of these principles all manifest certain critical similarities. However, before elaborating on the particular nature of these institutions, a more general look at the institutionalization process itself is warranted.

From a Weberian perspective, an institution can be defined as any established social entity that mandates both the organizational means and the ultimate ends of the activities pursued within its boundaries. Although Weber did not discuss institutions directly, S. N. Eisenstadt, in his elaboration of the relationship between charisma and institution-building, does provide a Weberian analysis of institutions.[62] What one can derive from Eisenstadt's work is that institutions are more than instrumental, practical, morally neutral task-oriented environments. In addition, they contain a sense of the "overall 'meanings' toward which the activities of the participants are oriented." Accordingly, social institutions are characterized by a "double aspect," comprising "their organizational exigencies on the one hand, and their potential close relations to the realm of meaning on the other."[63] It follows then that institution-building is defined in terms of

> the capacity to create and crystallize such broader symbolic orientations and norms, to articulate various goals, to establish organizational frameworks, and to mobilize the resources necessary for all these purposes (for example, the readiness to invest in the appropriate activities).[64]

The normative and contextual dimensions of this definition clearly sets it apart from the economically derived and procedurally oriented "rules of the game" conceptualization favored by Douglass C. North, among others. According to North:

> institutions are the rules of the game in a society or, more formally, are the humanly devised constraints that shape human interaction. In consequence they structure incentives in human exchange, whether political, social, or economic. Institutional change shapes the way societies evolve through time and hence is the key to understanding historical change.[65]

North goes on to add that "the rules of the game" may be written and formal, or unwritten, informal "codes of conduct that underlie and supplement formal rules."[66] While this formulation has been quite influential, especially in the literature on democratization, it is also quite narrow as it does not address how institutions come to be founded or legitimated. Specifically, North does not elaborate on the logically prior question of how the game itself is decided upon, since "rules" qua institutions can only be designed with a specific game in mind. Moreover, without this analytical distinction between the game and the rules, it is impossible to ascertain when decisive institutional change has taken place from one game to another, as opposed to periodic adjustments of the rules. Nor is it possible to highlight the conflict often seen in institutions between formal rules and informal behaviors. Informal behavior oriented toward one game will tend to subvert rather than to supplement the formal rules of another game. When analyzed from a Weberian perspective, however, these issues can be addressed. The kind of game that is established will depend on the symbolic orientations and norms prevailing in the institution-building process. The extent to which this new game can overcome informal resistance will depend on the strength and resources of the social groups that support its creation.

According to Eisenstadt, the successful establishment of an institutional framework based on a particular set of meanings and norms is contingent upon the "relative success of different competing groups of . . . leaders and entrepreneurs who attempt to impose, through a mixture of coercive, manipulative, and persuasive techniques, their own particular solution on a given situation."[67] As the appearance of such social actors is not always guaranteed, Eisenstadt goes on to indicate that

> the development of such "charismatic" personalities or groups constitutes perhaps the closest social analogy to "mutation," and the degree of their ability to forge out a viable symbolic and institutional order may be an important factor in the process of survival, or selection of different societies or cultural creations.[68]

These leading personalities or groups represent a core elite, defined not in terms of social hierarchy, but in terms of commitment to an ideology as experienced within the context of a charismatic community.

In other words, the essential features of political life sanctioned by such a community are selected and concretized in specifically agreed upon concepts—what I will term *institutional domains*—defined as the authoritative parameters or normative boundaries within which institution-building is to take place. Subsequently, these political actors attempt to identify the specific formal institutional arrangements that should be created and enforced as being consistent with the norms and meanings articulated by the community, as well as identifying the informal customs and practices to be promoted if they are similarly consistent. Correspondingly, the formal and informal institutions that are to be sanctioned as inconsistent with these norms and meanings are also identified. In short, whereas institutions can be either formal or informal, institutional domains are always formalized blueprints for the construction of a new order derived from a guiding ideology or set of meanings. To the extent that critical social groups support these domains as resonating with their interests, successful institutionalization will follow. As Eisenstadt summarizes:

> institution building is based not only on the direct or indirect exchange of various institutional resources between individuals or groups which attempt to use these resources for the implementation of their discrete, instrumental goals but in addition also necessarily includes interaction between, on the one hand, those individuals or groups who are able to articulate varied collective goals and crystallize acceptable norms and, on the other, those individuals, groups or strata that are willing to accept such regulations and norms.[69]

The willingness "to accept such regulations and norms" is, of course, enhanced if the new institutions retain enough of their charismatic origins to be considered legitimate. Here Eisenstadt's Weberian analysis dovetails well with Mary Douglas's more Durkheimian approach. For Douglas, institutions themselves represent "legitimized social groupings" that "rest their claims to legitimacy on their fit with the nature of the universe."[70] As Douglas elaborates:

> A convention is institutionalized when, in reply to the question, "why do you do it like this?" although the first answer may be framed in terms of mutual convenience, in response to further questioning the final answer refers to the way the planets are fixed in the sky or the way that plants or humans or animals naturally behave.[71]

As we have seen, natural law and the natural rights doctrine exemplify this type of legitimation. Natural rights were considered inalienable precisely because they correspond to the natural order of humankind—an order that is divinely sanctioned. In the case of the eighteenth-century democratic revolutions, new institutions were established and legitimated on this basis.

The heretofore natural hierarchies of monarchical rule and late feudal society were replaced with a new image of the true "nature of the universe." Accordingly, subjects were replaced with citizens, rule by divine right was replaced with representative government, and personalism was replaced with proceduralism. To a remarkable extent, informal institutional resistance to the new game of democratic government was also overcome as critical social groups were won over to the new game. Yet, the fact that the institutionalization of liberal democratic polities in Western Europe and the United States was successful should not blind us to the fact that the process is inherently a conflictual one, grounded in contingency not inevitability.

As democrats in the United States and Western Europe sought to organize political life in ways that would be consistent with the values and principles that had animated their struggle against absolutism, they established various institutional domains that reflected their conceptions of how best to guarantee individual freedom, and of how to construct the most rational form of government. Thus, for all of the undeniable differences among political institutions in liberal democratic countries, certain critical institutional domains are held in common. These shared domains constitute the essential characteristics of all modern democracies, without which we would not be able to analyze liberal democratic countries as belonging to the same category of political experience. Three characteristics in particular stand out: citizenship, representative government and procedurally defined public virtue.[72]

Modern democratic polities are based on a concept of sovereignty that enshrines the people as the constituent power. The members legitimately comprising this polity are thought of as free individuals acting as equally empowered citizens, not as hierarchically organized subjects. Furthermore, government in liberal democratic countries is supposed to be based on the principle of popular representation that mandates not only the validation of governing institutions via regularly held popular elections, but also allows for their transformation as a result of these elections. Finally, in all of these polities, public virtue is defined primarily in procedural and impersonal terms. Notions of personal honor prevalent in the old regime's conception of public virtue no longer provide the ethical basis for public service. While variations and differences do exist across countries within the parameters set by these institutional domains, the domains themselves are held constant. Taken together, then, these characteristics represent the defining attributes as well as the core achievements of the new political order.

Under the influence of the Enlightenment, and the culture of Reason it promulgated throughout Europe, both monarchs and their subjects began to conceive of alternative ways of reforming or transforming the political and social institutions inherited from feudalism. Whereas royal authorities used Reason to devise more efficient means of rule, groups negatively affected by increases in royal efficiency used Reason, as it was manifested in natural rights, as the justification for resistance. The words contained in a report of the Lille Bureau of Finances in 1788 speak for an entire era: "everywhere reason is combatting privileges, everywhere principles of natural equity are being raised."[73] Out of this process of reform, resistance, and ultimately revolution, a new political order emerged that, while building on the institutional legacies of feudalism and absolutism, was constituted along completely different lines.[74]

During the revolutionary era, the question of "who has the right to rule and on what basis?" was answered in such a way as to reshape fundamentally the institutional basis of the political community both in terms of its sovereignty and its constituent membership. In place of the old political community in which a divinely sanctioned monarch presided over his hierarchically organized subjects, a new political order was proclaimed on the basis of natural rights. Under these new conditions, divinely sanctioned free individuals agreed to permit themselves to be governed on the basis of equality, thereby replacing the old hierarchy of hereditary privilege with the associative principle of equal rights for all. Although the right to rule was still cast in divine terms, the people, not the monarch, were seen as the recipient of this divine favor. Sovereignty as the "supreme and independent political authority"[75] was thus vested in the population and not in the body of the monarch. In line with this new definition of sovereignty, the constituent membership of the political community (i.e. those individuals or groups that have a right to participate in public life) was transformed. In place of the hierarchically organized corporate bodies that had comprised the old order, all individuals, as citizens, now had the right to participate equally in the political community regardless of birth or occupational status.

At the center, therefore, of this newly envisioned order was the "creation of the juridical entity of the citizen"[76] as a free individual protected by formally proclaimed civil and legal rights. However, simply to declare the transformation of subjects into citizens was not enough. This transformation had to be grounded in actual events in order to achieve permanent validity. The writing and enacting of constitutions enshrining popular sovereignty and civic rights became the predominant means of establishing citizenship as a fundamental institutional domain common to all liberal polities.

In contesting the validity of the institutional structures of absolutism—structures that were legitimated by appeals to tradition and to the principle of the divine right to rule—democrats had to propose alternative ways of organizing public life. Constitutional conventions and the subsequent enacting of constitutions became the favored means of articulating a new vision of public life that revolved around the rights and duties of individual citizens and the states they had, in theory, freely chosen to constitute. These constitutions formalized the rules and guidelines that provided an authoritative institutional domain within which new patterns of behavior could emerge.

As two specialists on rights have noted:

> The United States Constitution and its first ten amendments, the Bill of Rights, not only are potent symbols of nationhood based on American understandings of the political ideals of the Enlightenment but also are working charters for the operation of increasingly powerful institutions—charters that are referred to constantly for guidance in sorting out social and political conflicts.[77]

Because the institutions of monarchy were based on the informal patterns of behavior embedded in traditional ways of doing things, democrats could not support their demands for new institutions on the basis of tradition. Instead, by basing their claims for legitimacy on the formally written and enacted rules of their constitutions, democrats hoped to achieve a decisive break with the informal, unwritten rules of monarchical government. Having enshrined the natural rights of citizens, these constitutions went on to lay a foundation for the governing institutions that would be appropriate for a new kind of political community.

Since modern democracy is based on the principle that all citizens comprising the nation have the right to be fully represented in its governance, democrats were faced with the challenge of deciding upon the means of representing these individuals. Clearly, it was no longer possible to apply ancient models of democratic government to large and populous states. It was decided, therefore, that the authority vested in every individual citizen to determine and judge the policies of his government was to be delegated to a small number of representatives. Moreover, since citizens in large states could no longer conduct the affairs of state themselves, state officials had to be entrusted with the implementation of government policies. Simultaneously, however, limits had to be defined for the authority exercised by both representatives and officials on behalf of citizens in order to protect against tyranny and abuse.

The governing bodies that emerged from these concerns were all based on the principle of popular representation. This principle is not, however, easily implemented in concrete organizational form since it requires the integration of two potentially contradictory components. On the one hand, given the liberal democratic vision that all citizens have an equal capacity for reason and, therefore, have an equal right to determine, pursue and promote their interests, government had to allow for the expression and representation of individual interests. On the other hand, government also had to promote the expression of the general interest wherein representatives set aside their particular interests in order to determine and to defend the general or common good.

Essentially, the integration of particular and general interests in liberal polities has taken place on the basis of assigning priority to the representation of citizens' interests.[78] According to changing needs and circumstances, the expression of these interests can lead to a reconceptualization of the common good. The common good in liberal polities is, therefore, not a static concept. Within the contours established by a constitution, different interpretations of the general interest have consistently been proposed and incorporated into government policy. Regardless of different institutional arrangements, all liberal governments are characterized by continuous efforts to attain and maintain a synthesis between the representation of individual interests and the determination of the common good.

These efforts are reflected in the two organizational features that have come to symbolize the institutional domain of government based on popular representation: regularly held popular elections and a stable balance of power between governing bodies. Whereas popular elections are to ensure the formal representation of individual interests, thereby providing the only appropriate validation of a government based on popular representation, an institutional balance between governing powers is intended to enhance the formation of a common good derived from these individually expressed interests. A multiplicity of interests, collectively expressed in different institutional settings, is supposed to generate an environment of protected diversity that will allow for the greatest possible common good to emerge. Through balanced competition and debate between the representatives of particular interests, the general interest can be determined without fear that it will be defined solely by one interest or set of interests. This hope is clearly exemplified by James Madison:

> Whilst all authority in it [the United States] will be derived from and dependent on the society, the society itself will be broken into so many parts, interests and classes of citizens, that the rights of individuals or of the minority, will be in little danger from interested combinations of the majority. In a free government, the security for civil rights must be the same as for religious rights.[79]

For the framers of democratic constitutions, the protection of citizens' rights represented the greatest common good a society and a free government could attain. Since their founding, however, liberal governments have had to go beyond this simple equating of the common good with the protection of civil rights to respond to new social demands ranging from the promotion of civil rights to the protection of certain social and economic rights. In the process of representing these new demands, the liberal common good has been redefined in broader and more inclusionary terms. Beyond the goal of achieving a synthesis between particular interests and the general interest, popular elections and a balance of powers were also intended to render impossible any permanent claim to represent the common good, thereby protecting against tyranny. Again to quote James Madison: "In a single republic, all the power surrendered by the people, is submitted to the administration of a single government; and usurpations are guarded against by a division of the government into distinct and separate departments."[80] Since, in theory, neither governing elites nor privileged portions of society can permanently monopolize power when government is divided in this way, popular elections should allow for the possibility of transforming government within the framework established by the Constitution. As representatives of different interests and constituencies take power, the composition and policies of governing institutions may change significantly. In other words, popular elections can have a substantive impact on politics far beyond their formal function of validation. It is this characteristic that separates liberal democratic states from façade democratic regimes that hold elections simply to validate a permanently existing monopoly of power.

Finally, in line with these efforts to constitute a new political order, public virtue itself was addressed in order to provide an image of how citizens were to behave in public life. Public virtue, in this context, can be defined as the ideal standard of moral behavior in a given political community—a standard that is also intended to provide the most appropriate means for the adjudication of conflicting interests in the polity. While this ideal standard is seldom consistently adhered to, it does provide an ethical base for public service and public life that officials and citizens are subject to as they seek to obtain the most just outcomes. Under monarchical rule, public virtue had been infused with aristocratic conceptions of personal honor, while the ethical base for public service derived from those conceptions had revolved around notions of personal loyalty and fealty. Under the new democratic political order, public virtue was increasingly defined in procedural terms, while an impersonally oriented vocationalism emerged as the ethical basis appropriate for public service in a modern democracy.

Having eradicated hierarchy, birth and privilege as the substantive criteria according to which interests were traditionally adjudicated, the builders of the new order were faced with the task of determining a new standard of adjudication. With their fundamental stress on the formal equality of all citizens, they resorted to procedural means for determining the outcomes of political and legal processes. Since the old means no longer provided guidelines for determining the best possible outcomes, outcomes that favored some individuals, interests or groups over others could no longer be justified with reference to the substantive correctness of the outcomes in favoring someone of the right birth or position. Instead, outcomes were justified with reference to the procedural correctness of the forms, procedures and rules that had provided the best possible means for adjudicating between the conflicting interests of formally equal claimants. Public virtue in a modern democracy is, therefore, characterized by notions of procedural fairness, rather than honor or loyalty.

Given the fact that "restraining, balancing and accommodating"[81] the multitude of interests represented in a liberal democratic state is a procedural task, it calls for public servants acquainted with these procedures and willing to submit to them even at the cost of personal honor. As Thomas Paine stated, "the government of a free country, properly speaking is not in the persons, but in the laws. The enacting of those requires no great expense; and when they are administered, the whole of civil government is performed."[82] In this setting, the virtuous public servant is characterized by rational, competent and purposive conduct within the context of impersonally oriented administrations. Over the course of time, the dilettantish and opportunistic attitudes of government officials under the old regime were replaced by a vocational orientation that elevated public service to the status of a profoundly felt secular calling. Instead of personal fealty to a king or to a lord, an impersonal dedication to the laws and to the Constitution of the state became the ethically appropriate standard of conduct for public service.

Taken together, these institutional domains—citizenship, representative government and proceduralism—comprise the essential political characteristics of all liberal democratic countries. As such, they represent an institutional expression of the spirit of modern democracy and, indeed, are derived from that spirit. For example, out of the "free individuals" celebrated by Thomas Paine, democrats created legally protected citizens with the right to participate equally in public life. Out of the abstract "social compact" he proclaimed as the sole appropriate foundation for government, democrats selected a system of representative government. The advance of proceduralism, as well, is foreshadowed in Paine's belief that an impersonal administration of laws provides the most appropriate means for governing a free country. Clearly, these critical institutional domains are a reflection of the synthesis between value rationality and instrumental rationality that characterizes the "historical individuality" of modern democracy. In the following case studies, we will examine how the value-rational belief in natural rights and the instrumentally rational conception of representative government were institutionalized historically in the United States and France. Such an examination entails two tasks: to outline in each case how charisma and natural rights are combined to create new institutional domains that simultaneously undermined the foundations of the ancien régime while laying the foundations for a new political order; and to explain how the institutional variations and differences developed in each country within the parameters established by the domains surveyed above.

Essentially, differences in how the institutional domains were conceptualized led to differences in institutional development. For example, although both American and French revolutionaries embraced the natural rights doctrine, thereby giving rise to the creation of citizenship as a new institutional domain based on the concept of naturally free individuals endowed with equal rights, the core elites of each revolution understood and experienced the doctrine differently. In the case of the American Revolution, where a formal natural rights interpretation held sway, citizenship was conceived of in highly individualistic terms. The freedom and autonomy of individuals was to be guaranteed above all else by the new political order. In the case of the French Revolution, on the other hand, a substantive natural rights interpretation prevailed, resulting in a more collectivistic understanding of citizenship in which the political order was to guarantee all individuals an equal ability to exercise their rights. As we shall see, guaranteeing the equality of all individuals leads to an emphasis on the collective rights of citizens over the individual rights of any one citizen. Eventually, the divinely sanctioned belief in the individual's capacity for autonomy (whether perfectly or imperfectly conceptualized) came under increasingly critical scrutiny. As the working class emerged in the nineteenth century, its leaders espoused an even more substantive and collectively oriented interpretation of natural rights that ultimately became part of the socialist doctrine. Meanwhile, traditional political and social forces (to which the German bourgeoisie belonged) mobilized to counter the revolutionary impact of natural rights with an alternative, conservative interpretation of natural law conceived in terms of a natural order of hierarchy and privilege.

It is this highly conflictual environment that latecomers to democracy must face, wherein democracy can more appropriately be described as the rational political organization of (formally) free individuals. For latecomers, the question becomes, then, can the conflict between formal and substantive natural rights principles be successfully resolved under these conditions in order to achieve a balance between individual rights and collective rights that would facilitate the institutionalization of democratic outcomes, or will the wholly collectively defined rights of either conservative or socialist origin predominate? In the following chapters this question will be addressed in historical terms. By applying the theoretical framework outlined in this chapter to the historical examples of how democracy has been legitimated and institutionalized in the American and French traditions, one can see how the balance between individual and collective rights was achieved in these cases.

This distinction between individualistic (Anglo-American) and collectivistic (French) understandings of citizenship is, of course, not novel and has most recently been analyzed in comparative historical context by Liah Greenfeld in her work on nationalism.[83] To a considerable extent, the following case studies of the American and French Revolutions reflect the outline developed by Greenfeld and historians such as R. R. Palmer in detailing the rise of discontent among critical social groups and their subsequent search for new ideas capable of addressing and solving the crises in which they found themselves. In the course of this search, the new identity of citizenship, in its individualistic and collectivistic forms, was forged. To a considerable extent, as well, the case studies follow the distinction between these two forms as described by Greenfeld. The analytical focus presented here differs, however, from Greenfeld's approach. Specifically, Greenfeld does not address the question of how ideas and identities are translated into institutions. For example, the idea of popular sovereignty that Greenfeld identifies as the central component of the original concept of the nation did not emerge automatically from "a profound change in structural conditions"[84] experienced by "influential social groups."[85] While such conditions are necessary, they are not sufficient. Ideas must be experienced as value-rational commitments within the context of charismatic communities in order to achieve a lasting influence first on the construction of institutional domains and then on the development of institutions. As the histories of the American and French Revolutions demonstrate, ideas such as popular sovereignty only became meaningful institutionally through the mechanism provided by the combined effects of value-rationality and charisma.

2 Formal natural rights and the American Revolution

"Justice," declared James Madison, "is the end of government. It is the end of civil society. It ever has been and ever will be pursued until it is obtained, or until liberty be lost in the pursuit."[1] For democratic revolutionaries of the eighteenth century, justice pursued meant the pursuit of natural rights, while justice obtained meant the establishment of governments founded on these rights. Yet, in spite of this clear consensus on what should be the end of government, the appropriate institutional means to that end were less apparent. It was easier, by far, to derive the philosophical principles that legitimated the struggle against absolutism from the natural rights doctrine than to derive specific institutional and organizational guidelines from that doctrine. Democrats, therefore, had to determine the means whereby natural rights were to be secured and protected in a new political order. In so doing, they struggled to harmonize their beliefs and convictions with the inevitable necessities and compromises of political life. During the course of this struggle, the defining institutional characteristics of liberal democratic government took shape—characteristics that are shared to a great extent by all democracies. However, liberal democratic countries are divided by considerable institutional differences as well. The task before us in these case studies is to provide a theoretically informed understanding of how both similarities and differences evolved during the founding period of modern democracies. A theoretical focus on the values proclaimed in opposition to absolutism, on the charismatic context in which they were proclaimed, and on the various political actors and social groups that adhered to these values, should illuminate the dynamics of how this new order was successfully institutionalized throughout Western Europe and the United States.

Accordingly, the following two chapters will present case studies of the American and French Revolutions in order to illustrate how the institutional similarities and differences emerged. While the case studies will cover well-known territory, it is to be hoped that new comparative light will be shed on these familiar historical processes. Specifically, both countries doubtlessly manifest features that allow us to classify them as liberal democratic. Yet they also manifest considerable differences in the way in which their respective governments are constructed. In both cases, the dynamic of institutionalization that resulted in these similarities and differences was determined by how the conflict between formal and substantive interpretations of natural rights was resolved. For while charisma and natural rights combined their revolutionary potential to generate a breakthrough to modern democracy in Western Europe and the United States, the outcomes varied according to the differing interpretations of natural rights held by the political actors taking part in the revolutionary upheavals.

In the ensuing chapter (Chapter 4), the significance of natural rights for the concomitant development of the capitalist free market will be elaborated. Here, as well, although the market economy is a shared institutional characteristic of democratic countries, variations have occurred in how the market is understood and regulated. These variations can also be explained by the differing interpretations of natural rights. In spite of these differences, the following account should make it clear that citizenship, representative government, proceduralism and the free market together comprise the essential institutional domains of liberal capitalism that latecomers to democracy must adopt and come to terms with.

NATURAL RIGHTS AND THE CHARISMATIC CREATION OF CITIZENS

> Subject is derived from the latin words, sub and jacio, and means one who is under the power of another; but a citizen is an unit of a mass of free people, who, collectively, possess sovereignty. Subjects look up to a master, but citizens are so far equal, that none have hereditary rights superior to others. Each citizen of a free state contains, within himself, by nature and the constitution, as much of the common sovereignty as another.[2]
>
> (David Ramsay, 1789)

In these few sentences, the South Carolina physician and historian David Ramsay has captured the fundamental aspects of the political and social transformation that took place as a result of the American Revolution. During the period between the signing of the Declaration of Independence in 1776 and the ratification of the federal Constitution in 1789, the traditional habits of deference and dependency that had characterized colonial life gave way to new standards of social and political interaction. Prior to the Revolution, sovereignty had been understood as the legitimate monopolization of power by those claiming hereditary rights. People without such rights were expected to defer, both in public life and in private life, to men of rank and breeding since it was assumed that they possessed superior talents and capabilities. This assumption and the understanding of sovereignty it was based upon were decisively undermined by the claim put forth during the Revolution that sovereignty resided in all citizens. As individuals endowed with natural rights that existed independently of birth and social standing, all citizens could legitimately partake in the exercise of power. Before, during and after the Revolution, large numbers of citizens from the formerly passive "lower" orders did indeed exercise their power by participating in government and by publicly pursuing their interests.[3] Subsequently, Americans would never again see government as a mysterious business best left to men with the right education, status and breeding.

This transformation, from passive subject to active citizen, has certainly not been overlooked in analyses of the American Revolution. Generally, these analyses can be divided into two approaches: those that focus on the social history of Revolutionary period, and those that focus on the history of the political ideas that animated the Revolution. While the former approach charts the changes in social, political and economic life as previously excluded social groups gained an active voice in the polity, the latter approach documents the political philosophy that accompanied these changes.[4] As a result of this division, analysts cannot do justice to the question of how ideas relate to changes in social, political and economic behavior. Ideas cannot, in and of themselves, prompt such widespread and wide-reaching changes. On the other hand, neither do these changes take place independently of ideas.

In the account offered here, a mode of analysis will be presented that should allow for a more nuanced exploration of the relationship between ideas and actions. Ideas can attain a binding validity for individual behavior when legitimated by a value-rational faith in the rectitude of these ideas. In conjunction with a charismatically oriented organization, ideas can then become binding for a collective and capable of determining the shape and direction of collective behavior.

The American Revolution resulted in profound social and political changes because the faith many individuals had in the natural rights doctrine became binding for critical collectivities in the context of the charismatic communities prevalent during that era. In the Committees of Correspondence, in the Minutemen militias, in the Sons of Liberty, members of two critical social groups—the gentry and the artisans—came face to face with one another. Animated by their shared faith in the values and principles of the natural rights doctrine, they began to act and to organize themselves in accordance with the democratic means mandated by the doctrine. Subsequently, institutional domains and governing institutions were established on the basis of the transformation in consciousness and conduct that took place in these charismatic communities. Before such a transformation could take place, however, conditions had to be present that brought the old categories of social and political life into question. This account will, therefore, begin with the antecedent conditions before elaborating on the changes wrought by the combined power of value-rationality and charisma.

ANTECEDENTS

In his recent work, Gordon S. Wood has characterized the mood of pre-revolutionary America as one of "uneasy prosperity."[5] The colonies may have been increasingly rich and successful, but pervasive fears about the permanence of these achievements generated an atmosphere conducive to "a popular revolutionary movement."[6] Many Americans had experienced the fruits of rapid upward mobility, but were insecure about their ability to retain these fruits in the face of the growing political, social and economic influence of the mother country. Through individual enterprise, endeavor and talent, people of the lower orders had broken through the traditional barriers to advancement to take their place among colonial society's "gentlemen." Their lives embodied what was to become a fundamental premise of the Revolution: "that people were not born to be what they might become."[7]

Prior to the mid-eighteenth century, colonial society had provided considerable support for such mobility. From the very beginning, the vicissitudes of colonial life had created degrees of social, economic and political equality unknown in the older, more rigidly constructed societies that had been left behind in Europe. The colonists governed themselves in small assemblies, they consorted and prayed with one another regardless of social rank, and the majority of them made their living in the same way as small landowners. This is, of course, not to claim that all social distinctions were eradicated. Compared to Europe, the relative absence of absolute hierarchies of birth, status and privilege simply meant that the colonists had a greater opportunity for advancement from one social grade to the next. Moreover, the Protestant religion, in which most colonists devoutly believed, provided considerable moral support, some would say even a moral imperative, for consistent efforts to advance oneself through hard work and discipline.

By the mid-eighteenth century, however, social hierarchies were beginning to solidify, at the same time as England began imposing greater political, economic and cultural control over the colonies. As the conditions of colonial life became more comfortable and more secure, it became easier to emulate European standards of social interaction. For many colonists, these standards still represented what it meant to be civilized and they were only too happy to replicate the hierarchies and patterns of patronage, the courtly manners and elaborate styles of dress in their own lives. Yet, in the course of a few decades, the desirability of this emulation came under increasingly critical scrutiny as England's power became more and more noxious to the Americans. Colonial governors appointed by the Crown were given ever greater authority, thereby diminishing the role of the colonial assemblies at the same time as the English parliament was attempting to increase the tax revenues collected from the colonies. The famous cry "no taxation without representation" emerged from this situation. Colonial Americans who were not represented in the parliament and whose local assemblies were coming under attack were in no mood to acquiesce quietly to England's demands. Furthermore, the ongoing efforts to elevate the Anglican Church to the role of the state church had not gone unnoticed by the ministers of other denominations. They, in turn, became very willing to sound the alarm among their parishioners against English conspiracies and English corruption. These fears of conspiracy and perceptions of corruption fell on fertile ground. All colonial Americans who owed their positions to the upward mobility made possible by the unique circumstances of colonial life felt threatened by the increasing influence of the old world.[8] Two groups, in particular, felt affected enough to provide the active core of revolutionaries who were to galvanize their more passive neighbors into open rebellion. From the first group, the colonial gentry, came the "founding fathers" of American democracy such as Thomas Jefferson, Alexander Hamilton, James Madison and Samuel Adams. By and large, they were professionals, lawyers and physicians, eager to culminate their careers by holding public office, yet frustrated by England's increasing control over the power of appointments. As Wood points out, "in an important sense the Revolution was fought over just this issue—over differing interpretations of who in America were the proper social leaders who ought naturally to accede to positions of public authority."[9] The second group, the mechanics and artisans, did not furnish history with many enduring names, yet they too felt their frustrated ambitions keenly enough to organize and to engage in revolutionary activity:

> Beginning with the Stamp Act disturbances and the formation of the Sons of Liberty in the several colonial ports in 1765, ordinary people—chiefly mechanics or artisans from many different crafts—came together to call for the boycotting of British goods. In 1772 the mechanics of Philadelphia, who comprised half the male residents of the city whose occupations are known, formed the Patriotic Society, the first organized nonreligious public pressure group in Pennsylvania's history. In New York the mechanics began convening in taverns but soon bought a meeting place for themselves and named it Mechanics Hall. . . . By 1775 the royal governor of Georgia could only shake his head in astonishment that the revolutionary committee in control of Savannah consisted of "a Parcel of the Lowest People, chiefly carpenters, shoemakers, blacksmiths etc. with a Jew at their head."[10]

Members of these two social groups joined together to form a core elite that promulgated revolutionary ideas, organized resistance to British rule and, ultimately, created new governing institutions. Without the presence of such a core elite, the general uneasiness and uncertainty prevalent in the colonies at the time would never have been sufficient to generate a revolution. For although structural conditions and social grievances are necessary antecedents, they are not sufficient, in and of themselves, to bring about a revolution. A committed core elite is necessary to provide leadership and direction, and to promote the revolutionary cause amongst the general population.

In the case of the American Revolution, the composition of this core elite provided access to all segments of society. Radical artisans could speak to their communities, while radical members of the gentry could speak to the upper ranks of society. Such widespread social penetration prevented the Revolution from disintegrating into a "private quarrel between rival gentleman leaders."[11] The extent to which the ideals and aims of the Revolution resonated with ordinary people became especially apparent during the debates between the Federalists and the Anti-Federalists over the ratification of the Constitution. Although this debate was in some danger of becoming an elite quarrel, the fact that artisan communities throughout the United States were actively in favor of the Federalist position had significant consequences. In the first place, artisan support was instrumental in ratifying the Constitution. For example, on 23 July 1788 in the city of New York, "between five and six thousand craftsmen—virtually every artisan in New York City—turned out for a grand procession to support ratification of the Constitution."[12] Beyond this, however, their participation in the debates vested the document with a validity amongst the general population that it might not otherwise have attained. Since ordinary Americans, artisans, mechanics and merchants, saw their interests supported and furthered by the Constitution, they were willing to live in accordance with the newly established governing institutions. The new polity was thereby inaugurated on the basis of a stable and broadly based social consensus.

THE NATURAL RIGHTS DOCTRINE

Having identified the social composition of the core elite and its significance to the American Revolution, we now turn to an examination of the beliefs that animated and legitimated the struggle of this elite. Men and women who endure the risks of taking decisive action in an environment characterized by uncertainty and turbulence need to be convinced of the fundamental rectitude of their actions. Structural conditions and interest-based grievances alone cannot provide such assurances. Rather, people must interpret their situation in such a way as to legitimate action and resistance. In the case of the American Revolution, the core elite readily embraced the language of natural rights in order to interpret their grievances as wrongs that had to be corrected at any cost—even at the cost of open rebellion against England.

While natural rights have not been ignored in studies of the intellectual origins of the Revolution, the doctrine has often been downplayed as only one influence among the many that played a role in animating the colonists to rebellion.[13] Indeed, Forrest McDonald finds that "those ideological historians who have concentrated on the tradition of civic humanism . . . have neglected the importance of theories of natural law and natural rights."[14]

Redressing this neglect does not, however, justify singling out the natural rights doctrine as the sole intellectual current of significance for the Revolution. Clearly, this would be foolish as numerous studies have attested to the multiplicity of intellectual influences on the colonial gentry. The claim made here is that, from among the multiplicity of influences, the natural rights doctrine proved to be the most influential *shared* language, providing a common set of beliefs capable of transcending differences in social standing and educational background.

In other words, while the classics and republican treatises were not commonly found among the lower orders, the natural rights doctrine was both readily available to *all* of the colonists, and well suited to provide solutions to the crisis generated by resistance to England. Consequently, once the doctrine was adopted by the core elite—the revolutionary gentry and artisans—it had a profound effect on the course of events. According to the historian Ernest Barker:

> There were two ways in which the theory of natural law affected American thought and action. The first was that of destruction. It served as a charge of powder which blasted the connection with Great Britain and cleared the way for the Declaration of Independence. The second way was that of construction. It served as a foundation for the building of new constitutions.[15]

Thinking in terms of rights came easily to the colonists since it was supported by their (non-Anglican) ministers and by the most profound philosophical works of the era. Protestant ministers such as John Wise, Jonathan Mayhew and Samuel Quincy sanctified a universally binding relationship between God, Nature and Reason and the rights derived from reason to such an extent that "there crept into the mind of the average man this conception of Natural Law to confirm his faith in the majesty of God while destroying his faith in the majesty of Kings."[16] As the "majesty of Kings" was undermined, so too was the traditional belief in the virtue and privileged rulership of the few "wellborn" and wealthy members of society. According to Mayhew, for example:

> To say that subjects in general are *not* proper judges when their governors oppress them, and play the Tyrant . . . is as great *treason* as ever man uttered;—'tis treason,—not against one *single* man, but the state—against the whole body politic;—'tis treason against God. . . . The people know for what end they set up, and maintain their governors; and they are the proper judges when they execute their *trust* as they ought to do it.[17]

Mayhew's argument was repeated throughout New England by other preachers who did not hesitate to tell their magistrates that government

> was not appointed, that some Men might enjoy Riches, Dignity, and Power above others, exclusive of the good of the Public. . . . That some

> might be clothed in Purple, and fine Linen, and fare sumptuously every Day; while others must be fed with the Crumbs that fall from the Table. No; Societies were not formed for the sake of Rulers, but Rulers were made for the sake of Societies.[18]

As Bushman summarizes in his study of Connecticut, "the familiar belief in the derivation of political authority from God was still repeated but with a new meaning. Emphasis shifted from the subject's obligation to obey to the ruler's obligation to serve."[19] Underlying this shift in emphasis was a decisive change in the colonists' understanding of the divinely sanctioned rights to which they were entitled. In this context, the words of the pamphleteer Daniel Fowle are significant:

> The Rights of the People are *certainly divine* as well as the Rights of Magistrates; and I hope no one will dispute, but the Rights of the People are *more divine* than the Rights of their Representatives, as the latter have no more than a *delegated* Power from . . . the People; and they receive and hold that Power only *from* them, and *by* them.[20]

Meanwhile, the colonial gentry were exposed, through the philosophical training of the time, to the works on natural law written by such authorities as Pufendorf, Burlamaqui, Vattel and Locke, from whom they drew guidance and inspiration. Given the prevalence of natural law, it is not surprising that Jefferson based the Declaration of Independence on the natural rights doctrine since his aim was "to place before mankind the common sense of the subject in terms so plain and firm as to command their assent."[21] Arguably, no other language was as "common," and as well understood.

Moreover, the natural rights doctrine provided the colonists with a strong legal foundation to legitimate their claims against the mother country. At the beginning of the conflict with England, the colonists derived their rights from the charters and the Bills of Rights that had accompanied the founding of their colonies. As Englishmen they felt that they could lay claim to specific rights that had been enumerated and guaranteed by royal covenant. Yet, as R. R. Palmer points out:

> When the highest English authorities disagreed on what Americans claimed as English rights, and when the Americans ceased to be English by abjuring their King, they were obliged to find another and less ethnocentric or merely historical principle of justification. They now called their rights the rights of man.[22]

Clearly, the doctrine provided a compelling solution to the crisis brought about by colonial resistance to English demands. The availability and suitability of the natural rights discourse should not, however, mislead us into thinking that the revolutionary core elite simply adhered to this discourse in a utilitarian or instrumental fashion. It is on the basis of faith and conviction that men such as Alexander Hamilton were prepared to risk their lives and their way of life. The force of this conviction is clearly present in Hamilton's ringing proclamation of 1774, originally written in bold, arresting capitals:

> THE SACRED RIGHTS OF MANKIND ARE NOT TO BE RUMMAGED FOR AMONG OLD PARCHMENTS OR MUSTY RECORDS. THEY ARE WRITTEN, AS WITH A SUNBEAM, IN THE WHOLE VOLUME OF HUMAN NATURE, BY THE HAND OF DIVINITY ITSELF, AND CAN NEVER BE ERASED OR OBSCURED BY MORTAL POWER.[23]

Conviction also infused the words of the lawyer John Dickinson when he rejected, in 1766, the notion that "the rights essential to happiness" can be given by kings and parliaments:

> We claim them from a higher source—from the King of kings, and Lord of all the earth. They are not annexed to us by parchments and seals. They are created in us by the decrees of Providence, which establish the laws of our nature. They are born with us; exist with us; and cannot be taken from us by any human power without taking our lives. In short, they are founded on the immutable maxims of reason and justice.[24]

Ultimately, such conviction sustained the revolutionaries as they faced death. This is exemplified by the response patriot prisoners made when confronted with British threats of execution: "we have only to regret that our Blood cannot be disposed of more to the advancement of the Glorious cause to which we have adher'd."[25] Not insignificantly, this particular group of Charleston prisoners contained artisans and mechanics, as well as planters and lawyers. In short, the "Glorious cause" to which the core elite adhered was liberty, and the cause of liberty was almost universally justified and vindicated as the pursuit of one of the fundamental natural rights of man. These natural rights were God-given, not man-made, and therefore inalienable. Nowhere is this more evident than in the Declaration of Independence:

> We hold these truths to be self-evident, That all men are created equal, that they are endowed by their creator with certain inalienable rights; that among these are life, liberty and the pursuit of happiness; that to secure these rights governments are instituted among men, deriving their just powers from the consent of the governed.[26]

While the pursuit of liberty was perhaps paramount during the years of the Revolution, the belief that men are created equal was also to prove highly influential both during and after the Revolution. During the Revolution, the concept of equality grounded in natural law legitimated the new habits of non-deferential intercourse between disparate social groups—habits which were to be consolidated in the charismatic communities. In the years following 1776, American social and political life proceeded in the direction of an ever more equalitarian democracy as evidenced by the successful Jeffersonian and Jacksonian responses to the rise of a new post-revolutionary aristocracy of wealth and privilege.[27] Again, not insignificantly, artisans and craftsmen participated actively in these efforts to promote the equality of rights across all social groups. As Wilentz indicates, "political equality, the right of all independent, virtuous citizens—including the artisans—to exercise their will without interference from a nobility of privilege, wealth, or title," was of primary significance for the artisan communities of New York.[28] Accordingly, "the craftsmen would insist on their equal rights and exercise their citizenship with a view to preserving the rule of virtue as well as to protecting their collective interests against an eminently corruptible mercantile and financial elite."[29] Not surprisingly, citizenship was understood by the artisans in terms of natural rights as this category of political membership "stood for men's obligations to exercise their natural political rights."[30]

The natural rights doctrine, as articulated during the Revolution, also had considerable influence on the abolitionist movement. For example, in 1779 two Connecticut slaves used the language of rights in the pursuit of their own cause of liberty:

> We do ask for nothing but what we are fully persuaded is ours to claim, for Reason and Revelation join to declare, that we are the Creatures of that God, who made of one Blood, and Kindred, all the Nations of the Earth . . . there is nothing that leads us to a Belief, or Suspicion, that we are any more obligated to serve them, than they us, and the more we Consider of this matter, the more we are Convinced of our Right . . . to be free . . . and can never be convinced that we were made to be Slaves.[31]

According to Gary Nash, "such statements . . . throwing the political theory being fashioned to justify the American challenge against English oppression in the face of American patriots, provide some of the most compelling language of the revolutionary era."[32] White abolitionists, as well, used the natural rights doctrine in support of their cause, as did David Rice in 1792:

> A slave claims his freedom, he pleads that he is a man, that he was by nature free, that he had not forfeited his freedom, nor relinquished it. Now unless his master can prove that he is not a man, that he was not born free, or that he has forfeited or relinquished his freedom, he must be judged free; the justice of his claim must be acknowledged. His being long deprived of this right, by force or fraud, does not annihilate it, it remains; it is still his right.[33]

In spite of the failure immediately to abolish slavery, a "tradition of protest" was kept alive in the black community "by holding up the principles of 1776 and 1787 before white petitioners and legislators in order to show them how far they had strayed from their own faith."[34] In the early 1800s, as white Americans, such as Noah Webster, began subjecting the natural rights doctrine to critical re-evaluation, black Americans still laid claim to the doctrine.[35] In 1813, for example, James Forten wrote:

> We hold this truth to be self-evident, that God created all men equal, is one of the most prominent features in the Declaration of Independence, and in that glorious fabric of collected wisdom, our noble Constitution. This idea embraces the Indian and the European, the savage and the Saint, the Peruvian and the Laplander, the white man and the African, and whatever measures are adopted subversive of this inestimable privilege, are in direct violation of the letter and spirit of our Constitution.[36]

Clearly, from the days of the Revolution and beyond, the natural rights doctrine encouraged the belief that Americans had a divinely mandated obligation to govern themselves with laws established in accordance with these rights. As the preacher Levi Hart stated in 1775, liberty was "a power of acting agreeable to the laws which are made and enacted by the consent of the PEOPLE, and in no ways inconsistent with the natural rights of a single person, or the good of the society."[37] If these laws and rights were violated, resistance was not only justified but imperative. On these philosophical grounds, both colonial resistance to England and subsequent civil rights movements demanding an extension of rights to previously excluded groups were justified.[38]

In terms of the Revolution itself, both the destructive and the constructive capacities of the natural rights doctrine as indicated by Barker are evident. On the one hand, the war against England that destroyed traditional ties and loyalties was legitimated by natural rights. On the other hand, the pursuit of these rights set in motion efforts to establish just and reasonable laws whereby liberty might be sustained once it had been attained. In this constructive endeavor, the role of the charismatic communities in transforming consciousness and conduct was critical.

CHARISMATIC COMMUNITIES

It was in the charismatic context of revolutionary communities that the ideas of the natural rights doctrine were given behavioral substance, or in Samuel Adams' phrase, "reduced to practice."[39] In other words, in the "communities of discussion,"[40] and later of action, that sprang up throughout the colonies in the years immediately preceding the Revolution, men began to act as if they were indeed free and equal with equal rights to participate in the formation of a movement of resistance. This transformation had two central components: a process of social leveling and the development of democratic rules and procedures. Both of these components would inform subsequent efforts to establish just governing institutions. After the Revolution, as members of the core elite faced the task of determining the appropriate form of government, they applied the principles and procedures that had governed their conduct in the charismatic communities to the governing of the country at large.

Charisma is inherently a leveling force. By subordinating oneself solely to a leader or to the cause embodied by a leader, the hierarchies and status relationships that had previously governed one's life are rendered meaningless and are ultimately dissolved. Followers or members of the community are then available for a complete reorientation toward "the different problems of the 'world.'"[41] In the American case, the "complete personal devotion" characteristic of followers was not oriented toward a preeminent leader, but toward the natural rights doctrine itself. Leaders certainly existed in the various communities, but they were subordinate to the mission they embodied. In other words, they derived their legitimacy as leaders from the doctrine, not from their personal vision. It was to the "Glorious cause" that the revolutionaries felt they owed their allegiance, their loyalty and even their lives. As natural law is "the sum total of all those norms which are valid independently of, and superior to, any positive law,"[42] it is also valid independently of any particular leader.

Yet this personal devotion to the cause needed to take place within the organizational structure of a charismatic community in order to have an effect on collective behavior. By providing a compelling context within which particular types of behavior are either promoted or sanctioned, a charismatic community can effect a transformation of social and political identities. Indeed, a general pattern of leaders, disciples (or, rather, active organizers) and followers was replicated in all of the communities of the American Revolution. Within these communities, hierarchies of birth, privilege and social standing lost their relevance and their power to inform behavior. Since all members of the community could make valuable contributions to the cause, contributions that were promoted and validated within the community, original social positions became meaningless. Out of this social leveling emerged a new status position, common to all adherents of the cause, that of citizen.

On the basis of their contributions to the cause, men of different backgrounds learned to accord one another trust and respect as citizens. This respect was most significant for the gentry members of the core elite. By working with artisans and mechanics they acquired a different attitude toward the lower orders. For example, in 1800 Christopher Gadsden, a Revolutionary gentry leader in Charleston, reflected on the contributions made by the artisans to the cause:

> From the first of, and throughout the revolution, none have shewn themselves more firm and steady in the most dangerous and trying occasions, in short, had it not been for their assistance, we should have made a very poor figure indeed.[43]

Overall, Gadsden referred to the Revolutionary artisans as "that useful body of citizens, whose worth, no man in the city, perhaps, is better acquainted with than myself."[44]

As documented by American historians, the social leveling that took place was extensive, pervading every aspect of Revolutionary activity and organization.[45] While the gentry learned to trust the masses, these formerly silent members of society began to act with self-confidence as they claimed their rights within the charismatic communities. As Barker describes this process:

> The town-meeting began to be crowded: a radical and popular wave of opinion came like a bore or an eagre into the channel hitherto occupied by the few—the few whose title had once rested on grace and election, but had latterly come to repose on money and merchandise. The caucus club altered its character: it "took in a large number of mechanics," and a mechanic was now generally chosen to be its president.[46]

Whether in the traditional assemblies or in new organizations such as the Sons of Liberty, men of different social standing came together bound by a common cause and by commonly held convictions. Perhaps the most famous relationship that exemplifies the leveling effects of these communities is the friendship between Paul Revere, an artisan, and Dr. Joseph Warren, a prominent Boston doctor. Between these two men "had grown a genuine affection, born of political rebellion and bonded by common cause and common peril."[47] Together as Mohawks they participated in the Boston Tea Party, together they alerted the countryside that the British army was on the march, and together they were celebrated in a street ballad: "Our Warren's there and bold Revere, With hands to do and words to cheer, For liberty and laws."[48] Without their membership in organizations devoted to the common cause, they never would have been able to "break down the social barrier that existed between the world of the mechanic and the circle of the well-born, Harvard-bred doctor."[49]

Together, then, men of different social backgrounds decided to fight a war for independence on the basis of shared principles. Guided by these natural rights principles, democratic means and procedures were consistently chosen to reach the common goal of independence. Perhaps the most remarkable feature of the American Revolution is the extent to which democratic procedures were followed even in the most adverse circumstances of war. Committee meetings and public meetings were generally conducted in a sober and reasonable manner. Propositions were voted upon, leaders and representatives were nominated and elected. Considerable effort and maneuvering went into rendering these leadership tickets as representative as possible of the community. All constituencies felt they had a right to be represented in the deliberations by leaders of their own choosing. Thus, the mechanics of Philadelphia stated unequivocally in 1770 that although they had, in the past, allowed themselves to be ruled by others, this submission was now at an end:

> this we have tamely submitted to so long, that those Gentlemen make no Scruple to say, that the Mechanics (though by far the most numerous, especially in this County) have no Right to speak or think for themselves. But I would beg Leave to ask, have we not the same Privileges and Liberties to preserve or lose as themselves? Have we not an equal right of electing, or being elected? If we have not the Liberty of nominating such Persons whom we approve, our Freedom of voting is at an End. . . . I would not be understood that we should unite to oppose them, but with them, in chusing upright Men, who will promote the public Good; at the same Time I think it absolutely necessary, that one or two Mechanics be elected to represent so large a Body of Inhabitants.[50]

Ernest Barker has drawn attention to the extent to which there was a belief in the "congruity of political democracy with the religious democracy of God's Church"[51] (especially with the principle of elected leadership espoused by Congregationalism) in colonial America. The Congregationalist minister John Wise concluded in 1717, after his study of the natural rights philosophy of Pufendorf, that "a democracy in church or state is a very honorable and regular government according to the dictates of right reason."[52] Already prior to the Revolution, the Congregationalist practice of elected ministerial leadership had made itself felt in other domains. During the Seven Years' War, for example, the British were considerably frustrated by the lack of hierarchical discipline among the colonial militias that elected their own officers and decided by majority vote whether or not they would continue to fight.[53] Here, we find support for Weber's thesis that the "inalienable personal right of the governed against any power" emerged under the charismatic influence of the Protestant sects.[54] This right, among others, was further amplified and put into political practice by a socially mixed core elite in the charismatic communities of the revolutionary period.

Subsequently, men who had participated on equal terms in the planning and making of a revolution fought for the right of all men to life, liberty and the pursuit of happiness were ready to create and acknowledge new ways of organizing social and political life. As the democratic habits and principles of interaction sanctioned by these charismatic communities stripped away the traditional forms of social hierarchy, privilege and patronage, they paved the way for the formation of a new government based on the right of all individuals to be represented in the polity's decision-making process.

Moreover, the tradition of community self-government was continued as the preferred means of civic action linking individual citizens in the pursuit of a common cause outside of the direct realm of the government. As de Tocqueville noted in the early nineteenth century:

> The citizen of the United States is taught from infancy to rely upon his own exertions, in order to resist the evils and the difficulties of life; he looks upon the social authority with an eye of mistrust and anxiety, and he claims its assistance only when he is unable to do without it. This habit may be traced even in the schools, where the children in their games are wont to submit to rules which they have themselves established, and to punish misdemeanors which they themselves have defined. The same spirit pervades every act of social life. If a stoppage occurs in a thoroughfare, and the circulation of vehicles is hindered, the neighbors immediately form themselves into a deliberative body; and this extemporaneous assembly gives rise to an executive power, which remedies the inconvenience before anybody has thought of recurring to a pre-existing authority superior to that of the persons immediately concerned. . . . In the United States, associations are established to promote the public safety, commerce, industry, morality and religion. There is no end which the human will despairs of attaining through the combined power of individuals united into a society.[55]

Divested of their charismatic content, yet still imbued with more legitimacy than any external "social authority," post-revolutionary communities now acted as "political associations" in which being a concerned citizen was enough to guarantee membership.

In the wake of the Revolution, citizenship thereby became the fundamental category of social and political interaction. By de Tocqueville's time the political equality of American citizens, combined with a lack of deference toward social hierarchies, had resulted in a particularly dynamic society wherein "the image of an ideal but always fugitive perfection presents itself to the human mind."[56] Since castes and ascriptive status positions had disappeared:

> Continual changes are then every instant occurring under the observation of every man: the position of some is rendered worse; and he learns but too well that no people . . . can lay claim to infallibility: the condition of others is improved; whence he infers that man is endowed with an indefinite faculty of improvement. His reverses teach him that none have discovered absolute good—his success stimulates him to the never-ending pursuit of it. Thus, forever seeking, forever falling to rise again, —often disappointed, but not discouraged—he tends unceasingly towards that unmeasured greatness so indistinctly visible at the end of the long track which humanity has yet to tread.[57]

Accordingly, one can conclude that under the influence of the social leveling and the civic equality fostered in the charismatic communities, Jefferson's natural right to the pursuit of happiness soon expressed itself as the continuous pursuit of progress embedded in the idea of the "indefinite perfectibility of man."[58] In this pursuit, the primary initiative was retained by individual citizens, acting alone or in associations, not by the government. As this fact had already been recognized by the constitutional framers, the best and most just government in their opinion would be one that was limited in the exercise of power. A representative, but also unobtrusive and noninterventionist, government was clearly called for. Consequently, the question of how to limit government, while simultaneously ensuring it sufficient strength and capacity to carry out its tasks, became the main preoccupation of the new political leadership in the aftermath of the war for independence.

INSTITUTIONAL CONSEQUENCES

The Constitution of 1789 established a government that embodied all of the three institutional domains presented above: citizenship, popular representation and proceduralism. These domains were, however, constituted in a particular manner, one that corresponded to the interpretation of natural rights held by the political actors seeking to distill authoritative guidelines for institution-building from the ethos that had legitimated their struggle against the British monarchy. Essentially, the famous natural rights triad of "life, liberty and the pursuit of happiness" proclaimed by Thomas Jefferson in the Declaration of Independence already embodied the formal interpretation of rights that was to remain paramount in the American deliberations over the creation of a government. In other words, the American rights formulations did not identify or mandate any specific substantive collective outcomes toward which government should be oriented. Instead, they specified the realms of conscience, action and endeavor that government was to leave in the hands of individual citizens. Government, according to these formulations, was simply to guarantee the lives and liberty of its citizens, as well as promising non-interference with the lawful means chosen by individuals in the pursuit of happiness and property. Outcomes would thereby be the result of any given individual's proclivities, talents and fortunes.

The extent of the individualism inherent in the American natural rights doctrine is exemplified by the following quotation from a 1772 declaration of the rights of the colonists written under the supervision of Samuel Adams:

> Among the Natural Rights of the colonists are these. First a Right to Life; Secondly to Liberty; thirdly to Property; together with the Right to support and defend them in the best manner they can. Those are evident Branches of, rather than deductions from the Duty of Self Preservation, commonly called the first Law of Nature.[59]

Lest there by any doubt as to the locus of these rights, the document goes on to elaborate by stating that "the absolute Rights of Englishmen, and all freemen in or out of Civil society, are principally, personal security personal liberty and private property."[60]

The formal quality of these rights is apparent from the way in which subsequent state Declarations worded their understanding of the rights that were to form the "basis and foundation of Government."[61] For example, the Virginia Declaration of 1776 states:

> That all men are by nature equally free and independent, and have certain inherent rights, of which, when they enter into a state of society, they cannot, by any compact, deprive or divest their posterity; namely, the enjoyment of life and liberty, with the means of acquiring and possessing property, and pursuing and obtaining happiness and safety.[62]

What is significant in this understanding of rights is its emphasis on individual means as opposed to collective outcomes. No attempt is made to define a collective good or outcome such as "*solidarité*," one of the famous watchwords of the French Revolution, toward which a government should direct its policies. Even the potentially collective and substantive notion of equality is relegated to an ancillary position. Jefferson, in the Declaration of Independence, was quite clear on that point. To reiterate:

> We hold these truths to be self-evident, That all men are created equal, that they are endowed by their creator with certain unalienable rights; that among these are life, liberty and the pursuit of happiness; that to secure these rights governments are instituted among men, deriving their just powers from the consent of the governed.[63]

Since the creator had already created men to be equal, there was no need for government intervention in the matter of equality according to Jefferson and the "founding fathers." Beyond guaranteeing civic equality and equality before the law, government was to be limited in scope. As the constitutional historians Kelly and Harbison have pointed out:

> Jefferson did not intend to lay down any broad premise of extreme democratic equality. Natural-law theory did indeed hold that in a state of nature all men were equal in the possession of certain inalienable rights. . . . Government was instituted to protect those rights and could not impair them. It was in this sense that all men were created equal—equal, that is, before the law. This concept did not imply intellectual, moral, or spiritual equality, although a later generation imbued with the spirit of democracy might read it so.[64]

A government based on formal rights is thereby legitimate as long as it guarantees life and liberty and the means to pursue happiness and property, and as long as it does not interfere with the life-chances of its citizens. Accordingly, it is the duty and obligation of citizens not to interfere with others in their quest for "Self Preservation." Again to quote Jefferson:

> Of liberty then I would say that, in the whole plenitude of its extent, it is unobstructed action according to our will, but rightful liberty is unob-

> structed action according to our will within limits drawn around us by the equal rights of others.[65]

Given the relative equality of colonial society, there was little disagreement either before or after the Revolution over this formal interpretation of natural rights. A society without great disparities of wealth and income, a society founded on the principle of individual enterprise, could readily see its interests served by this elaboration of rights. Samuel Adams' Declaration of 1772, for example, was disseminated throughout Massachusetts and received widespread acclaim. The township of Truro was typical of the many local communities that met to vote their endorsement of the document, agreeing "that our Rights as Men, as Christians, and as Subjects are therein well stated."[66]

The institutional domains that emerged from this formal interpretation of rights were also broadly accepted. Citizenship, as we have seen, was understood as an individual rather than a collective property. Moreover, since citizens were already animated by the drive for "Self Preservation" and self reliance, there was no need for government to assist in the task of preservation beyond the guarantees of life, liberty and the means to pursue property and happiness. This understanding also had an impact on the way in which the principle of popular representation was received. Clearly, government had to be representative as citizens had a right to be represented, but this right had to be balanced with the imperative of constructing a government that would not meddle overmuch in the lives of its citizens, thereby preserving the essential individual right to liberty.

Finally, the procedural and impersonal conception of public virtue was also profoundly influenced by the formal natural rights interpretation. Indeed, submission to laws and procedures was critical for the new polity, since laws and procedures were the predominant, and perhaps the only, means of forming a cohesive society from the multitude of individuals endowed with natural rights. As Jefferson elaborated in 1816:

> No man has a natural right to commit aggression on the equal rights of another; and this is all from which the laws ought to restrain him; every man is under the natural duty of contributing to the necessities of the society; and this is all the laws should enforce on him; and, no man having a natural right to be the judge between himself and another, it is his natural duty to submit to the umpirage of an impartial third. When the laws have declared and enforced all this, they have fulfilled their functions; and the idea is quite unfounded, that on entering society we give up any natural right.[67]

Not only the political elite acknowledged the vital significance of laws. Quite average Americans did so as well. For example, Harbottle Dorr, a Boston shopkeeper and the son of an artisan, agreed fervently with a 1771 newspaper article written by Samuel Adams in which he extolled the fact that "laws and the constitution alone are the basis of public tranquility, the firmest support of public authority, and the sole guarantors of the liberty of the citizens."[68] Underneath the article Dorr wrote: "This is orthodox, and is *my* political creed."[69]

Another example can be drawn from the writings of William Manning (1747–1814), a self-professed "laborer" who began writing essays in opposition to Hamilton's financial policies which, in his opinion, threatened the lives and livelihood of the "middling sort" on behalf of the powerful "Few." In spite of his fears that "Gog and Magog are gathered together to destroy the rights of man and banish liberty from the world,"[70] he did not advocate or support unlawful opposition activities. Instead, he remained steadfast in his conviction that the laws had to be obeyed and that popular resistance to the administration had to be undertaken in a lawful way. In this effort, knowledge and learning played a key role:

> only by pursuing learning and knowledge—including the "knowledge that when laws are once constitutionally made they must be obeyed"—could the Many secure their rights and keep the Few from "putting darkness for light, and light for darkness, falsehood for truth, and truth for falsehood."[71]

Accordingly, Manning advocated the establishment of "Democratic Societies" which were to

> watch over the Republican interest both in State and National Governments, especially as to elections and appointments, convey intelligence, confute false rumors, confirm the wavering in right principles, prevent delusion of weak brethren, and fight the most formidable enemy of civilized men, political ignorance.[72]

In no other revolutionary setting has public faith been vested so clearly in the virtue of reason and the impersonal laws grounded in reason rather than in the virtue of particular leaders. In this context, it is worth recalling that even George Washington, a leader of unquestioned virtue and integrity, was not spared attacks in the press or increasingly critical popular scrutiny during his tenure as President. Nor did average Americans treat him with much awe and deference, many coming to his house during the early months of his presidency "simply to gawk at the Great Man," and all acting "as if they had every right to be there."[73] This behavior contrasts sharply with the deference accorded to impersonal laws. Such a broad social consensus over the importance of laws and procedures is a reflection of the larger consensus that emerged during the course of the Revolution over which elements of the natural rights ethos should define the authoritative boundaries and parameters of the new polity. Disagreements did, however, come to the fore in the Constitutional debates over the specific type of government that would best conform to the agreed upon domains. The institutional outcomes of these debates represent the distinctive features of the American system of government that set it apart from the liberal democratic governments of Western Europe. Essentially, what is distinctive about the American system is the extent to which the powers of government (executive, legislative and judicial) have been divided and placed beneath the absolute authority vested in the Constitution.

The Constitutional debates were predominantly oriented around the question of what kind of government would interfere least in the lives of its citizens, while protecting their essential rights. James Madison and the Federalists believed that a strong central government with its powers equally divided among the three branches would best protect the rights of the individual and of minorities both from government interference and from the dictates of a popular majority.[74] On the other hand, critics such as the Anti-Federalists maintained that a weak central government combined with strong state governments would promise the best protection for the rights of all citizens. At issue was also a conflict over whether or not parliamentary sovereignty was the best means to secure the rights of the people by representing their collective will. For Madison, rule by parliament would simply replace the despotism of the monarchy with the despotism of pure democratic rule. In which case, there would be nothing to prevent a majority from infringing on the rights of the minority. His critics, on the other hand, felt that a strong central government, headed by a strong executive, would replicate the tyranny of the British monarchy. In the end, Madison's position prevailed because of two factors: the power of his ideas, and the extent to which the Federalist vision was able to gain the support of average citizens.

Ideologically, Madison was rigorously consistent with the formal natural rights interpretation that had animated the Revolution. Whereas the Anti-Federalist position was ultimately perceived as an effort to protect the collective rights of the states, the Federalist position was based on the perception that the protection of individual rights was at stake in the new polity.[75] This consistency strengthened the ability of the Federalists to claim that their proposals, although radical and innovative, embodied the only appropriate means to consolidate the Revolution's accomplishments. The cornerstone of Madison's entire intellectual enterprise was the protection of the rights of the individual, both from the tyranny of government and from the tyranny of the majority. He had no faith in the rights of any collectivities, be they parliaments, states or factions.[76] His solution to the problem of individual rights was the creation of a giant republic that would distribute power so effectively that any dangerous accumulation of factional interests would be impossible. The creation of such a giant republic, in turn, resonated with the commercial interests of average citizens. They could see possibilities for advancement and enterprise that were well worth the potential risks of supporting the Federalist position.[77]

However, not just interests but also principles were involved in gaining popular acceptance for the Federalist Constitution. As Michael Merrill and Sean Wilentz point out in their introduction to the writings of William

Manning, it is likely that "Manning came fully to support the Constitution only after the inclusion of the Bill of Rights in 1791, a common trajectory for plebeian democrats."[78] Consequently, while the Bill was debated mainly in instrumental terms among the Federalist and Anti-Federalist leadership, for "plebeian democrats" issues of substance were at stake: namely, the rights and liberties they had fought for in the Revolution. For Manning, this was clearly the case as the battles for independence represented "an all-important personal turning point":

> "I saw almost the first blood that was shed in [the] Concord fight and scores of men dead, dying and wounded in the cause of liberty, which caused serious sensations in my mind." From then on, he claimed, he was deeply interested in politics—"a constant reader of public newspapers" who "closely attended to men and measures."[79]

As we have seen, "the cause of liberty" was understood in terms of natural rights, therefore, although the framers based their constitutional deliberations on instrumental rationality, the value-rationality embodied in the natural rights doctrine still served to legitimate the new Constitution in the eyes of many average citizens.

Eventually, the Federalist victory resulted in institutional arrangements that distributed power not just between the branches of government, but also between two levels of government—the federal level and the state level. Given the critical significance ascribed to laws in holding together the disparate individuals comprising American society, it is perhaps not surprising that the role of holding together the disparate powers of government fell to the Constitution. Since the Constitution was devised as the fountainhead of all governmental authority, standing above the reach of any particular government or political leader, it was to regulate permanently the relationship between citizens and their government, as well as mandating a stable separation of powers between the various branches and levels of government. The power that this document holds over the fate of a nation is perhaps best understood in terms of the particularly democratic understanding Americans have of the rule of law. As de Tocqueville observed:

> However irksome an enactment may be, the citizen of the United States complies with it, not only because it is the work of the majority, but because it is his own, and he regards it as a contract to which he is himself a party. In the United States, then, that numerous and turbulent multitude does not exist, who, regarding the law as their natural enemy, look upon it with fear and distrust. It is impossible, on the contrary, not to perceive that all classes display the utmost reliance upon the legislation of their country, and are attached to it by a kind of parental affection. . . . Besides, the people in America obey the law, not only because it is their work, but because it may be changed if it be harmful; a

> law is observed because, first, it is a self-imposed evil, and secondly, it is an evil of transient duration.[80]

Recent cross-national surveys of popular attitudes regarding the rule of law still find that the citizens of the United States stand alone in their near absolute commitment to the law and to "legal rigourism."[81] Apparently, even successive generations have, by and large, been willing to abide by the constitutional "contract" to which the original colonists were party.

The fact that the Constitution has successfully fulfilled its functions for over two hundred years, and that Americans have retained their "respect for the law,"[82] is a testimony to the transformatory power generated during the American Revolution. The natural rights doctrine achieved a lasting impact on conduct and consciousness when it was brought to life in the charismatic communities of the Revolution. The concept of citizenship as a universal right was only rendered meaningful by the habits of democratic intercourse acquired in these communities. By bringing together men of different social standing and exposing them to the leveling experience of charisma—wherein everyone must submit equally to the dictates of faith in the cause—the communities were able to make the crucial natural rights premise that all men have an equal capacity for Reason into a concrete reality. The interests of all citizens regardless of social standing thereby became legitimate in both theory and practice.

The constitutional framers subsequently made room for the actual, as opposed to symbolic, representation of these interests in the polity. Moreover, they established the public nature of American political life by soliciting the reasoned support of all interests in their debates. Such reasoned support demanded the free flow of information that would allow citizens to reach reasonable decisions on matters of public policy.[83] Thereafter, politics could never be successfully confined to the narrow realm of a permanent political elite and an administrative bureaucracy. Considerations of virtue, ability and efficiency have consistently given way to the principle of public access to government. In a very real sense, the United States government is the property of its citizens. They have the right to participate in it, to pursue their interests through it, and even to corrupt it—if they so choose. While this degree of accessibility would have been frowned upon by the "founding fathers," the principles of government they established, by departing from every precept of political life known at the time, led to the creation of a very permeable democracy.

The permeability of American democracy is particularly evident in the way in which government administration has evolved. From part-time amateur efforts to corrupt machines, from affirmative action to recent downsizing and privatization efforts, government bureaucracy has never been elevated into a realm of public service above the heads of ordinary citizens. Indeed, the belief that ordinary citizens, active in small communities or in associations, can better accomplish the tasks of government has been with us since de Tocqueville's time.

Elsewhere, in the West European democracies, the realm of government in many ways became the bastion of a political and administrative elite that, while embracing and accepting the principles of modern democracy, still believed that a government of guardianship would best serve these principles.[84] While governing elites have at times sought to create a government of virtuous guardianship in the United States, most notably in the Hamilton era, such efforts have consistently run aground. Popular mistrust of a restricted elite-based government and of government bureaucracies run by "mandarins" has historically fueled opposition to these efforts.

As we shall see in the following study of the French Revolution, the tendency toward guardianship in France is an outcome of the conflictual process whereby democracy was established in that country. Apart from the military engagements with Britain, the American Revolution is remarkable for its lack of conflict. After the loyalists were expelled, there was no significant internal resistance to the new government.[85] The clergy had been overwhelmingly supportive of the Revolution, and considerable portions of the population were already experienced in the sober exercise of self-government during the colonial years. Nor were there any significant conflicts among the revolutionaries themselves over how to interpret the natural rights doctrine. Therefore, there were no grounds, other than formal ones, for preventing citizens from exercising their rights to the fullest extent in the new polity.

This is not to say that the United States has not experienced subsequent conflicts, most notably in the Civil War, over citizenship rights. For the most part, however, these have been conflicts over the extension of rights to new categories of citizens, rather than conflicts over the very definition of citizenship and its attendant rights.[86] Needless to say, France experienced a completely different set of circumstances during its Revolution, leading to different outcomes.

3 Substantive natural rights and the French Revolution

Coming so soon in the wake of 1776, the French Revolution was inevitably compared to the prior revolution that had taken place across the Atlantic. For example, as the delegates to the Constituent Assembly debated the Declaration of the Rights of Man in 1789, they made explicit references to the American Declaration of Independence. Not surprisingly, both documents represent manifestations of the natural rights doctrine, anchoring revolutionary demands in the inalienable rights of individuals.

In spite of such similar philosophical origins, however, the French went on to experience a long and tumultuous period of institution-building. As Maurice Agulhon points out:

> the end of the eighteenth century had seen a great and necessary revolution take place in France, but that social revolution had not been able to find its political expression. It had inaugurated little short of a century (1789–1879) of trial and error and bloody chaos before witnessing the emergence of a stable political regime.[1]

While American post-revolutionary history is certainly not free from conflicts and struggles, "the emergence of a stable political regime" based on the ideals and principles articulated in 1776 appears relatively unproblematic when placed against the French experience.

These disparate developmental paths have, of course, been the subject of continuous conjecture and analysis. Furet, for example, maintains that a fundamental difference between the French and American cases lies in the fact that the declaration of natural rights in France was not "in harmony beforehand with the social state."[2] Whereas the American colonies were "peopled by minor landowners with democratic customs, who from the start had cultivated the spirit of equality, unhampered by external enemies or a feudal or aristocratic heritage," in France, rights were proclaimed "after a violent break with the national past, and against the corruption of an old society which had for so long trampled on the mere idea of a contract."[3] From these differences in the "social state," flow the two major strands of opposition to the successful institutionalization of a government based on natural rights. On the one hand, the aristocracy and the Church retained enough force and influence to form a strong counter-revolutionary tradition based on conceptions of natural order rather than natural rights. On the other hand, the lower classes plagued by "poverty, inequality, class distinctions," could not readily see the value of "the proclamation of theoretical rights possessed equally by all individuals."[4] Accordingly, the French Revolution also gave birth to a socialist tradition that insisted on the institutionalization of substantive natural rights such as the right to work.

Seen from this perspective, the fact that natural rights were proclaimed in an inhospitable social and religious context accounts for the turbulent century following the Revolution. Indeed, class struggles and the resistance of the Church did much to contribute to the problems of the post-revolutionary era. Yet, these social and cultural factors represent only one facet of the explanation of why the social revolution took so long to find its expression in a stable political regime. The problematic nature of the revolutionary ideals themselves, and the nature of their articulation in the charismatic communities of the Revolution, should not be overlooked as a crucial explanatory variable. From the very beginning, ideas—specifically the natural rights doctrine—played an active role in shaping both the changes and the conflicts of the revolutionary era. Even the great Marxist historian of the French Revolution, Georges Lefebvre, recognized that

> we would commit . . . an error in forgetting that there is no true revolutionary spirit without the idealism which alone inspires sacrifice. Undoubtedly the interest of the bourgeoisie, which was the first to profit from the new order, can easily be detected beneath the philosophy of the 18th century. But the bourgeoisie believed sincerely that it worked for the good of humanity. It was persuaded that it prepared the way for the advent of justice and right. . . . The men who rose on the great "days" of the Revolution . . . would not have risked their lives had they been thinking only of themselves.[5]

Since interests and grievances alone do not propel revolutionary action and sacrifice, they must be interpreted in such a way as to legitimate opposition to the existing state of affairs. Revolutionary actors were motivated by a value-rational adherence to natural rights which provided the legitimation for their actions. Furthermore, this value-rationality attained an independent influence on collective behavior in the context of the charismatic communities of the revolutionary era.

The following quotations are illustrative of the transformation of consciousness and conduct that took place in the French Revolution:

> The Third Estate is the People and the People is the foundation of the State; it is in fact the State itself; the other orders are merely political categories while by the *immutable laws of nature* the People is everything. Everything should be subordinated to it (the People); its safety should be

> the first law of the State. . . . It is in the People that all national power resides and it is for the People that all states exist.[6]
>
> (Comte d'Antraigues, 1788)

> When I found myself in the middle of the district assembly, I thought I could breathe fresh air. It was truly a phenomenon to be something in the political order and by virtue alone of one's capacity as a citizen . . . that assembly, an infinitely small fraction of the Nation, felt nonetheless part of the power and rights of the whole.[7]
>
> (Sylvain Bailly, 1789)

The subjects of an absolutist monarchy were being transformed into the citizens of a nation constituted by the people. The nation that had previously belonged to the kings of France by divine right, became the property of the people by virtue of natural right. Citizenship was thereby conceived of as a collective attribute of the people, while citizens' rights were derived from the natural right of the people as a whole to constitute the state. As pundits of the time put it, France as a nation could exist without kings, but what would the nation be without the people?

This elevation of the people as the sole legitimate source of sovereignty had profound consequences for social and political life. As Simon Schama points out in regard to the work of the 1789 National Assembly in abolishing feudal privileges:

> it was one of the most astonishing collective personality changes in political history, this transformation from a realm based on ceremonially defined orders and corporations to that of the uniform entity of the sovereign nation.[8]

The society of estates and corporate orders wherein everyone knew their place as ordained by their birth, gave way to a society whose individual members could determine their place according to merit and achievement. The realm of political authority which had, in the past, been coterminous with the monarchy, was redefined as a realm of responsible leadership, accountable to the people. During the turbulent history of France's political institutions, this definition was, however, subject to numerous interpretations as different leaders such as Robespierre and Napoleon claimed to represent the will of the people. Specifically, the charismatic presentation of natural rights in France resulted in a highly conflictual environment that made the process of determining the appropriate institutions and institutional domains for the new polity a very lengthy one. Unlike the American case, during the course of the French Revolution, the natural rights doctrine both united and separated the various political actors taking part in it. Although all revolutionaries were united by their shared adherence to the principles of the doctrine, *liberté*, *égalité* and *fraternité*, they were also divided by the fact that these principles were interpreted differently in the charismatic communities that carried the Revolution forward. These communities subsequently developed separate and distinct claims to embody the essence of the revolutionary endeavor. Since each community claimed to be the sole repository of revolutionary virtue, an over-arching strategy for institution-building was precluded.

While the ensuing tensions between revolutionary actors did not undermine the doctrine's "destructive" impact in serving as "a charge of powder" with which to destroy the old regime, the conflicts and tensions did prevent the emergence of a unified political elite capable of determining a ready consensus for the "constructive" task of creating new governing institutions. The divisions, and ultimately the Terror, experienced in the early years of the Revolution, left behind a weakened democratic core elite that was vulnerable to attacks from the counter-revolutionary forces as they, in turn, rallied. In the face of this weakness and lack of unified political will, social and cultural resistance to the Revolution could take on greater significance. This chapter will, consequently, focus primarily on the revolutionary period (1780s to 1799) as the crucial point of departure for understanding both the similarities and differences of the American and French Revolutions and their institutional outcomes.

ANTECEDENTS

Between the reigns of Louis XIV (1643–1715) and Louis XVI (1774–92), French society underwent considerable changes in economic development, social mobility and cultural attitudes. These changes resulted in a weakening of the rigid social distinctions and corporate hierarchies characteristic of the feudal legacy. Such a weakening was a vital precondition to the revolutionary transformation of West European societies. Unlike the American colonies where feudal institutions had never taken root, European societies were divided by immense disparities of wealth and privilege. These disparities led to such differences in the conditions of life for various social groups that any common action or common understanding of grievances was severely impeded. The revolution in France was made possible by the partial breakdown of these social barriers; it was also made problematic by the ardent desire of revolutionaries to eradicate completely the remaining barriers and distinctions.

As the monarchy struggled to maintain the political supremacy established by the absolutist Sun King, social and economic life began to manifest a new vitality. Alongside traditional wealth derived from land, considerable wealth was being generated by commercial enterprises from which both bourgeois merchants and aristocratic entrepreneurs profited. R. R. Palmer maintains, for example, that French foreign trade increased fivefold between 1713 and 1789.[9] This new prosperity allowed members of the bourgeoisie to buy admission into the ranks of the nobility by purchasing the public offices put up for sale by a perpetually fiscally embattled monarchy. Social mobility was also apparent in the cultural realm. As the ideals of the Enlightenment were disseminated, the nobility of birth began to accept middle-class intellectuals and artists of merit and talent as their equals.[10] In all realms of life—economic, political and cultural—a fusion of elites was taking place between the nobility and rising members of the bourgeoisie. Unlike a similar fusion of elites in England that led to a relatively peaceful transformation of political, economic and social institutions, developments in France were inherently unstable since economic development and social mobility were progressing within the parameters of the traditional hierarchies of privilege, prestige and patronage.[11] Just as guilds and corporate privileges continued to govern economic life, so too did personal patronage networks dictate the terms whereby one might advance in the political and cultural realms. Not only did this result in structural inconsistencies as the old hierarchies "no longer corresponded to the [new] hierarchies of wealth, education, and power,"[12] it also created serious social divisions and antagonisms. By and large, members of the bourgeoisie who had attained equal status with the nobility shared the latter's belief in the old hierarchies. They were willing to acquiesce, therefore, to the "aristocratic reaction" of the middle eighteenth century that closed previously available avenues of social mobility. In reaction to what was perceived as a monarchical effort to dilute their strength, the nobility closed its ranks to the upwardly mobile bourgeoisie. Both military and civil service positions were increasingly restricted to members of the nobility, while their feudal rights vis-à-vis the peasantry were more strictly enforced.[13] Unfortunately, the passivity of the bourgeoisie who had arrived in "*le monde*" of the aristocracy did not reduce their own status uncertainty as second-class members of an elite still ultimately defined by birth.[14] Furthermore, the dynamic of closure animated the anger and frustrated ambitions of those members of the bourgeoisie who wished to emulate the success of their peers in rising to the top of the social hierarchy. This frustrated ambition was felt quite keenly by members of the professional bourgeoisie such as lawyers, writers and intellectuals, who wished to become the next Voltaire or Rousseau, and instead became the Robespierres, Brissots and Marats of the Revolution.[15]

Frustrated hopes and ambitions were not, however, monopolized by members of the upwardly mobile bourgeoisie. Status anxieties were also felt by members of the middle orders who were being adversely affected by the changing patterns of economic production. Independent craftsmen, artisans and small shopkeepers, who wished to retain their status as productive members of the bourgeoisie, were threatened by downward mobility as the introduction of factory production reduced increasing numbers of them to the status of a wage-earning proletariat.[16]

In all, one can identify numerous social groups that were frustrated, disaffected and alienated by the existing circumstances of the ancien régime. Reform-minded members of the fragilely fused elite were frustrated by the intransigence of both the monarchy and the reactionary nobles. Upwardly ambitious professionals and intellectuals became so profoundly disaffected by the fact that the world of the elite was closed to them, that they began to question the validity of that world itself. Finally, ordinary people, artisans, craftsmen and peasants, were increasingly aware of the threat to their existence as small independent producers—a threat they ascribed to the machinations of the old order, rather than to the dawning of a new economic era.

Under the impact of Louis XVI's efforts to reform the feudal system of taxation, the precarious social and political stalemate that had prevailed between these disaffected social groups was shattered. At the end of the American Revolution, the French government found itself greatly in debt as a result of the assistance it had rendered to the American cause. Various ministers attempted to reform the fiscal affairs of the realm, but to no avail. The king was finally forced to call the old medieval corporate assembly, the Estates-General, into session in order to gain their approval for new taxes.

United in resistance to the king and his ministers, a common understanding of the problems facing France and the appropriate solutions to these problems began to emerge throughout the diverse social strata comprising the traditional three corporate orders (the nobility, the clergy, and all other subjects of the third estate). The corrupt system of privileges was widely identified by regime opponents as the central problem plaguing France. In their view, both the monarchy and the aristocracy were clinging to this system and protecting it by the use, or rather abuse, of state power. Whether in learned treatises or in the gutter press, the corruption and dissipation of the Court was held up to public scrutiny and ridicule. The emptiness of Court life was invidiously contrasted to the moral and virtuous way of life prevalent under republican systems of government where citizens could be free and equal, and the state worked for the common good of all citizens. The proposed solution to the current dilemma was to reclaim the state from the dissolute elite and to base state sovereignty on the citizens of France, not on the monarchy.

As documented by Simon Schama, a veritable "passion of citizenship"[17] preceded the May 1789 convening of the Estates-General. For example, in the audiences for public spectacles such as balloon ascensions, social hierarchies were broken down and transcended by a "kind of temporary fellowship in the open air."[18] This fellowship was subsequently validated by the widely read writings of Rousseau and popular plays such as *The Marriage of Figaro* that fostered a new image of "virtuous citizenship bullied by aristocratic arrogance."[19] Furthermore, "communities of discussion,"[20] whether in the cafés of the Palais-Royal in Paris or in the Masonic lodges, spread throughout France, and also contributed to the growing perception of a common destiny shared by all members of French society as equal citizens. The rigid feudal distinctions between social strata that had previously prevented concerted action were thereby decisively undermined. The ultimate manifestation of this process was the transformation of the

Estates-General into a National Assembly wherein all delegates, regardless of their "order," were to sit and deliberate together.

By the late 1780s, then, a broad audience existed for the revolutionary ideal of a government founded on natural rights principles such as articulated by the young lawyer Martin de Marivaux:

> Man is born free. No man has any natural authority over his peer; force alone confers no such right; the legislative power belongs to the people and can belong only to the people.[21]

A core group of active revolutionaries was, however, needed to provide leadership and direction for the generally disaffected population. By and large, this core group was drawn from the middle ranks of French society with radically inclined nobles and priests participating as well.

Studies of the Jacobin clubs, for example, indicate a mixed membership of radical nobles and clergy, "sober, steady" artisans, prosperous shopkeepers and merchants, and rather less well-to-do lawyers and intellectuals. Although the Revolution has often been analyzed in class terms, Crane Brinton, in his pioneering study of the Jacobins, concluded that they were not obvious representatives of a class, if class meant "a group of persons having a common social standing and social background, a common standard of life, and common economic interests."[22] He proceeded to draw the conclusion that what held these disparate social elements together was a shared community of faith in the ideals of the Revolution. As we shall see below, charisma not class was the basis of action for this core elite.

Like the American Revolution, the revolutionary elite in France was drawn from different social groups which facilitated their ability to promulgate the revolutionary cause throughout French society. As in the American case, such widespread social mobilization prevented the Revolution from becoming limited to a dispute between differing political elites. Unlike the American case, however, the political awakening of previously silent members of the polity did not result in a broadly shared consensus on the establishment of, and adherence to, new institutions. Part of the explanation for this lack of unity lies in the nature of the social composition of the core elite.

In spite of their different social standings, the American revolutionaries shared a relatively common way of life which facilitated understanding and compromise within the charismatic communities. The French core elite, comprised as it was of people with widely diverging life experiences, had to rely more on demonstrations of absolute faith and commitment to the cause as the basis of mutual cooperation. These manifestations of faith escalated rapidly as embattled revolutionaries demanded ever more stringent and exacting demonstrations to ensure unity and the same degree of fervent commitment within the community. Ultimately, even violence was considered an appropriate means to purify the membership and the nation of "contaminating" social elements that questioned or threatened the revolutionary cause. Unfortunately, the beliefs that animated and legitimated the struggle of these revolutionaries also had a profound impact on the creation of this conflict-ridden environment.

THE NATURAL RIGHTS DOCTRINE

Although the influence of the Enlightenment on the French Revolution has been the subject of debate and controversy, recent studies have documented the widespread dissemination and impact of these philosophical principles on French society. The ideals of the Enlightenment, specifically the natural rights doctrine, were readily available, and provided compelling solutions to the problems faced by the core elite as they sought to conceptualize a new political identity for the French nation. Regime opponents faced a choice, however, between two variations of the doctrine. The Enlightenment *philosophes* had articulated a secularized interpretation of formal natural rights based on the fundamental freedom and equality of individuals. This interpretation was challenged by Rousseau's more substantive interpretation of the rights of the collectivity. Eventually, Rousseau's definition of rights proved to be the more powerful variant of value-rationality in the French context.

In spite of the censorship policies of the French monarchy, the reading public had direct access to the major works of the Enlightenment. The famous *Encyclopédie* edited by Diderot, for example, sold about 13,000 multivolumed sets in France. R. R. Palmer indicates that this particular work was widely disseminated throughout France. In the provincial city of Besançon, 137 sets of the *Encyclopédie* were sold to local residents:

> of whom 15 were members of the clergy, 53 were of the nobility, and 69 were lawyers, doctors, merchants, government officials, or others of what was called the Third Estate. The privileged groups of whom the Encyclopedists were the most critical, that is, the clergy and the nobility, read it or at least purchased it far out of proportion to their numbers in the population as a whole.[23]

Assuming that the work was indeed read, members of these privileged groups were exposed to the individually oriented expression of rights characteristic of Enlightenment thought. Turgot, for example, wrote in his contribution to the *Encyclopédie* that

> the citizens have rights, rights that are sacred for the very body of society; the citizens exist independently of society; they form its necessary elements; and they only enter it in order to put themselves, with all their rights, under the protection of those very laws to which they sacrifice their liberty.[24]

While the reach of this Enlightenment expression of natural rights seems to have been limited to the upper echelons of French society, Robert

Darnton has documented the extent to which Rousseau's work was disseminated throughout the lower echelons of society as well. Accordingly, he suggests that "Rousseauistic reading was an important phenomenon in prerevolutionary France."[25] By studying the letters Rousseau received in 1761, Darnton shows how Rousseau's writings touched average readers and helped them to make sense of their lives in new ways. Readers became so dependent on Rousseau's wisdom that they felt somewhat lost when he died. For example, upon hearing of Rousseau's death, an average bourgeois writes:

> So, Monsieur, we have lost the sublime Jean-Jacques. How it pains me never to have seen or heard him. I acquired the most extraordinary admiration for him by reading his books. If some day I should travel near Ermenonville, I shall not fail to visit his grave and perhaps shed some tears on it. Tell me, I pray, what you think of this famous man, whose fate has always aroused the most tender feelings in me, while Voltaire often provoked my indignation.[26]

Furthermore, Rousseau had an immense impact on the thought of young intellectuals who found themselves excluded from the world of the *philosophes*. Brissot, the future Jacobin leader, identified so completely with Rousseau that he wrote: "I suffer myself when I read him. I enter into his suffering, and I say to myself: why was I not fortunate enough to have known him? How I would have opened up my soul to him!"[27] These young intellectuals, filled with rage at their exclusion from the fashionable salons and lucrative state sinecures enjoyed by the fortunate members of "le monde," proceeded to write highly critical pamphlets decrying the vices of the ancien régime from a Rousseauist perspective of republican virtue. They subsequently distributed these pamphlets to the artisans and working people of the urban centers. In this highly popularized form, even ordinary Frenchmen had access to Rousseauist ideals.

These ideals embodied a more collectivist interpretation of rights, both natural and civil. Rousseau believed that the collectivity of the general will, or of the will of the nation as he later termed it, represented the common interest. The general will should be the basis upon which society is governed. In the social contract, the natural rights of individuals were to be replaced by a higher order of civil rights realized collectively in the social order through the general will. Rousseau is still, however, within the tradition of natural rights discourse since the following principles lie at the core of his philosophy:

> I believe I perceive in it [the human soul] two principles that are prior to reason, of which one makes us ardently interested in our own well-being and our self-preservation, and the other inspires in us a natural repugnance to seeing any sentient being, and principally our fellow men, perish or suffer. It appears to me that the ability of our mind to coordinate and

> combine these two principles . . . gives rise to all the rules of natural right, rules that reason is then forced to reestablish on other foundations, when by its successive developments, it has succeeded in smothering nature.[28]

His social contract theory represents an effort to reestablish the rules of natural right, as he perceived them, on the basis of "other foundations," namely that of mutual agreements.

For Rousseau "the social order is a sacred right which serves as the basis of all the others. Yet this right is not derived from nature; it is, therefore, founded upon agreements."[29] On the basis of these agreements the social contract is formed wherein men give up their "original rights and natural liberties" in favor of civil liberty and the protection of life and property. In its essential elements, the social contract requires that "each of us puts his person and all his power in common under the supreme control of the general will, and, as a body, we receive each member as an indivisible part of the whole."[30] According to this vision:

> the social pact establishes such an equality among the citizens that they all commit themselves under the same conditions and should all enjoy the same rights. Thus, by the very nature of the pact, every act of sovereignty, that is to say, every authentic act of the general will, obligates or favors all citizens equally, so that the sovereign knows only the body of the nation and makes no distinctions between any of those who compose it.[31]

In other words, the natural rights that the individual possesses before he enters into the social pact are transformed into civil rights of equality and liberty within the context of the general will. As Rousseau goes on to declare:

> instead of destroying natural equality, the fundamental pact, on the contrary, substitutes a moral and legitimate equality for whatever physical equality nature had been able to impose among men, and, although they may be unequal in strength or in genius, they all become equal through agreements and law.[32]

Natural rights are, therefore, not inalienable, in the sense that they can be altered or transformed. Instead, it is the exercise of the general will or popular sovereignty that "can never be alienated."[33] Rousseau makes this point crystal clear when he states that if the sovereign should ask a particular citizen to lay down his life for the state, the citizen "should die, since it is only on this condition that he has lived in safety up to that time, and since his life is no longer merely a blessing of nature, but a conditional gift of the state."[34]

The notion that the state as the embodiment of the general will transcends the will of its constituent citizens and becomes a separate entity with the right to usurp the individual citizen's natural rights is indeed a far cry from the formal natural rights interpretation. As elaborated by Thomas

Paine, for example, that interpretation postulates the following relationship between the individual and the public good:

> Public good is not a term opposed to the good of individuals; on the contrary, it is the good of every individual collected. It is the good of all, because it is the good of every one: for as the public body is every individual collected, so the public good is the collected good of those individuals.[35]

In the French context, however, this rigorous individualism with its attendant formalism proved much weaker than in the American context where it reigned uncontested.

Essentially, there are three reasons for the strength and popularity of Rousseau's interpretation of the rights doctrine. First, the privileged groups of French society that were most familiar with the formal interpretation were not united in their support of this version of the natural rights doctrine. Within their ranks, as well, Rousseau had made substantial inroads. R. R. Palmer goes so far as to say that

> Rousseau estranged the French upper classes from their own mode of life. He made many of them lose faith in their own superiority. That was his main direct contribution to the French Revolution.[36]

Simon Schama also documents the degree to which bourgeois values in general, and Rousseauist visions of virtue in particular, had gained ground among the social elites.[37] While members of the core revolutionary elite drawn from these privileged groups were divided and insecure in their reasoning about rights, members drawn from other social groups manifested a firm commitment to the substantive interpretation of rights.

The second reason for the popularity of Rousseau's works resides in the extent to which his thinking resonated with the interests of the small independent producers of the middle and lower echelons of French society. As Jacobin and sans-culottes revolutionaries, these small producers would attempt to implement Rousseau's vision of a republic without great disparities of wealth and opportunity. Buttressed by the strength of their belief in the substantive interpretation of rights, these revolutionaries were able to dismiss the formal rights doctrine as an expression of the self-interest and egoism of the privileged members of society. Formal individual rights could only benefit those who already possessed the means to be independent citizens in thought, spirit and action. During the course of the Revolution, adherents of formal rights actually acknowledged the charges of self-interest and egoism, but postulated that even "if self-interest is not the 'purest' of social bonds, it is nonetheless the most realistic and appropriate to France's condition."[38] Such an instrumental justification of formal rights demonstrates the degree to which this interpretation lost its ability to claim legitimacy on the basis of value-rationality.

Finally, Rousseau's interpretation provided more compelling solutions to the problems of defining a new political identity in opposition to the monarchical order. The French revolutionary elite needed to find legitimation for an assault, not just on the status of the king, but also on the socially embedded system of hierarchically organized estates, corporate orders and privileges. To base this assault on the rights of the individual citizen alone was considered insufficient because the system of the ancien régime had created too few citizens. In their view, the ability to act as a good citizen was connected to the possession of independent means. Revolutionaries were fully aware that the feudal legacy had resulted in large networks of personal patronage that rendered people dependent, not independent. Faced with active resistance on the part of the monarchy and its allies, and with apathy on the part of the lower orders, the revolutionaries, not surprisingly, reached the conclusion that people needed to be "forced to be free."

According to the logic of Rousseau, the best way to establish freedom for all individuals would be to embed them in new social and political relationships that guaranteed an equal distribution of the means to support citizenship. In order to create these new relationships, revolutionaries believed that the power of the state was absolutely essential. Unlike the American case, where the power of the state was curtailed to provide individual citizens with maximum liberty, the French state was retained as a powerful weapon of change. The equality and rights of the people had to be guaranteed by the state as a precondition to the exercise of individual rights and liberties. Collective rights, therefore, took precedence over individual rights in the minds of many revolutionaries.

Given the nature of the struggle that the revolutionary elite was seeking to legitimate, Rousseau's emphasis on embedding the rights of the individual within the rights of the collective provided a compelling new political identity. The state would no longer secure the rights of the privileged few, but would work to attain the rights of all. Not only would the people be treated equally by this newly constituted state, they would also be assisted by the state in acquiring the means necessary to become independent citizens. This new identity is apparent in the following statement made by the president of the Sauveterre Jacobin club in his inaugural speech:

> Members of the social body, we cannot be happy as individuals except as society shall be in the state of prosperity which the Constitution is preparing—Citizens, it is not permitted to the individual to prefer, even in secret, his private interests to those of society.[39]

In the process of extricating the population from the legacies of feudal dependencies, the formal natural rights of man, without the substantive conditions of equality promoted by the state, were considered insufficient by a majority of the core elite.

The conviction of many middle-class revolutionaries that the right of collective equality was a precondition to the right of individual liberty goes against the common assumption that the Revolution was the product of an upwardly mobile French bourgeoisie fulfilling its class destiny. On the basis of their faith in the revolutionary cause, these revolutionaries were willing to go against their material interests by advocating substantive rights, such as the right to subsistence, for all citizens. They were as convinced as the small independent artisans that the creation of a republic, in which the causes and consequences of the existing disparities of wealth and opportunity would be remedied, embodied a cause worth dying for. This faith was exemplified by Condorcet, an aristocratic revolutionary leader killed during the Terror, who wrote the following analysis of the Revolution shortly before his death:

> the Americans, satisfied with the code of civil and criminal legislation which they had derived from England, having no corrupt system of finance to reform, no feudal tyrannies, no hereditary distinctions, no privileges of rich and powerful corporations, no system of religious intolerance to destroy, had only to direct their attention to the establishment of new powers to be substituted in the place of those hitherto exercised. . . . In these innovations there was nothing that extended to the mass of the people, nothing that altered the subsisting relations formed between individuals; whereas the French Revolution, for reasons exactly reverse, had to embrace the whole economy of society, to change every social relation, to penetrate to the smallest link of the political chain.[40]

Ultimately, the many nobles and prosperous members of the Third Estate who became members of the revolutionary core elite acted on the basis of their faith in the principles of *liberté*, *égalité* and *fraternité*, not on the basis of calculated class interest.

In short, the revolutionary cause to which the core elite adhered was the imperative of changing "every social relation" in order to obtain a more just social and political order constituted by citizens rather than subjects. This imperative was legitimated on the basis of a doctrine of natural and civil rights that emphasized collective and substantive rights over formal individual rights. Such an interpretation not only strengthened the sense of common destiny amongst the citizens of France, regardless of social and economic standing, it also mandated a belief in the desirability of active state intervention to create and maintain conditions of equality between citizens.

Unfortunately, the beliefs that animated and legitimated the struggles of the core elite had negative implications that rendered the task of establishing a new order more difficult. By embracing a vision of citizenship based on collective rights protected through the formation of a general or national will, the revolutionaries constructed a highly abstract standard against which to measure progress in institution-building. Consequently, the question of *how* the general will was to be determined and institutionalized was ultimately reduced to the question of *who* would best be able to determine and embody that abstract will in concrete form.

Conflicts, therefore, ensued between different revolutionary groups and leaders, all speaking as the definitive voice of the people's will. These conflicts were rendered absolute and non-negotiable as each group claimed to embody the substance or the virtue of the collectivity. This statement made by Robespierre is typical of revolutionary thinking: "the soul of the Republic is virtue, love of country, the generous devotion that fuses all interests into the general interest."[41] As the sole appropriate reflection of that virtue and devotion, each group maintained that it, and it alone, had the right to determine the character and composition of the nation and its new institutions. Although Robespierre and the Jacobins are best known for their attempt to embody revolutionary virtue, all revolutionary groups, and many individual leaders, from the National Assembly to Napoleon, presented themselves as the only true representatives of the people's will. Thus the core elite, animated by a particular vision of collective rights, was engaged in a revolutionary struggle with two fronts. On the one front, feudal legacies had to be overcome and demolished, while on the other front the most appropriate representatives of the collective had to be determined on the basis of demonstrated virtue. These struggles were augmented by the nature of the charismatic communities within which the collective understanding of citizenship rights was given concrete form and substance.

CHARISMATIC COMMUNITIES

> We have respected, for centuries, the will of one man; shall we not learn to respect our own? Without virtue, you will make revolutions in vain—now slaves, now subjects, now royalists, now republicans, but never free—for why make of public officials repositories of the fixed law which is your will, if each one of you does but wish to follow his own caprices, his own passions?[42]

This statement made in the Toulon Jacobin club represents the essence of the transformation in consciousness and conduct that took place in the charismatic communities of the French Revolution. Within these communities, men were able to act upon their convictions and engage in the overthrowing of an entire social and political order. While the familiar old order was decisively delegitimated, the unfamiliar and untested new order was given shape and substance within the political clubs and assemblies that dominated the revolutionary era. The will of the monarch was replaced by the will of the people who were infused with a spirit of public virtue. Three central components can be identified in this process of transformation: the complete undermining of hierarchical authority, the development of substantively oriented rules and procedures, and the extensive leveling of social relationships.

Like the American revolutionaries, the French core elite attempted to apply the principles and procedures that governed their conduct in the charismatic communities to the governing of the country at large. Unlike the

American case, these efforts were unsuccessful and of short duration. The reason for this inability to institutionalize their political vision by creating stable structures of authority lies in the particular nature of these communities. On the one hand, each community claimed to embody the general will. On the other hand, the reach and influence of each community was limited since participation was restricted to members with specific qualities. The particularistic desire for members of proven virtue came into conflict with the universalism each group aspired to. The resulting inconsistency weakened the organizational strength of the charismatic communities by curtailing their ability to recruit new members from the population at large, and by diminishing their ability to command widespread loyalty and respect beyond the immediate ranks of the "chosen." Furthermore, the way in which the general will itself was embodied in the communities led to highly unstable forms of authority. This instability rendered the task of extrapolating stable and consistent principles and procedures from community life highly difficult.

To begin with, the charismatic communities of the French Revolution did not just challenge the hierarchical authority of the ancien régime, they proceeded to question the principle of authority itself. While the old social and political hierarchies were also undermined in the American Revolution, the French revolutionaries went beyond this to an almost complete rejection of delegated political authority in any shape or form. As is well known, the king and the aristocracy, visible representatives of the old hierarchies, were put to death as the "contaminating" remnants of a despised way of life. Popular sovereignty was proclaimed to have replaced monarchical authority. Yet the process of ruling through popularly elected representatives was rejected as well. The revolutionaries were unwilling to submit to the authority of even their elected or delegated representatives. Authority removed from the direct control of the people had become as discredited as monarchical rule within the charismatic communities.

Extreme hostility toward any external source of authority beyond the control of the community is typical of charismatic relationships. In an atmosphere of intense emotions, "of transport and of rapture,"[43] supreme authority is given over to the leader and/or to the principles he represents. The charismatic communities of the French Revolution allowed people to experience the principle of popular sovereignty in a very direct and immediate way. Consequently, the old authority structures lost their ability to regulate conduct, while the new structures were highly volatile and resistant to routinization. The following oath, taken in a Jacobin club "amid an 'indescribable delirium,' " illustrates the absolute way in which the ancien régime was rejected:

> I call down anathema upon kings and tyrants, anathema upon dictators, upon triumvirs, upon false defenders, upon false protectors of the people; anathema upon any who under the title of chief, general, stadholder,

> prince or any other name whatsoever would usurp a superiority, a pre-eminence over his fellow-citizens; and I swear to pursue him to the death.[44]

To fill the vacuum left by the passing of "kings and tyrants," the revolutionaries advocated direct popular participation on the basis of the rights doctrine derived from Rousseau. As the sans-culotte leader Leclerc wrote:

> Above all, remember that when people are "represented" they are not free, so do not use this term loosely . . . there is no way of "representing" the General Will . . . your magistrates, whatever their function, are only your mandataries.[45]

That many of his followers took him very seriously is indicated by the fact that they signed their letters to elected officials, "your equal in rights."[46] This new identity as activist-citizens required members of the charismatic communities to engage in self-government. Indeed, the extent to which the communities either governed their neighborhoods and towns directly by establishing parallel centers of authority, or by intervening consistently in the formal structures of government, is remarkable.[47] Clearly, the legacies of feudal authority structures were destroyed within the charismatic communities. Unfortunately, the ability to generate new stable structures of authority was severely undermined by the way in which these communities brought the principle of popular sovereignty to life.

The substantive orientation toward rules and procedures fostered by the communities also rendered the process of extrapolating stable principles and procedures from community experience difficult, if not impossible. The rules and procedures of any group regulate the relationship between group leaders and group members, as well as between the members themselves. By adhering to a substantive rather than formal interpretation of these rules, the charismatic communities of the French Revolution experienced unpredictable and dramatic changes in leadership as leaders were enthroned and deposed according to shifting perceptions of how the substantive criteria should be defined and applied. This volatility was augmented by periodic membership purges as these criteria were subsequently used to ferret out the unworthy. Ultimately, substantively oriented perceptions of who could be identified as a proper citizen were used to limit membership to the "elected" few, thereby further weakening the organizational strength of the communities.

Like the American case, the leaders of the French charismatic communities were subordinate to the doctrine of rights they served. Since the doctrine was, however, based on a collectively oriented understanding of rights, there was a tendency to elevate particular leaders to the status of concrete embodiments of the abstract will of the collectivity. These leaders were chosen according to a substantive criterion of demonstrated virtue. Initially, Robespierre represented such a leader, as the young revolutionary Saint-Just attested:

> You who sustain the vacillating country against the torrent of despotism and intrigue, you whom I know as I know God by your miracles, I address myself to you, monsieur, to beg you to join with me in saving my poor region. I don't know you but you are a great man. You are not merely the deputy of a province, you are the representative of humanity and the republic.[48]

The adulation of virtuous leaders was, however, inherently tenuous. If a leader could no longer demonstrate his virtue, he was removed regardless of his formal elected status. Since he no longer represented the General Will, his tenure as an elected official was meaningless. The unpredictable nature of changing perceptions of virtue meant that this test of leadership ability could not provide a stable basis upon which to formalize the relationship between citizens and their elected representatives.

An absolute emphasis on virtue as a substantive criterion of leadership was extended to the membership, and governed every aspect of the rules and procedures with which the communities operated. Crane Brinton illustrates this preference for substantive over formal criteria in regard to the Jacobin clubs:

> This insistence on an inner, emotional conviction or righteousness rather than on external rules . . . comes out again in the proceedings of the Paris club. "One must distrust," says the speaker, "liberty unaccompanied by virtue"; and by virtue he understands "not the mere practice of moral duties, but also an exclusive attachment to the unalterable principles of our constitution." The club at Limoges was told: "It is not enough, in order to belong to a truly republican society, to call oneself republican, to have done guard duty, to have paid one's taxes; one must have given sure indications of hatred for kings and nobles, for fanaticism; one must have passed through the crucible of perilous circumstance."[49]

Brinton goes on to show that this was not just empty rhetoric. Candidates who wished to be admitted to the clubs or members who wished to be recommended by the clubs for public office had to demonstrate their virtue in every sense of the word. The Jacobin club of Boulogne, for example, turned down the candidacy of the citizen Décadi since they did not want "merely men who love the Revolution. All members of our Society must be moral. Décadi has not treated his wife decently, has abandoned her without motive to carry on with another woman."[50]

Such considerations obviously limited the number of people who could gain and retain entry into the charismatic communities. Since virtue was of such preeminent importance, membership became restricted to particular social milieux where members could vouch for one another—or denounce one another—on the basis of familiarity. Membership was further restricted by the blanket rejection of entire categories of individuals deemed inherently unvirtuous due to their social standing (e.g. the nobility and the clergy) or due to their incomes (e.g. servants and wage-earners or the very wealthy bourgeoisie).

As a result of this exclusionary dynamic, different charismatic communities came to represent separate and distinct manifestations of virtue. The faultlines that divided Robespierre's Jacobins, Le Chapelier's Feuillants, Brissot's Girondins and Hebèrt's sans-culottes have less to do with socioeconomic divisions than with differing interpretations of civic virtue. The struggles between these communities took on a zero sum quality as each group claimed an absolute right to embody the collective virtue of the nation. Boundaries between the communities were solidified in the process, rendering alliances problematic and fragile. In this atmosphere, the social leveling that took place was of a particularly contingent nature.

Although the Jacobin clubs, for example, have been called "temples of equality,"[51] the charismatic communities of the French Revolution created trust and respect only between the members of a given community. Unlike the American case, where men of different backgrounds learned to trust and respect each other universally on the basis of a shared identity as citizens, a dual identity was created in the French communities where one became a citizen in good standing only by becoming a sans-culotte or a Jacobin first. One's identity as a citizen was contingent upon membership in a particular—and therefore exclusive—community.

As a result, members of the upper social orders did not acquire a different attitude toward the lower orders taken as a whole. A radical noble sans-culotte citizen learned to esteem the artisans of his community, while a radical noble of another charismatic community continued to mistrust and fear people of the lower orders who were not members of his community. Intense suspicions and hostilities toward those outside the group were ultimately only alleviated by a shared consensus that all citizens, regardless of group affiliation, were French. As a Jacobin stated unequivocally: "Republicans are neither from Lyons nor from Paris, nor from any city, nor from any department; they are Frenchmen, they are all brothers."[52]

This all-encompassing national identity still left open the question of who had a right to be represented in the governing of France. Theoretically, all social groups could be accepted as French citizens while denying certain groups a concrete right to represent their interests because they had not demonstrated the requisite amount of virtue. The stage was thereby set for the ensuing struggles over whose interests would legitimately be served in the new polity. That these struggles took place in an environment of intense conflict rather than cooperation is a result of the problematic way in which the charismatic communities transformed the conduct and consciousness of their members.

Due to the organizational weaknesses elaborated above, the French communities did not have a direct and unmediated influence on the creation of lasting political institutions that reflected their vision and their way of life. These charismatic communities did, however, successfully overthrow the old order by providing secure and compelling havens within which members could reject their previous identities as aristocrats or artisans in favor of a new identity—that of citizen. As we shall see below, by creating the institutional domain of citizenship, the French revolutionaries did ultimately have a lasting impact on institutional outcomes.

INSTITUTIONAL CONSEQUENCES

> It [the French Revolution] replaced arbitrary power by law, privilege by equality; it freed men from class distinctions, the land from provincial barriers, industry from the handicaps of corporations and guilds, agriculture from feudal servitude and the oppression of tithes, property from the constraints of entail; and it brought everything together under a single state, a single law, a single people.[53]

This summary of the Revolution's achievements was written in 1824 by F. A. Mignet, one of the earliest historians of the French Revolution. It remains representative, however, of most subsequent interpretations of the Revolution's positive institutional outcomes. In spite of France's post-Revolutionary turmoil, analysts from all schools of thought, from Marxists to conservatives, agree that a decisive break with the past had occurred. Whether this is seen as a matter for celebration or regret, France was clearly no longer dominated by feudal institutions. Feudalism with all of its constraints, divisions and distinctions had been replaced by an emerging constellation of institutions, generally deemed bourgeois in orientation, that enabled a "single people" to pursue their interests within a "single state," under a "single law."

The precise nature of these institutions and their origins in the Revolutionary era have not, however, received much careful attention. By and large, it has simply been assumed that the bourgeoisie emerged institutionally victorious. Since the events comprising the Revolution are both complicated and contradictory, it is perhaps natural that analysts have focused on what is clearly evident, namely the destruction of feudalism, rather than on the more complex question of the nature of the institutionalization process that followed. A more nuanced understanding of the type of liberalism that emerged from the Revolution can, however, be achieved by a careful examination of the natural rights doctrine that legitimated the Revolutionary struggle, and that subsequently informed the efforts of political actors to institutionalize a new political order.

All of the three institutional domains associated with liberalism—citizenship, representative government and procedurally defined public virtue—have been marked by the substantive interpretation of natural rights that dominated the Revolutionary effort. Already in the 1789 Declaration of the Rights of Man and Citizen, a collectivistic and substantive, as opposed to an individualistic and formal, interpretation of citizenship and government prevailed. Unlike the American case where just government essentially meant non-interference in the lawful lives of individual citizens, just government for the French revolutionaries implied a commitment to maintaining the "general welfare" of the citizens collectively comprising the nation. This is made clear in Article III of the Declaration which states that: "The principle of all sovereignty rests essentially in the nation. No body and no individual may exercise authority which does not emanate from the nation expressly."[54]

The concept of sovereignty residing in the over-arching collectivity of the nation was further bolstered by the way in which the Declaration tempered its statements of individual rights with clauses based on the rights of the collective. In Article I, it is written that: "Men are born and remain free and equal in rights. Social distinctions may be based only on common utility."[55] In other words, as long as differences in social standing serve the collective good, they may be tolerated. Conversely, if social distinctions do not serve the "common utility," they may be abolished. In Article IV, the attempt to establish an appropriate balance between individual and collective rights is further highlighted:

> Liberty consists in the ability to do whatever does not harm another; hence the exercise of the natural rights of each man has no limits except those which assure to other members of society the enjoyment of the same rights. These limits can only be determined by law.[56]

That this balance is decisively cast in favor of collective rights is clear, however, since Article VI goes on to state unequivocally that "law is the expression of the general will."[57] The ultimate arbitrator of the scope and range of the individual's rights is thereby the collective will of the nation. As one analyst has put it, "the concept of the nation had actually absorbed the concept of the individual."[58]

This orientation toward the collective is complemented by a substantive, as opposed to a formal, understanding of natural rights. From this understanding, the revolutionaries derived their views on how government should legitimately act to protect the rights of citizens. The substantive nature of the French interpretation of rights is apparent in Article II of the Declaration which states that: "The aim of all political association is to preserve the natural and imprescriptible rights of man. These rights are liberty, property, security and resistance to oppression."[59] While the rights of liberty and property are also to be found in the American understanding of rights, along with an implied right to rebellion, the substitution of security for the pursuit of happiness is an important distinction. Whereas American government simply had to guarantee non-interference as its citizens pursued their individual definitions of happiness, French government, in order to be seen as legitimate, had to guarantee the minimal requirements for the security of all of its citizens. Enshrining the right to security as a natural right commits government to providing a number of ancillary substantive rights such as the right to subsistence, i.e. food at affordable prices, and the right to work, as well as to the maintenance of law and order. Given this perception of natural rights, citizens have an eternally legitimate claim on the government to provide them with the means of achieving their security however broadly or narrowly defined. Moreover, government can legitimately intervene in the lives of its citizens in order to achieve the greatest degree possible of individual and collective security.

Seen from this perspective the sans-culotte demands for "practical equality" (*l'égalité de fait*), as a necessary companion to the equality of rights, were consistent with the overall tenor of the substantively and collectively oriented natural rights doctrine. Although most revolutionaries would not have taken the logic of the doctrine to the following extreme, they were largely in agreement with its underlying spirit of egalitarianism:

> Take away everything which a citizen has no use for, because excess is an open violation of the rights of the people. Every man who has more than he needs cannot use his surplus, he can only abuse it. Consequently, after leaving him simply what he needs and no more, the remainder belongs to the Republic, and to its less fortunate citizens.[60]

Although neither the Jacobins nor the sans-culottes denied the individual's right to property, they believed it should be circumscribed by the collective's right to security through an equitable distribution of resources. As a sans-culotte leader stated in 1792, "find a government which will lift the people above their meagre resources and deny to the rich the unrestricted exercise of their wealth and the balance of society will be perfect."[61]

Given the general desire to overcome the great disparities of wealth and opportunity that characterized French society, this substantive interpretation of natural rights remained uncontested until the end of the Terror (1793–94). In the wake of this tumultuous period in which revolutionary egalitarianism was carried to excess, moderates attempted to formulate a different vision of "the balance of society," one that would not lead to such radical extremes. They were, however, unable to base this vision on the language of rights—not even a formal interpretation of rights—since the substantive interpretation was widely considered to be the only appropriate definition of natural rights. Instead, the leaders of the Directoire period (1795–99) used the more utilitarian language of self-interest in order to protect what they believed to be the essential component of a stable social and political order, namely the individual's right to accumulate property. It was their opinion that "liberty must contribute to the advancement of commerce if it is to have a secure foundation."[62] Needless to say, this stark realism did not recommend itself to the still numerous revolutionary idealists who dismissed it as a blatant justification for rampant egoism and the development of a new oligarchic political, social and economic elite. After the end of Bonaparte's empire, such instrumental justifications for oligarchic rule were revived during the Restoration period (1814–30) and the July

Monarchy (1830–48). Ultimately, even moderate liberals such as de Tocqueville were disturbed by such persistent efforts to substitute the pursuit of wealth for the retention and expansion of revolutionary rights and liberties:

> Most of the politicians who have ruled us for the past ten years have changed principles and parties so many times that we are entitled to conclude that they have no principles and are incapable or unworthy of having a party. Witnessing their sterile debates, the people become more and more indifferent; it would seem that the rights which have cost the French most dear have ceased to be precious to them; that they are not worried to see the violation or evasion of those laws which they have had the most difficulty in obtaining, and that they are allowing to slip from their memories everything that their fathers and they themselves have done for liberty. The great liberal cause which triumphed momentarily in 1789 seems compromised once more.[63]

In short, the revolutionary articulation of the natural rights doctrine resulted in a widely accepted understanding of the collective nature of citizenship, while engendering a conflict between a vision of government based on substantive natural rights and a vision of government based on the self-interest of its most influential elites. The stage was thereby set for subsequent conflicts between the ideologically uninspiring but powerful large property owners on the one hand, and the small property owners and the emerging working classes on the other hand. The latter two groups were inflamed by a sense of righteousness derived from the founding premises of the Revolution. As Furet notes, the restoration of the monarchy and the apparent victory of the counter-revolutionary forces gave rise to an "extra-parliamentary republicanism . . . which imperfectly distinguished between Jacobinism and Bonapartism, mingling the two traditions round images of the nation, equality and a strong state."[64] In addition, the utopian writings of Saint-Simon, criticizing the bourgeois individualism of the Rights of Man but welcoming the revolutionary ideals of equality and fraternity, marked the emergence of a socialist movement in which "the idea of regenerating man by means of reason" was upheld, "but by organizing his social existence instead of picturing him in the anarchy of individual rights."[65] Accordingly, Furet concludes, "the extraordinary revolutionary insistence on equality thus resurfaced in the new garb of the era, having become the science of history and progress."[66] Finally, the Church and the nobility weighed in with a proposed "alliance of Throne and Altar," justified, in the writings of the Vicomte de Bonald for example, by "a theologico-political system of natural order."[67] This "system of natural order" was to legitimate the restored monarchy beyond the instrumental terms of self-interest. According to Furet, Bonald's philosophy "conceived the social element only as organized in bodies linked hierarchically in dependent relationships; it challenged modern individualism, the Rights of Man and civil equality."[68]

The resulting conflicts between republicans, socialists and conservatives, all adhering to different conceptions of how political and social life should be organized, were ultimately only contained by governments and political leaders that could successfully represent the nation in its collective unity.

In this context, the "man-on-horseback" syndrome in post-Revolutionary French history is a reflection of the ability of certain leaders to transcend the conflicts associated with class and government, and to tap into the understanding of citizenship as the collective attribute of a single people. Men such as Napoleon, Louis Bonaparte and, finally, De Gaulle embodied the disinterested and virtuous citizen par excellence and were, therefore, able to legitimate their governments on the basis of representing the collective national interest as opposed to the narrow interests of particular factions. They were thereby able to echo the revolutionary effort to achieve "the unity and indivisibility of the nation."[69] Even though, as Furet indicates, "in French history, class consciousness was a legacy of the Revolution before it became the product of industrial development,"[70] a division of society into the "haves" and "have-nots" was not acceptable by the standards of justice articulated during the Revolution. Consequently, persistent efforts to actualize "the legend of a national community united in egalitarian brotherhood"[71] coexisted with "bourgeois panics in the face of the poorer classes."[72] Clearly, the tension between these two legacies of the Revolution, class struggle on the one hand and national unity on the other hand, was best resolved by political figures who could suppress the former in the name of the latter.

However, even under the conditions of empire or restored monarchy, the institutional domain of citizenship still set the parameters of what was politically possible. As Patrice Higonnet points out:

> A great deal is implied by Napoleon's basic inability to withdraw ordinary rights of citizenship from even his weakest subjects, namely, Jews, whose outmoded, particularist, and even privatist customs he so disliked. And the Restoration was no more able to achieve on behalf of the landowning nobility as a whole what Napoleon had tried to impose on the Jews, namely, a distinct social existence recognized by law.[73]

Indeed, Furet elaborates this theme:

> The example of the French Revolution illustrated just how vain it was to try to reconcile the institution of royalty with the sovereignty of the people: Louis XVI, rechristened a constitutional king, had remained a prince of the ancien régime, the man of Varennes and betrayal. For the Republic was also the nation, that collective image of the citizenship of each person, one and indivisible, the bearer of an international right as well, since it was the promise of sovereignty for every people.[74]

In the name of the Republic, the restoration of the monarchy was brought to an end during the "July flash of lightning"[75] in 1830 as Paris took to the barricades in protest against the king's intention to establish a new regime by violating political and civil liberties. Although this uprising ended with a new, albeit constitutional, monarchy—that of Louis-Philippe—it did end the concept of legitimate royalty. As Chateaubriand observed, "The idolatry of a name is abolished; monarchy is no longer a religion."[76] In turn, the July monarchy fell as it too "revealed a will to cut back the principle of political citizenship," by refusing to widen a restricted electoral body and by attempting to evade parliamentary control.[77] Ironically, it was the bourgeois ministers of the July monarchy who were most passionately committed to restricting representation to the wealthiest, and therefore most enlightened, members of society. Not surprisingly, this eventually left the regime "open to the accusation of wanting to reestablish an aristocracy of wealth in a country which, for the second time, had just driven out the aristocracy of birth."[78]

Evidently, the French polity could only be distracted for so long with the prospects of the "enrich yourself" policy that both regimes maintained while attempting to restrict political rights to the privileged few. De Tocqueville need not have worried. Although the French Revolution established a collective understanding of rights, the individual citizen, irrespective of birth and social standing, was still seen as the fundamental component upon which the political order rested. Therefore, in the wake of the Revolution, the "political representation of corporate values" based either on inherited privilege and status or on acquired wealth and status became impossible.[79]

Unfortunately, given the conflicting visions of just government, the institutional domain of representative government was a long time in the making. From 1789 until 1958 constitutions came and went, as did various types of government. Since the ultimate source of authority resided with the nation, each new representative of the national will could enact a new constitutional interpretation of that will. Yet these interpretations were not haphazard or randomly expressed. Post-revolutionary regimes oscillated between giving either the executive or the legislature supreme authority. The effort to achieve a lasting constitutionally sanctioned balance of governing powers was consistently undermined by supporters of absolute executive authority, on the one hand, and by supporters of absolute legislative authority on the other. Consequently, until De Gaulle's Fifth Republic, political elites were unable to achieve a lasting consensus on how the institutional domain of popular representation was to be constituted.

Essentially, the regimes based on executive dominance (Napoleon 1799–1814; the Restoration period 1814–48; Louis Bonaparte 1852–70) attempted to derive their legitimacy from the post-Terror vision of government allowing its citizens to pursue their self-interest in an environment of social stability. By suppressing demands for redistributive justice and by providing avenues for middle-class advancement in the state bureaucracy, these governments did succeed in providing a considerable degree of stability. As the French historian Marc Richir has pointed out:

> the bourgeoisie did not make the Revolution (in 1789). It was the failed universalist Revolution of 1793–94 that brought into being a particularist, law-abiding, and unimaginative middle class that even privileged writers (Constant, Stendhal, Balzac, Flaubert, Baudelaire) instinctively knew to hate.[80]

Because these regimes represented a specific synthesis of a political leader claiming to embody the national will while being supported by an openly self-interested social class, the bourgeoisie, they became vulnerable both to self-criticism and to criticism from opponents. By and large, this criticism was derived from the substantive vision of government and of natural rights that had predominated during the years preceding the Terror. Obviously, the social class most amenable to this vision was the emerging working class. The 1848 Revolutionaries and the 1871 Paris Commune supporters were fueled by a sense of popular outrage that the ideals of the Revolution had been betrayed by a newly entrenched elite.

To a less extreme extent, the Second (1848–52), Third (1870–1940) and Fourth (1946–58) Republics were led by political leaders who shared this vision of government. In their opinion, democratic popular sovereignty and substantively oriented government could best be accomplished by a supreme legislature collectively embodying the national will. Needless to say, the forging of a social and political détente between the political representatives of hostile social classes was rendered exceedingly difficult by the factionalism and turbulence of parliamentary politics. Against all odds, however, the Third Republic was able to "domesticate democratic republicanism"[81] by building on key elements of the pre-Terror revolutionary legacy. Instead of denying substantive natural rights any validity in the political order, republican political leaders embraced a moderate understanding of natural rights and implemented laws designed to enhance the security and well-being of all French citizens. They were able to hold both political extremes (conservatives and radical socialist leaders) at bay by drawing on the support of small property owners, such as shopkeepers, who were now organized into the single most important political party of the era, the Radicals. This was precisely the social group that had formed the backbone of the original Jacobin clubs and that had been most supportive of democratic republican ideals. Moreover, the sale and redistribution of Church property during the Revolution, from which many members of the middle class and peasants had profited, had long bound the interests as well as the principles of this group to the fate of the Revolution. Their support became critical for the eventual institutionalization of a stable polity. According to Furet, the Third Republic can be characterized as "a municipal democracy of small property-owners and minor notables, backed up by 1789 against 1793. An immeasurable society, at last bound together by a strong civic spirit which combined equality and liberty."[82]

Yet each of the regimes surveyed above was exceedingly vulnerable in times of crisis. By rejecting a separation of powers, these regimes were not fully representative of political, social and economic interests. Some groups always felt themselves to be substantively excluded from the political process. Therefore, during crisis periods they chose to mobilize against the entire existing system of government, rather than expressing their grievances within the system. De Gaulle's lasting accomplishment was to embed an empowered executive *within* the framework of a republican government, thereby merging, for the first time, the two visions of government inherited from the revolutionary period. While it may be argued that during his presidency De Gaulle functioned as "an uncrowned republican monarch,"[83] his successors have acted more like American presidents than like sovereign rulers.

During the turbulent evolution of representative government in France, the institutional domain of procedurally defined public virtue provided a considerable source of stability. The French interpretation of the natural rights doctrine resulted in a vision of public virtue that proved to be remarkably steadfast, even in the context of rapidly changing regimes. What emerged subsequently is an apparent anomaly: the development of a stable, impersonal and procedural civil service in the midst of an unstable political order that oscillated between substantively oriented republics and instrumentally oriented executive rule.

The procedural and impersonal ethos of this bureaucracy was the result of a specific amalgam of formal proceduralism and substantive notions of equality that took shape during the Revolution. Just as in the American Revolution, French revolutionaries believed that formally enacted laws and legal procedures were the only appropriate means of adjudicating between conflicting interests in the new polity. Unlike the American case, however, these laws and procedures were to be oriented toward the attainment of a substantively defined goal, namely the equality of all citizens before the law. Given the great disparities of wealth and status in pre-revolutionary France, equality before the law meant more than equal treatment—it meant a certain equality of condition, as well. For example, even prior to the Revolution, members of the privileged orders, such as the administrative elite of the ancien régime, realized that they would have to give up their prerogatives, and perhaps even their offices, if true equality before the law was to be achieved for all citizens. In 1788, the Bureau des Finances at La Rochelle made the following suggestion in a declaration addressed to fellow administrators throughout the country:

> Let us sacrifice the exemptions dearly bought; let us offer to share with our fellow citizens the burden of public taxes . . . let us remember that before being Magistrates, we must be Men, French, citizens, and that the prerogatives, the exemptions of a corps must be forgotten when it is a question of the great interest of humanity and *la Patrie*.[84]

In other words, under the influence of the natural rights doctrine, privileged members of society were willing to give up their corporately defined status positions in exchange for an equality of *all* French citizens before the state. In place of the previous hierarchies and status positions, an ability to serve the state, through individual merit and talent, was to become the sole hallmark of true membership in the political community. As the magistrates of Dijon had stated already before the Revolution: "the first obligation of the citizen is that which attaches him to the State. This is the law of every social contract, the spirit of all civilized nations."[85] Consequently, after the Revolution, impersonally and impartially rendered service to the state was considered the ultimate manifestation of public virtue.

While, at first glance, it may seem paradoxical that a procedural and impersonal conception of public virtue and public service developed on the basis of this substantive preoccupation with equality, a closer examination reveals the way in which proceduralism derived its strength from the substantive notions that prevailed during the Revolution. First, the social and political leveling of all feudal hierarchies made possible by the Revolution destroyed the social bases of support for the competing notions of public virtue associated with the ancien régime. Furthermore, this leveling provided opportunities for previously excluded social groups to achieve greater status and dignity in the polity. In the context of rapid social mobility, the new conception of public virtue provided a powerful and compelling guide for professional conduct for newcomers to public office. By generating rules and standards for appropriate public behavior, procedurally defined public virtue attained a very immediate relevance for the many individuals who found themselves in positions of authority for the first time. Finally, and most importantly, the widespread acceptance of this definition of public virtue is due to the fact that it was derived from the substantive interpretation of natural rights that had legitimated the Revolution itself. Subsequently, privileges and inequalities of rank were considered legitimate only if they had been earned by serving the state in some capacity. In this process:

> the justification for social ranks . . . was moving from characteristics ascribed to individuals or associated with the traditional monarchy—divine decree, birth or personal honor—toward strictly utilitarian grounds embedded in an impersonal state. A Frenchman was to earn his place in society; he was to achieve his position through merit or, more specifically, through service to the nation.[86]

Both the substantive nature of the French natural rights doctrine and its collectivism combined to produce a conception of public virtue that set impersonal loyalty to the state, as the embodiment of the general will, above loyalty to particular leaders, political parties or constitutions. As one historian has stated: "allegiance to the state was to be the starting point from which all other relationships in society flowed. Citizenship defined participation in that state; privilege was the reward for it."[87] Seen from this perspective, the stability of state bureaucracies in the face of continuously changing regimes is no longer such an anomaly. If anything, such rapid turnovers simply served to emphasize the transcendent quality of the state and "*la Patrie*" in the eyes of citizens and civil servants.

Indeed, the permanent civil service that France is so famous for was made possible by the fact that it was imbued with a spirit of impersonal, bureaucratic professionalism. This meant that each post-revolutionary regime could rely on public officials to be impartial and efficient. Regimes, therefore, had little incentive to tamper with the existing structures of state bureaucracy. Furthermore, due to its ethos—an ethos which was grounded in the notion of service to the state—the civil service proved to be resistant to corruption in a personalistic or particularistic direction. Taken together, these two features facilitated the development of a permanent, apolitical state bureaucracy. According to analysts of French history, this bureaucracy subsequently provided continuity and stability during the post-revolutionary period.[88]

As in the American case, the institutional domain of procedurally defined public virtue represented a cohesive force in the polity. There are, however, important differences in emphasis. In the American case, laws, procedures and the Constitution were considered critical for the cohesion of a polity based on free and equal individuals. Since the Constitution created the state, it, and not the American state, became the transcendent object of loyalty. This emphasis on a legal source of authority superseding the state led to the development of an independent judiciary—an institution that is unknown in the French liberal democratic tradition. In the French case, laws, procedures and the state were considered critical for the cohesion of a society and a polity based on free and equal individuals. The creation and maintenance of social harmony was an overriding concern of the French *philosophes* and of the French revolutionaries. They ultimately came to believe that harmony would be assured if the interests of rights-bearing individuals could be transcended by the "great interest of humanity and *la Patrie*." In the words written by Robespierre in 1792: "the soul of the Republic is virtue, love of country, the generous devotion that fuses all interests into the general interest."[89]

In conclusion, what is distinctive about the French institutionalization of liberalism is the extent to which power and authority have been concentrated in the institutions of the state, regardless of whether these institutions were defined by executive or legislative supremacy. The American concept of limited government does not have an analogue in the French experience. Unlike the American concern with the formal rights of the individual, French revolutionaries were concerned with the substantive rights of individuals taken collectively. Not only was a strong state needed to achieve substantive goals such as an equality of condition, the state itself became the very embodiment of the collective will of all of its citizens. As Higonnet has stated, the Declaration of the Rights of Man

> emphasized less the specific and inherent, imprescriptible rights of the citizen, than his total empowerment in the context of the nation-state. It was indeed this simultaneously naturalized and nationalized quality that in the eyes of its makers essentially differentiated the French statement from its inferior and more positivistic Virginian antecedents.[90]

Just as the king had once been the head, both literally and figuratively, of the body politic, "*la Patrie*" now became the transcendent object of loyalty. As we have seen, the struggles and conflicts over who was to represent this state politically dominated French history from the Revolution to the Fifth Republic. The state itself was, however, largely uncontested. Both revolutionaries and counter-revolutionaries accepted it as the ultimate goal or objective of their political struggles.

The only constraint the Revolution imposed on this all-powerful state was the institutional domain of citizenship. The state was both to embody and serve the citizenry. Gross violations of civic rights by government officials were, therefore, rendered difficult, if not impossible. Conversely, citizens had both a right and a duty to serve the state. The notion that a Frenchman had to earn his place in society through service to the state eventually separated those citizens actively serving the state from those citizens who did not hold public office or somehow serve the common good. Ultimately, a political elite and an administrative bureaucracy emerged that perceived government in terms of guardianship and not in terms of public accessibility and accountability. Only those who served the state had a right to dictate the terms upon which the collective will of all citizens would be determined and implemented. In this process, the determination of the general or national interest took precedence over the representation of the interests of individual citizens. Consequently, France has had a weak tradition of representative government.

The conflicts engendered by the substantive natural rights doctrine and by the charismatic communities of the French Revolution were, thereby, resolved in a particular way. Over time, the zero-sum conflicts between different groups within the political elite, all claiming to embody the general will, gave way to a unified elite claiming guardianship rights on the basis of its public service. In effect, this was the solution Napoleon proposed after the turbulent years of the Revolution. His policy of attempting to unite the old political and social elites with the new elites of the revolutionary era on the basis of service to the state, foreshadowed the evolving "social compact" between elites that ultimately stabilized the new polity.[91] This compact was only made possible, however, as competing elites accepted the institutional domains of citizenship and procedurally defined public virtue that determined the parameters of the post-revolutionary French state.

Whereas the institutional impact of the natural rights doctrine and the charismatic communities of the French Revolution is not as direct as in the American case, citizenship and proceduralism could not have taken root in the French polity without the transformatory power generated during the Revolution. The civic identity of liberally oriented political elites and the critical social groups that supported them, such as small property owners, was in effect created by the natural rights doctrine and given behavioral substance in the charismatic communities. Without the unequivocal commitment fostered in these communities, the legacies of feudalism would not have been decisively undermined, nor would the new political identity have attained the status of a faith capable of altering people's consciousness and conduct.

4 Natural rights and liberal capitalist development

An overview

At this point in our analysis, it might be useful to recapitulate the most significant features of liberal democratic revolutions and institution-building in comparative terms. The following two questions will guide this endeavor: which conditions are necessary for the successful revolutionary articulation of modern democracy, and which conditions subsequently determine the character of the institutionalization process? Distilling these conditions will make it easier to examine the extent to which the Solidarity experience either replicates or deviates from the ideal typical model of the historic emergence of liberal regimes.

The emergence of such regimes cannot, however, be considered in isolation from the development of capitalism. Indeed, the relationship between liberalism and capitalism is a central issue for latecomers to democracy in Eastern Europe as they attempt to change simultaneously both the political and economic institutions inherited from Leninism. Accordingly, this chapter will subsequently address the origins of the free market as an institutional domain legitimated by natural law. Just as citizenship, representative government and procedurally defined public virtue were legitimated on the basis of the natural rights doctrine, so too did John Locke and Adam Smith provide a philosophical justification for the free market grounded in natural rights and the natural order of things. The market is thereby an integral component of the ideal typical model of what has become known as liberal capitalist development.

REVOLUTIONARY CONDITIONS

In order for a liberal democratic revolution to take place, four conditions would appear to be critical.[1] First, our survey of the antecedents to both the American and French Revolutions reveals a period of social mobility followed abruptly by a period of stalled social mobility. This dynamic affected the middle strata of society most intensely. Members of these strata, who had been able to improve their status and living conditions, suddenly found themselves deprived of possibilities for further advancement. Consequently, they were disenchanted with the existing state of affairs and became available for participation in groups or movements that proposed radical remedies.

The term "middle strata" is important to note. It would be a mistake to associate the making of liberal democratic revolutions with the pursuit of bourgeois or middle-"class" interests. As the Marxist historian Eric Hobsbawm has pointed out in regard to the French Revolution, "if by bourgeoisie we understand essentially a class of profit-making business people, then we shall certainly not rate their social importance and economic wealth in 1789 highly."[2] He goes on to define the social group that actually played the most significant role in the French Revolution as

> a stratum of people who owed their position in the social order not to birth or privilege but to individual worth, open to all suitable recruits . . . situated, by status and income, between the nobility above and the (manually) laboring classes below.[3]

In both Revolutions, small, non-industrial, property owners and independent producers hoping to advance themselves through initiative and talent represented the strata most negatively affected by the closure of opportunities for social advancement. In this context, property is defined broadly in a Lockean sense to include the property individuals owned in themselves such as special skills or a special education. Both artisans and intellectuals, as well as shopowners and landowners, were hampered in their quest to improve their social and economic positions. The existence of disaffected middle strata, therefore, appears to be the first condition necessary for the emergence of an environment conducive to the revolutionary articulation of a new political order.

The second vital condition is the crystallization of a core revolutionary elite drawn largely from these disaffected strata. This elite represents the political actors who are motivated enough actively to oppose existing circumstances and to proclaim the birth of a new order. While core elites are the organizational and motivational locus of all revolutions, what is significant about the American and French Revolutions is the extent to which the core elite embraced both the upper and lower echelons of the middle strata. The participation of both gentry and artisans, for example, in the core elite provided a broad social base that prevented the revolutionary endeavor from remaining on the level of elite-based political conflict. A core elite comprised of various components of the middle strata can convince wide segments of the population to pursue their political, social and economic interests within an alternative framework, thereby furthering revolutionary outcomes.

This brings us to the third condition, namely the existence of a natural rights doctrine articulated by religious or secular philosophers that can provide a liberal democratic framework, both for the destruction of old institutions and for the creation of new ones. As we have seen, the American and French core elites legitimated their struggles against the existing order on the basis of a value-rational belief in the fundamental rectitude of the principles derived from the natural rights doctrine. To quote Georges Lefebvre again: "there is no true revolutionary spirit without the idealism which alone inspires sacrifice." The revolutionaries believed they were fighting for the "advent of justice and right,"[4] not simply for the advance of their material interests.

"Justice and right" were given form and content in the charismatic communities of both Revolutions. Such communities represent the fourth condition necessary for the revolutionary articulation of a new order. Without the existence of these communities, the core elite would not have been able to translate their value-rational beliefs into a new understanding of the broader political community, its membership, purpose, principles and code of conduct. Within the charismatic communities, the Sons of Liberty and the Jacobins attained a concrete realization of what they were fighting for, as well as what they were fighting against. They were able to act and to conduct themselves as if their vision of a new order was already in existence. Under the impact of these communities, established behavioral patterns were transformed, status distinctions were eroded and a new category of identification, citizenship, took their place. Subsequent visions of how to institutionalize a new order were drawn directly from the conduct political actors had come to accept as appropriate and desirable in the communities.

Of the four conditions listed above, three are a matter of revolutionary form, while one is a matter of revolutionary content. In other words, while the existence of disaffected middle strata, a core elite and charismatic communities might well, in and of themselves, lead to a revolution, only the belief of a core elite in the natural rights doctrine will result in a revolution oriented toward liberal democratic principles. As we have seen, the doctrine provided a democratic standard according to which the old order could be invalidated and the new order proclaimed. The revolutionary cause itself was defined by the natural rights doctrine. Moreover, belief in the doctrine generated compelling grounds for both struggle and sacrifice on behalf of the cause. The basis upon which a revolution is legitimated, therefore, has profound implications for the way in which revolutionary struggle against an existing order is articulated and conducted. The content of the revolutionary doctrine also shapes the character of the institutionalization process after the old order has been overcome. In the case of the liberal democratic revolutions analyzed above, the way in which the natural rights doctrine was interpreted by the core elite determined the nature of the new institutional domains, and whether the process of constructing new institutions would be conflictual or relatively uncontentious. A formal understanding of natural rights in the United States resulted in a highly individualistic conception of citizenship, a rigorous separation of governing institutions, and a procedural conception of public virtue firmly oriented toward the Constitution as the ultimate manifestation of political authority. In France, where a substantive interpretation of natural rights prevailed, citizenship was conceived of in collective terms: governing institutions tended toward an unitary expression of the general will (embodied either in the executive or the legislature), while procedurally and impersonally defined public virtue was oriented toward the state as the supreme manifestation of political authority.

By leading to the development of two conflicting images of just government, the substantive natural rights interpretation also resulted in a highly conflictual process of institutionalization wherein the institutional domain of representative government remained contested until the Fifth Republic. Indeed, if it had not been for the firm entrenchment of the institutional domain of citizenship in the polity, it is doubtful whether a stable liberal democratic government would ever have emerged in France. Citizenship provided the parameters and constraints within which the various post-revolutionary regimes had to operate.

The mass of small property owners and independent producers that had been mobilized by the revolutionary core elite embraced the institutional domain of citizenship as serving their status aspirations and their economic interests. As citizens they had achieved, for the first time, a secure equality of social status, and as citizens they could make legitimate claims on the state to protect their substantive right to subsistence. Citizenship thereby opened an avenue for the protection of their economic interests. Any regime choosing to contest this institutional domain would have risked alienating a considerable portion of the population; a portion that had shown itself capable of active resistance during the Revolution.

In short, whereas the formal articulation of natural rights leads to a relatively uncontested institutionalization of all three of the institutional domains associated with liberalism, the substantive articulation leads to a highly conflictual process, the successful outcome of which depends on the strength of the domain of citizenship. If the articulation of citizenship as a natural right by the core elite resonates with the social and economic interests of critical social groups such as the small property owners, this domain, in and of itself, would appear to be a sufficient condition for the eventual institutionalization of a liberal democratic government. An analysis, therefore, of which natural rights interpretation, if any, legitimated Solidarity's opposition to the existing order, and of the extent to which the movement's conception of citizenship has resonated with particular social groups, should provide us with some insight into the future development of liberal democratic institutions in Poland.

On the whole, the relationship between rights and interests is crucial for understanding not just the development of liberal democracy, but for understanding the accompanying rise of the capitalist free market as well. In a recent article, Furet states that the democratic citizen maintains two faces, one as the "man of interests" and the other as the "man of rights."[5] This imagery echoes the ideal type definition of modern liberal democracy developed in the preceding chapters. As a synthesis of the value-rational commitment to natural rights and the instrumentally rational orientation toward the representation of interests, modern democracy itself has two faces or facets that are inseparably linked. Without a commitment to rights, the rational pursuit of interests alone cannot generate a legitimate foundation for political organization. Taken in isolation, instrumental rationality is too easily attacked as the naked pursuit of selfish interests on the part of particularistically inclined elites.

Conversely, without a "rational system of representative government"[6] based on the interests of citizens, rights cannot be entrenched and protected. As Thomas Paine noted, "the common interests of society and the common rights of man"[7] represent the joint foundations for a just government. By allowing individuals the freedom to determine, pursue and represent their interests, both publicly and privately, governments protect the natural rights of their citizens. The pursuit of individual interests consequently serves as a vital means of preserving rights for all members of the political community.

As we have seen, the institutional domains of citizenship, representative government and proceduralism were established and legitimated on the basis of this understanding of the relationship between rights and interests. Within this context, the pursuit of economic interests as well came to be justified as serving the general "good of all," rather than simply serving the selfish needs and desires of particular individuals. According to the well-known ideas of Adam Smith:

> the natural effort of every individual to better his own condition . . . is so powerful a principle, that it is alone, and without assistance, not only capable of carrying on the society to wealth and prosperity, but of surmounting a hundred impertinent obstructions with which the folly of human laws too often encumbers its operations.[8]

Less well known, however, is the extent to which conceptions of natural law and natural rights provided the philosophical justification for the free market, as the systemic outcome of individuals pursuing their material interests, as well as influencing both the moral and the legal codes that generated the enabling conditions for the emergence of the free market. Ultimately, natural law and the natural rights doctrine legitimated the institutional domain of the free market, thereby establishing the critical domains of the political and economic system we know as liberal capitalism.

ORIGINS OF THE FREE MARKET

In his classic work, *The Protestant Ethic and the Spirit of Capitalism*, Weber defines "capitalistic economic action" as resting

> on the expectation of profit by the utilization of opportunities for exchange, that is on (formally) peaceful chances of profit. . . . The important fact is always that a calculation of capital in terms of money is made, whether by modern book-keeping methods or in any other way, however

> primitive and crude. Everything is done in terms of balances: at the beginning of the enterprise an initial balance, before every individual decision a calculation to ascertain its probable profitableness, and at the end a final balance to ascertain how much profit has been made.[9]

Weber goes on to note that the Occidental form of capitalism, "which has appeared nowhere else," is based on "the rational capitalistic organization of (formally) free labor."[10] According to Weber, "exact calculation—the basis of everything else—is only possible on the basis of free labor."[11] In other words, without being able to calculate the cost of labor inputs against the expected productivity of labor, the ability to utilize "opportunities for exchange" for maximum benefit or profit are severely impaired. Given that labor costs are integral to the calculation of prices, and therefore to the calculation of profit, labor costs must be predictable and calculable in monetary terms. Such calculations are only possible to the extent that labor has become commercialized, that is, to the extent that labor can be bought and sold freely, just as any other commodity is bought and sold on the market. The supply of labor must be rendered constant and predictable, unfettered by feudal practices that restricted mobility and enforced servitude on the land.

The rational organization of labor, therefore, takes place within the parameters of the free market, just as all other commodity and capital exchanges take place within the market. Consequently, the free market represents the essential field of action or domain of Occidental capitalism. Recalling the definition of institutional domains presented in Chapter 1, the free market can be said to constitute the normative boundaries for "capitalistic economic action," thereby establishing the parameters within which the institutions of capitalism have developed. Although Weber notes that markets have always existed and are not unique to capitalism, Polanyi has argued that a self-regulating or free market represents *the* critical underlying feature of capitalist development. According to Polanyi:

> A market economy is an economic system controlled, regulated, and directed by markets alone; order in the production and distribution of goods is entrusted to this self-regulating mechanism. An economy of this kind derives from the expectation that human beings behave in such a way as to achieve maximum money gains. It assumes markets in which the supply of goods (including services) available at a definite price will equal the demand at that price. It assumes the presence of money, which functions as purchasing power in the hands of its owners. Production will then be controlled by prices, for the profits of those who direct production will depend upon prices, for prices form incomes, and it is with the help of these incomes that the goods are distributed amongst the members of society. Under these assumptions order in the production and distribution of goods is ensured by prices alone.[12]

It would appear, then, that a particular type of market, namely the self-regulating market, is unique to capitalism. That this market also determines the parameters within which the rational calculation of profit can take place peacefully is indirectly acknowledged in Weber's work as well. For example, Weber states that: "Rational industrial organization, attuned to a regular market, and neither to political nor irrationally speculative opportunities for profit" represents a "peculiarity of Western capitalism."[13] Indeed, the other notable peculiarities of capitalism, the development of individual private property, the development of an "ethic of endless accumulation"[14] of money, the separation of business from the household, the emergence of rational bookkeeping are all attuned to the mechanisms of the free market.

Contrary to what prominent theorists of capitalism, such as Hayek, would have us believe, the development of the free market was not inevitable nor was it a simple evolutionary development from one type of market to another. Instead, as Polanyi notes:

> just as the transition to a democratic system and representative politics involved a complete reversal of the trend of the age, the change from regulated to self-regulated markets at the end of the eighteenth century represented a complete transformation in the structure of society.[15]

Consequently, just as the revolutionary transition to a democratic system had to be legitimated, so too did the transition to a free market system. Given their novelty, the "extraordinary assumptions"[16] underlying the self-regulating market had to be validated as representing the best possible course of economic action.

The philosophical terms chosen by early theorists such as Locke and Smith to justify new conceptions of property and economic enterprise were couched in the language of natural rights and natural law. The impact of their arguments can be seen to this day in the widely accepted view that the free market is a natural reflection of the innate tendencies of human beings to engage in acquisitive behavior. From Hayek to Sachs, theorists, unaware or dismissive of natural law and natural rights, nonetheless implicitly take as their point of departure the fundamental propositions of Locke and Smith—that the rights of private property and the law of the market are founded in the law of nature. Although economists such as Sachs make explicit arguments about the utility of the free market in providing the greatest good for the greatest number, these arguments are based on the underlying assumption that all human beings are inherently capable of capitalist economic action.[17] Accordingly, all societies are capable of choosing, creating and sustaining the free market. As in the case of modern democracy, capitalism is now justified almost exclusively on instrumental, utilitarian grounds, while the value-rational basis of liberal capitalism is overlooked or taken for granted. A direct and unmediated sense of the value-rational principles that originally rendered this form of economic conduct compelling enough to effect a "reversal of the trend of the age" has been lost.

The works of Locke and Smith, however, do provide a value-rational justification for capitalism, grounded in the natural law tradition. For example, in his *Second Treatise of Government*, Locke examines three principal components of the free market—private property, wage-labor and monetary exchange—and places them in the context of the manifest laws of nature. From the very beginning, Locke defines the "perfect freedom" found in the state of nature in terms of ownership and the disposition of property:

> To understand political power right, and derive it from its original, we must consider what state all men are naturally in, and that is a state of perfect freedom to order their actions and dispose of their possessions and persons as they think fit, within the bounds of the law of nature, without asking leave, or depending upon the will of any other man.[18]

For Locke, both "possessions and persons" were considered property: "By property I must be understood here, as in other places, to mean that property which men have in their persons as well as goods."[19] It is to preserve this property that man leaves the state of nature where he is "absolute lord of his own person and possessions, equal to the greatest, and subject to nobody,"[20] and enters into political society:

> The great and chief end, therefore, of men's uniting into commonwealths, and putting themselves under government, is the preservation of their property, to which in the state of nature there are many things wanting.[21]

Having established the right to property and its preservation as the only *raison d'être* for just government, it is not surprising that Locke considers the appropriation of property by individuals to be a divinely sanctioned activity:

> God commanded, and his [man's] wants forced him to labor. That was his property which could not be taken from him wherever he had fixed it. And hence, subduing or cultivating the earth and having dominion, we see are joined together. The one gave title to the other. So that God, by commanding to subdue, gave authority so far to appropriate. And the condition of human life, which requires labor and materials to work on, necessarily introduces private possessions.[22]

The accumulation of private property is thus considered both a fact of nature as man's needs force him to work, and a divinely sanctioned occupation. It follows, for Locke, that man acquires a natural right to the property that is produced by "the labor of his body, and the work of his hands."[23] Land enclosures are thereby justified as the outcome of man acting in obedience to the "command of God." The enclosed land subsequently becomes a man's private property that "another had no title to, nor could without injury take from him."[24]

In addition to material possessions, Locke maintains that "every man has a property in his own person. This nobody has any right to but himself."[25]

Given that Locke's theoretical point of departure includes the right to dispose of one's person as one sees fit, any personally determined use of such property is in accordance with natural law. Accordingly, Locke places the traditional master–servant relationship on a new footing, one based on the concept of a wage-labor contract:

> Master and servant are names as old as history, but given to those of far different condition; for a free man makes himself a servant to another by selling him for a certain time the service he undertakes to do, in exchange for wages he is to receive. And though this commonly puts him into the family of his master, and under the ordinary discipline thereof, yet it gives the master but a temporary power over him, and no greater than what is contained between 'em.[26]

Men have the right to dispose of their persons as they see fit, including entering into contractual arrangements for the sale of their labor. Having done so, however, the fundamental "equality of men by nature"[27] attenuates the inequalities inherent in the master–servant relationship. What was once a relationship of complete domination has become a limited and contingent one in Locke's opinion. Presumably, one of the factors constraining the master's power is his ability to fulfill the contractual obligations by paying the agreed upon wages. In the event that wages are not forthcoming, the servant has every right to dispose of his labor elsewhere. On the other hand, the unequal distribution of monetary wealth means that labor will always be for hire—thus the master–servant or master–tenant relationship is perpetuated, albeit in different moral and commercial circumstances.[28]

Along with the role played by money in the contractual exchange of labor for wages, Locke was concerned with the overall role of money and its place in the laws of nature. Money, for Locke, became the means whereby men could fulfill the divinely sanctioned mandate of accumulating property without violating the equally important divine prohibition against the waste or spoilage of goods. As "nothing was made by God for man to spoil or destroy,"[29] money became the means whereby property could be accumulated without the danger of waste. According to Locke, money arose out of the imperative need to find a commonly agreed upon unit of measure to facilitate more durable and numerous commodity exchanges: "and thus came in the use of money, some lasting thing that men might keep without spoiling, and that by mutual consent men would take in exchange for truly useful but perishable supports of life."[30] While it has been maintained that Locke invests money and capital with the standing of a natural right by placing the initial moment of "mutual consent" in the state of nature, it is perhaps more accurate to say that Locke values money as he values all other forms of property to which men have an inalienable right.[31] Indeed, money is doubly blessed, not only as property in and of itself, but also as the means with which God's commands to accumulate and not to waste can be reconciled.

In short, Locke validates the accumulation of private property, wage-labor and monetary exchange as being derived from the original state of nature in which men are born free and equal and with a natural right to preserve and protect their property:

> Man being born, as has been proved, with a title to perfect freedom, and an uncontrolled enjoyment of all the rights and privileges of the law of nature, equally with any other man or number of men in the world, hath by nature a power not only to preserve his property, that is his life, liberty and estate, against the injuries and attempts of other men, but to judge of and punish the breaches of that law in others as he is persuaded the offense deserves, even with death itself in crimes where the heinousness of the fact, in his opinion, requires it.[32]

While men may unite and render unto political society the right to punish those that threaten "life, liberty and estate," the inherent God-given rights to property, freedom and equality cannot be given up when men leave the state of nature. Rather, these rights, in Locke's view, form the only legitimate basis for a properly constituted government or political society. A government is legitimate only to the extent that it protects these rights. By conceptualizing natural rights in economic as well as in social and political terms, Locke provides a powerful natural rights justification for the emerging free market. Just as liberty and equality are inseparable from property, so too is the market in which private property is exchanged inseparable from the liberal "umpire" state.

Specifically, against the prevailing customs of the time, Locke maintains that private property, rather than collectively or commonly held property, is a natural right. Land enclosures are therefore legitimate as the divinely sanctioned pursuit of this right. Furthermore, Locke's concept of all men having property in themselves, which they have a right to dispose of as they wish, legitimates a wage-labor market by invalidating all traditional restrictions on employment and labor mobility. Even if wages do not rise above subsistence levels in this labor market, as Locke believed, the right to dispose freely of one's property, no matter how impoverishing the outcome might be, is derived from the state of nature and is, therefore, to be upheld in all circumstances by positive law.[33] According to Locke, man only has a natural right to subsistence, not to a full and rewarding existence. Grounded in both "natural reason" and "revelation," men "being once born, have a right to their preservation, and consequently to meat and drink, and such other things as nature affords for their subsistence."[34] This right is, however, linked to the obligation men are under to work for their own preservation. Neither the state nor the community have a duty to provide for those who can, through their own labor, maintain themselves. Locke is adamant that poverty resulting from idleness and the avoidance of work should not be tolerated:

> If the causes of this evil [the multiplying of the poor] be looked into, we

> humbly conceive it will be found to have proceeded neither from scarcity of provisions, nor from want of employment for the poor, since the goodness of God has blessed these times with plenty. . . . The growth of the poor must therefore have some other cause; and it can be nothing else but the relaxation of discipline and corruption of manners: virtue and industry being as constant companions on the one side as vice and idleness are on the other.[35]

It follows from this that work embodied in the contractual exchange of labor–property for wages, even if only for subsistence wages, is the only course of action consistent with the natural rights and duties men are born with.

Finally, Locke's validation of money as both a means of exchange and a form of property legitimated the use of money as capital, thereby undermining any religiously derived prohibitions against interest and usury. In Locke's view, money is a form of property equal to that of land:

> Money therefore, in buying and selling, being perfectly in the same condition with other commodities, and subject to all the same laws of value, let us next see how it comes to be of the same nature with land, by yielding a certain yearly income, which we call use, or interest.[36]

Consequently, just as the appropriation of land as private property is legitimate as a natural right, so too is the accumulation and use of money as capital legitimate. As C. P. Macpherson notes, Locke's theory of property "is a justification of the natural right not only to unequal property but to unlimited individual appropriation."[37] Macpherson goes on to state that this "individual right of appropriation" overrides any moral claims that society as a whole might have. A collective sense of rights and obligations embedded in "the traditional view that property and labor were social functions, and that ownership of property involved social obligations," is thereby decisively undermined in Locke's work.[38]

Whereas Locke was still within the mercantilist tradition, and, therefore, used natural rights to justify elements of what would later become the free market, Adam Smith, writing over eighty years later, was concerned with describing and justifying the free market itself. Interestingly, however, Smith continues the use of natural law propositions to legitimate his understanding of how economic relations should be constituted. Early in *Wealth of Nations*, for example, Smith echoes Locke's views on property: "The property which every man has in his own labor, as it is the original foundation of all other property, so it is the most sacred and inviolate."[39] More explicitly than Locke, Smith goes on to invalidate all restrictions placed on labor as being in violation of that which is "sacred and inviolate":

> The patrimony of a poor man lies in the strength of his hands; and to hinder him from employing this strength and dexterity in what manner he thinks proper without injury to his neighbor, is a plain violation of this

> most sacred property. It is a manifest encroachment upon the just liberty of the workman, and of those who might be disposed to employ him.[40]

Indeed, throughout the book, Smith questions both the validity and the utility of feudal and mercantile restrictions, regulations and duties by juxtaposing the negative results achieved by these "human institutions" to the positive results obtained when the "natural order" is allowed to develop. For example, in his overview of economic history, Smith finds that:

> Had human institutions . . . never disturbed the natural course of things, the progressive wealth and increase of towns would, in every political society, be consequential, and in proportion to the improvement and cultivation of the territory or country.[41]

For Smith, the "natural course of things" corresponds to a "natural system of perfect liberty and justice,"[42] that is, the natural system of a free, self-regulating market. In this system

> every man, as long as he does not violate the laws of justicc, is left perfectly free to pursue his own interest his own way, and to bring both his industry and capital into competition with those of any other man, or order of men.[43]

It is here that the famous "invisible hand" comes into play. For when man pursues his own interests, his own gain, he is "led by an invisible hand to promote an end which was no part of his intention." As Smith elaborates, "By pursuing his own interest he frequently promotes that of the society more effectually than when he really intends to promote it."[44] Accordingly, once all restrictions and regulatory systems are removed, and "the obvious and simple system of natural liberty establishes itself of its own accord,"[45] men are free to pursue their natural inclinations to their own benefit and the benefit of society at large.

Given that men have a natural tendency to better their condition, only the proper circumstances are needed to unleash the inherent potential of unregulated human industry. Smith illustrates this proposition with reference to the debilitating effects of mercantile restrictions on colonial trade in the North American colonies. He concludes that "some moderate and gradual relaxation of the laws which give to Great Britain the exclusive trade to the colonies" is necessary to restore the colonial economy to "that natural, healthful, and proper proportion which perfect liberty necessarily establishes, and which perfect liberty can alone preserve."[46] Correspondingly, Smith views any laws that undermine this "perfect liberty" by regulating and/or restricting commerce and manufacturing as "evident violations of natural liberty, and therefore [as] unjust."[47]

Although Smith does not legitimate his preferred economic system with explicit references to the natural rights obtained from the state of nature and divine grace, he does consistently equate the free market of competing interests with what is natural and, therefore, correct. In other words, Smith validates his vision of the free market with reference to the natural laws of economic conduct that he has brought to light. By using the authority of natural law, Smith is able to "impose the arrangements of the free market as both inevitable and in accordance with the uninhibited workings of human nature."[48]

In addition, the free market is given moral undertones by virtue of being linked to the realization of a "comprehensive social ethics of 'natural liberty.' "[49] For Smith is also consistent in elaborating how the free market frees the common man from dependence and arbitrary servitude. Not just the wealthy merchant and the great landowner are to benefit from the "natural liberty" of the free market, average small proprietors are to prosper as well. Indeed, for Smith, the small proprietor

> who knows every part of his little territory, who views it with all the affection which property, especially small property, naturally inspires, and who upon that account takes pleasure not only in cultivating but in adorning it, is generally of all improvers the most industrious, the most intelligent, and the most successful.[50]

In short, without employing the language of natural rights directly, Smith still legitimates the free market "in terms of a whole range of naturalizing strategies"[51]—in terms of human nature, and in terms of natural economic processes. This simply represents a more secularized version of natural law, in contrast to Locke's more religiously based worldview. The absence of references to divinely mandated natural rights in Smith's work is not surprising given that he was heavily influenced by the natural law traditions of the Stoics. As Raphael and Macfie note: "Life according to nature was the basic tenet of Stoic ethics, and a Stoic idea of nature and the natural forms a major part of the philosophical foundations of *The Theory of Moral Sentiments* and *Wealth of Nations* alike."[52] In Stoic thought, natural laws reflect the properties of nature as a "cosmic harmony" wherein all elements are in balance, and the world appears as "one immense and connected system." Given these influences, Raphael and Macfie maintain that Smith's "invisible hand" should be understood in the context of the "Stoic idea of harmonious system, seen in the working of society."[53] Thus, even the most famous of Smith's insights has its origins in the natural law tradition.

Taken together, both Locke and Smith provide different, albeit complementary, natural law justifications for the free market. Using natural law arguments allowed them to invalidate existing conventions, customs and legal practices by contrasting them to the purity of a prior state of nature or, in the case of Smith, an underlying state of natural harmony, that was being corrupted. The harmful effects of this corruption could only be alleviated by returning to natural principles and practices. The revolutionary impact of the free market system was thereby obscured behind a recognizable form of argumentation. The social audiences that Locke and Smith were addressing found their works intelligible as part of the natural law discourse promulgated by numerous seventeenth-century philosophers such as Grotius and Pufendorf. On a deeper level, their natural law arguments resonated with the ingrained religious metaphors of the time. Essentially, Locke and Smith were promising nothing less than a return to a state of grace. By rediscovering and following the laws obtaining in the pure state of nature, people could overcome the negative consequences of the Fall, thereby coming closer to Paradise. The power of arguments for the free market was, therefore, enhanced by being linked to the power of religious faith. The social groups most susceptible to this linkage were, of course, those influenced by Protestantism. Indeed, Locke and Smith have an affinity with Protestant thought, given their emphasis on the virtues of labor, self-discipline, and frugality.[54] In general, Protestantism, especially the Puritan Revolution, prepared the ground for emergence of the free market and its philosophical legitimation. According to Michael Walzer, although "liberalism and capitalism appear fully developed only . . . after Puritanism is spent as a creative force," it seems clear that Puritanism shaped the "disciplinary basis of the new economy and politics."[55] As Walzer elaborates:

> The moral discipline of the saints can be interpreted as the historical conditioning of the capitalist man; but the discipline was itself not capitalist. It can be argued that the faith of the brethren, with its emphasis upon methodical endeavor and self-control, was an admirable preparation for systematic work in shops, offices, and factories. . . . And by teaching self-control, it provided the basis for impersonal, contractual relations among men.[56]

On the basis of this "historical conditioning," Locke and Smith could assume that methodical endeavor, self-control and impersonal, contractual relations represent the natural inclinations of men. Correspondingly, due to the impact of Puritanism, a social audience existed that was inclined to agree with them. In addition, their use of natural law, as the philosophical basis for the legitimation of the free market, resonated with Protestant conceptions of natural law.

The extent to which natural law contributed to the traits that shaped the moral and behavioral foundations for capitalism can be seen by drawing on Weber's work in *The Protestant Ethic and the Spirit of Capitalism*. While Weber emphasized the doctrine of predestination as the critical dimension in his elaboration of the changes Protestantism wrought in the individual and his relationship to the world, he also addressed the "*lex naturae*" of the Protestant sects to explain integral components of this ethos and its effects. Specifically, he mentions the *lex naturae* in connection with the Protestant validation of labor as a calling, the individual's personal responsibility before God, and the impersonal nature of brotherly love fostered by the Protestants.

Protestantism decisively reinterpreted the traditional Catholic view of natural law as a reflection of the natural order of the world into a doctrine of "natural morality."[57] The emphasis of the Catholic Church on an earthly order that is divinely ordained and, therefore, natural inculcated a passive submission to that order in its believers. The Protestant understanding of natural law, on the other hand, demanded of its believers an active quest for the grace of God. Natural morality, in this sense, indicated the natural instinct to please God. A decidedly voluntaristic dimension was thereby added to the religious understanding of natural law. The exercise of man's will in the service of God as an expression of his natural morality became a guiding leitmotif of the Protestant faith.

In this context, labor or work in one's calling was validated as a moral injunction binding on all individuals; as the purest expression of their search to please God. The objective and material results of ascetic action in one's calling thus became proof of the power of one's faith. An adherence to this natural morality did not, however, ordain a uniform order that had to be obeyed uniformly: "In principle there could be no general rules, no moral code, for the calling which everyone had, and which is different for every individual, is revealed to him by God through his conscience."[58] The personal way to serve God was thereby determined by one's own will as "revealed either directly through the Bible or indirectly through the purposeful order of the world which he (the individual) has created (*lex naturae*)."[59] In the latter case, not metaphysical speculation, but "natural reason," was to be used to acquire an "empirical knowledge of the divine laws of nature to ascend to a grasp of the essence of the world."[60] According to Weber, "the empiricism of the 17th century was the means for asceticism to seek God in nature."[61] Furthermore, the redefinition of natural law had profound implications for the concept of brotherly love which was transformed from a personal relationship to an impersonal one:

> Brotherly love, since it may only be practiced for the glory of God and not in the service of the flesh, is expressed in the first place in the fulfillment of the daily tasks given by the *lex naturae*; and in the process this fulfillment assumes a peculiarly objective and impersonal character, that of service in the interest of the rational organization of our social environment.[62]

In terms of Weber's major concern, the contribution of Protestantism to the development of capitalism, natural law obviously had a considerable impact in validating the impersonalism, the rationalism and the individualism that fostered a new economic order. As we have seen, these themes: the value of work, the primacy of the individual, the presumption of rational conduct, and the impersonalism inherent, for example, in the wage-labor contract are all echoed in the later works of Locke and Smith. In both the writings of these philosophers and in Protestant thought, natural law provides the value-rational legitimation for the fundamental moral, social and economic reorientation required for capitalist development.

The impact of the Protestant *lex naturae* was most immediately manifested in the realm of ethical and moral conduct, since it changed the internal conditions of life for the believers. Yet these internal changes had external consequences. For example, the disciplined, rational and methodical approach to work, characteristic of capitalism, had its origins in Protestantism as a means to the end of spiritual salvation. According to Walzer, the saints "sought in work itself what mere work can never give: a sense of vocation and discipline that would free them from sinfulness and the fear of disorder."[63] These behavioral manifestations of the Puritan Revolution and the moral code they were based on were accepted as natural by Locke and Smith. Indeed, as Walzer notes, "Lockeian liberals found it possible to dispense with religious, even with ideological controls in human society. . . . But this was only because the controls had already been implanted *in men*."[64]

Consequently, Locke and Smith could take much for granted regarding the nature of man. In this context, their use of natural law arguments had an entirely different impact on the development of a worldview conducive to capitalism. By presenting a natural law foundation for what was originally the purview of specific religious sects, Locke and Smith achieve nothing less than a philosophical universalization of the Protestant ethic. The conduct and the ethical code of the saints was now seen as binding for all men due to an assumed "naturalness." In locating attributes derived from Protestantism in the state of nature or in the system of natural liberty, the religious boundaries and restrictions are removed. Any man can now be a "saint," any political society can now be "saintly"—to the extent that they follow the course of conduct outlined by Smith and Locke.

This potent combination of religious and philosophical foundations for the free market was given added strength and depth by the natural-law-based legal codes of the eighteenth century. The significance of these legal codes for the development of a capitalist economic order attracted Weber's interest in the *Sociology of Law*. In his view, modern natural law, under the impact of the "rationalistic Enlightenment" and of "powerful religious, particularly Anabaptist, influences," created abstract "norms of a formal type" which provided the legitimation for revolutionary changes in positive law.[65] These changes, in turn, provided the legal framework for the emerging free market.

As we recall from our previous discussion of natural law in Chapter 1, Weber defines this type of law as

> the sum total of all those norms which are valid independently of, and superior to, any positive law and which owe their dignity not to arbitrary enactment but, on the contrary, provide the very legitimation for the binding force of positive law.[66]

He goes on to note that: "The natural-law legitimacy of positive law can be connected either with formal or with substantive conditions."[67] The formal axioms of natural law are, in Weber's opinion, particularly conducive to capitalist development in that they protect individual rights, contract rights and property rights. Accordingly:

> the essential elements in such a natural law are the freedoms, and above all, "freedom of contract." The voluntary rational contract became one of the universal formal principles of natural law construction, either as the assumed real historical basis of all rational consociations including the state, or, at least, as the regulative standard of evaluation. Like every formal natural law, this type is conceived as a system of rights legitimately acquired by purposive contract, and, as far as economic goods are concerned, it rests upon the basis of a community of economic agreement created by the full development of property. Its essential components are property and the freedom to dispose of property, i.e. property legitimately acquired by free contractual transaction made either as primeval contract with the whole world, or with certain other persons. Freedom of competition is implied as a constituent element. Freedom of contract has formal limits only to the extent that contracts, and social conduct in general, must neither infringe upon the natural law by which they are legitimated nor impair inalienable freedoms. This basic principle applies to both private arrangements of individuals and the official actions of the organs of society meant to be obeyed by its members. Nobody may validly surrender himself into political or private slavery. For the rest, no enactment can validly limit the free disposition of the individual over his property and his working power.[68]

This passage has been quoted at length to demonstrate the extent to which Lockean principles were translated into the legal constructs of the eighteenth century under the legitimating influence of formal natural law. Weber also provides evidence for the legal codification of Smithian principles by commenting on the transformation of the concept of the "just price" from the "subsistence principle" characteristic of canonist economic doctrine to the notion of a just price based on free competition: "The price which was to be rejected as 'unnatural' was now one which did not rest on the competition of the free market, i.e., the price which was influenced by monopolies or other arbitrary human intervention."[69]

The specific consequences of these formal natural law axioms can be seen in the country where they arguably had the greatest influence, namely, the United States. Weber, himself, points to one example regarding the difficulties of enacting social welfare legislation in the United States. Given that "every act of social welfare legislation prohibiting certain contents of the free labor contract, is on that account an infringement of freedom of contract,"[70] social welfare legislation was originally declared invalid as violating the due process clause of the Fourteenth Amendment of the

Constitution. It was not until after the turn of the century that "the Supreme Court of the United States was able to free itself from formal natural law so as to be able to recognize the validity of certain acts of social legislation."[71] Even so, the Supreme Court continued to declare unconstitutional basic welfare legislation such as state minimum wage laws. In 1936, for example, in *Morehead* v. *Tipaldo*, a New York law establishing a minimum wage for women was struck down as a violation of the due process clause. Justice Butler defended the ruling by stating that

> the right to make contracts about one's affairs is a part of the liberty protected by the due process clause. . . . In making contracts of employment, generally speaking, the parties have equal rights to obtain from each other the best terms they can by private bargaining.[72]

Similar arguments have recently been made in regard to the Clinton administration's plan for national health care. According to this line of reasoning, a national health care program would limit people's choices and inhibit them from obtaining, through private bargaining, the "best terms" possible. The history of the United States, therefore, demonstrates that a complete break from the dictates of formal natural law has never been achieved, and that formal natural law continues to dominate American legal and economic thought. In any effort to introduce social welfare legislation, the burden of proof has always been on those who would go against the established rights and freedoms of the free market.

Roosevelt, for example, was well aware of this burden when he attempted to justify his New Deal legislation. In this effort, he sought to redefine basic rights in order to give government a greater role in protecting the public welfare. Accordingly, he declared that the right to life should be broadened to include the "right to make a comfortable living," while the right to property should include the right to be secured against the privations of old age, disability and unemployment.[73] In his 1933 inaugural address, Roosevelt explicitly criticized the "practices of the unscrupulous money changers" and demanded "an end to a conduct in banking and in business which too often has given to a sacred trust the likeness of callous and selfish wrongdoing."[74]

Nonetheless, in spite of Roosevelt's considerable rhetorical skills, critical components of the New Deal were ruled unconstitutional. The Supreme Court in fact continued to declare regulatory legislation designed to enhance social welfare unconstitutional until the late 1930s to early 1940s. Justice Sutherland indirectly countered Roosevelt's logic by declaring that: "It has been proved by centuries of experience, under all conceivable circumstances that government should confine its activities, as a general rule, to preserving a free market and preventing fraud."[75] Sutherland went on to uphold his belief in the workings of the invisible hand:

> [I believe] in certain fundamental social and economic laws which are

> beyond the power, and certain underlying governmental principles, which are beyond the right of official control . . . [such laws] are entirely outside the scope of human power.[76]

Although the Supreme Court eventually acquiesced to federal regulatory powers and to social welfare legislation, contemporary battles over national health care, environmental protection and gun control indicate that potential legal infringements on private property rights and on free market competition are still likely to meet with political and/or judicial resistance, even when the public interest stands to benefit.

In a more positive sense, the American commitment to free market competition and to formal natural law has resulted in consistent efforts legally to curtail the power of monopolies, and to prevent or restrict government policies favorable to "big business." From Jefferson's battles against Hamilton, from the Progressives' antitrust campaigns to the present scrutiny of Microsoft by the Justice Department's Antitrust Division, American political, economic and legal history has maintained a firm commitment to safeguarding the rights of small interests as well as large. Huntington, for example, notes that in the American tradition:

> money becomes evil not when it is used to buy goods but when it is used to buy power. Large accumulations of wealth are acceptable until they are transformed into monopolies and trusts, which exercise economic power by dominating the marketplace. The American antitrust mania, unique among industrialized societies, focuses precisely on the point at which wealth becomes power. Similarly, economic inequalities become evil when they are translated into political inequalities. As a result, considerable effort has been invested over the years to exposing and regulating lobbying and political contributions.[77]

Here, we see a perfect example of how both the economic interests and the political rights of even the most insignificant individuals are to be safeguarded as mutually reinforcing components of the democratic citizen. What makes the American case unique is the extent to which these components have been legally protected and fostered on the basis of formal natural law axioms. The political rights and economic freedoms of the individual have consistently been upheld over the collective rights of the community. During the mid-1930s, economic freedoms were protected so assiduously by the legal system that Supreme Court Justice Stone was moved to critical reflection: "there is grim irony in speaking of freedom of contract of those who because of their economic necessities, give their services for less than is needful to keep body and soul together."[78] Yet even this criticism is couched in Lockean terms, given that only the right to subsistence is a matter for concern, not the fundamental validity or justice of the principle of freedom of contract as anchored in formal natural rights.

Overall, the theoretical and practical consequences of formal natural law axioms, would appear to be highly conducive to capitalist development. As illustrated by the American example, the free market has been defended, upheld and legitimated by the legal codes derived from formal natural law. When these legal codes are combined with the religious and philosophical natural law legitimations of the free market, a very powerful synthesis has been the outcome. As Weber points out:

> Throughout the whole puritanically influenced Anglo-Saxon world this principle [free competition] has had a great influence up to the very present. Because of the fact that the principle derived its dignity from natural law, it remained a far stronger support for the ideal of free competition than those purely utilitarian economic theories which were produced on the Continent.[79]

In addition to the more tepid legitimation of the market provided by Continental utilitarian theories, Weber notes the debilitating impact of substantive natural law axioms on Continental European capitalist development. Accordingly, he analyzes how, under the influence of socialism, the revolutionary force of substantive natural law which was "connected primarily with socialist theories of the exclusive legitimacy of the acquisition of wealth by one's own labor"[80] began to challenge the formal natural law axioms that had supported the expansion of the free market.

Before the advent of Marxism, economic and social demands made on behalf of the emerging working class were largely legitimated with reference to substantive natural law, which, Weber maintains, is in its pure form incompatible with a capitalist economic order. Specifically, substantive natural law

> rejects not only all unearned income acquired through the channels of inheritance or by means of a guaranteed monopoly, but also the formal principle of freedom of contract and general recognition of the legitimacy of all rights acquired through the instrumentality of contracting. According to these theories, all appropriations of goods must be tested substantively by the extent to which they rest on labor as their ground of acquisition.[81]

In economic terms, three natural rights can be derived from this understanding of natural law, namely, the right to work, the right to a minimum standard of living and the right to the full product of one's labor.[82] As these rights were formulated for an entire class, they were understood collectively as opposed to the individualism inherent in formal natural law. For example, the right to a minimum standard of living, expressed as a minimum wage, is meaningless without the ancillary right to collective bargaining. Although Weber concludes that these "substantive natural law doctrines could not achieve practical influence over the administration of justice," as they were destroyed in part by the "evolutionary dogmatism of Marxism," before they could influence the development of legal codes,[83] this substantive challenge to formal natural law did have an indirect impact on the way in which the free market developed beyond the borders of the "Anglo-Saxon world."

The impact of the challenge can be seen in two critical areas. First, the very fact that a challenge emerged from within the natural law tradition served to weaken the power of the formal natural law legitimation of the free market. In general, this weakening resulted in attenuated commitments to the principles of free competition, freedom of contract and, at times, private property. The most evident manifestation of this tendency can be seen in the prevalence of cartels and monopolies in Continental European economic development. Rather than being prosecuted as gross violations of the free market, such restrictions on competition were tolerated and even encouraged as normal business practices. The second area of impact can be seen in the enhanced role of the state. Substantive natural law legitimated extensive social welfare legislation and state regulation of the economy by mandating state intervention into the economy on behalf of the general welfare of the population. The economic freedoms and interests of the individual were thereby relegated to a secondary position as the collective interests of particular groups and classes were given priority. The capitalist market that developed under the influence of substantive natural law principles was, therefore, less free as it was regulated by the state in the public realm and by special interest groups in the private realm.

The country that best exemplifies this development is France—a country that has, as we have seen, been exposed to substantive natural law principles since the days of the Revolution. On the one hand, France developed a capitalist market characterized by private property, wage-labor and monetary exchanges. This "commodification of land, labor and capital,"[84] typical of the self-regulating market, was justified with reference to natural rights. Indeed, the 1789 Declaration of the Rights of Man and Citizen specifically included property as one of the "natural and imprescriptible rights of man."[85] In other ways as well, French economic development is similar to the American case. For example, in both countries small proprietors, small business and farming interests played a significant economic role. Of course, these interests were prevalent in France much longer than in the United States, but in both cases small proprietors, just as Smith believed, benefited from the emerging market in the eighteenth century. Even later, when their interests were threatened by the onset of advanced capitalism, small property owners chose, by and large, to use democratic legal and political structures to fight for economic protection. In contrast to Germany, where liberals and conservatives alike dismissed the interests of small proprietors as antithetical to capitalism, the American and French political structures remained open to their interests throughout the nineteenth and twentieth centuries.[86] This is not surprising given that liberalism in both countries was established on the basis of a social coalition that included both upper and lower middle orders. As a result, right wing, fascist political groups had less success in translating the economic distress of the small property owners into political mobilization. In Germany, however, small proprietors were available for recruitment by anti-liberal parties from 1848 on. The failure of German liberals to include the lower middle orders in the revolutionary effort of 1848 had disastrous consequences not only for the revolution itself but for the future of liberalism in Germany.[87] In the United States and France, however, a broad commitment to democratic political processes served to ameliorate the social costs of transition to advanced capitalism.

On the other hand, the extent to which the market itself was regulated to preserve and protect certain social interests represents a crucial difference between the two countries. In France, a preference for a "limited but stable market"[88] consistently dominated economic policy making from the turn of the century on. For example, the high protectionist tariffs adopted during the Third Republic, which made French tariff rates the fourth highest in the world in 1910, served both the interests of small domestic producers and the large industrialists who preferred to limit production, often through cartel arrangements, as well as imports in order to keep domestic prices high.[89] Gordon Wright explains the political and social factors that underlay these economic policies:

> Politically, most of the Third Republic's leaders consistently tended to favor the little man—both by necessity and by choice. A successful politician could hardly avoid such an attitude in a country with so many voters who were little men. But it was a genuinely appealing attitude as well, for it fitted the honest prejudices of most French politicians, the bulk of whom were themselves of middle- or petty-bourgeois origin. The Opportunists and Moderates, with their conservative social philosophy, saw the small producer and distributor as the source of social stability. The Radicals were even more deeply committed to defending the little man, by doctrine and interest as well as by family background.[90]

In the early 1930s, high tariffs and domestic cartels, in which "participating producers agreed to cut production, share the shrinking home market, and keep prices at the predepression level,"[91] were again used to counteract the effects of the global depression. By the mid-1930s, labor was added to the protected social groups, as a French "new deal" brought together labor and employer representatives under government auspices. The subsequent agreements included immediate wage increases and the introduction of collective bargaining, the forty-hour week in industry, paid vacations for workers and compulsory arbitration of labor disputes.[92] What Roosevelt failed to do, Blum accomplished without any legal or political hindrances.

Overall, French policy makers in both the private and public sectors preferred to limit competition and regulate the market in order to preserve social well-being. As a consequence, the rural population was not proletarianized, the small independent producers survived until well into the twentieth century and, most importantly perhaps, French society did not succumb to the totalitarian temptations of the 1930s. Unrestricted capitalist economic growth was thereby sacrificed for social objectives. Accordingly, a self-regulating market never managed completely to "subordinate the substance of society itself to the laws of the market."[93] Nor was the total "institutional separation of society into an economic and political sphere" achieved in France.[94] To this day, politics, in the form of state intervention in the economy, continues to influence French economic development.

Immediately after World War II, for example, the French government undertook "the world's first experiment in national economic planning by a democracy."[95] Under the leadership of Jean Monnet, a Planning Commission was created with "authority to lay out a four-year plan of investment in key branches of the economy."[96] In addition, strategic sectors of the economy (including energy, banking and insurance) were nationalized. Social welfare was again taken into consideration as an extensive social security system was put into place. While some of the regulatory practices established by the Fourth Republic have been attenuated over the years, the French state still plays a major role in directing the economy—often violating the principle of free competition in the process. One need only recall the recent scandal when it was determined that a government ministry prevented the licensing of American blood testing technology, thereby allowing HIV-contaminated blood to remain in circulation until a French company developed similar technology.

These departures from the ideal of the self-regulating market can be explained, in large part, by the impact of substantive natural law axioms on French political and economic development. Although both state regulation of the economy on behalf of social well-being, and the pursuit of collective interests over individual interests, represent violations of formal natural law, they are legitimated by substantive principles that emphasize collective rights, interests and obligations. For example, the substantive natural right to a minimum standard of living implies an obligation on the part of the state to provide for this minimum standard if the individual or group in question cannot. As R. R. Palmer points out, the post-war welfare state in France was already envisioned in and mandated by the French Resistance charter which called for a "more just social order," including the right to suitable work, unemployment compensation, social security, free or subsidized health care, and the redistribution of wealth through progressive taxation.[97] This emphasis on a just social order guaranteed by the state is clearly reminiscent of the sans-culottes' substantive rights agenda; an agenda that has been a prevalent aspect of French political discourse since the days of the Revolution.

Moreover, the right to the full product of one's labor, while difficult to achieve in a wage-labor economy, did resonate deeply with the French. The tradition of family firms, which often cooperated in cartels to assure their collective survival, and the persistence of small property owners illustrate this tendency. French economic actors were well aware that only by being one's own boss, no matter how small, could one be assured of the right to the full product of one's labor. Wright points to the following French maxim as "more revealing of a generalized attitude toward life": *Mon verre est petit, mais je bois dans* mon *verre* ("My cup may be small, but I drink from my own").[98] As a consequence of the impact of substantive natural rights, during the nineteenth-century heyday of unrestricted capitalist entrepreneurship in Britain and the United States, economic growth was sacrificed in France for social stability and a "fairer distribution of the product of reasonable growth."[99]

In sum, natural law in its philosophical, religious and legal manifestations legitimated the domain of the free market as the only form of economic conduct consistent with the rights and liberties inherent in a just and natural social order. No longer could feudal or mercantile restrictions, regulations and relations of social dependency be tolerated. Instead, individuals should be free to pursue their own calling and their own interests in peaceful competition for goods and services. However, within this institutional domain, different patterns of market development have taken place. Under the combined impact of philosophical, religious and formal natural law influences, a truly self-regulating market emerged in Britain and the United States. As these two countries evolved into the most powerful members of the international community, they were in a position to create an international economic order based on the free-trade principles consistent with their domestic economic institutions. Given their power and influence, it is not surprising that this type of market is often considered the norm or standard against which marketization should be measured.

The case of France, however, demonstrates an alternative pattern of market development. To a large extent, France lacked a philosophical and religious natural law foundation for the free market. Therefore, the eighteenth-century natural rights doctrine, as it was reflected in legal codes and in political life, provided the dominant form of legitimation for the free market. In these circumstances, the conflict between the formal and substantive elements of the natural rights doctrine—what Weber calls the formal and substantive axioms of revolutionary natural law—resulted in a contingent, rather than unconditional, commitment to the free market. Free-market principles validated by formal natural law, such as competition, contract and private property, were combined with principles derived from substantive natural law. The outcome, as we have seen, is a semi-regulated market in which capitalist economic interactions are constrained by social and political institutions.

In both cases, however, it is clear that natural law, in one form or another, provided a common basis of legitimation for liberalism and capitalism to emerge together as complementary political and economic systems. This commonality is drawn out by Weber in the following passage:

> The other Rights of Man or civil rights were joined to this basic right [the freedom of conscience], especially the right to pursue one's own econ-

> omic interests, which includes the inviolability of individual property, the freedom of contract, and vocational choice. This economic right exists within the limits of a system of guaranteed abstract rules that apply to everybody alike. All of these rights find their ultimate justification in the belief of the Enlightenment in the workings of individual reason which, if unimpeded, would result in the at least relatively best of all worlds, by virtue of divine providence and because the individual is best qualified to know his own interests. . . . It is clear that these postulates of formal legal equality and economic mobility paved the way for the destruction of all patrimonial and feudal law in favor of abstract norms and hence indirectly of bureaucratization. It is also clear that they facilitated the expansion of capitalism. The basic Rights of Man made it possible for the capitalist to use things freely, just as this-worldly asceticism—adopted with some dogmatic variations—and the specific discipline of the sects bred the capitalist spirit and the rational "professional" who was needed by capitalism.[100]

Having acknowledged the Rights of Man as the common point of origin for both capitalism and liberalism, Weber goes on to question the likelihood of such a confluence ever occurring again. On the one hand, Weber notes that natural law and its "metajuristic axioms" have been "subject to ever continuing disintegration and relativization."[101] The advance of legal positivism and "the disappearance of the old natural law conceptions has destroyed all possibility of providing the law with a metaphysical dignity by virtue of its immanent qualities."[102] In other words, the natural law foundations for the legal codes conducive to liberal capitalist development are no longer available. Concomitantly, Weber is skeptical about the possibility of securing political freedoms in an era of advanced capitalism, given the nature of the rationalization and bureaucratization that accompanies the modern economic order. Accordingly, he states that: "We are individualists and advocates of democratic institutions against the stream of material interests."[103] The danger to individual freedom is present in both existing liberal capitalist states as the "iron cage" threatens to overwhelm them, and in latecomer states hoping to establish liberal capitalist institutions. For example, in reviewing the chances for democracy to develop alongside capitalism in the wake of Russia's 1905 Revolution, Weber is profoundly pessimistic:

> It is ridiculous to ascribe to present day advanced capitalism as it is currently being imported to Russia and as it exists in America—this inevitability of our economic development—an elective affinity with democracy or even with freedom, in any sense whatsoever.[104]

In his famous "iron cage" passage at the conclusion of *The Protestant Ethic and the Spirit of Capitalism*, Weber elaborates on the characteristics of advanced capitalism that render it incompatible with democracy. Specifically, he notes the negative consequences of the "technical and economic conditions of machine production" which determine the lives of all individuals whether they are "directly concerned with economic acquisition" or not. Furthermore, under the "modern economic order . . . material goods have gained an increasing and finally an inexorable power over the lives of men."[105] Given the mechanization, the bureaucratization and the materialism of modern life, Weber is forced to conclude, in his observations on Russia, that only the "determined will of a people not to be ruled like a herd of sheep" can safeguard liberty.[106] As to how this "determined will" is to be upheld against the "stream of material interests," remains unclear.

Weber thus leaves us with the conclusion that what once was is never to be again: "The historical origin of modern 'freedom' is based on unique, never to be repeated, conditions."[107] The legitimation provided by natural law and the natural rights doctrine for both liberalism and capitalism is a relic of the past. Consequently, while capitalism is likely to continue progressing, even without principled legitimation, modern democracy is just as likely to suffer as the conditions of advanced capitalism narrow the scope of rights and liberties. Only a "spiritual deadening" ("*geistige Stumpfheit*") is to be expected after generations have been forced to keep "their fists fruitlessly clenched in their pockets and to bare their teeth to the heavens."[108]

Yet these conclusions can be criticized on two levels. First, from a theoretical perspective, there is no reason to rule out a new charismatic manifestation of value-rationality, even in a world dominated by the "iron cage." As Weber himself admits:

> No one knows who will live in this cage in the future, or whether at the end of this tremendous development entirely new prophets will arise, or there will be a great rebirth of old ideas and ideals, or, if neither, mechanized petrification, embellished with a sort of convulsive self-importance.[109]

A rebirth of natural rights, with all of its attendant consequences for the legitimation of democracy and capitalism, therefore, cannot be precluded. Secondly, on an empirical level, Weber's conclusions are overdrawn in regard to the original liberal capitalist states. Given the validation provided by a value-rational commitment to the preservation of rights and liberties, and the existence of institutional domains based on that value-rationality, the histories of France and the United States demonstrate that, while personal freedoms may have been curtailed by modern socioeconomic conditions, political freedoms have consistently been upheld. Based on these examples, one can conclude that the "determined will of a people not to be ruled like a herd of sheep" is best upheld when the natural rights doctrine is successfully institutionalized.

In other words, once the institutional domains mandated by the doctrine have been established in both the political and economic realms, the formation and the articulation of subsequent social interests will reinforce, or at least not threaten, the overall institutional structure. For example, class interests threatened by capitalist development, such as those of the working class and the small independent producers, were articulated within the institutional framework established by liberalism. From the English Chartists to the American Progressives to the French Radicals, parties and movements have arisen to voice and protect the political and the economic interests of the "common man." That they have done so within the parameters established by representative government is due both to political self-interest, in terms of satisfying a voting constituency, and ideological inclination, as Wright determined in regard to the Radicals, who were "deeply committed to defending the little man, by doctrine and interest as well as by family background."[110] In this context, the equality of citizenship has consistently served to ameliorate the inequalities inherent in capitalism.[111]

It follows, then, that the relationship between advanced capitalism and modern democracy cannot be assumed a priori to be either conflictual or compatible.[112] In the event that a charismatic manifestation of value-rationality provides the legitimation for the institutional domains of liberal capitalism, a compatible relationship is the likely outcome as social interests will be articulated within the established domains, both by political necessity and ideological choice. However, without a value-rational foundation for the institutionalized preservation of rights and liberties, Weber's conclusions regarding the incompatibility of advanced capitalism and democratic freedoms are likely to be accurate. The impact of capitalist development will create social and economic interests that are unconstrained by a value-rational commitment to universal rights and freedoms, while simultaneously being subjected to the processes of bureaucratization. Consequently, both the winners and losers of the capitalist economic order will promote their interests on a purely instrumental basis within bureaucratic structures that are unfettered by democratic controls and oversight mechanisms.[113] In such an environment, empty populist or nationalist rhetoric, whether of upper- or lower-class origins, replaces the institutional rights and freedoms guaranteed by representative government. Given that a peaceful and predictable means for representing both general and particular interests does not exist, social groups will increasingly engage in a Darwinian struggle for survival, with the result that society becomes ever more fragmented and divided.

According to Lipset, such "a society divided between a large impoverished mass and a small favored elite results either in oligarchy (dictatorial rule of the small upper stratum) or in tyranny (popular-based dictatorship)."[114] In these circumstances, capitalism itself is likely to be deformed by "populist economics," entailing:

> the maintenance of a sizable state industrial sector, the provision of consumer subsidies on a large scale, the granting of inflationary wage increases for groups such as workers in key industries, and the imposition of selected price controls—all leading to severe macroeconomic imbalances.[115]

Yet these imbalances will be tolerated as governments seek to protect the interests of the elite, while pacifying the demands of labor in critical sectors.

Clearly, a social coalition encompassing both upper and lower echelons of the middle ranks of society is difficult to forge in an environment that systematically prevents even the emergence of a middle class. Yet precisely such a coalition is a necessary condition for the emergence of a value-rational commitment to democracy that is capable of fusing the ethical and material interests of these critical social groups in a charismatic context. In short, the social, political and ideological foundations for maintaining the "determined will of a people not to be ruled like a herd of sheep" are increasingly undermined by the effects of advanced capitalism.[116]

Given the possibility of such a negative outcome, the importance of a natural-rights-based legitimation for liberal capitalism that has broad social support, and that is capable of generating stable institutional domains, looms large. Therefore, an analysis of how the domains of liberal capitalism were originally established under the auspices of the natural rights doctrine is of continued theoretical significance. Having provided an overview of this process, we are now in a position to turn to a comparatively informed examination of the ethos of Solidarity, and the extent to which it provides a value-rational foundation for liberal capitalist development in Poland.

Before moving on to such an analysis, the following chapter will present Marx's critique of the natural rights doctrine, and the consequences of this critique for the evolution of Leninist regimes. Marx demystified and set aside the natural rights that democratic revolutionaries believed in as the only legitimate foundation for political order. This left an analytical door open for Lenin's conceptualization of the Party, rather than the rights-bearing citizen, as the sole appropriate frame of reference for political conduct and institutional development. After World War II, Poland was forcibly exposed to political, social and economic institutions based on Lenin's vision. These institutions subsequently shaped the environment that generated the antecedent conditions for Solidarity's emergence.

5 The Marxist–Leninist response to natural rights and liberal capitalism

By the mid-nineteenth century, a new wave of revolutionaries had become active throughout Europe. Defining themselves as socialists, rather than as democrats, these revolutionaries were no longer preoccupied with the central issues and demands that had animated the previous century's liberal democratic revolutions. According to the socialist vision of just government, concern for the social and economic rights of workers took precedence over the civic and political rights of man. Originally, early socialists did use the familiar language of substantive natural rights to legitimate their demands. In this effort, they followed the lead of Babeuf, one of the most famous sans-culottes leaders of the French Revolution, who had demanded economic and social justice for the lower orders with the justification that economic and social rights were as self-evident and natural as civic rights. Although Babeuf made only a brief appearance during the Revolution, his influence on the nascent socialist movement was considerable.[1] By the end of the century, however, Marx's growing stature among socialists resulted in a reorientation within the movement. Marx's scathing critique of the natural rights doctrine combined with the new, scientifically determined basis he proposed for the legitimation of a workers' revolution led socialists and, subsequently, communists to make their revolutionary claims in scientific terms rather than in the terms of moral or natural rights.

Moreover, Marx decisively rejected the individualism of liberalism in favor of elevating the collectivity of the working class into the social entity which required emancipation and liberty. Just as the liberal revolutionaries believed that guaranteeing the individual's liberty would benefit all of society, Marx and his followers believed that freeing the working class would ultimately emancipate all of society. The Marxist response to the doctrine of individually based natural rights that lies at the heart of modern democracy can, therefore, best be understood as the creation of an alternative doctrine that enshrined the collectivity of the working class as the harbinger of a new order in which the need for natural rights would be transcended once and for all. In addition, this new order was to do away with what even Marx termed "the natural laws of capitalist production,"[2] by replacing the "blind, natural,"[3] necessities of market exchange with a rational allocation of economic resources. As Walicki points out, Marx conceived of human freedom

> as the opposite of the spontaneous, quasi-natural order of the market, as the liberation of human beings, as rational creatures capable of conscious self-determination, from the rule of the "invisible hand." Of course, he regarded this task as achievable only through the communist regulation of production and exchange on a world scale.[4]

Consequently, the revolutionary path toward this new order would be determined and legitimated by scientific rationality rather than by divinely inspired morality.

Lenin subsequently developed the Communist Party into an organization that was to capture and embody this scientific rationality as the highest level of revolutionary consciousness attainable by the working class. In Lenin's thinking, the Party would be comprised of the leading representatives of this class, thereby becoming the very essence of proletarian will and consciousness. As the sole appropriate vehicle through which the rational truth could be channeled, the Party was able to demand continuous and total loyalty from its members. Consequently, the authority of the Party as an impersonal organization dedicated to scientifically illuminating the revolutionary path became absolute and unquestionable under Lenin's leadership. Lenin ultimately created a novel type of political party that can best be conceptualized as a permanent charismatic community of disciplined revolutionaries acting in accordance with principles they believed to be objectively determined.

While it may appear to be simply an arcane, not to mention redundant, exercise in intellectual history to trace the evolution of Marxism–Leninism, one cannot understand the nature of the institutions built in post-World War II Poland without some knowledge of how this ideology, as articulated and implemented by the Communist Party, established the parameters within which these institutions developed. The first part of this chapter will, therefore, examine Marx's critique of natural rights and the radically different basis of legitimacy he proposed for a revolutionary transformation of the political, social and economic orders. Next, Lenin's creation of the Communist Party as the "organizational weapon"[5] that was to lead and direct such a revolution will be addressed, along with the nature of the institutional domains created under his auspices. Finally, institutional developments in Poland will be assessed with reference to the antecedent conditions created by these developments for the emergence of Solidarity.

Unlike other post-Stalinist rebellions both within Poland and throughout Eastern Europe, Solidarity provided a coherent ideological and institutional alternative to the Party and the institutional domains established under Marxism–Leninism. Recalling Jowitt's assessment:

> If part of a Leninist Party's uniqueness rests in its political conflation of the state and public realms; in its effort to have the cadre fuse the roles of

> state official and citizen, then Solidarity's challenge is immediately apparent. Solidarity was more than a threat to Party power. Solidarity offered an opposing definition of political leadership and membership. It confronted the Party cadre with the national citizen. As a politically "self-limiting" movement, Solidarity was an organized public whose membership consisted of voluntarily associated individual citizens opposed to a hierarchical, corporate Party polity. Solidarity and the Party were mutually exclusive *ways of life*.[6]

Yet, how and why did such a powerful alternative to Leninism emerge in Poland? As we shall see, part of the answer to these questions is to be found in the unique features of the Polish polity that eventually facilitated the rise of an alternative "way of life" based on a restoration of the rights that Marx had rejected.

MARX'S CRITIQUE OF NATURAL RIGHTS

> *Political* emancipation is of course a big step forward. True, it is not the final form of human emancipation in general, but it is the final form of human emancipation *within* the hitherto existing world order.[7]

> The limits of political emancipation are evident at once from the fact that the *state* can free itself from a restriction without man being really free from this restriction, that the state can be a *free state* without man being *a free man*.[8]

These two passages are taken from Marx's *On the Jewish Question*, the 1844 essay in which he develops his most significant critique of natural rights. Although much has been written about Marx's critical view of rights, the significance of the context in which he places his critique has generally not been recognized.[9] Because Marx embeds this critique within an overall discussion on the relationship between political emancipation and human emancipation, he achieves a far more nuanced depiction of rights than he is commonly given credit for. By ignoring the context represented by Marx's concern with emancipation, it has been too readily assumed that Marx is completely dismissive of rights. In the essay, however, Marx recognizes that natural and civic rights form the foundation for the political emancipation of the individual, of the citizen and of the state. He then analyzes each of these realms of *political* emancipation with reference to the potential consequences for *human* emancipation. As Walicki observes, Marx's understanding of human emancipation is centered on "a mode of existence in which humans are integrated and self-determining—that is, in which their actions correspond to their true self, their innermost identity."[10] This view of freedom as collective self-actualization unfettered by considerations of material necessity "depends on the extent of humankind's domination over nature and the degree of rational, conscious control over social relations."[11] Consequently, control over the socioeconomic realm is of greater importance for emancipation than any given set of political or legal rights. Not surprisingly, Marx's most scathing criticism is reserved for the rights and realms of political emancipation he believes have a negative impact on human emancipation. Before assessing the implications of this analysis, Marx's discussion of rights needs to be examined in detail.

Marx begins his essay by noting that "only the criticism of *political emancipation* itself would have been the conclusive criticism of the Jewish question and its real merging in the 'general question of the time.' "[12] In this context, the "Jewish question" was whether or not Jews should be granted civil and political rights as Jews. For Marx, however, the quest politically to emancipate particular categories of people is misleading and distracting since the human emancipation of all people represents the true question of the age.

Essentially, Marx maintains that the political emancipation brought about by the eighteenth-century revolutions should be seen only as a stage in the struggle for complete human emancipation. According to this view, political emancipation taken by itself is an insufficient end for human endeavor. As Marx notes in his 1843 essay "Critique of Hegel's Philosophy of Law":

> It is an historical advance which has transformed the political estates into social classes so that, just as the Christians are equal in heaven but unequal on earth, so the individual members of the nation are equal in the heaven of their political world, but unequal in the earthly existence of society.[13]

Consequently, the benefits provided by political emancipation, such as universal suffrage, should not be seen as ends, in and of themselves, rather they must be seen as means to further the true goal of social emancipation.

Within this quest for a general, human emancipation, Marx argues, the question of the particular emancipation of the Jews must be seen in a different light. Since he equates "the empirical essence of Judaism" with "the market and the conditions which give rise to it," he is able to conclude that "the social emancipation of the Jew is the *emancipation of society from Judaism.*"[14] In Marx's view, both "the narrowness of the Jew" and the "Jewish narrowness of society"[15] are manifestations of particular, selfish interests that inhibit man's ability to supersede his "sensuous, individual immediate existence";[16] thereby inhibiting man's ability to achieve complete human emancipation. As Marx states categorically:

> because you [the Jews] can be emancipated politically without renouncing Judaism completely and incontrovertibly, *political emancipation* itself is not *human* emancipation. If you Jews want to be emancipated politically without emancipating yourselves humanly, the half-hearted approach and

> contradiction is not in you alone, it is inherent in the *nature* and *category* of political emancipation.[17]

In the course of his analysis, Marx reaches a similar conclusion regarding the natural rights of man. They, too, have had a negative impact on the quest for human emancipation by turning man into an individual; an "isolated monad, withdrawn into himself,"[18] and, ultimately, only concerned with his particular well-being. In this context, we find one of Marx's most trenchant observations on the nature and the origins of individualism:

> Political democracy is Christian since in it man, not merely one man but every man, ranks as *sovereign*, as the highest being, but it is man in his uncivilized, unsocial form, man in his fortuitous existence, man just as he is, man as he has been corrupted by the whole organisation of our society, who has lost himself, been alienated, and handed over to the rule of inhuman conditions and elements—in short, man who is not yet a *real* species-being. That which is a creation of fantasy, a dream, a postulate of Christianity, i.e., the sovereignty of man—but man as an alien being different from the real man—becomes in democracy tangible reality, present existence, and secular principle.[19]

The most negative consequences of this secular maxim are not, however, to be found in the realm of the political state. Rather, it is in the realm of civil society as the "state of need and of reason" that the most antisocial behavior takes place, since it is here, in Marx's opinion, that "egoistic man . . . man separated from other men and from the community" exists.[20] Furthermore, Marx maintains that the existence of sovereign man in civil society is founded on the natural rights of man. These rights to equality, liberty, security and property simply serve to legitimate and reinforce the selfish and particularistic conditions of life in civil society. Marx's basic point of attack is that each of the fundamental natural rights separate men from one another, rather than joining men in a common community. For example, in regard to the right to liberty, he observes that

> the right of man to liberty is based not on the association of man with man, but on the separation of man from man. It is the *right* of this separation, the right of the *restricted* individual, withdrawn into himself.[21]

Following this line of analysis, Marx concludes his discussion of natural rights with the following, definitive statement:

> None of the so-called rights of man, therefore, go beyond egoistic man, beyond man as a member of civil society, that is, an individual withdrawn into himself, into the confines of his private interests and private caprices and separated from the community. In the rights of man, he is far from being conceived as a species-being; on the contrary, species-life itself, society, appears as a framework external to the individuals, as a restriction of their original independence. The sole bond holding them together

> is natural necessity, need and private interest, the preservation of their property and their egoistic selves.[22]

Interestingly, Marx goes on to evaluate the impact of civil rights—the *droits du citoyen*, as opposed to the *droits de l'homme*—in a more positive light. By separating rights into two categories, Marx is able to reach the conclusion that whereas the natural rights of man have alienated man from his species-being, the political rights of citizens represent a positive contribution to the cause of human emancipation by, at least in the abstract, creating a moral category of shared membership, of shared species-being, in the political community. The problem, as Marx sees it, is that

> the political emancipators go so far as to reduce citizenship, the political community, to a mere means for maintaining these so-called rights of man, and that, therefore, the citoyen is declared to be the servant of egoistic homme, that the sphere in which man acts as a communal being [*Gemeinwesen*] is degraded to a level below the sphere in which he acts as a partial being, and that, finally, it is not man as citoyen, but man as bourgeois who is considered to be the *essential* and *true* man.[23]

Contrary, then, to simplistic interpretations of Marx's analysis of rights, he does not reject all rights as meaningless abstractions distracting men from the true goal of human emancipation. Instead, he notes that the "abstract citizen" endowed with civil rights is really the "true man," the "moral person" that needs to be actualized in man's species-being.[24] In Marx's opinion, political emancipation dichotomized man into an "egotistic, independent individual" living in civil society, and a moral citizen interacting with others in the political community. The goal of human emancipation is to transcend this dichotomy by allowing "real, individual man [to] re-absorb in himself the abstract citizen."[25] Marx goes on to state that

> only when man has recognized and organized his forces propres as social forces, and consequently no longer separates social power from himself in the shape of *political* power, only then will human emancipation have been accomplished.[26]

From this statement, and from the whole thrust of Marx's argumentation, it is clear that the motor of human emancipation is not to be found in the political realm. For not only did political emancipation decisively subordinate the citizen to the bourgeois, it also resulted in the creation of a deceptively "free state." A freely constituted state did not, for Marx, equal a freely constituted society. Since citizens merely abdicate their freedoms to the state, the political emancipation of the state becomes simply a substitute for the true emancipation of man-in-society. Marx illustrates this point by drawing attention to the fact that the state can be freed from religious particularism, while society is still riddled with religious distinctions and divisions.

While acknowledging that the state could be seen as a realm of universality, standing above the particular elements comprising it, Marx maintains that this would be an "unreal universality"[27] since distinctions and divisions still exist on the social level. Indeed, they have to exist in order for the political state to exist at all. In his opinion:

> Far from abolishing these *real* distinctions [such as those based upon private property, education and occupation], the state only exists on the presupposition of their existence; it feels itself to be a *political state* and asserts its universality only in opposition to those elements of its being.[28]

Not surprisingly, Marx concludes his discussion of the state by contrasting its "fictitious sovereignty" to the "immediate reality" of civil society. The political emancipation of the state simply amplifies the above-mentioned dichotomy between abstract universality and concrete particularities. In this context, Marx states that:

> Where the political state has attained its full degree of development man leads a double life, a life in heaven and a life on earth, not only in his mind, in his consciousness, but in reality. He lives in the political community, where he regards himself as a communal being, and in civil society, where he is active as a private individual, regards other men as means, debases himself to a means and becomes a plaything of alien powers.[29]

Again, the goal of human emancipation is to transcend this dichotomy by removing the particularities embedded in civil society that sustain the political state. Ultimately, the state itself would cease to exist as "the real harmonious species-life of man"[30] achieves a heaven on earth.

In short, Marx's critique of rights cannot be separated from his overall discussion of emancipation in its political, economic and human forms. The consequences of political emancipation for the individual, for the citizen and for the state are significant for Marx solely to the extent that they help or hinder the goal of human emancipation. In this context, only the realm of citizenship and the rights associated with it are somewhat positively evaluated. For Marx, the "abstract citizen" as a *Gemeinwesen* shows some potential for achieving a true sense of fellowship, thereby contributing to the universality of human emancipation. Moreover, Marx appears to have been favorably disposed toward the concept of political democracy as expressed in the "people's sovereign will."[31] According to Walicki, however, Marx maintained that

> it was necessary to extend the democratic principle of popular sovereignty to the economic sphere through subjecting economic relations to collective control. In other words, no sphere of life should remain exempt from public regulation, and, consequently, all legal safeguards of private freedom, freedom from intervention, should be abolished.[32]

It follows that natural rights, as the foundation for these "legal safeguards," are decisively rejected by Marx as the basis upon which egotistical and selfish individuals interact in civil society, inhibiting the full expression of popular sovereignty. Ultimately, such rights only serve artificially to separate man from his true self as a social being. The political state as well, in spite of its claims to universality, only serves to perpetuate the "factual distinctions" that separate man from his fellowman.

The question that emerges from this analysis of rights and emancipation, is how the dichotomies between civil society and the political community are to be resolved and transcended. In order to achieve human emancipation, the citizen must realize his "social forces"; his identity as a social being in order to free himself of the egotistical confines of civil society. Yet on what basis was such a struggle to be legitimated? Whereas other socialists such as Ferdinand Lassalle continued to legitimate their calls for a program of human emancipation by employing the language of rights, Marx decisively rejected this basis of legitimation as a recourse to bourgeois methods. His analysis of rights had already demonstrated that natural rights only legitimated the inequalities of civil society, while civil rights, and the political community in general, were too weak to effect revolutionary change.

In the *Critique of the Gotha Program*, Marx later concretized this view of rights in the process of envisioning the nature of communist society that would replace bourgeois society. While the "first phase of communist society" would have to live with the "defects" of "bourgeois rights," these rights would eventually be transcended:

> In a higher phase of communist society, after the enslaving subordination of the individual to the division of labor, and thereby also the antithesis between mental and physical labor, has vanished; after labor has become not only a means of life but life's prime want; after the productive forces have also increased with the all-round development of the individual, and all the springs of common wealth flow more abundantly—only then can the narrow horizon of bourgeois right be crossed in its entirety and society inscribe on its banners: From each according to his ability, to each according to his needs![33]

In Marx's opinion, the equality of rights espoused by both bourgeois and socialist reformers as a means of legitimating the struggle for human emancipation was a mere chimera. Because individuals are, by nature, unequal, any attempt to apply rights according to an equal standard inherently advantages some individuals while disadvantaging others. Given that liberal ideology is based on an acceptance of the unequal capacities of formally equal individuals, Marx is quick to point out that even an equal right to the proceeds of labor is "a right of inequality, in its content, like every right."[34] Therefore, a recourse to rights as a means of legitimating the creation of a more just society or polity is misplaced since "right can never be higher than the economic structure of society and its cultural development which this determines."[35] A revolutionary endeavor based on rights cannot transcend existing socioeconomic circumstances in order to legitimate a newly evolving set of socioeconomic conditions. Herein lies the most significant implication of Marx's critique of rights. The rejection of rights as a basis for the revolutionary transformation of society called for a new basis of legitimation. In this context, Marx's theory of the dialectical evolution of history evolved into a "scientific" basis for legitimating revolutionary struggles on behalf of human emancipation, largely under the influence of Engels. In contrast to the utopian and/or rights-based language of other socialists, Marxists, such as Lenin, could subsequently point to objectively determined historical truths that mandated their cause.

Marx's theory rests on a particular interpretation of the patterns and causal factors that underlie historical development. As is well known, this interpretation was developed in critical dialogue with Hegelian philosophy. Essentially, Marx accepts the dialectical pattern developed by Hegel in which a given phase of historical development generates antithetical tensions and contradictions. As these tensions and contradictions are resolved, a higher stage of development is achieved. Unlike Hegel, however, Marx maintains that the critical causal factors in this dialectical progression are material rather than ideal in nature. In other words, Marx replaces Hegel's emphasis on the self-actualization of the *Geist* with an emphasis on the material conditions men create and live with.

According to Marx, as men "produce their means of subsistence" they produce a mode of production that

> must not be considered simply as being the reproduction of the physical existence of the individuals. Rather it is a definite form of activity of these individuals, a definite form of expressing their life, a definite mode of life on their part. As individuals express their life, so they are. What they are, therefore, coincides with their production, both with what they produce and with how they produce. Hence what individuals are depends on the material conditions of their production.[36]

It is in this material realm that the "empirically perceptible process of development under definite conditions"[37] can be observed. Philosophical speculations cease to have any relevance since "where real life starts, there consequently begins real, positive science, there consequently begins the expounding of the practical activity, of the practical process of development of men. Empty phrases about consciousness end, and real knowledge has to take their place."[38]

On the basis of such scientifically based observations, Marx went on to determine the dialectical dynamics of the capitalist mode of production that would ultimately pave the way for a final stage of development—communism—in which complete human emancipation would be realized. As Marx elaborates:

> Communism is for us not a state of affairs which is to be established, an ideal to which reality will have to adjust itself. We call communism the

real movement which abolishes the present state of things. The conditions of this movement result from the premises now in existence.[39]

Marx's subsequent analysis of these premises is quite detailed and sophisticated. At the heart of this analysis, however, lie three pivotal assumptions that informed the worldviews of both early and later Marxists.

First, Marx assumes that the division of labor, which encompasses both the forms of property ownership and the relations of individuals to one another, leads, under capitalism, to the progressive alienation and exploitation of the labor force. Workers are forced to endure degrading forms of work while being deprived of the true value of their labor by the ruling class, the bourgeoisie. Under these conditions

> a class is called forth which has to bear all the burdens of society without enjoying its advantages, which is ousted from society and forced into the sharpest contradiction to all other classes; a class which forms the majority of all members of society, and from which emanates the consciousness of the necessity of a fundamental revolution.[40]

This, then, leads to the second assumption Marx makes, namely, that the working class, the proletariat, represents the universal interest. Unlike previous classes that had risen up against oppression on behalf of their particular interests, the proletariat has achieved a universal consciousness due to the conditions of its existence. As Marx notes:

> only the proletarians of the present day, who are completely shut off from all self-activity, are in a position to achieve a complete and no longer restricted self-activity, which consists in the appropriation of a totality of productive forces.[41]

That such an appropriation would take place within the context of a revolutionary upheaval represents Marx's third pivotal assumption. Indeed, Marx goes so far as to claim in *The German Ideology* that a revolution is not only necessary to overcome the resistance of the bourgeoisie, it is also necessary to alter the consciousness of the proletariat:

> the revolution is necessary, therefore, not only because the ruling class cannot be overthrown in any other way, but also because the class overthrowing it can only in a revolution succeed in ridding itself of all the muck of ages and become fitted to found society anew.[42]

In short, Marx considered the basis of legitimacy he proposed for this revolutionary struggle to be rational, as opposed to utopian, since it was deduced from empirically observable patterns of historical development. The undeniably transcendent qualities of communism, as Marx envisioned the final stage of this development, were thereby firmly rooted in logic and analysis. As Lenin was to say later:

> There is no trace of utopianism in Marx, in the sense that he made up or

> invented a "new" society. No, he studied the birth of the new society out of the old, and the forms of transition from the former to the latter, as a natural-historical process.[43]

After subjecting the concept of rights to careful scrutiny, Marx concluded that rights were inadequately emancipatory and deceptively utopian, in the sense that rights promised more than they could deliver. Therefore, they provided an inadequate basis for revolutionary struggle.

Ironically, although Marx rejected natural rights, his vision of history, especially after it was codified by Engels into "scientific socialism," did provide his followers with a related, though decisively different, form of legitimacy. Belief in either the Marxist doctrine or the natural rights doctrine is based on a value-rational adherence to the values and principles deduced from the doctrine. These values and principles are considered absolutely binding on the conduct of believers precisely because they are rationally deduced from a given body of work.

Yet as we have seen from our discussion in previous chapters, value-rationality in and of itself is unlikely to result in collective action. It would appear from Marx's comments regarding the need to change consciousness in a revolutionary context that he was intuitively aware of the difficulties of translating the abstract communist consciousness of proletarians into actual collective conduct and consciousness. He, therefore, considered the transformatory capacity of a revolution to be essential, at least in his early work. At other points in his writings, Marx maintained that the material conditions of the proletariat alone would be sufficient to attain a collective transformation of consciousness. In either case, however, a mediating element is foreseen that would be capable of transcending individual particularities in order to achieve a collective drive toward emancipation. Here, Marx's analysis is analogous to Weber's opinion that a particular social context is necessary to translate individually based value-rationality into collective action. Marx was simply incorrect about the type of context. Neither revolution nor material conditions provided the setting within which the value-rationality of Marxism was translated into collective conduct. Instead, Lenin's party organization generated a charismatic community in which both consciousness and conduct were transformed.

LENIN'S CREATION OF A CHARISMATIC PARTY

In creating a party devoted to the pursuit of Marxist principles, Lenin established an authoritative organization that could legitimately sanction and reward the behavior of its members. On the basis of their intense personal devotion to Lenin and the Marxist cause he represented, individual members of the Party experienced a transformation of consciousness and conduct that enabled the Marxist doctrine, as interpreted by Lenin, "to gain an independent influence on the conduct of life."[44] Subsequently, during the revolutionary upheavals in Russia, this organization proved itself capable of gaining power and transforming the existing conditions by establishing the institutional domains and the actual institutions that reflected the value-rational commitment of the Bolsheviks to the Marxist–Leninist doctrine. Before elaborating on the general nature of the institutional domains mandated by the doctrine, and on the particularities of post-World War II institutional development in Poland, the nature of Lenin's Party needs to be addressed. Since the Party set out to create a society and a polity in its own image, the Party itself captures the essence of the Marxist–Leninist response to liberalism.

Whereas Marx himself had been ambivalent about the need or desirability of a revolutionary party organization, Lenin had no doubts that a party was necessary to enhance and direct the struggles of the proletariat. In *What is to be Done?* Lenin crisply asserts that even the spontaneous nature of the working-class movement does not relieve socialists of the duty of creating an organization of revolutionaries:

> On the contrary, this movement imposes this duty upon us, because the spontaneous struggle of the proletariat will not become its genuine "class struggle" until this struggle is led by a strong organization of revolutionaries.[45]

Lenin goes on to call for "an all-Russian organization of revolutionaries that stands undeviatingly on the basis of Marxism, that leads the whole of the political struggle and possesses a staff of professional agitators."[46] Only on this basis could scientific socialism be saved from the vulgarization it was suffering at the hands of Russian Social Democrats who were veering toward trade unionism in the last years of the nineteenth century. Under the pernicious influence of this trade unionism Lenin maintains that

> scientific socialism ceased to be an integral revolutionary theory and became a hodgepodge "freely" diluted with the contents of every new German textbook that appeared; the slogan "class struggle" did not impel them [the Russian Social Democrats] forward to wider and more strenuous activity but served as a soothing syrup . . . the idea of a party did not serve as a call for the creation of a militant organization of revolutionaries, but was used to justify some sort of a "revolutionary bureaucracy" and infantile playing at "democratic" forms.[47]

In response, Lenin organized a militant, vanguard party dedicated to the pursuit of a revolutionary class struggle. This "wider and more strenuous activity" on the part of disciplined revolutionaries was legitimated on the basis of Lenin's interpretation of scientific socialism as "an integral revolutionary theory." Furthermore, the Party itself was to embody and preserve the true nature of scientific socialism against the negative influences of trade unionism and revisionism.

In contrast to the morally based philosophy of the natural rights doctrine, which did not "claim to conquer and systematize the whole of human knowledge,"[48] scientific socialism provided party members with the assurance and the conviction that all realms of life, both public and private, could be revolutionized and improved. Consequently, nothing was to stand outside the domain of the Party's authority, for everything was to be transformed. Moreover, given that the Party was considered the only appropriate agent of transformation, dissenting opinions either inside or outside the party organization were sanctioned and suppressed once the Party had reached its verdict on any given "call for action." Accordingly, "in the heat of the battle, when the proletarian army is straining every nerve, no criticism whatever can be permitted in its ranks."[49]

The ability to legitimate party decisions on the basis of their "scientific" status, enabled the Party to suppress dissent as a fundamental error rather than as a simple difference of opinion. Scientific socialism thereby provided the party leadership with unassailable grounds upon which to discipline members. This disciplinary ability generated unprecedented organizational power as the leadership could control and deploy party members in any given realm of action. As A. J. Polan maintains, to be a member of Lenin's Party was to be all things: representative, legislator, civil servant, warrior, and missionary.[50] Indeed, given the vast transformation of all aspects of human life mandated by scientific socialism, a tightly controlled and multidimensional party organization was crucial.

The Party's power and authority as the collective representative of the "accumulated wisdom" of scientific socialism was further enhanced by the intense loyalty members felt toward the organization. Undoubtedly, Lenin himself, as a charismatic leader, was the object of considerable personal loyalty, yet he systematically elevated the Party into the appropriate locus of loyalty, devotion and sacrifice. As a Marxist, Lenin could not allow the glorification of an individual over the collectivity of workers' representatives. Consequently, he insists that "all our lives we have carried on an ideological struggle against the glorification of personality, of the individual. We long ago solved the question of heroes."[51]

In short, Lenin created not just a party, but a charismatic community of dedicated revolutionaries that provided a compelling context for the transformation of social and political identities. The Marxist doctrine of scientific socialism was thereby able to gain, in Weber's words, an "independent influence on the conduct of life." Like the value-rational commitment of the French and American revolutionaries, first to the cause and only secondarily to the leaders representing the cause, "the complete personal devotion"[52] of party members was also primarily directed toward the revolutionary cause as embodied and represented by the Party. As Stefan Staszewski, a former Polish Communist, explains:

> For the party is simply the party: it is a word which replaces all known concepts and expressions; it is an absolute, an abstraction. It is always

> right; it is our honor, our happiness, our life's goal. And if you ask any communist about its infallibility, and if you also prove to him that for the past 38 years of its existence in Poland all it has done is commit mistakes, he will say to you: the party didn't commit mistakes; people committed mistakes. The leadership, abusing our trust, committed mistakes.[53]

Under the influence of this uncritical devotion, party cadres of all nationalities were willing to risk their lives in the struggle to overthrow the old order.

However, unlike the communities of the French and American revolutions, the Party was not to abdicate its position as the organizational locus for revolutionary transformation once the transfer of political power was completed. Instead, Lenin's Party was to remain in place until economic, social, political and cultural life conformed to the norms and principles established by the Marxist doctrine. The doctrine of scientific socialism consequently justified the elevation of the Party to a supreme position in the polity. Ultimately, loyalty to the revolutionary cause and loyalty to the Party were conflated to such an extent that the two became virtually indistinguishable. The Party could thus evolve into a permanent and monopolistic charismatic community. In contrast, the charismatic communities of the French and American revolutions remained dedicated to the pursuit of rights such as the freedom of conscience and the freedom of speech. The natural rights doctrine itself provided no legitimate basis upon which one community could monopolize power permanently by silencing dissent both externally and internally. Such a silencing would have entailed violating the very doctrine to which the community was committed.

Moreover, given that the Party's mission was to revolutionize all realms of life, it was a far more invasive organization with a far more pervasive mandate. The private morals of members were not simply to be scrutinized, as in the case of the Jacobin clubs, they were to be *transformed* in the name of scientific socialism. The Party thereby claimed a permanent monopoly over both public and private realms. This monopoly had considerable consequences for the institutional domains the Bolsheviks derived from the Marxist doctrine. Essentially, the central domains of Leninism were designed to establish and protect the Party's monopoly position in political, social and economic life.

THE INSTITUTIONAL DOMAINS OF LENINISM

Under the auspices of the all-encompassing ethos of scientific socialism and the all-encompassing organization of the Leninist Party, institutional domains were created that were decisively different from those established under liberal auspices. Since this ethos and organization were directed against the liberal capitalist bourgeois state of the West, as well as against the old order of Tsarist Russia, it is not surprising that the institutional domains that emerged after the Russian Revolution represented a direct response and challenge to the institutional domains of liberal capitalism.

Instead of the free and equal citizens mandated by the natural rights doctrine, under Marxism–Leninism the party cadres became the only actors legitimately participating in public life. In place of representative government, the Party established the "dictatorship of the proletariat" advocated by Marx, that was to guide and control the transformation of public and private realms. Furthermore, public virtue was not defined in terms of impersonal proceduralism; rather, the ideal standard of moral behavior and the ethical basis for public service and public life were cast in terms of "charismatic impersonalism."[54] In response to the free market with its "blind" and "irrational" exchange mechanisms, the economy was decisively subordinated to the rationality embodied by political control. As the Party moved to establish the "conscious control over economic forces"[55] desired by Marx, the economy, as a whole, ceased to function as an autonomous institutional realm—instead becoming an organizational expression of the dictatorship of the proletariat.

As we have seen, charismatic communities are capable of decisively reorienting the worldviews of their members. Within the communities, previous sociocultural identities are rendered meaningless and, ultimately, are replaced by new identities and new principles of conduct. Just as the American and French charismatic communities recast the identities of their members, so too did the Leninist Party. The difference, however, lies in the nature of the new identities. Whereas the democratic revolutionaries replaced their previous hierarchically defined and circumscribed identities with the novel identity of citizenship that allowed all members of society to interact with one another on the basis of equality, the transformation of consciousness in the Leninist case replaced the sociocultural hierarchy of the old order with a new one.[56] This new hierarchy was based on the distinctive nature of the party cadre as the creator, bearer and implementor of scientific socialism.

Although traditional, status-oriented identities were set aside when an individual joined the Party, the new identity provided was also status based. As a party cadre, one became an integral member of an heroic and extraordinary collectivity that was embarked on an historic mission to further the revolutionary struggles of the proletariat. Since this collectivity was superior to all other social and political groupings, it stood at the pinnacle of a new social and political order that was conceived of in hierarchical terms.

Generally speaking, the new hierarchy placed the proletariat above its class enemies and above society at large, while the Party stood above the proletariat due to its vanguard mission. Within the Party, as well, an organizational hierarchy was developed to distinguish between higher and lower levels of consciousness and competence. Ideological zeal and commitment combined with demonstrated ability were rewarded with greater positions of authority within the Party. Lenin's organizational principle of democratic centralism further solidified the internal order of the Party by imposing strict standards of discipline and hierarchical decision-making.

Invidious distinctions between higher and lower members of society and of the polity were thereby built into the political system. In place of the fundamental question posed by liberal democratic revolutionaries—Who has the right to rule and on what basis?—Lenin asked the famous question "*kto kovo*?" or "who over whom?" The answer, as mandated by his interpretation of Marxism, was quite clear: the party cadres represented the "*kto*" that would rule over the "*kovo*"—"over all others"—in the name of scientific socialism. The appropriate institutions of rule were to be derived from the domain established by the "dictatorship of the proletariat" upon which the monopoly rule of the Party was based.

The dictatorship of the proletariat is quite tersely defined by Lenin as the "rule—unrestricted by law and based on force—of the proletariat over the bourgeoisie."[57] During the period of revolutionary transformation, it is to be expected that the Party will be confronted by an unreconstructed society ranging in attitude from hostile to indifferent. In these circumstances, absolute vigilance and force is needed in order for the Party to effect the massive changes foreseen by the guiding doctrine while itself remaining free from contamination and corruption. Such an unrestricted conception of rule mandates the establishment of a form of government that, in Polan's words:

> allows for no distances, no spaces, no appeals, no checks, no balances, no processes, no delays, no interrogations and, above all, no distribution of power. All are ruthlessly and deliberately excluded, as precisely the articulations of the disease of corruption and mystification.[58]

Specifically, under the dictatorship of the proletariat, the Party was to control all aspects of political, economic and social life. Power in the Leninist state was thereby to be highly centralized, not distributed. Yet how, precisely, was the Party to exercise both control and vigilance simultaneously?

To address this need, three organizational features came to characterize the dictatorship of the proletariat: a dual political authority structure, a command-driven, centrally planned economy, and a set of "transmission belt" organizations designed to facilitate social mobilization. By establishing, formally, autonomous realms such as state governments, central planning bureaus, and trade unions that were, however, under the complete control of the cadres, the Party ideally acquired both a means of remaining separate from the mundane, routine tasks of modern life, and a means of fulfilling its transformatory mission.

In keeping with Marx's relatively positive assessment of citizenship and civic rights, Leninist regimes developed a political structure that resembled liberal forms of government. Constitutions guaranteeing certain civic rights, regularly held elections, and the branches of modern government—the executive, the legislative and the judicial—were all established and maintained.

However, this structure did not exist independently of the Party. Indeed, since, in the words of the Polish communist Edward Ochab, "no democratic rights can ever override the right of the proletariat to its class rule,"[59] the Party had to ensure its control over the polity. The Party functioned, therefore, both as a separate political entity dedicated to transformation and as the sole administrative basis for the government. The dual nature of Leninist political structures, wherein the Party and the state exist as formally separate entities even as they are fused under the leadership of the Party, was to provide the degree of control and intervention needed to transform the polity, while keeping the cadres aware of their special identity as revolutionaries, not state functionaries.

A similar logic was applied in the economic realm under Stalin's leadership, although the scope of even formal autonomy was more restricted than in the formation of the state government. Again, following the Marxist doctrine, private property, property rights and the capitalist market were abolished during the course of the 1930s. The Party subsequently became the sole de facto owner of the means of production. As Lenin envisioned:

> Accounting and control—that is mainly what is needed for the "smooth working," for the proper functioning, of the first phase of communist society. *All* citizens are transformed into hired employees of the state, which consists of the armed workers. *All* citizens become employees and workers of a *single* country-wide state "syndicate."[60]

Yet, even in this context, a certain duality was maintained as the central planning organs that provided for the "accounting and control" of the economy were nominally independent of the Party. In actuality, of course, the cadres determined and controlled the means of economic development in order to achieve the end of socialist transformation.

Finally, the Party also dominated all other significant organizations such as trade unions and professional organizations that were, however, organized as nominally autonomous and spontaneous representations of the interests of the social groups involved. In actuality, these organizations served primarily as transmission belts conveying the Party's message to selected social groups, while controlling their activities. The interests, needs and aspirations of social groups outside of the Party were thereby relegated to political insignificance.

In short, unlike the representative governments of liberal states, wherein citizens could express their interests via regular elections and wherein governing institutions were separated to prevent the monopolistic exercise of power, Leninist regimes were characterized by an invidious separation between an all-controlling Party and a society deemed unworthy of participation in public life. Indeed, according to Lenin's reasoning, social participation would only serve to dilute and corrupt the Party by exposing the cadres to the undesirable influences of overt or covert class enemies. Nor were the cadres to lose their specific revolutionary identity by becoming directly involved in the mundane regulatory tasks associated with modern life. Instead, they were to preserve their unique status as the instigators of the great transformation by "overseeing" the tasks of formally autonomous realms.

In keeping with this exclusive and exclusionary conception of the Party cadre, and with this coercive conception of the dictatorship of the proletariat, the ethical basis for public conduct under Leninism was also developed in opposition to liberalism. Rather than the notions of procedural fairness and predictable rules and regulations that characterize liberal states, public virtue in a Leninist state is based on a conceptualization of the Party that Ken Jowitt has termed "charismatic impersonalism." According to Jowitt, "the novelty of Leninism as an organization is its substitution of charismatic impersonality for the procedural impersonality dominant in the West."[61] Within the context of charismatic impersonalism, the Party is free to determine the means, however arbitrary, unpredictable or coercive, whereby the end of socialist transformation is to be achieved. Laws and rules exist in a Leninist polity, but they can be set aside at any given moment if this furthers the Party's mission.

In terms of the theoretical framework developed by Jowitt, "Lenin took the fundamentally conflicting notions of individual heroism and organizational impersonalism and recast them in the form of an organizational hero—the Bolshevik party."[62] Jowitt goes on to say that the Party created by Lenin "was distinctive in its *novel recasting* of elements—heroism, arbitrariness, and absolute certainty, along with impersonal discipline, planning and empirical investigation."[63] This fusion of organizational impersonalism and arbitrariness within the charismatic community of the Party is exemplified by the concept of the correct line.

As established by Lenin, the correct line or program of action for the Party is to reign supreme as the "authoritatively compelling and exclusive ideological-political statement that must be adopted and adhered to."[64] The authoritative qualities of the norms and policies mandated by the Party's correct line renders the impersonalism of this organization arbitrary and unpredictable in nature. In other words, the Party, rather than a constitution, is the sole source of authority in the polity—hence the charismatic component of its organizational impersonalism.

As embodied in the correct line, this charismatic impersonalism provides the basis upon which conflicting views or interests within the Party are to be adjudicated. Prior to the Party's adoption of a particular policy or statement, debate between conflicting interests and points of view are, at least theoretically, encouraged. However, once a decision is made about the correct line or policy, all differences must evaporate as the cadres lay aside their previous positions in order to adhere wholeheartedly to the new line. For example, Roman Werfel, a committed Polish communist, declares:

> Look, when a resolution is passed, it's the duty of a communist to carry it

out. So we were taught discipline and unity of action. That's not important when the party only has an election battle to deal with, but it's essential when it comes to organizing the masses for revolution. We were preparing the ground for that revolution, so we had to act as a unit.[65]

In this context, the appropriate standard for public conduct on the part of the cadres as defined by charismatic impersonalism is reflected in the cadre's ultimate loyalty to the Party and its dictates, no matter how arbitrary or contrary to the individual cadre's views and interests. Furthermore, the correct line supersedes all existing laws and regulations. They, too, can arbitrarily be set aside in the pursuit of the Party's objectives. Again, like the other institutional domains established by Leninism, this definition of public virtue is invidious given that the only legitimate interests are located within the Party. Only the cadres can demonstrate public virtue by adhering unquestioningly to their Party's correct line. By limiting the capacity to demonstrate public virtue to the party cadres, society is further held at bay; is further removed from public life.

Taken together these institutional domains—the party cadre, the dictatorship of the proletariat and charismatic impersonalism—comprise the core attributes of all Leninist regimes. The viability of these regimes is contingent upon establishing and maintaining the Party's monopoly position in all realms of life. As we have seen, only by maintaining this position can the Party fulfill its revolutionary task of complete social, political and economic transformation, as mandated by scientific socialism. Consequently, the cohesion and purpose of the polity is grounded in the transcendent authority of the Party, rather than in the state, as in the French case, or in the constitution, as in the American case. The institutional domains established during the first decades of Soviet rule were, accordingly, designed to secure the Party's authority by protecting the cadres from corruption and contamination.

The cadres as a permanent community of revolutionaries had to be prevented from pursuing narrow or particular goals and interests that were in conflict or at odds with the general task of transformation. Since a communist society would not emerge overnight, revolutionary élan and self-sacrifice among the cadres had to be maintained over several generations. Consequently, in order to protect the cadres, the institutional domains of Leninism all maintained an invidious distinction between the Party and society.[66]

Society, as a potentially hostile realm of unreconstructed groups and forces, had to be confined to a passive role in public life. In this process of confinement, those outside the Party were discriminated against on a routine basis, while those inside the Party enjoyed a privileged status. By creating such a gap between party and non-party status, the Bolshevik leadership hoped to render the cadres immune from the competing interests and claims that might be placed upon them by family, by regional, and/or by ethnic loyalties. Furthermore, rigorous internal vigilance and discipline (taken to the extreme of the purges under Stalin) were to be continuously exercised at all levels of the party hierarchy to maintain compliance with the Party's objectives. Discipline and a superior status vis-à-vis society were, therefore, essential to the Party's monopoly position and to its ability to perform a revolutionary transformation. While the Party's base in the working class was continuously proclaimed by Soviet leaders, the Party's vanguard role was thought to justify its tutelary, and ultimately superior, position vis-à-vis this social class as well.

These essential attributes, and the institutional domains they were embedded in, were, however, substantially weakened by Khrushchev's 1956 de-Stalinization campaign. Khrushchev's efforts to mitigate and correct the worst excesses of the Stalin era led to the unintended consequence of decisively undermining the Party's monopoly position. By declaring an end to the class war that had guided party policies up to that point, and by declaring a "state of the whole people," Khrushchev set in motion a process that would ultimately result in the very corruption and contamination of the Party that his predecessors had feared. As Jowitt points out:

> In fact, Khrushchev's repudiation of class war in his 1956 de-Stalinization speech was an ideologically mortal blow to the integrity and vitality of Leninism as a Soviet and international phenomenon. With this action, Khrushchev removed the ideological and political rationale for juxtaposing the Party as the locus of a superior, more "real" way of life to an "unreconstructed culturally contaminating" Soviet society. With his ideas of "state of the whole people" and "Party of the whole people," Khrushchev diluted the ideological and political tension between the Party and its host, Soviet society. He weakened the Party's conviction that it had a still-unfulfilled mission requiring internal discipline. Khrushchev's revisions left a Party increasingly unable to distinguish between the Party "City of God" and the Soviet "City of Man"—between the cadres' particular interests and the Party's general interest.[67]

Even by symbolically including the people into a political community that had heretofore been restricted to the Party, Khrushchev undermined the Party's monopoly position as the sole legitimate agent of administration and transformation. As the Party's superior status was relativized, its organizational integrity declined as well. Without a sense of purpose, corruption and the selfish pursuit of privileges began to characterize the cadres. By the end of the Brezhnev era, the Soviet Union was being ruled by a "banquet regime,"[68] rather than a revolutionary regime. While the cadres toasted themselves, social frustrations and economic problems began to mount. Ultimately, the institutional domains of Leninism disintegrated into façades behind which a "parasitical Party, a booty economy and a scavenger society"[69] were taking shape. The consequences of these developments were not, however, felt first in the Soviet Union. Instead, the Communist Party in

Poland was the first to feel the effects of growing social opposition to the levels of corruption and mismanagement that characterized Gierek's version of the Brezhnevite banquet regime.

POLAND: ANTECEDENTS

The generalized corruption to which all Leninist regimes were subject after de-Stalinization, combined with the particular features of postwar development in Poland, resulted in a set of institutions that precipitated a pattern of destabilization unique in the Leninist regime world. These institutions were: an organizationally weak Communist Party, a strong Catholic Church, and the spontaneous, informal organizations established in opposition to existing authorities. In the wake of de-Stalinization, the Polish Party's organizational integrity was fatally weakened, while alternative organizations grew in strength and purpose. These autonomous realms provided a strong foundation for oppositional activity, since participants received the necessary support and protection to sustain their activities as they acquired organizational and leadership experience.

The inability of the Polish Party to marginalize and neutralize such organizations rendered the Party's monopoly position insecure and readily contestable in the years after 1956. Consequently, by the time Gierek was appointed General Secretary in 1970, Polish society had already undergone numerous upheavals as various aspects of party rule had been opposed with some frequency. Indeed, Gierek owed his very appointment to the worker protests of 1970 that had driven his predecessor Gomułka from office. Gomułka in turn, had been brought to power by the events of 1956, when a worker uprising had precipitated a serious regime crisis by challenging a shaken and disoriented Party.

In the aftermath of Khrushchev's 1956 speech, the Polish United Workers' Party (the PUWP) was clearly cast into a disarray from which it never recovered. The moral sense of mission and purpose that had animated Poland's first generation of communist leaders evaporated as the revelations of Stalin's abuses against Poland and against Polish communists became known. Apparently, even the older leaders who had been in regular contact with Stalin and with the Soviet party apparatus were shaken to the core. For example, Bierut, head of the Party during the immediate postwar era, found it very difficult to come to terms with the knowledge that good Polish communists had been put to death in the Soviet Union on Stalin's orders during the purges. Indeed, it is widely believed that the shock of reading Khrushchev's speech at the Twentieth CPSU Congress in Moscow contributed to Bierut's death of a heart attack a few days later.[70]

The original sense of mission that had infused the lives of postwar communists with meaning can be said to have died along with Bierut. Pelczynski, for example, points out that the effects of Khrushchev's speech were widely felt in Poland, since the speech was read in open meetings to the rank and file members of the Party. Elsewhere in Eastern Europe, the speech was presented to only a select few in closed meetings. Not surprisingly, "the effect on the younger Party members was shattering. The hero they had been trained to worship was now shown to be a bungler and a murderer."[71] Ironically, the organizational unity of the Party was subsequently lost as efforts to reclaim a sense of moral purpose divided the cadres. Henceforth, the internal discipline of the Party was irredeemably undermined by the continuous struggles of reformers attempting to infuse new purpose into the Party's existence by following the path of "democratization." Such reforms were, in turn, opposed by ideological "hard-liners" and betrayed by more opportunistic wielders of power, such as Gomułka and Gierek, who rose to prominence by proclaiming their support for reforms, only to revert to traditional power politics once their positions of authority were secured. Roman Werfel, an old Polish communist, describes the extent of the damage done to the organizational integrity of his party by de-Stalinization:

> something began to go wrong from about 1952, and the apparatus alienated itself from the masses. Take Gomułka, for instance: a totally honest man who once, over the radio, confessed his surprise at hearing there were no tights to be had, because his wife found no difficulty in buying them. What did that imply? Surely not that he was stupid, but rather that he didn't know Poland: he simply didn't know the things I knew. . . . Gomulka didn't know . . . although he himself was beyond reproach, which you couldn't say about Gierek.[72]

In this context, the 1956 crisis in Poland represents a pivotal turning point in postwar Polish development. During the succession struggle after Bierut's death, the Party experienced its first factional battles, battles which were subsequently to become, more or less, institutionalized. Although the names and the reform programs were to change in the course of the following decades, factional strife within the Party was to become a consistent feature of Polish political life, thereby limiting the Party's ability to maintain the monopoly position mandated by Marxism–Leninism. This, in turn, limited the Party's ability to retain control over "the masses."

The year 1956, therefore, also marked a turning point in the evolution of organizations and institutions capable of competing with the Party. During the course of the crisis, the Party was forced to make long-term and far-reaching concessions to defuse popular discontent.[73] Attacks on the Catholic Church ceased, as did the drive to collectivize agriculture. Control over cultural and intellectual life was abandoned, never to be completely reimposed. In the aftermath of 1956, for example, five organizations existed for children and young adults—a situation not found anywhere else in Eastern Europe. Of these five groups, only two were directly controlled by the Party, while one, the Polish Students Association which included most university students, was completely nonparty in orientation and in membership[74] 1956 also saw the birth of independently organized discussion clubs for young intellectuals throughout the country. The most famous of these clubs, Warsaw's Klub Krzywego Koła (the Crooked Circle Club), provided an important forum for open, uncensored discussions on significant matters of the day. As noted in *Po Prostu*, the student weekly and organizational fountainhead for the Klub: "We are a group of young hotheads, students and graduates. We are people who cannot stop meddling with all that happens around us. We are a group of the discontented. We want more things, wiser things, better things."[75]

Although the Klub was forced to dissolve in 1962, the regime was unable to prevent the emergence of other organizations dedicated to free expression. A pattern was thereby established of a continuous struggle to maintain autonomous fora for free expression that the regime was ultimately unable to cope with. If one organization was shut down, another would emerge to take its place at a later date. While this pattern is best known in connection with Polish intellectual life, it was also well established amongst Polish workers.

For example, although control over the autonomous workers' councils that emerged in opposition to the communist trade unions was reimposed (by coopting them into the Party-led Conference of Workers' Self-Management), the Party never managed to stifle the tendency toward workers' self-organization that crystallized during the 1956 crisis. Not surprisingly, during the 1970 period of worker unrest, workers again formed independent councils, thereby continuing to establish the organizational precedents that would eventually culminate in the struggle to establish Solidarity as an independent trade union.[76] Clearly, the concessions made in 1956 decisively undermined the Party's ability to maintain its "leading role" in society.

This seemingly rapid and complete erosion of the Party's ability to exercise monopoly control over social, economic, cultural and political life was actually the result of the incomplete or attenuated nature of Stalinism in Poland. As has been pointed out by numerous analysts, Stalinism in Poland was short in duration, lasting from 1949 to 1953, and failed to achieve the objectives mandated by Stalin's program of transformation.[77] The collectivization of agriculture was, for example, only half-heartedly attempted. As Staszewski, deputy minister of agriculture in 1954–55, recalls in a 1982 interview:

> I maintained that it would take a civil war to cooperativize the countryside and that even if we won it, it would lead the state to bankruptcy, because as it was we were spending horrific sums of money subsidizing existing cooperatives, and if any more were created we would finally run out of funds.[78]

A similar fear of generating unrest amongst the country's elites may also have kept the purges of oppositional figures in check. Unlike the Soviet Union and other East European countries, the Polish Party did not "physically liquidate" its opponents. For example, Gomułka and Cardinal Wyszyński were simply arrested, not put to death, for their oppositional activities (the former in 1951 for his "nationalist deviations" and the latter in 1953 for his religious opposition to the Party).[79]

The scarcity of both financial and human resources in postwar Poland clearly constrained the Party's ability to follow the dictates of the Soviet model of Stalinist development. In coping with the tremendous dislocations resulting from wartime destruction and the changing of the country's borders, Polish communists preferred circumspect policies over revolutionary ones. Resistance wherever and whenever possible to Soviet pressures and dictates appears, early on, to have become second nature to Poland's leaders. As Staszewski again recalls with reference to the Stalinist policy of socialist realism:

> And I assure you that's why we were able to reject and get rid of socialism realism with such relative ease: because first of all it was not rooted in our cultural tradition, and secondly we weren't excessively enthusiastic in implementing it. Wherever it was possible to wriggle out of some act of servility, we wriggled out of it.[80]

While this attenuated version of Stalinism certainly did not encourage the development of autonomous forms of expression, it did provide a less terror-filled environment in which independent initiatives were not completely stifled. Localized workers' strikes, for example, were already taking place in the late 1940s and early 1950s. According to Staszewski, "brutal solutions were not resorted to then." Instead, accords were apparently reached peacefully.[81]

In the cultural realm, as well, the relatively "humane treatment" of the "creative intelligentsia" seems to have allowed for some degrees of autonomy.[82] The Catholic University of Lublin, for example, was amazingly enough allowed to continue, providing an institutional safe haven for non-Party academics and students. In regard to the Catholic Church, the Polish Party was forced to register its greatest defeat since the Church was able to maintain an independent institutional existence throughout the Stalinist period, as well as maintaining its influence on Polish social life. As Pelczynski observes, "even Party members secretly married in church and had their children baptized, confirmed and instructed in religion, yielding to tradition and social pressure rather than to the Party's orders."[83]

The continued existence of the Catholic Church, as well as the growing tendency toward the creation of autonomous, informal organizations, rendered the post-1956 weakness and corruption of the Party particularly damaging in the Polish context. Since the Party had not managed to destroy or subordinate these alternative independent loci of organized expression during the Stalin era, its monopoly position in public life could readily be challenged once the Party's internal unity and sense of mission were undermined by de-Stalinization. Without a viable sense of mission, the distance maintained between society and the Party, along with the cadres' privileges, no longer seemed valid—even in the eyes of some communists such as Werfel. Therefore, the Party's position was potentially open to attack.

Only in Poland, however, did the existence of independent institutions provide the basis for challenging the Party's privileges and corrupt practices. Elsewhere in Eastern Europe and in the Soviet Union, corrupt Communist Parties were relatively successful in retaining their positions of privilege in social, political and economic life. As Jowitt, quoting Hirschman, elaborates, they became, in effect, "lazy monopolies" characterized by "an oppression of the weak by the incompetent, an exploitation of the poor by the lazy."[84] The destruction or marginalization of all independent realms of action and organization during the Stalin years allowed the corrupt and "lazy" party cadres to rule in peace, at least in the short run.

In sum, the half-hearted and brief implementation of Stalinist policies, combined with the disruptive impact of de-Stalinization both on the Polish Party and on Polish society, led to a period of chronic instability as the weakened, and increasingly corrupt, Party was unable successfully to suppress or coopt autonomous institutions. After 1956, for example, the Church's position in Poland was never again seriously in question. According to some observers, such as Jerzy Wiatr, the Church eventually functioned as a "political opposition" to the Party, thereby "rendering the Party's legitimacy and authority highly unstable."[85] Moreover, after that watershed year, autonomous forms of social expression could crystallize into independent organizations. In these organizations, activists received the necessary experience and the confidence needed to sustain their efforts to create autonomous realms of expression.

The experiences of Solidarity leaders Adam Michnik and Lech Wałęsa are paradigmatic in this regard. Both men had long histories of involvement in the founding of independent organizations before the birth of Solidarity in August 1980.[86] For example, Tadeusz Nowak, a former shipyard worker, recalls that when he first met Wałęsa in 1979, the latter made a point of reciting his opposition "pedigree":

> I am an activist for the Free Trade Unions. . . . I am a shipyard worker who took part in the strike of 1970 and I was a member of the advisory board. In 1976 they fired me from the shipyard because I became too uncomfortable. However, I left behind my people in well organized groups.[87]

Predictably, Wałęsa immediately began to organize groups again at his new place of employment, the Lenin Shipyards.

Wałęsa's activities demonstrate how the weakness of the Polish Party, in conjunction with the existence of organizational alternatives, resulted in a unique pattern of destabilization as workers periodically attempted to redress their grievances through the creation of independent workers' councils, and as intellectuals attempted to widen their scope for the freedom of expression. These attempts would be met by the Party with a mixture of repression and inducements; a mixture that proved ineffective in either suppressing or coopting dissent. The stage would subsequently be set for the next round.

The fact that these periodic upheavals eventually produced the most powerful challenge to Leninism is partially a result of the confluence of two processes. On the one hand, the opposition was gaining organizational strength and experience while, on the other hand, the nature of the opposition itself was changing. Changes in the social structure of Poland were generating the preconditions needed for the emergence of a powerful core elite drawn from the middle strata of society. As we have seen in the case of the American and French Revolutions, a core elite comprised of upper and lower echelons of the middle strata can convince broader segments of the population to pursue their interests in an alternative framework, even in opposition to existing authorities. In the case of Poland, a "new middle class,"[88] comprised of skilled workers and intellectuals, provided the social base for the emergence of an elite dedicated to the radical improvement of Polish society. Ultimately, Solidarity became "the organizational as well as the ideological manifestation" of this new class.[89] For example, in analyzing the social origins of the events of 1980, Kurczewski notes that

> a new class started the fight, a class composed of people who directly confronted the authorities in companies, offices, and institutions run by them. This new middle class consists of the best-educated and most highly paid people in comparison with the lower, truly proletarianized classes. . . . The cultural and economic advancement of millions of people led to the situation in which a new middle class was formed, blocked in its aspirations on the one hand by the closed borders of the ruling class, and on the other by the misgovernment of the country and its economy.[90]

While the "cultural and economic advancement" associated with communist-led development was not unique to Poland, Kurczewski points out that these social processes "came to the fore with full force much earlier, and influenced thus both Polish history and the further developments in the region."[91] Consequently, what is unique about Poland is the earlier impact of the social consequences of development, and the overall political context in which these developments took place.

From 1945 onwards, an emphasis on individual achievement and mobility was slowly replacing traditional conceptions of static, hereditary corporate identities. Middle strata in the Hobsbawmian sense of owing "their position in the social order not to birth or privilege but to individual worth"[92] and talent were emerging. Peasant sons were becoming skilled workers or white collar bureaucrats, while peasant daughters were becoming doctors or teachers. Although these new, upwardly mobile occupational groups did retain their links to the countryside, this resulted in "the functional (or professional) urbanization of the countryside" with the accompanying spread of "urban outlooks and habits in the country."[93] During this initial period of increased mobility and migration from rural to urban areas, the direct influence of the Catholic Church, traditionally a barrier to individuation, was attenuated. Pelczynski, for example, points out that the "lack of churches in the new suburbs" or near the factory hostels "encouraged laxity in religious practice."

However, he notes that the "full [sociological] impact" of this distancing from the Church would "become noticeable somewhat later."[94] According to Kurczewski, the eventual impact can be seen in the attitudes of the emerging middle class:

> More often, members of what I call the "new middle classes" in socialist society feel themselves personally free moral agents, in that it is up to them to decide their own conduct even if this contradicts the teachings of the Church. This, in a way, could provide a bridge between their attitude towards religion and their political engagement.[95]

While the majority continued to "believe in God and the other elements of the Judaeo-Christian world-view," a "strong feeling of agency and subjectivity" had clearly taken shape.[96]

As a result of these processes, the autonomous organizations that developed after 1956 were largely independent of the Church, as well as of the party-state. In other words, the traditional social forces that had influenced Polish public life for so long—the clergy and the small and large landowners—were increasingly being undermined. Urbanization and industrialization, even under communist auspices, had weakened the influence of peasant culture on the one hand, and of aristocratic culture on the other hand. In the past, only the Church and the Polish nationalist tradition had been able to negotiate the gap between these two worlds. Catholicism and nationalism had provided the only links between the two Polish "nations."

By 1955, however, Chałasiński, a noted Polish sociologist, observed three major currents in contemporary Polish political culture: "communist, liberal-progressive, and Catholic-progressive."[97] The very fact that Catholicism was now increasingly linked to progressive tendencies testifies to the changing nature of Polish society. The doctrine of the Polish Catholic Church had evolved, under the leadership of Cardinal Wyszyński, to reflect the needs and aspirations of an increasingly urban, mobile and educated population. As Michnik noted, in the Church "jeremiads against 'Godless ones' have given way to documents that quote the principles of the Declarations of Human Rights."[98] Ultimately, the Church itself was forced to compete for influence in public life with the Party on the one hand, and with autonomous organizations on the other.[99]

While the Church remained the most visible symbol of Polish resistance to communism, its influence was increasingly attenuated. Consequently, the decline of the Church's position as an unquestioned arbiter of private and public conduct, combined with the scope allowed by the Party for independent organizations, meant that the newly emerging social strata could develop and express in organizational terms, autonomous perceptions, values and interests as "free moral agents."[100] During the Gierek years, under the impact of his policies, these social strata became increasingly frustrated and open to alternative visions of political life that could infuse such independent organizational efforts with new purpose and direction. By the late 1970s, a core elite drawn from this middle class was in a position to provide both leadership and vision.

Gierek came to power in the wake of another crisis precipitated by workers' strikes and demonstrations throughout Poland. Essentially, the Gierek regime attempted to stabilize the Party's position by reducing the causes for social frustration, thereby reducing the attractiveness of alternative organizations. Simply put, Gierek attempted to solve the problem of social unrest by throwing money at it. The ready availability of Western funds appeared to be heaven-sent for the purpose of achieving a level of prosperity that would diffuse popular discontent with the Communist Party. In the short run, Gierek's policies did result in a period of social mobility and economic well-being that was, unfortunately, unsustainable over the long run. The Party's corruption and economic mismanagement undermined any chance of sustained prosperity and upward mobility which also reduced its ability to maintain social peace. If anything, social frustrations only became worse as the failure of the regime's promises became apparent.

Gierek began his tenure in office with an economic offensive designed to generate new jobs and improve consumption levels for the new entrants into the labor force. By the early 1970s, Poland was facing a demographic explosion of its work force. In 1970, for example, 21.2 percent of the population was between the ages of ten and twenty.[101] Optimistically, Gierek hoped to take advantage of increased access to Western financial markets and government loans in order to finance the levels of investment needed to achieve his goals. On the basis of foreign capital, enhanced export potential and administrative streamlining, Gierek intended to "address the problems of an aging industrial plant, falling growth rates, a sclerotic administrative structure, restless workers and a new generation."[102]

During the first half of the 1970s, Gierek's policies succeeded in improving the standard of living for most Poles. Consumer products, largely imported from the West, became more readily available. Meat consumption, for example, rose, becoming a symbol of the new prosperity. The pattern of social mobility continued as the new generation was absorbed into the workforce. Gierek's administrative reforms, however, proved to be less successful. Instead of enhancing the control of the Party and rendering the decision-making processes more efficient, the concentration of industrial enterprises initiated in 1971 was counterproductive. According to one analyst:

> Gierek's administrative reforms had paved the way for a powerful weakening of the PZPR as a device for controlling and "leading" the country

at lower levels. His primary political intention had apparently been to reduce the stature of voivodeship party secretaries—his potential rivals either singly or in alliance with other local secretaries or even Politburo figures. But in so doing he rendered them impotent to master the growing bureaucratic autonomy of Polish industrial enterprises.[103]

The subsequent evolution of "localism" in the 1970s, came as a result of the growing "collusion between local economic decision makers and party-state authorities."[104] This collusion facilitated the development of widespread, almost systemic corruption, which further undermined the central leadership's control over the periphery. Not that the center was impervious to corruption. By the late 1970s, for example, it was common knowledge that a close advisor to Gierek, Maciej Szczepanski, was one of the most corrupt public officials. Charges later leveled against him included "embezzlement, personal enrichment at public costs (ownership of villas, luxurious yachts, etc.) and moral depravity (financing of concubines, a library of 900 pornographic films, etc.)."[105]

As the economic situation worsened in the mid-1970s, the Party's organizational weakness, political corruption and economic mismanagement became issues of widespread public concern. It was becoming increasingly evident that the hard-won prosperity and mobility of the postwar era was in jeopardy. The events of 1976, when the regime attempted unsuccessfully to raise prices, yet managed successfully to suppress workers' protests through the use of force, simply underscored the ultimate inability of the Party to generate constructive solutions to the country's growing problems.[106] In the wake of this painful episode, a common understanding of the problems facing Poland, and of the appropriate solutions to these problems, began to emerge. Public opinion research, for example, documented a widespread perception that the following values should be "realized in a good and just social system": "equality of life opportunities, satisfaction of people's basic needs, freedom of speech, and influence of citizens on the way society is being governed."[107] Meanwhile, a consensus was growing that non-party public interests needed to be represented in the decision-making process in order to combat the Party's diminishing ability to govern effectively. For example, in an influential 1976 article, Michnik called for the increased participation of independent social institutions in public life.[108] However, whether such participation and representation was possible, and how it was to be achieved without violating the formality of the Party's leading role in society, remained open questions.

In this context of growing uncertainty and confusion, almost all members of Polish society were negatively affected by declining standards of living and diminishing expectations about the future. As Nowak notes, "in the late 1970s, the Polish people were evincing political irritation and social apathy at the same time. The combination turned out a few years later to be explosive."[109] In all, one can identify numerous social groups that were frustrated, disaffected and alienated by the existing circumstances. Reform-minded members of the Party were frustrated by the intransigence and immobility of their conservative or corrupt colleagues. Non-party intellectuals were increasingly alienated and disaffected by the regime's inability to effect positive reforms and to act in the nation's interests. Skilled workers were becoming fed up as their productivity was impeded and impaired by senseless and arbitrary party interference in economic management. Indeed, Nowak's survey research in the late 1970s found that "freedom of speech proved to be more highly prized among workers, and particularly among highly skilled workers, than it was even among people with a university education."[110] Clearly, the ability to speak out freely, without reprisals, about the miserable state of one's living and working conditions was becoming a primary concern. Finally, peasants were provoked into resistance as the Gierek regime attempted to impose an extremely disadvantageous pension system on the rural population.

True to the Polish tradition of autonomous organization, opposition groups began to organize after 1976 both in rural and in urban settings. Workers along the Baltic coast, for example, persisted in their efforts to establish genuinely autonomous councils for the representation of their interests, while peasants began to organize rural self-defense committees.[111] As yet, however, these organizations represented discrete and generally isolated efforts on the part of particular social groups to address and redress particular wrongs. The obstacles to a broadly based, concerted effort to initiate a general reform of the governing system were still formidable. Apart from the Party's ability to repress, at least in the short run, unwanted oppositional activity, Polish society was segmented, separated into various strata removed from and suspicious of one another. The Party had managed, with considerable success, to implement a "divide and rule" strategy whereby suspicions between various social groups such as workers and intellectuals were fanned and encouraged. Nowak's studies, for example, "revealed a kind of social vacuum between the level of primary groups and that of the nation."[112] In other words, Poles tended to identify, first, with their families and immediate friends and, second, with the Polish nation as a whole. No intermediate groups, associations or organizations evoked "the kind of identification that comes out most plainly in interviews when the respondent says 'we.' "[113] This social isolation was undermined and transcended by two developments: the election of a Polish pope, and the emergence of a core elite drawn from the middle ranks of society.

The election of Cardinal Karol Wojtyła to the papacy in October 1978 provided Poles with a national symbol of hope and pride. As has often been pointed out, his subsequent visit to Poland in 1979 provided an opportunity to demonstrate independent organizational abilities on a nationwide scale. In the words of one analyst, the Pope's visit "revealed how able Poles were to organize and respond to an unprecedented national event relatively independently of state direction and control."[114] Moreover, the Pope's visit, similar to the public spectacles that preceded the French Revolution, gave Poles a renewed sense of common destiny, and a shared identity as Polish citizens—regardless of previous grievances or suspicions. Consequently, in the aftermath of the Pope's tour of Poland, a relatively unified and receptive national audience existed for a program of substantial, even radical, reform based on the representation of social interests and respect for civil rights.

Such an audience could only be galvanized into concerted action, however, under the leadership and direction of a core elite. This elite was drawn largely from the two social groups—skilled workers and intellectuals—that occupied the middle of the social scale. At the top of this scale were, of course, party members and the nomenklatura, while at the bottom one could locate the very unskilled and poorly educated workers and peasants. These middle strata were marginal in status yet relatively secure in economic position, thereby manifesting both the frustration and the resources needed to mount an opposition to the existing state of affairs.[115] Organizationally, the autonomous Social Self-Defense Committee (or KOR), established by intellectuals in the wake of the 1976 strikes to assist workers against state reprisals, provided the initial meeting ground for workers and intellectuals. In the words of one observer, the work of this committee

> convinced many worker activists that the interests of both social groups were identical, their purposes coincided and that realization of the desires of one particular group could not be brought about without achievement of those of the other.[116]

Subsequently, in 1977, workers and intellectuals began jointly to edit and produce an independent journal, *Robotnik* (*The Worker*). This journal became something of a symbol of mutual cooperation and respect between the two groups, as well as a forum for the development of more intense collaborative efforts. According to the founding appeal of *Robotnik*, both groups were well aware of the significance of their cooperation:

> In Poland's postwar history there have been many attempts to organize resistance against the measures and moves taken by the authorities. Various social groups, however, went singly into action. An example of this which ended in defeat was the student protest in March 1968 and the passive attitude of the intelligentsia milieux during the workers' revolt in December 1970. This lack of solidarity was partly overcome in June 1976. We want our joint cooperation to start on the project of realizing our aspirations towards a just and independent Poland.[117]

Throughout the latter part of the 1970s, the intellectuals associated with KOR and the workers associated with the free trade union movement were in constant contact with one another. In the course of these contacts, a shared sense of injustice and a shared conviction that substantial reforms were necessary became solidified amongst the newly emerging leadership—a leadership comprised of both workers and intellectuals.[118]

Due to the composition of this core elite, a broad range of the recently created middle strata of Polish society were mobilized to support the reform program subsequently advanced by Solidarity. As in the French and American cases, this broadly based mobilization prevented reform efforts from being limited to a debate between various factions of the ruling elites, as had been the case in Czechoslovakia in 1968. Czech workers, for example, only mobilized to support the revisionist leadership after the Soviet invasion.[119] Moreover, the character of the Polish core elite also had considerable consequences for the type of reform advocated. Rather than supporting a return to the "status quo ante" of prewar conservatism, as did many participants in the Hungarian uprising of 1956, Polish workers and intellectuals—as members of the Hobsbawmian middle strata—were in favor of creating political and economic structures that would represent and liberate the individual's interests and productive capacities.[120] In the ongoing effort to create such structures, the preservation of civil rights, such as the right of association and freedom of speech, loomed large in the minds of Polish reformers. As, for example, in a July 1980 statement:

> in accordance with its aims, the Social Self-Defense Committee "KOR" draws attention to the necessity of restoring fundamental civil rights which are guaranteed in the Pacts of Human Rights ratified by Poland. The authorities' respect for these rights will favor an agreement concerning the most urgent economic, political and social reforms. Workers' meetings should be allowed to appoint workers' committees, independent trade unions and other representations able to defend the interests of employees. Citizens should be able to organize themselves and defend their rights, to act with a view to public good. To facilitate this, the law concerning public gatherings and associations should be changed.[121]

In short, the character and composition of the core elite in Poland had a considerable impact on both the scope and the nature of resistance to party misrule in the latter half of the 1970s—resistance that ultimately culminated in the Solidarity movement to which ten million Poles belonged. Consequently, the emergence of this core elite from a new social class represents part of the answer to the question posed at the beginning of this chapter, namely: How did Solidarity mount such a powerful challenge to Leninism? The fact that this elite legitimated its resistance to the Party by using the language of rights, rights that were subsequently translated into a civic conception of citizenship in the context of the charismatic communities of the movement, constitutes the second part of the answer. In the following chapter, the extent to which Solidarity embraced a natural rights doctrine, and the extent to which this doctrine was given form and content in the charismatic communities of 1980–81, will be examined.

6 Solidarity's articulation of natural rights

In the process of resisting Communist Party rule, Polish dissidents had to determine a legitimate basis for their opposition. As we have seen in the cases of the American and French Revolutions, only on the basis of grounds considered legitimate will people risk their lives and livelihood in the struggle against an existing order. In the years after 1956, therefore, dissidents explicated and legitimated their activities with reference to various values as embodied, for example, by Polish national culture, or by Catholicism, or by democratic socialism. However, none of these approaches, developed largely in isolation from one another, provided the unifying appeal needed to legitimate a sustained, broadly based struggle. It was not until the language of rights came into usage in the 1970s that the potential for a more coherent value-rational basis for the legitimation of resistance emerged. With its universal appeal and applicability, the language of rights united dissidents of all inclinations and orientations, and provided them with the motivation and conviction that their newly discovered *common* cause was one worth sacrificing for.

Initially, however, dissident groups remained divided by the differing conceptions of rights they employed.[1] Until the mid-1970s, the general language of rights consisted of two separate strands: a focus on secular civil rights and a focus on sacred natural rights. Dissidents associated with the non-communist Left espoused the former interpretation of rights, while dissidents associated with the Church employed the latter interpretation. Under the auspices of the newly emerging core elite, these two strands were fused by the late 1970s to create, in Adam Michnik's words, "a community in humanist values"[2] that embraced workers and intellectuals, believers and non-believers, nationalists and cosmopolitans alike.

Ironically, this community in values represented a return to the linkage between natural rights and civil rights that Marx had so vehemently rejected. Only by restoring the natural rights of individuals to the notion of citizenship were dissidents able to infuse civil rights—rights that had been granted but divested of all content by the communist regime—with new meaning. In the context of communist Poland, citizenship, as a *meaningful* category of political membership, was thereby created on the basis of a natural rights doctrine articulated in the late twentieth century. This doctrine was subsequently given practical form and content in the charismatic communities forged under the banner of Solidarity.

In contrast to the Protestant roots of the American natural rights doctrine, and in contrast to the "enlightened" anticlerical secular roots of the French natural rights doctrine, the Polish doctrine was based on a synthesis of Catholic and socialist humanism. This chapter will, therefore, begin by documenting the evolution of this synthesis and the extent to which it resonated with the beliefs, needs and interests of large segments of Polish society. Ultimately, the Polish doctrine resulted in a substantive and collectively oriented interpretation of rights in which formal rights were linked to substantive rights, and individual rights were seen as inseparable from collective rights. Next, the question of how this interpretation was concretized in Solidarity's charismatic communities will be addressed. In the following chapter, the charismatic presentation of natural rights in Poland will be compared to the American and French Revolutions in order to lay the groundwork for a comparatively based analysis of the institutional consequences of Solidarity's ethos, both in the political and the economic realms.

THE NATURAL RIGHTS DOCTRINE

Based on a fusion of Catholic and socialist humanism, representatives of Solidarity's core elite articulated a new vision of public life that elevated man, as the ultimate bearer of rights and dignities, to the highest position in the political community. Clearly, this elevation of man stood in direct conflict with the elevation of the Party to the highest position in the Leninist polity. Solidarity's vision does not, however, represent a simple return to, or reiteration of, the natural rights doctrine of the eighteenth century. In many ways, Poland's dissidents circumvented the Enlightenment era by unconsciously replicating the traditions and the struggles of the humanists of the Italian Renaissance, who had elaborated a new vision of the centrality of mortal man. Based on a conception of human dignity derived from the study of rediscovered classical texts and philosophers, this new vision guided the efforts of Renaissance humanists to enhance man's this-worldly well-being.[3]

During the course of these efforts, the religiously based world view of the Middle Ages, in which man's other-worldly well-being was paramount, came into increasing conflict with the focus on man's earthly existence and dignity. Subsequently, Renaissance scholars struggled to find a common ground between the Christian traditions they had been raised with and the Greco-Roman traditions they were fascinated with. Renaissance humanists, such as Pico della Mirandola, ultimately achieved a synthesis of the two traditions by proclaiming that "man as the creator of himself," a concept derived from Stoicism, is based on the resemblance between man and God, a concept that is readily derived from Catholicism. Accordingly, the humanists firmly believed

> that no being can dignify himself: dignity is a quality with which one is *invested*; it must be conferred. For human dignity to exist, there must be a Master who can raise Man above the brute creation. If that Master is denied, then dignity for Man is unattainable.[4]

Given the nature of the time, when religious principles were no longer unquestioningly accepted, but were not yet criticized or rejected, it was essential for Renaissance humanists to find an "*Ausgleichsformel*" between the secular and sacred realms in order to validate their perception of man.[5]

Polish dissidents, as well, attempted to find a balance between "trust in man and trust in God"[6] in order to validate their elevation of man, and to unify their opposition to communism. The two traditions of opposition to Polish communism—democratic socialism and Catholicism—had for too long been hostile to one another, as well as to the Party. It became clear to dissidents, such as Adam Michnik, that if the secular principles of the former and the sacred principles of the latter tradition could somehow be reconciled, a stronger basis for opposition would emerge. Such an effort to bridge sacred and secular worlds was foreign to the anticlerical Enlightenment *philosophes*, nor did it form part of the intellectual agenda of the American revolutionaries. In the French case, any linkage between the Church and the polity was decisively rejected, while in the American case, a positive and mutually reinforcing relationship between the sacred and secular realms was considered natural and beyond the need for debate or reflection. The American colonists, many of whom were members of Protestant sects, unquestioningly believed in the sacred nature of divinely mandated rights—rights that were to be protected by secular authorities.

Yet in Poland, finding an *Ausgleichsformel* was crucial for the emergence of a unified opposition, and for the development of a rights doctrine capable of restoring the linkage between natural and civic rights that Marx had severed philosophically and Lenin had severed institutionally. By the late twentieth century, the natural rights doctrine that had animated the American and French Revolutions had been discredited and relativized to such an extent— not only by Marx but by liberals such as Bentham—that a new philosophical basis for the validation of natural rights had to be found.[7] Polish dissidents found this basis in the fusion of Catholic and socialist humanism.

Central to this fusion was a mutual recognition on the part of both secular and Catholic Poles of the need to proclaim and reclaim the dignity of man; a dignity which had been lost in the corrupt and alienating environment of Gierek's Poland. Again, given an analogous situation, the Polish focus on dignity resembles the efforts of fifteenth-century humanists to establish firmly the sacred dignity of mortal man as the guiding principle of secular life. The following quotations, although diverging in time and place, illustrate the extent to which dignity became the guiding principle of Solidarity:

> The ultimate goal of Solidarity is to create dignified conditions of life in an economically and politically sovereign Poland. By this we mean a life free from poverty, exploitation, fear and lies, in a democratically and legally organized society.[8]
>
> (Solidarity Congress, 1981)

> The 1980–81 events were a revolution for dignity, a celebration of the rights of the vertebrae, a permanent victory for the straightened spine. Whatever happens, one fact cannot be erased from the twentieth century history of this nation: that the downfall of the totalitarian communist order began here in Poland.[9]
>
> (Adam Michnik, 1988)

The concept of dignity is clearly central to an understanding of both the goals and the accomplishments of Solidarity. In large part, the impact of Solidarity is due to the presentation of a particular conception of citizenship based on the natural right of man to live in dignity. This conception, in conjunction with the charismatic communities of the movement, provided Poles with new principles of civic consciousness and conduct. Humanist values such as the God-given dignity of man served to reinfuse formal civic rights with a binding ethical or value-rational component. The value-rationality represented by a natural rights doctrine was thereby reintroduced into political life two centuries after the American and French Revolutions—with similarly consequential outcomes, but with a different philosophical basis.

In Michnik's terms, the struggle for dignity provided people with a new sense of not just the possible, but also the imperative. Once a spine has been straightened, it can no longer return to being stooped—rights must be asserted and claimed. For Poles, rights were accordingly derived from a humanistic conception of dignity, encompassing both a spiritual *and* a temporal dimension, as opposed to the contemporary Western experience in which human dignity is increasingly derived from rights—a legacy perhaps of the eighteenth-century natural rights doctrine and its residual power. According to Feinberg, for example:

> respect for persons (this is an intriguing idea) may simply be respect for their rights, so that there cannot be the one without the other; and what is called "human dignity" may simply be the recognizable capacity to assert claims. To respect a person then, or to think of him as possessed of human dignity, simply *is* to think of him as a potential maker of claims.[10]

As we shall see, this sober and despiritualized rendition of the dependent status of human dignity is very different from the transcendent status accorded to dignity by Solidarity.

In order to document the evolution and content of Solidarity's powerful and unique understanding of rights, the following section will draw on three key sources. First, the works of Adam Michnik, a leading proponent of socialist or secular humanism, and the works of Father Józef Tischner, a highly influential proponent of Catholic humanism, will be examined as exemplary manifestations of the philosophical or theoretical basis of the Polish doctrine. In the works of these two philosophers, one can see the evolving synthesis between the two traditions of humanism. Subsequently, the major Solidarity documents will be examined as the practical reflection of this philosophical synthesis.

Adam Michnik: secular humanist

> In searching for truth, or, to quote Leszek Kolakowski, "by living in dignity," opposition intellectuals are striving not so much for a better tomorrow as for a better today. Every act of defiance saves some degree of freedom, dignity and truth; saves values without which no people can exist. Every act of defiance helps us build the framework of democratic socialism, which should not be merely or primarily a legal institutional structure but a day-to-day community of free people.[11]
>
> (Adam Michnik, 1976)

The above quotation exemplifies Michnik's commitment to both democratic socialism and humanist values. Indeed, the two are seen as mutually reinforcing and interdependent. This seemingly natural synthesis is, however, the result of a lengthy personal and intellectual odyssey on Michnik's part. In this odyssey, the Polish philosopher Leszek Kolakowski played a pivotal role by redefining Marxist humanism in such a way as to render humanism and socialism compatible. By divesting Marxism of its rigid collectivism, egalitarianism and class basis, Kolakowski's work influenced an entire generation of young Polish Marxists, including Michnik and Kuroń, to think in new categories such as "human individuality," "ethical individualism," and, ultimately, human dignity.

Since Marxist humanism had been rooted in visions of collective emancipation and in egalitarian claims that "one man is as good as another,"[12] the Leninist polity was able systematically to violate the dignity of the individual and to vitiate the individual's moral responsibility and initiative. In the pursuit of the greatest end—human emancipation—all means, no matter how debilitating or morally questionable, could be justified. This relativization of morality, combined with the denigration of the individual, is decisively rejected by Kolakowski in his 1968 work *Toward a Marxist Humanism*, in which he presents an agenda of the Left not linked to class but to intellectual conviction. In other words, Kolakowski's aim is to universalize the Left by divesting Marxism of its militant and, ultimately, particularistic claim to represent one class.

Furthermore, by elevating the ethical and moral components of human individuality into the central attributes of a new Leftist humanism, Kolakowski places the individual, as opposed to a class or collectivity, at the center of this recasting of socialist humanism. In this context, Kolakowski presents a doctrine of individual responsibility:

> Thus we profess the doctrine of total responsibility of the individual for his deeds and of the amorality of the historical process. In the latter we avail ourselves of Hegel; in the former of Descartes. It was he who formulated the famous principle, whose consequences are not always visible at first glance, "there is not a soul so weak that it cannot, with good guidance, gain an absolute mastery over its passions." This means that we cannot explain away any of our actions on the grounds of emotion, passion, or the moral impotence to act differently, and that we have no right to transfer the responsibility for our conscious acts to any factor which determines our behavior; because in every instance we have the power to choose freely.[13]

In accordance with this doctrine, Kolakowski concludes with a call for ethical action based on his vision of principled, responsible individualism. Inspired by Stoicism, and in direct contrast to the moral relativism and determinism of Marxism–Leninism, Kolakowski maintains the primacy of free will in guiding ethical action. Given the individual "will snatched from destiny . . . man must situate his own behavior in the world of possible things, not that of necessary things."[14] Such principled action must, however, be based on certain criteria for determining moral choice and responsibility. Here Kolakowski advocates an "humanistic interpretation of values,"[15] rather than Marxist determinism, as the basis for moral judgment. In doing so, he challenges the unquestioning loyalty and obedience demanded of the party cadres for the "good of the cause." Indeed, Kolakowski is adamant that the individual's moral responsibility cannot be attenuated by the claims of a cause or movement:

> Real social involvement is moral involvement. For although a great political movement that seeks to shape the world in its own image is called to life by the world's needs, and though its fundamental direction is determined by the development of social relations, nevertheless each individual's participation in any specific form of political life is a moral act for which that individual is wholly responsible.[16]

Kolakowski's recasting of socialist humanism in terms of ethical individualism, as opposed to egalitarian collectivism, provided the philosophical background for Michnik's own reappraisal of Marxism. This reappraisal led to the articulation of a program of principled action based on the defense of human dignity. For Michnik, dignity could be reclaimed and protected through the non-violent, self-organization of society into autonomous institutions. Perhaps due to Kolakowski's call for ethical action and individual responsibility, Michnik's work is not that of a purely abstract thinker.

Instead, his writings are infused with the need to determine the ethical and practical grounds for individual and collective action.

Michnik himself came of age in a household that believed deeply in Marxism. Indeed, Michnik ascribes his critical stance toward the Communist government to his upbringing:

> In Poland people feared the communists. I was not afraid because I considered this to be my organization. And since it was mine, I had nothing to fear. I was not afraid to criticize the government, because it was my government, and if it did something wrong then it was up to me to speak critically. It didn't occur to me that there were people in Poland who thought a lot worse about the government, but were afraid to say anything. My courage was the product of a lack of imagination.[17]

In this process of critical engagement, Michnik, ultimately, came to the conclusion that "Communism is above all antihumanitarian, aimed at the destruction of the human personality."[18] Human dignity, the most fundamental of humanist values, was consistently violated and denigrated under this system of government. Acting on this realization soon brought Michnik into conflict with party authorities as his conduct reflected his convictions. Yet, even in the face of reprisals and imprisonment, Michnik was unwilling to give up his "natural right to dignity." As Michnik wrote later in one of his *Letters From Prison*:

> Impotence in the face of armed evil is probably the worst of human humiliations. When six hulks pin you to the ground, you are helpless. But you do not want to give up your natural right to dignity: you are not going to reach any agreements with the ruffians, you are not going to make any commitments . . . your ordinary instinct for self-preservation and your basic sense of human dignity will make you say NO.[19]

Michnik subsequently concluded that "to forsake your dignity is not a price worth paying to have the prison gates opened for you."[20] Based on these principles, Michnik spent a considerable amount of time in prison:

> My personal experience is the experience of a man . . . who was imprisoned for the first time twenty-five years ago in March 1965, who participated in the 1968 student uprising in protest against the anti-intellectual and anti-Semitic hue-and-cry organized by the Communist bureaucracy in Poland, who stubbornly wanted to be part of the independent community, and who saw that this community was being systematically disrupted by the force of police crackdowns.[21]

From the very beginning of his public career, Michnik linked the destruction of the human personality to the disruption of independent communities. Having divested himself of the rigid principles of Marxist collectivism, Michnik still believed that the fate of the individual and the fate of the community could not be considered in isolation. In searching for a way to release both the individual and the community from degradation, for a way to defend human dignity, Michnik turned to the works of another Polish socialist, Edward Abramowski (1868–1918). According to Michnik, Abramowski was a philosopher who, "in the name of humanist values . . . wanted to overcome the merciless atmosphere of his time."[22] Abramowski's strategy for overcoming "political practices that degraded man to the role of an unthinking creature" was based on the vision of a "movement of social liberation"[23] that would take the shape of grass-roots cooperatives formed independently of state structures. In these cooperatives, both individual self-determination and social self-determination would be fostered since "new forms of management, a new work ethic, new moral values"[24] would allow people to liberate themselves from the "apparatus of coercion." In Michnik's view, Abramowski "trusted the good in the human condition, he trusted the sense of humanist values, he trusted the potential of man's labor, he trusted friendship." What man could not accomplish in isolation, he could accomplish through the "ties of friendship."[25]

The idea of individuals cooperating in the formation of voluntary associations independent of the state was to become pivotal in Michnik's thinking. If the government would not defend human dignity, society would have to defend itself through autonomous self-organization initiatives. In his highly influential 1976 article, "A new evolutionism," Michnik maintains that "an expansion of civil liberties and human rights is the only course East European dissidents can take."[26] Such liberties and rights can, however, only be protected and expanded in the context of independent organizations, "addressed to an independent public."[27] Following Abramowski, Michnik proposes a break with the policies of revisionism that were addressed to those in power. Instead, the state and the Party should be pressured "from below" as people organize to protect themselves. In this program of ethical conduct, Michnik envisions an emphasis on social solidarity replacing an "acceptance of the government as the basic point of reference" for oppositional activities.[28]

The main pillar of this social solidarity is, in Michnik's opinion, the working class. Indeed, he maintains that "pressure from the working classes is a necessary condition for the evolution of public life toward a democracy."[29] Again, although Michnik has divested himself of the rigid Marxist view of the absolute centrality of the working class, he still places this class at the heart of his program of evolutionary resistance, since it is the social group most feared by the power elite. In accordance with this insight, Michnik hopes for a convergence between the intellectual opposition, striving to "form an independent public opinion with nonconformist attitudes,"[30] and the activities of the working class.

This hope became a reality with the founding of KOR (Committee for Workers' Defense) in the same year. Michnik himself took part in the founding of this independent organization in which intellectuals and workers would break through the "accursed barrier of isolation" that had separated them in the past. As Michnik recalls, KOR was

> formed on the initiative of a dozen or so people of different ideological leanings, different traditions, different backgrounds, and different generations, who shared the desire to defend the persecuted workers, to defend the people who, in June 1976, went out into the streets of Radom and Ursus to demonstrate their disapproval of the social policy of the Communist bureaucracy.[31]

Beyond the defense of workers, KOR was united by the desire to "wage a war for human dignity without hatred."[32] In this war without hatred, violence was rejected as morally inappropriate. This rejection was based on the awareness that "there are causes for which it is worth suffering and giving one's life, but there are no causes for which it is permissible to cause suffering and to kill."[33] Accordingly, KOR "wanted to prove that it is possible to challenge force and deception, to reject force, consciously choosing conflict without force, and to reject deceit by speaking the truth."[34]

In the effort to counter force with ethical action and to counter lies with the truth, the Catholic Church was regarded as a model by KOR. As Michnik attests, "the KOR campaign as a whole had a model in Polish civic life: the Catholic Church."[35] Overall, Michnik ascribes great significance to the role of the Catholic Church in "defending the civil liberties of the working people, and particularly their right to strike and to form independent labor unions."[36] As the Church evolved into a "more broadly antitotalitarian stance," Polish bishops began "defending the right to truth and standing up for human freedom and dignity."[37] Given this evolution, Michnik ultimately considers the Church to be "the most important institution in Poland because it teaches all of us that we may bow only before God."[38] On the basis of this realization, Michnik was at the forefront of efforts to effect a reconciliation between the secular intellectuals of the Left and the Church.

In his book, *The Church and the Left*, written in 1975–76, Michnik reexamines "the complex relationship between the Catholic Church and the secular intelligentsia."[39] By documenting the extent of the Polish Church's commitment to humanist values, and its persistent resistance to totalitarian rule, Michnik prepares the ground for a common defense of human dignity. As Michnik notes, "European humanism, after all, arose from the seed of Christian morality."[40] In this context, he goes on to quote Stefan Kisielewski, a leading Polish journalist, who states that:

> Although much of the religious ritual and dogma is alien to many secular activists, the core of Christian morality contained in the Ten Commandments is and will remain the most brilliant and most concise expression of the moral achievements of the European citizen.[41]

Michnik's vision of a society defending humanist values through the self-organization of independent institutions is, therefore, predicated on the social solidarity made possible by bridging the barriers between workers and intellectuals, and between secular and religious humanists. In Michnik's opinion, these barriers could only be overcome through "a uniquely Polish synthesis of Christian and democratic ideas."[42] A doctrine of natural rights based on humanism provided such a synthesis. In a 1989 article, Michnik asked himself

> whether there was some kind of religious background to this antitotalitarian struggle in which I had the good fortune to be a participant. And I answer yes, there was such a background. We are all witnesses to something that I would call a religious renaissance. This is not simply an increase in the power of the Church and a mass return to religious practice. . . . It is simply a collective return to issues of transcendence . . . I personally think that . . . people like Andrei Sakharov (who was not at all a believer) lived and acted as if they were bathed in the light of religious reflection and the struggle for fidelity to natural law. It was as if God were watching over them continuously from on high, as if they were aware of the presence of God. We might say that the experience of these people involved in the antitotalitarian opposition was of an ineluctably transcendent nature.[43]

This quotation makes clear the extent to which sacred and secular principles became fused in Michnik's version of an "*Ausgleichsformel*" between the Church and the Left. By moving from an understanding of human dignity grounded in socialist humanism to an understanding of human dignity that embraced both secular *and* sacred realms, Michnik helped to create a powerful fusion of the two traditions. For Michnik, the "revolution of dignity" achieved by Solidarity itself was a reflection of the power of transcendence generated by this fusion. In his opinion, Solidarity was able to transcend the "psychology of captivity," of apathy and of isolation in order to give people "a taste of freedom; they forged their solidarity and discovered their strength; they again felt themselves to be a civic and national community."[44] We thereby come full circle from the 1976 article in which Michnik proposed "living in dignity" as the way to attain a "community of free people" to the "revolution of dignity" achieved by Solidarity in 1980–81.

Józef Tischner: Catholic humanist

> The concept of human dignity defies simple definition. Human dignity is a value that can be seen and felt but one about which it is difficult to speak. One can, however, turn attention toward this value by pointing out its context. The context of the concept of human dignity is human rights. Human dignity expresses itself through the rights afforded to human beings.[45]
>
> (Józef Tischner, 1980)

While this linkage between dignity and rights is likely to appear self-evident and natural to a secular audience, it is a remarkable indicator of the intellectual journey taken by the Catholic Church in general, and the Polish Church in particular, during the latter half of the twentieth century. Paralleling Michnik's journey from rigid Marxism to socialist humanism to an acknowledgment of the sacred, the Polish Church moved from rigid "jeremiads against 'Godless Ones' " to Catholic humanism to an acknowledgment of secular principles as embodied in rights, both human and civic. In the course of this evolution, the Church stepped away from its primary preoccupation with man's immortal soul and his other-worldly salvation to embrace a concern for man's this-worldly dignity and conditions of life. Although Tischner himself was critical of Michnik's secular "Leftism," his work nonetheless reflects this parallel philosophical evolution and, therefore, is exemplary of the path taken by the Polish Church.

The fundamental component in the progression toward humanism, whether it be of the Catholic or socialist variant, would appear to be a respect for human individuality. Just as Kolakowski reclaims the individual from the Marxist collective, so too does Tischner reclaim the individual from the community of believers:

> Not everything can be organized. A human being must have some area of freedom and liberty. The concept of humanity is also the personal and spontaneous creation of an individual. The richness of a person is expressed through freedom, a richness that should not be limited by any assigned function. Human beings are the artists of their own lives and shape them according to their own perceptions of happiness and honor.[46]

Indeed, Tischner defines human dignity itself as the product of conscience, which, by definition, is an individual attribute.

In a 1980 sermon, Tischner expands upon this definition:

> Today we are living through unusual times. People are discarding their masks; they are emerging from their hiding places and showing their true faces. From under the dust and out of oblivion their consciences are emerging. Today we are as we truly are. Believers are believers, doubters are doubters, and non-believers are non-believers. There is no point in assuming someone else's role. Everyone wants to be called by his or her own name. What we are living through is not only a social or economic event but one that touches us all personally. The problem impinges upon human dignity, human dignity that is based on the conscience of human beings. The deepest solidarity is solidarity of consciences.[47]

The final sentence of this passage returns us to the concept of Christian community, but from a different perspective, that of a community based on the solidarity of human beings aware of their individual consciences; aware, therefore, of their individuality as well as of their commonality. As Tischner explains in the same sermon:

> What does it mean to be in solidarity? It means to carry the burden of another person. No one is an island all alone. We are bound to each other even if we do not know it. The landscape binds us, flesh and blood bind us, work and speech bind us. However, we are not always conscious of these bonds. When solidarity is born, this consciousness is awakened, and then speech and word appear—and at that point something that was hidden becomes manifest. All our bonds become visible. . . . Then the burden of one's fellow human often becomes greater than one's own. In this way the disciple of Christ fulfills His law.[48]

While the emphasis here is on the commonalities binding human beings, Tischner's understanding of conscience is rooted in the individual's ability to reason: "After a person has seen the world of values that surround him, he himself is capable of formulating prohibitions and directives; he himself is able to counsel himself; and when the need arises, he is also able to evaluate himself."[49] Therefore, the ethical imperative that Tischner puts forward, of determining and acting on one's conscience, is similar to Kolakowski's understanding of individual responsibility and the exercise of free will. As Tischner states, "conscience constitutes an independent reality within an individual, something like the mind and the will. We can exercise our will and mind, or we can neglect to exercise them. Likewise, we can listen to our conscience, stifle it, or even deny it."[50] If enough individuals were to exercise mind, will and conscience, this would, in Tischner's opinion, lead to a solidarity of consciences. This solidarity would ultimately serve to create a "natural bond of human beings with those who suffer" needlessly.[51]

Tischner's recasting of the individual and the individual's relationship to the community leads to a conclusion similar to Michnik's. On philosophical grounds, both men agree that the fate of the individual and the fate of the community cannot be considered in isolation. While human individuality must be respected as the foundation of human dignity, only on the basis of collective solidarity can dignity be defended against the infliction of needless pain and suffering by the state. Consequently, both Michnik and Tischner advocate collectively based action such as the self-organization of society or strikes in order to reclaim human dignity. According to Tischner:

> People who want to do something good become members of a spontaneously formed communion of people of goodwill. They have love in their hearts for those for whom they work. They feel the taste of courage on their lips. . . . In growing to the point of striking, they grow to their full humanity. Participation in *such* a strike becomes a moral act, that is, an act dictated by the order of the ethics of work. Humanity rises from the Fall and regains a human horizon and human dignity.[52]

Overall, Tischner ascribes a similar significance to the working class as does Michnik. However, while Michnik values the strategic position of the workers in the social order, Tischner is, above all, concerned with the "moral exploitation of work."[53] In his opinion, "a strike is a protest against the moral exploitation of work," the consciousness of which "reaches its peak at the moment when working people discover that they work senselessly."[54] To safeguard against such exploitation and the resulting diminishment of dignity, protest actions must be sanctioned. For "senseless work, regardless of its form, strikes at the sense of dignity of the working person. It is a form of betrayal."[55] However, the means of protest must "not be contrary to conscience."[56] The means must be commensurate with human dignity:

> Human dignity does not imply pride and empty ambition. One who thinks so does not understand human beings. Since treachery has occurred, fidelity must follow. Since humiliation has been inflicted, respect must ensue. Since there was degradation, equality must come.[57]

Echoing Michnik, Tischner supports protest actions, such as strikes, only within the context of non-violence and a moral transcendence of existing conditions.

Tischner goes beyond Michnik, however, in stressing the "right to meaningful work" as a critical goal of the "mutiny of conscience against the moral exploitation of work." In Tischner's work, the solidarity of consciences, and the solidarity of work complement one another, are integral to one another, as both are aspects of human dignity. While conscience is a manifestation of spiritual dignity, work is the manifestation of physical dignity. Accordingly, Tischner points out that "work is above all an agreement. . . . A spirit of solidarity is the spirit of work. Human solidarity is not a supplement to work but a flower produced by the wisdom of work."[58] Given the centrality of dignity, Tischner maintains that "human dignity outlines the ethical perspectives of human development. It speaks of the need for a social system that would provide the possibility for human development starting from within. What is external should take its beginning from what is internal."[59] A social system should, therefore, be devised that can guarantee both the freedom of conscience and the right to meaningful work. For Tischner, an "ethical democracy" based on freedom, rationality and human dignity would represent such a system.

Individual freedom is central to the idea of democracy in Tischner's opinion. "An idea is democratic when it delineates for the largest number of people the greatest possible sphere of individual freedom and responsibility, simply, when it enables everyone to be himself in his life."[60] In conjunction with freedom, "an idea is democratic to the degree . . . that it determines the need to realize values indispensable for the life and survival of people."[61] These values are best realized in a rational social order in which there is "harmony between social functions and their bearers."[62] In other words, a social order should function rationally so that "in exchange for carrying out a function useful to others, one receives from others the means to satisfy one's own needs."[63] Clearly, both freedom and rationality were violated in Gierek's Poland.

Beyond the immediate circumstances creating a barrier to the implementation of an ethical democracy, Tischner recognizes an additional barrier. Namely, "rationality and freedom are opposites. The more there is freedom, the less things can be predicted. The more there is rationality, the more things are regulated a priori."[64] In order to join these two opposites into a synthesis capable of gaining the support of the majority, a third element is needed—the idea of human dignity. Accordingly, "the idea of dignity is the background for all concrete hopes. Even in this call for bread, there is a call for the recognition of dignity."[65] The demand for dignity, in both its spiritual and physical forms, thereby becomes the central idea linking individual freedom and socioeconomic rationality in Tischner's ethical system of democracy.

In the pursuit of such a system, Tischner is willing to re-evaluate the relationship between the Church and its traditional foe, socialism. To the extent that the same ethical commitment to human dignity is shared by members of both communities, a dialogue can ensue. As Tischner points out, "dialogue is possible only when there is a common grammar. Ethics are the grammar of relationships between people, and their principle, human dignity."[66] Based on the insight that both Christianity and socialism "want to make people happy," Tischner concludes that:

> One must say that there is a profound difference [between the two], but there is no contradiction. What does it mean to say that there is no contradiction? It means we are dealing, not with one ethos, but with two different ones—however, it is not that one proclaims "evil" what the other calls "good." One should not confuse the difference between something ethical and something unethical with the difference between something ethical in one way and something ethical in another way. Not every difference must be a contradiction.[67]

Tischner goes on to distinguish between open and closed socialism. While the latter refuses to recognize the legitimate claims of the workers, the former is open to the needs and interests of working people. It follows from this that Tischner, while not directly advocating dialogue, would not be averse to the possibility of communication and cooperation. Although this reappraisal of socialism is by no means as fargoing as Michnik's positive reassessment of the Church, it does pave the way for a coming together of dissidents from formerly distinct and separate circles on the basis of a shared adherence to the principle of human dignity.

This adherence to a shared principle is especially evident in the assessments Michnik and Tischner make of Pope John Paul II's impact on Poland. Both men emphasize that the Pope's message of dignity and his vision for Poland contain universal truths that "everyone can accept" whether believer or non-believer. As Tischner states:

> Choosing the fatherland today, we also choose this point of view [the

> Pope's] on Poland. It does not mean that from now on everyone in Poland should be Catholic—No! This is not the issue. Faith is a grace, whereas freedom is a basic human right. The issue is that in this pope there is something that everyone can accept.[68]

Michnik echoes this sentiment in a 1979 essay on the Pope's visit entitled "A Lesson in Dignity":

> Let me just say that when I listened to John Paul II's homily in Cracow, I had a strange feeling. When the Pope asked the faithful Catholics "never to forsake Him," he was also addressing me: a pagan.[69]

Indeed, Michnik justifies his reconstruction of the Pope's ideas by indicating that his efforts are undertaken "with the conviction that Pope John Paul II spoke to all of us and to each one of us individually. To me, too. So I will try to relate what I heard, what I understood, and what I am applying to myself."[70] As Michnik understands the Pope, he did not simply ask his listeners to choose between Catholicism and atheism. Instead, the Pope posed a more general question. In Michnik's words:

> "What are you in favor of?" we were all asked. "Of conformist consent to totalitarian coercion or of the inviolable right in God's and man's order of things for human beings to live in freedom and dignity?" An overwhelming majority of Poles chose the latter.[71]

Given the centrality of the fight for freedom and dignity, and the undeniable contributions of Christianity to the Polish understanding of these values, Michnik concludes with a final question he poses to himself and to his fellow non-believers:

> Can one reject Christ and all that he has contributed to mankind's history? Of course one can. Man is free. Man . . . can say no to Christ. But the fundamental question then is this: Is one allowed to? And "allowed to" in the name of what? What argument of reason, what value of will and of the heart can one use with oneself and with those one is close to, with one's fellow-Poles, and with the nation . . . to say no to all that which we have been living for a thousand years? Therefore: Am I allowed to reject this culture based on Christian values, on faith, love and hope?[72]

In the wake of the Pope's visit, Michnik is clearly moved to affirm his acceptance of Christian culture, especially in light of the tolerance and inclusiveness emphasized by the Pope.

In short, both Tischner and Michnik heard the same truths proclaimed in the Pope's homilies. Whatever else the Pope might have said, the essential truths he proclaimed, as understood by Tischner and Michnik, were dignity, freedom, tolerance and inclusiveness. These very similar assessments of the Pope's words are a reflection of the extent to which the evolving synthesis of

Catholic and socialist humanism had, by the late 1970s, crystallized into a coherent ethos.

This ethos, or natural rights doctrine, was comprised of three critical elements: the primacy of the natural right of all human beings to live in both spiritual and physical dignity; the ancillary civil rights of people to associate freely and to organize and represent themselves in independent organizations in defense of human dignity; and the corresponding duty of such organizations to use only means commensurate with human dignity. Essentially, organizations must be devoted to non-violence, and they must be democratic in Tischner's sense of allowing participants the "greatest possible sphere of individual freedom and responsibility." The extent to which this duty was acknowledged and supported by tactical considerations is evident in the following statement issued by KOR in July 1980:

> We also appeal to workers throughout Poland and warn them against those forms of protest which may be utilized by the authorities to provoke riots. The most effective but also the safest form, from the point of view of the nation, of looking after the interests of workers and of society as a whole, is to organize ourselves at work places, to elect democratically independent workers' representatives who will formulate demands on behalf of the workers, who will conduct talks with the authorities and lead the workers in a responsible, but also a determined way.[73]

In general, the Solidarity statements and documents of 1980–81 reflect the understanding of rights presented by the above synthesis. The very demand for "free trade unions independent of the Party and employers," which was at the heart of the August strikes along the Baltic coast, represents an effort to implement the right to organize in defense of human dignity. Underlying this demand, however, is a clear commitment to the broader ethical and moral context of the pursuit of the natural right to dignity and freedom. The strikers themselves made this point in the following statement issued in August 1980:

> Our strike enjoys the support and sympathy of all the country and of other countries in the world, because our 21 demands are deeply humanitarian. The strikers and society at large are well aware of this and it is a source of our strength. The workers are not fighting for a mere pittance for themselves but "for justice for the whole nation." We have to oppose the local authorities' attempts to disrupt the unity of our strike movement. We are living up to the words: "Man is born free."[74]

The broader context of the strike was also clear to observers, such as KIK (Clubs of Catholic Intelligentsia), who issued statements in support of the strikers:

> Once again it became clear that it is impossible to rule the Polish nation without listening to its voice. With determination and maturity,

> Polish workers are fighting for the right to a better and more dignified life.[75]

As an anonymous verse, circulated in the main hall of the Gdańsk strike, adds:

> Put back our words to what they mean,
> Words which grew empty and obscene,
> So we can live with dignity
> And work in solidarity.[76]

Subsequently, in the founding documents of the Independent Labor Union, Solidarity, the linkage between the right to representation and the right to live in dignity is reiterated:

> As it fights for the interests of its members, the union strives at the same time for the improvement of the working, pay, and living conditions of all working people. Our proposed activity is motivated by our firm belief that the effective defense of workers' rights and the authentic representation of the interests of different professional groups is essential to the well-being of the country, society as a whole, and each individual inhabitant.[77]

The Solidarity Statute goes on to state clearly that "the purposes of the Union are to protect the jobs, dignity, and interests of workers."[78] In early 1981, Solidarity's Center for Social and Labor Tasks issued a comprehensive document outlining the Union's general aims and principles in which the same theme is amplified:

> We were born of the protest against wrongs, humiliation and injustice. We are an independent, self-governing labour union of the working people from all regions and all trades. We defend the rights, dignity and interests of the entire labour world.
>
> Defending the working people, which is our basic labour union job, is based on the principle of observing social justice. . . . We base social justice on the principle of the natural dignity of the person of man, of the working man and of his toil. It is our wish that the principle of man's dignity permeates everything about our union and serves as the foundation on which relations in the new society are built.[79]

Beyond an adherence to the abstract principle of human dignity, the document goes on to present a more concrete catalogue of the issues and reforms that need to be addressed in order to ensure the conditions of dignity. What emerges from this catalogue is a collectively and substantively oriented program of Solidarity's aims. For example, the document goes on to state that "the principle of social justice and of man's dignity makes it obvious that in their most essential nature all people are equal. That is why we will seek social equality."[80] From the essential equality of men as individuals endowed with dignity, Solidarity derived a mandate to secure the collective well-being of society at large. In accordance with Michnik's and Tischner's views that the individual cannot be considered in isolation from the community, an emphasis on unity and solidarity prevailed from the first days of the August strikes. As with the commitment to non-violence, the belief that "only in unity can we find strength" had both a moral and a tactical dimension. In regard to the latter, KOR issued the following advice in July 1980:

> Workers must be made aware that only common action can bring positive results. It is most important to prevent the authorities from victimizing the strikers and the people who are, or are thought by the authorities to be, the leaders of the workers' protest.[81]

The focus on collective solidarity went beyond simple tactical concerns, however, to become a moral imperative. Based on the notion that the "universal bond of solidarity imparts a special stamp upon our union," union members were required to act "in keeping with the principle of solidarity."[82] Specifically, the Solidarity Statute lists "to cooperate in helping to create real community feeling among members of work teams" as one of the duties of a union member.[83] As the 1981 document concludes:

> The idea of uniting working people imparts great importance to the qualities produced by common efforts. Those qualities are represented by Solidarity—a term that we have adopted as the name of our labour union—and by good fellowship and the ability to make sacrifices and to do everything for the labour union community and for broader social interests. The idea of the working people's brotherhood in their common front against exploitation, no matter what slogans are used to disguise such exploitations, should also be this sort of virtue.[84]

In regard to political life, as well, there is an emphasis on uniting citizens into a community. For example, the demand for a return to legality is simultaneously a demand for the restoration of a general "will of society":

> We consider it a matter of fundamental importance to restore full legality to relations between the authorities on the one hand, and the citizen on the other, in order to enhance self-government and openness in public life. . . . Legality means that the law should express the interests and will of society and should, by its precepts, bind together authority and the citizen. Nobody must stand above or beyond the law. . . . All should be equal before the law. The law should be one and offer justice to everybody, irrespective of position in society and the state.[85]

The language of "binding together authority and citizen" clearly indicates a concern with the creation of a community united on the basis of legal and social equality.

Consequently, in the pursuit of collective well-being and social equality as derived from the natural right to live in dignity, the document goes beyond the demand for formal equality before the law, to support a substantive leveling of the conditions of life and work for all Poles. Those at the top of the social hierarchy, specifically the nomenklatura, were to lose their privileges, while those at the bottom were to receive more in the form of a social minimum. As the authors explain, "meeting the social minimum means satisfying not only elementary needs in food, clothing and housing, but also all those social and cultural needs that make it possible to lead a dignified life in order to develop one's personality."[86] The union itself was to "check both the level of the minimum and the standards for fixing it as well as the way the state implements the programme for ensuring the social minimum for all citizens."[87] Even the "universal right to work" is maintained, albeit with the recognition that economic restructuring is likely to necessitate some unemployment. In this event, "vocational retraining programmes financed by the state and endorsed and supervised by the union" are to be put into effect.[88] It is evident that this Solidarity program of practical reforms was intended to establish and maintain the minimum conditions for a life of dignity for all citizens. Since individuals alone cannot ensure these conditions, the substantive rights to meaningful and safe work, and to state-funded, minimum levels of subsistence, represent a collective responsibility of the community. The community, as represented by Solidarity, hereby takes on the crucial task of administering and allocating public resources according to these rights and principles.

Solidarity subsequently determined that worker self-management in the enterprises and community self-government represented the most democratic and efficient means of administration and allocation. During 1981, culminating in the first Solidarity Congress's program in October, the concept of the self-governing republic emerged as the primary focus of a reform agenda that would ensure citizens and workers maximum levels of participation in public life, and control over public resources. Indeed, in Solidarity's vision of a reformed political community, social participation is a critical component of democracy:

> Only under a truly democratic system will we be able effectively to fight for our labour union and workers' interests. Only under such a system will it be possible to fulfill the principle of genuine participation by the working people in the country's social and public life. That is why we will seek to expand the forms of social participation in public decision-making and in reviewing what the authorities do.[89]

This understanding of democracy is reiterated in the introduction to the October program:

> We regard democracy as a principle that must not be desisted from. Democracy must not be rule exercised by groups placing themselves above society and claiming the right to determine the needs and to represent the

> interests of society. Society must be able to speak with its full voice, to express various social and political opinions; it must be able to organize in such a way as to guarantee a fair share in the material and spiritual achievements of the nation for all, as well as to liberate all the nation's possibilities and creative forces. We aspire for the real socialization of the administration and management system. For this reason our objective is a self-governing Poland.[90]

The program goes on to clarify that democratic self-government is based on participation and representation at two levels—the workplace and the government. First, "genuine self-management of employees will be the basis of the self-governing republic."[91] In order to prevent the "unceasing interference by party elements in the functioning of enterprises," the program maintains that only the creation of self-management groups would "make the workforces true masters of enterprises."[92] Second, both local and central government were to be brought under the control of self-governing bodies that were to be freely elected and fiscally independent. Whether in the local People's Councils or in the national Sejm, freely elected representatives were to exercise administrative oversight and to make policy decisions independently of the Party. Essentially, this program for a self-governing republic is based on the natural rights doctrine that animated Solidarity's struggles. As postulated by the doctrine, independent organizations are critical for the defense of dignity; for the representation of social interests, and for the social participation that will guarantee the implementation of reforms. Within these organizations, the individual, acting in concert with others, becomes part of a powerful new community bound by a common desire to overcome needless suffering. The republic, therefore, should be comprised of a plurality of such organizations:

> Pluralism of views and social, political and cultural pluralism should be the foundation of democracy in the self-governing republic. Public life in Poland requires profound and comprehensive reforms which should result in a permanent introduction of the principles of self-government, democracy and pluralism. This is why we will seek both to transform the structure of the state and to create and support independent and self-governing institutions in all spheres of social life. Only such a direction of changes will ensure the agreement of the organization of public life with the needs of the human being, society's ambitions and the Poles' national aspirations. These changes are also necessary to overcome the economic crisis. We regard pluralism, democratization of the state and the opportunity to make full use of constitutional freedoms as the basic guarantee that the working people's toil and sacrifices will not be once again wasted.[93]

In short, citizenship in this republic was to be protected and defined by participation in such organizations. Only by acting collectively, within organizations, can individuals, in relative safety, exercise the greatest degree of civic "freedom and responsibility." Aside from the protection offered by collective action, participation itself acquired the character of a moral imperative since only the collectivity of citizens, as represented in these organizations, could ensure the substantive conditions for the dignified existence of all individuals. Individuals, acting in isolation, could simply not achieve what the community, acting in solidarity, could. The rights and duties of individual citizens were thereby dependent on the collective defense of civic freedoms and responsibilities.

Overall, a formal understanding of rights as embodied by the enactment of legal safeguards for individual rights and liberties is secondary in significance. While formal laws and procedures are not neglected, as in Solidarity's October program, for example: "the system must guarantee basic civil freedoms and respect the principles of equality before the law as far as all citizens and all public institutions are concerned,"[94] there is an overriding concern with establishing both the formal *and* substantive conditions of equality. By exercising social control, via independent organizations, over all aspects of public life (including the judicial system), Solidarity hoped to assure the appropriate substantive outcomes, as well as the appropriate formal means.

Consequently, given the centrality of "independent and self-governing institutions," participation in these institutions represented more than simple reform activism or protest. In a larger, symbolic sense, participants were rediscovering and reclaiming human dignity itself. In Tischner's words, "humanity rises from the Fall and regains a human horizon and human dignity" on the basis of participation in a "communion of people of goodwill."[95] In this context, "communion" and the God-given dignity of man are greater components of citizenship than the purely legal aspects of one's status as citizen. Therefore, although Solidarity's vision of citizenship is civic in orientation, since it is based on an inclusive definition of the rights to which all individuals are entitled (e.g. all human beings have the right to live in dignity), it goes beyond a narrow concern with man's rights as citizen to encompass man's rights in all dimensions—as worker, as consumer, as believer, as student, and so on. Dignity, after all, cannot be limited to any one sphere of existence.

This understanding of citizenship, grounded in the natural right of human beings to live in dignity, clearly resonated throughout Polish society. As is well known, Solidarity ultimately had ten million members. Given this all-encompassing vision of rights and membership (even Communist Party members could join), Solidarity must be viewed as more than a trade union bent on protecting the rights of workers alone. Although Solidarity did function as a trade union in its daily activities, the universal nature of its mission and the multiplicity of organizations and organizational forms that comprised Solidarity rendered it the most powerful social movement in the history of post-World War II Poland and, one might add, of Eastern Europe in general. According to Bogdan Borusewicz, a longtime Solidarity activist, even today Solidarity still manifests a dual character:

> Solidarity is not just a trade union, it is a movement which embodies values that are more general, democratic, rejecting xenophobia and nationalism. Within Solidarity there is an ongoing struggle with those who want to get rid of values for the sake of efficiency.[96]

The reasons for the broad social resonance that further facilitated Solidarity's dual nature as both trade union and social movement are twofold. First, the articulation of a natural rights doctrine based on a synthesis of Catholic and socialist humanism had a strong affinity with the historical, philosophical and religious traditions associated with resistance, democracy and social responsibility. Second, this doctrine addressed the needs and interests of large segments of the Polish population. The continuity between past and present traditions is stressed in the Solidarity documents themselves:

> The nation's best traditions, Christianity's ethical principles, democracy's political mandate and socialist social thought. These are the four main sources of our inspiration. We are deeply attached to the heritage of Poland's whole culture, which is merged with European culture and has strong links with Catholicism but which contains various religious and philosophical traditions. The ties with the generations of Poles who fought for national freedom and social justice and who handed over to us traditions of tolerance, brotherhood and civil responsibility for the republic and of equality before the law are alive in us. That is why there is room among us for everyone regardless of his world outlook, nationality, or political convictions.[97]

Beyond this broad context, a specific point of continuity is represented by the philosophical tradition of humanism. Historically, humanism has deep roots in Polish culture, dating back to the sixteenth century. Miłosz, for example, in his *History of Polish Literature*, documents the extent to which Erasmus was venerated in Poland:

> Erasmus of Rotterdam was regarded throughout Europe of the sixteenth century as the fountainhead of all wisdom. In Polish intellectual circles his name was surrounded by genuine veneration. . . . The Polish king, Sigismund I, when writing to Erasmus used to treat him as a kind of monarch. Polish humanists addressed him as "the only adornment of our age, . . . the prince of humanities and of ancient, purest theology." One of them says in his letter, "Oh would that I could kiss not only that hand, but also that head which has contrived so much, that heart which has conceived works that have spread your glory all over the earth and over this Poland, our dear country."[98]

Erasmus is perhaps best known for his advocacy of "tolerance and accommodation in the face of extremism and deep division."[99] In the pursuit of the "common good," he counseled his contemporaries to set aside petty vices and sterile disputes. The following examples from Erasmus' writings are typical in this respect:

> How much more Christian it would be to put aside all conflict and bring forward with good spirit whatever is of advantage for the common good, learning what you do not know without pride and teaching what you do know without jealousy.[100]

> But in every kind of life let this be the common endeavor of all, that we strive, each according to his own ability, toward that target, which is Christ, set up before us all; and let us exhort and also aid one another toward this goal, neither envying those who hasten on before us in this race nor disdaining the weak who are not yet able to overtake us.[101]

In the sixteenth century, Polish elites did more than pay lip service to the ideals articulated by Erasmus, as Poland was, at that time, considered a country of remarkable religious tolerance anchored in law (the Polish law "*de pace inter dissidentes*" was enacted in 1573); a tolerance that was rooted in the humanist "respect for the dignity of the human person." As Walicki illustrates:

> This attitude (of respect) found beautiful expression in the words of the Crown Chancellor, Jan Zamoyski (1542–1605): "If it would lead you back to Catholicism I would gladly give up half of my life and with the other half I would live rejoicing this union. But if anyone should try to compel you, then I would give up all my life, rather than be obliged to witness this compulsion."[102]

Moving into the modern era, humanism, in both its philosophical and political manifestations, continued to have a profound impact on Poland. Ultimately, whereas Poland's historical experiments with democracy, such as the May Constitution of 1791, left little in the way of lasting institutional or ideological achievements (albeit much was left in the way of symbolism),[103] the intellectual traditions of humanism were carried forward into the late twentieth century by important literary figures who developed humanistic themes in their writings. As most contemporary Poles are very familiar with the works of these writers and poets, a "transmission belt" from the past to the present was made possible. Interestingly, the latest poet to participate in the traditions of Christian humanism is Miłosz himself. In this context, it is noteworthy that Michnik and Tischner both maintain that Miłosz, the Pope and Wałęsa are the three most important figures of the 1980–81 period.[104] Echoing Erasmus, all three advocated tolerance and accommodation in the pursuit of a higher common good that was to elevate people above the corruption and venality of the times they found themselves in. Accordingly, the tradition of tolerance mentioned above in the Solidarity document is more likely to be a reflection of the humanism of the Renaissance, than of the Enlightenment.

In contrast to humanism, the Enlightenment has had a weaker impact on Poland. The inalienable Rights of Man, for example, were not supported by contemporary Poles without qualification. Polish intellectuals and revolutionaries believed that these rights either paid insufficient attention to the question of national liberation, as opposed to the question of the liberation of the individual, or that they ignored the substantive conditions required for equality and liberty. Accordingly, in the mid-nineteenth century, Polish socialists such as Wiktor Heltman attempted to

> unite the postulates of the eighteenth century with the postulates of the nineteenth century in a harmonious synthesis. The eighteenth century emphasis on the rights of man and on the pursuit of individual happiness should be combined with the nineteenth century emphasis on the duties of man and on the pursuit of collective happiness.[105]

Other socialists went on to condemn outright the doctrine of inalienable human rights as sanctifying egoism, and therefore providing an inadequate basis for social justice. "Social justice cannot stem from the doctrine of rights, it needs Christian sacrifice, selflessness, the emphasis not on one's legal rights but on one's moral duties."[106] Moreover, the Enlightenment's revolutionary application of reason to the task of building a new political and social order completely divorced from all that had gone before, was unlikely to appeal to Poles who, no matter how "enlightened," were taught to venerate, if not all, then certain aspects—cultural, religious, intellectual, institutional—of the national past.

Given the historical strength of Christian and socialist humanism in Poland, affinities with the doctrine animating Solidarity are clear. Tapping into historical traditions of tolerance, "Christian sacrifice" and the "pursuit of collective happiness," gave Solidarity a broadly based appeal that it might otherwise not have possessed. Since the synthesis of Catholic and socialist humanism that comprises the Solidarity ethos was intelligible in philosophical terms, and inclusive of the major themes of Polish history, all political proclivities could see themselves reflected in the ethos. Therefore, "everyone regardless of his world outlook, nationality, or political convictions" could find something compelling in Solidarity's natural rights doctrine.

Beyond the feelings of familiarity and continuity evoked by the doctrine, the needs and interests of large segments of Polish society were also addressed. As we have seen in the previous chapter, the traditional social hierarchies in Poland, similar to the American and French cases, had given way to a more modern social order based not on birth or privilege but on "individual worth." Unlike the American and French cases, however, these new middle strata of society were not occupied as independent producers, professionals or property owners. Instead, they were dependent on the employment provided by the state. Overall, this dependence was accepted, and "the distribution of resources and employment undertaken by the state was deemed necessary and desirable."[107] What was deemed unnecessary and undesirable was the interference, corruption and mismanagement of the Party. If the Party could be removed from the workplace and circumscribed in public life, people would be able to go about their productive and private lives in a more efficient, relaxed and dignified manner. Solidarity's emphasis on ensuring the conditions for dignity for all citizens assured a more equitable and just distribution of resources *within* the structures of dependency that people were accustomed to.

Furthermore, if the privileged Party nomenklatura could be prevented from automatic access to positions of responsibility, these positions would be open to anyone with the requisite skills and talents. Indeed, the social equality mandated by Solidarity's ethos led to demands that appointments to high level positions be made on the basis of talent and fair competition rather than Party affiliation:

> Cadre policy has thus far failed to guarantee the proper selection of persons for executive positions, which have almost exclusively been reserved for members of the party which has the decisive say in appointments. Such a state of affairs circumscribes civil rights because the overwhelming majority of citizens are discriminated against so far as access to executive positions is concerned, and society has no influence on appointments made to them. . . . Under such circumstances it is essential, as soon as possible, to open up access to executive positions for all citizens possessing the proper professional qualifications and guarantee the public a say on appointments to these positions. It follows that executive positions should be held by persons who are competent and accepted by an enterprise's employees.[108]

In short, Solidarity's natural rights doctrine resonated with the personal ambitions, the material interests and the philosophical convictions of the social strata seeking to protect and improve their conditions of life within the structures of dependence established by the Leninist state. Aside from the fact that the redistributive role of the state was widely accepted, external constraints imposed by Yalta meant that the character of the state and the leading political role of the Party could not be challenged directly without violating Solidarity's commitment to non-violence. Accordingly, a doctrine based on human dignity and participatory democracy oriented people toward change within the existing system, as opposed to a radical transformation of political, social and economic institutions. The doctrine itself makes no a priori judgments of any given set of institutional arrangements. Institutions are instead to be judged according to their ability to provide for human dignity. If they do not provide for this fundamental natural right, they are to be reformed. By working peacefully from below to transform the decision-making process in a democratic direction that would ensure policy outcomes commensurate with human dignity, the content, but not necessarily the form, of existing institutions was to be changed.

This strategy of peaceful transformation, as mandated by the doctrine, provided a compelling solution to the problems of the late Gierek era. The critical problems of corruption, economic mismanagement and shortages in every realm could all be addressed within a reform process that was capable of constructively channeling people's frustrations, as well as their ambitions.

Without the added element of conviction, however, it is doubtful whether even the most frustrated or most ambitious of Poles would have risked their lives, livelihoods and family well-being in order to pursue a reform agenda that was still vigorously opposed by the Party and its security apparatus. It was on the basis of belief in the doctrine itself that people were motivated to participate in the risky business of founding Solidarity, and later of compelling the Party to accept Solidarity's reform proposals. As one participant in the strikes of August 1980, J. Szylak, recalls:

> Some people from the management were very indignant with the strikers and just left ostentatiously making insulting comments about the strikers on their way. Our guards were at the gates, but they did not want to stop anybody by force nor to force anybody to strike. Many people probably could not imagine how important that strike was, and others probably did not want to run the risk, because it was not yet clear whether the strike would succeed. There might have also been such persons who thought, let others fight for these demands, and if they win, everybody will benefit from that anyway. But more than half of our personnel remained on the premises.[109]

Those that remained did so because they believed that the strike "was over just and important causes" as Szylak concludes. Another striker, J. Gajda, recalls his confusion and bitterness when the Polish primate delivered a speech in August which seemed to discourage the strikes:

> Deeply embittered, I took a pass from the strike committee and went to see my family. I told my wife of my distress and doubt, she advised me to get a sick leave . . . and to stay home. But a few hours later I nevertheless went back to the port. When all had betrayed our cause, I thought embittered, I would remain faithful to myself and to my workmates. The call of solidarity was stronger than all temptations.[110]

Gajda explains his commitment to the cause in the following words:

> We were ready to take the cross upon our own shoulders, the cross in the form of the caterpillar tracks of the tanks, if it came to an assault on us. To understand that one has to be a mystic or to have experienced that oneself. These are two different things: to be a Hamlet and to experience what the alternative to existence means, and to be an onlooker and to sympathize with Hamlet. The people of the coastal region took upon

themselves the responsibility for the whole nation without knowing what was ahead.[111]

In his conclusion, Gajda challenges future analysts of the strike to remember the crucial element of faith:

> In the future learned historians, sociologists, economists and others will write bulky volumes with analyses of the causes and effects [of the strikes]. They will formulate theses and axioms. . . . They will be extremely wise. After the fact. But how much of all that was known by an uneducated and handicapped docker at the time of the strike, before the fact? Nothing. He had at his disposal neither the results of Gallup polls, nor a staff of scholars and scientists, nor time to be concerned with all that. . . . But the uneducated and handicapped docker had faith. Faith in the broad sense of the word.[112]

This faith in the cause of solidarity allowed the strikers, and later Poles around the country, to relinquish their fears in order to reclaim their dignity and their rights as citizens and as workers. Michnik, for example, relates the continued existence of Solidarity in post-martial law Poland to the fact that "the people are relaxed, unafraid, and their backs are straight."[113] People that had fought for the right to live in dignity and for "dignified conditions of life" continued to do so even after the suppression of Solidarity in December 1981. It is this achievement that, Michnik believes, sets the events in Poland apart from Hungary in 1956 and from Czechoslovakia in 1968:

> I am convinced that while the events of 1917 signaled the rise of the communist system, the meeting at the Gdańsk shipyards in August 1980 began its destruction. Six years after the Hungarian Revolution there was no trace of the revolution. And six years after the invasion of Czechoslovakia there was no trace of the Prague Spring. But six years after the declaration of martial law in this country Solidarity exists along with a civil society.[114]

In other words, victory had been snatched from the jaws of defeat by the power of a "revolution of dignity." As we have seen, the compelling nature of Solidarity's doctrine of natural rights is, in part, responsible for this unique revolution. Taken in isolation, however, a doctrine cannot effect changes in the consciousness and conduct of a given group of people. Since it is only in conjunction with charismatic communities that the value-rationality of a natural rights doctrine can achieve such a permanent impact, it is to the charismatic communities of Solidarity that we now turn.

CHARISMATIC COMMUNITIES

"Nothing has changed, and everything has changed."[115]

(anonymous Pole, 1981)

During the legal period of Solidarity's existence (August/September 1980–December 1981) and beyond, Poles from every walk of life were inspired to act and to speak without fear. As Wałęsa states:

> In fact our souls contain exactly the opposite of what they wanted. They wanted us not to believe in God, and our churches are full. They wanted us to be materialistic and incapable of sacrifices: we are antimaterialistic and capable of sacrifice. They wanted us to be afraid of the tanks, of the guns, and instead we don't fear them at all.[116]

A divided and atomized society was able to unite on the basis of the values articulated by Solidarity. Yet, even in the midst of these momentous changes in the conduct of average Poles, the external conditions of life remained the same. The "revolution of dignity" did not redistribute property, nor did it remove a privileged elite from political power. The seemingly contradictory assessment of Solidarity's accomplishments: "nothing has changed, and everything has changed," is a reflection of this ambivalent outcome. Within the charismatic communities of the movement, everything changed, while on the outside, nothing changed. Within the movement, fear was overcome and the authority of the Party was completely invalidated; the public virtues of civic responsibility, mutual respect and tolerance were acted upon, and democratic rules and procedures were formulated and followed. Citizenship was thereby rediscovered as a meaningful identity.

Outside the movement, grim conditions continued to prevail. Shortages, economic disintegration and the political obstructionism of the Party could not be alleviated or removed. Moreover, there did not appear to be any visible progress in positive directions. Even the promise of progress appeared too remote at times. Ultimately, the tensions generated by this disjuncture between internal and external realities, in conjunction with the specific attributes of the communities themselves, severely attenuated the transformatory capacity of Solidarity's charismatic communities. This section will begin by addressing the positive and negative features of these attributes, and will conclude with an analysis of the incomplete nature of the transformation accomplished by Solidarity.

Two attributes in particular stand out as critical components of the charismatic experience generated by Solidarity. First, the principal communities of the movement, formed during the initial strikes in the fall of 1980, were based on the preexisting enterprise structures that, in many ways, already resembled self-contained communities. In general, the large Leninist enterprises represented more than a place of employment. Schools, shops, vacations, cultural and political activities were all available or arranged within the confines of the enterprise. Once the strikers decided to engage in sit-down occupation strikes, rather than taking to the streets as in the preceding years, they were able to draw on the resources of the enterprise community. These resources ranged from the practical—e.g. printing presses, paper, intra-factory communications systems—to the psychological, as a sense of common destiny could readily be evoked on the basis of familiarity and shared lifestyles. The very fact that most enterprises were physically enclosed, and that the gates could be controlled by the strikers, enforced feelings of intimacy, mutual responsibility and collective discipline.

The second critical attribute is the extent to which Lech Wałęsa emerged as *the* charismatic leader of the movement. For many participants in the strikes, and later for many Poles around the country, Wałęsa himself was the embodiment of hope and moral renewal. The values he represented were often less important than the fact that he, Wałęsa, was articulating them in a novel and powerful way. As Wałęsa, a simple worker, negotiated successfully on a basis of equality with Party bureaucrats and national leaders, a miracle appeared to take place in which average Poles could share by identifying themselves with him. The seemingly impossible dream of breaking the Party's stranglehold on public and productive life, was suddenly becoming a reality under the leadership of Wałęsa. Taken together, these two attributes had both positive and negative aspects. In the short run, the infusion of charismatic content into preexisting community structures and the added conviction generated by people's faith in Wałęsa did effect remarkable changes. In the long run, however, the negative aspects became increasingly evident. For example, the particular nature of the strike communities rendered insider–outsider distinctions more acute, often resulting in suspicion of and hostility toward anyone that could be defined as an outsider. Those who had not been members of the preexisting community or enterprise, such as intellectual advisors, were particularly prone to being labeled outsiders. Moreover, faith in Wałęsa, as in any charismatic leader, was contingent upon his continuous performance of miracles. As Wałęsa was ultimately unable to follow up the miracle of founding Solidarity by miraculously improving the state of the economy and the polity, faith in the entire cause represented by Solidarity began to wane. In order to understand how both positive and negative outcomes could be generated by the same attributes, a closer examination of the strike communities and of Wałęsa's charisma is necessary.

The strike communities

One of the participants in the August strikes along the Baltic coast closed his account of the strike with the following words:

> I just wanted to show how people coped with the situation in the closed premises of the shipyard, away from their families. It was a great and

> unforgettable experience. One has to experience much to be able to comprehend things, and even to understand oneself.[117]

In regard to positive outcomes, what he and his co-workers experienced within the "closed premises of the shipyard" was the creation of a charismatic community in which old fears were broken and new behaviors were established on the basis of a shared belief in the "just and important causes" that animated the strikes. The feelings of fellowship that emerged from this shared belief were given organizational expression in meetings, informal discussions and in the outdoor masses that were held on a regular basis during the strikes:

> At 10 a.m. the square near the gate is filled with people. A field altar has been set up on a lorry for the transportation of sheet metal, and a wooden cross painted white has been placed at its side. It is a sublime moment. All those who are in the shipyard have come here to attend the mass in such extraordinary circumstances. There are believers and non-believers among them, PUWP members and people of other opinions. But there is some force which drew all of them to listen to the Word of God. There are some ten thousand people here. . . . During the sermon emotion overpowers all. I see tears in the eyes of sturdy men. Many of them wipe tears with their sleeves.[118]

On a more mundane level, fellow feeling was promoted by the daily, routine conditions of life in the communities. For example:

> We started organizing cultural life: there were film shows and artistic events. In my section we had an ad hoc ping-pong table, some people played soccer in the yard in front of the building of our section, and others played tennis. . . . We also strove to provide more caloric food, but that was not a problem, because our families took care of us, and we in turn took care of those workmates who had no families in the area.[119]

Overall, there is a consensus among both participants and observers that the "cohesion and solidarity of the personnel [i.e. strikers] were really imposing."[120] As one striker recalls, in spite of anxieties and uncertainties:

> the cohesion of the personnel and the conviction that their attitude was the correct one had a calming effect. It is also to be noted that the personnel trusted the members of the strike committee. That trust and mutual understanding were very much needed by the members of the committee. The important point was that we did not make any decisions that had not been approved by the personnel.[121]

In experiencing such intense, concrete manifestations of fellowship and mutual trust, the strikers began to come to an understanding of their own strength and efficacy. In the words of one participant, "workers today are not a mass of benighted people, they know how to think, they have drawn conclusions from their experience, they can tell truth from lies."[122] In spite of having been spoken to and treated like passive children by the authorities in the past, the workers became more assertive and self-confident during the strikes. "We were fighting for a good cause and our strength was growing and [the authorities] had to reckon with that strength."[123] The barrier of fear that Party members and managers had formerly hidden behind was thereby overcome. Numerous reminiscences of the strikes recount how workers were suddenly able to stand up for themselves against managers and Party secretaries. The following account is representative:

> A moment later I see the first secretary coming, led by a group of people. He walks in the midst of them, next to Kołodziej. . . . He resembles a convict, does not look around, his eyes are turned down. . . . Kołodziej introduces him. He does so with great satisfaction. "Listen shipyard workers," he says, "here is one of those who take your money, you work for such idlers, who only sit behind their desks and want to remote-control you." At that moment he makes the first secretary climb the truck. . . . He stands on the truck like a statue. He does not budge, his legs are motionless, his face looks stony. Kołodziej continues speaking all the time. "Workers, what shall we do with such a man? He is a thief of your wages, a loafer. . . . What shall we do with such a guy? Decide that yourselves." At that moment people on the square burst out laughing and hooting, somebody runs up to the truck and spits toward him, some other man calls "take him away through the gate with his feet forward." There is no end of hooting, name-calling, and shouts "away with him . . . we don't want such people among us."[124]

By taking part in such scenes of public humiliation, workers were able to express directly their frustrations over "all the misfortunes caused by the authorities," and over "their hypocrisy and [the] arbitrary decisions that did not take public opinion into account."[125] Remarkably, these incidents took place without physical violence; those humiliated were simply escorted off the premises. In other confrontations, workers took their managers to task for their arrogance and disinterest:

> SJ, one of the recently employed workers, who had been a storehouse keeper in another enterprise, boldly and courageously expressed what others felt but found it difficult to express adequately. He said more or less this: "Mr. Manager, when I or anyone like me has a case then I write an application to you on a fine sheet of paper; and what do you do? You come to your people with a crumpled slip [of paper]; you thereby show that you despise us."[126]

On the basis of the confidence gained in such encounters, workers were ready to agree with the exhortations of a fellow striker: "Don't fear, we won't suffer for that [for presenting demands to management]. They will do us nothing because we demand our just rights. The rights of respect for the workers."[127]

As the authority of the Party and its managerial minions was undermined and invalidated, the strikers took over the responsibility for protecting their enterprises, as well as for organizing the strike itself. In this process, democratic rules and procedures were introduced and put into practice. Representatives to the strike committees were elected, while critical decisions were voted upon by all strikers. As one participant recalls:

> We now split into groups by the departments and elected the delegates to the strike committee in open voting. I was reelected in my department, but this time it was formal [in the past semi-conspiratorial conditions workers' representatives had not been "elected in a fully democratic way"]. . . . We were elected by open vote to perform the functions of the chairman and its two deputies; we were also the board of our Strike Committee. . . . Somebody said that before we announce a sit-down strike, the departmental delegates should go to their respective departments and ask their people whether they would agree to a sit-down strike. We did so and it turned out that a large majority of the departments was in favor of a sit-down strike and the other departments agreed to subordinate themselves to the will of the majority.[128]

Furthermore, a code of conduct was agreed upon by the strikers that would sanction dangerous, criminal or unbefitting behavior. Guards were posted to protect the enterprises, alcohol was prohibited, while unauthorized behavior was censored. In one case, a worker even censored himself for using the copier for unauthorized, i.e. not validated by the Strike Committee, purposes.[129] In general, the discipline, fortitude and democratic practices of the strike communities were quite remarkable given the unfavorable circumstances: "Every night members of our strike committee made tours of the guards and found that order and discipline prevailed despite fatigue and tension. People understood that now we had to stay to the end."[130]

In short, the strike communities gave birth to the democratic mode of conduct observers would later note as a constituent feature of Solidarity. The following assessment of the Solidarity Congress by Alain Touraine is typical:

> The whole Congress was organized in such a way that no infringement of democratic procedures was possible; the contrast with the political mores of the Communist bloc was striking, and had indeed been consciously intended by the organizers. It was even the occasion for a joke: when the time came to elect the president, the ballot boxes were held aloft upside down, to show that they were really empty and had not been interfered with. A complex procedure had been adopted, whereby any delegate could intervene, ask for a vote to be taken, and in certain cases have extra time to speak. At the same time the organizers had taken steps to prevent the Congress from deviating too much from the agenda. This meticulous

> formal democracy was a guarantee of the movement's legitimacy and put the Congress's decisions beyond all possible dispute. Obviously it also had its disadvantages: it was cumbersome and often slow.[131]

Given the fact that democratic procedures were put into practice first by the strike communities and then by the movement, and the fact that the virtues of non-violence, civic responsibility and mutual respect were fostered and upheld by the communities, Solidarity has been understood as a "school for citizenship." In this "school," the conception of citizenship mandated by Solidarity's natural rights doctrine was given a degree of behavioral substance as people were able to act as if they were indeed free of the Party's constraints and coercion. Within the realm of freedom provided by the movement, the pursuit of the natural right to dignity could take place. Solidarity's multidimensional conception of citizenship, in which all aspects of one's public life, political, social and economic, were addressed as equally important components of a dignified existence, could thereby gain something of an "independent influence on the conduct of life." Consequently, a powerful alternative to the Party's definition of political leadership and membership was created. The Party's monopoly on public life, together with that of its cadre, was finally broken under the joint influence of a natural rights doctrine and the charismatic communities that concretized it.

Notwithstanding this enormous achievement, the charismatic communities also resulted in certain negative outcomes that have implications for the extent to which the communities were able to effect a sustainable transformation of people's consciousness and conduct in directions compatible with the doctrine. Two outcomes are particularly significant in this context. First, given the self-contained nature of the communities and their difficulties in accepting outsiders, the status distinctions between, for example, workers and intellectuals were never completely overcome. The extensive social leveling characteristic of the American and French communities was not replicated. Instead, traditional hostilities between social groups were retained—albeit on a somewhat muted level. In the interests of the common cause, and in the face of a common enemy, such hostilities were discouraged and subsequently appeared openly only on a sporadic basis. The following account by a striker provides an example of one such occasion:

> At about 6 p.m. a gentleman who wore dark spectacles came to us from the Gdańsk Shipyard. He was a member of the KOR, whom our strike committee did not let address us through the microphone. He said that we should not surrender.... He was greatly applauded. When the members of our strike committee heard the applause they said that we should not side with him so much, because he represented the KOR and the men who stayed in the Gdańsk Shipyard for political goals, for their advantages.[132]

The suspicion that outsiders, such as KOR, were representing their own interests, and were not truly concerned with the workers' needs and interests remained a latent feature of Solidarity's existence. At the first Congress, for example, another incident of open hostility toward intellectuals and KOR took place as a motion to thank KOR for its contributions was subjected to hostile criticism.[133]

In spite of the fact that the ethos of Solidarity was based on tolerance, inclusiveness and mutual trust between social groups, the charismatic communities that originally put the ethos into practice were based on the self-contained worlds of the enterprises. In this environment, mutual trust was fostered among the workers of any given strike community but was hampered from developing between "outside" advisors and the workers. On an instrumental basis, the two groups certainly did cooperate, but the genuine feelings of mutual respect and trust envisioned by the ethos were not readily translated into a widespread reality in these circumstances. Consequently, already in 1981, the question emerged as to which group bore the primary responsibility for the existence of Solidarity. Since Solidarity was so closely associated with civic virtues and democratic practices, the subtext of that question revolved around the issue of which group was more democratic and, therefore, comprised of the better citizens. Unlike the French and American revolutions, the linkage between particular social or class standings and the right to citizenship was not overcome.

The second negative outcome that needs to be addressed concerns the question of political authority. Although the formal democratic procedures introduced in the strike communities created a stable basis for delegated authority, the level at which that authority was to be exercised—at a central or decentralized level—remained a contested issue. The strike communities themselves created a model of cooperation between autonomous, decentralized units. As we have seen, each community elected a strike committee to represent and coordinate the needs of that particular constituency. However, in order to strengthen the negotiating position of the strikers vis-à-vis the central authority of the Party, the Interfactory Strike Committee was established. This committee consisted of two representatives from each of the striking enterprises along the Baltic coast, and was empowered to conduct negotiations with the Party authorities. It was later to evolve into the central coordinating body of Solidarity.

The fundamental question that emerged at the First Congress was how much decision-making power was to be granted to this central body, and how much to the regional bodies of the union? The debate over decentralized versus centralized power was ultimately resolved in favor of the latter. Again, in the interests of a strong negotiating position vis-à-vis the Party, the delegates decided that the union should be able to formulate policies as quickly and as efficiently as possible. Moreover, it was decided that there should be no separation of powers between "rule-making and executive powers." Yet this was not an uncontested victory for the proponents of centralized power. The legacy of the autonomous, self-contained strike communities resulted in considerable resistance to the imposition of central control. In response, those in favor of centralized decision-making advocated ever more stringent control over the union's "periphery." An unhealthy dynamic was thereby set in motion as the "center" and the "periphery" accused one another of undemocratic means.

As in the above tensions between workers and intellectuals, advocates of each position considered themselves to be the true democrats. Unlike the American and French cases, a sovereign uncontested source of political authority that could determine a stable relationship between center and periphery—such as the American Constitution or the French state—could not develop given the particular nature of Solidarity's charismatic communities. The vision mandated by the doctrine, of a plurality of independent, self-governing organizations cooperating in harmony, was thereby unable to take hold even within the more limited scope of Solidarity's internal organizational structure.

The charisma of Wałęsa

In place of an impersonal source of political authority, the personal leadership of Lech Wałęsa provided the major source of authority and arbitration during the legal period of the union's existence. Ultimately, it was Wałęsa who arbitrated between the various interests comprising the union, who defused tensions and resolved conflicts. That he was able to take on this role is, in large part, due to the charismatic nature of his leadership. A critical mass of Solidarity members believed implicitly in Wałęsa's abilities, thereby making him the only viable source of authority even for those in the union that remained skeptical of Wałęsa himself.

The absolute faith that people had in Wałęsa originated in the early days of the August strikes. What struck workers immediately was Wałęsa's public speaking style. Unpolished and not particularly original in content, his style nevertheless had a powerful impact on the strikers. One striker recalls waiting for the official announcement of the signing of the Gdańsk Accords—waiting for what, in his opinion, was a "miracle of the Baltic":

> We were afraid of a provocation to the very end. For if they did not sign them, why was there no report, no speech by Wałęsa? And if they substitute an actor who would imitate the voice of the chairman of the Interfactory Strike Committee? That seemed rather impossible. Wałęsa has his specific way of speaking in public. . . . Finally it is there: Wałęsa's coarse and stuttering voice. How much different from the smooth, monotonous and watery speeches of those in power. And this was why it was beautiful. Beautiful in its ugliness.[134]

The association of Wałęsa with the "miracle" of the Gdańsk Accords represents the foundation of Wałęsa's charisma. As his role in Gdańsk became public knowledge throughout Poland, average Poles—unconnected with the strike communities—attached their awe and admiration to him personally. He became more than just a symbol of what had been accomplished, he became the very embodiment of Solidarity for those who had not been able to participate directly in its founding. Selections from letters written to Wałęsa in 1980–81 illustrate the status he had acquired:

> Mr. Wałęsa, I consider you to be second only to God Himself, here on this earth, of course . . . Mr. Wałęsa, I look upon you as the liberator of the Polish workers and farmers; I look upon you as a Great National Hero, Mr. Wałęsa [Kielce province]. I'd like to start my letter with the words: A man of the people will perform a miracle [Warsaw]. . . . Without a word of exaggeration I can describe you as a Savior [Silesia]. . . . And in a letter to Mrs. Wałęsa another writer says: He is so important to us! I don't know if you realize just how many people love and adore him. I am a fanatical worshipper of the chairman. I would gladly tear anyone who dared to say something bad about Mr. Wałęsa into little pieces. But people like that are just simpletons or downright evil [Łódz].[135]

The compiler of these letters, Grzegorz Fortuna, goes on to add that:

> Very often, people confide in Wałęsa in their letters. All sorts of people describe their hard and sometimes tragic lot, convinced that he is the one person who can help them and set them free. This trust and belief that Wałęsa represents the ideals of a caring and, at the same time, a fulfilling compassion are of a very intimate nature. That is why I have refrained from quoting the relevant extracts.[136]

This absolute faith in Wałęsa's abilities and virtues helped make membership in Solidarity compelling to people all over Poland. As one letter states, "you have shown us that we mustn't be frightened off by police truncheons, nor by ridicule, nor lack of faith. The other thing that really impresses me is your profound faith."[137] Undoubtedly, Wałęsa's charisma, and the direct, unmediated and personal devotion people felt toward him, helped the movement achieve an impact on the lives of people who might otherwise have remained untouched by the events on the Baltic coast. In this context, the wave of strikes that took place across Poland in the wake of the August strikes—strikes that were considered unnecessary by the Solidarity leadership and in which Wałęsa often had personally to intervene—represent unconscious efforts to replicate the charismatic experience of the original strikes, complete with the presence of Wałęsa himself.

While these positive aspects of Wałęsa's charisma were most evident in the early stages of the movement, the negative aspects became increasingly evident during the latter half of 1981 when a certain disenchantment with Solidarity in general, and with Wałęsa in particular, began to manifest itself. Amongst the general population, faith in Wałęsa's leadership began to diminish as his inability to improve the conditions of life became increasingly apparent. As Wałęsa was considered the embodiment of Solidarity by many, commitment to the union and the cause it represented began to wane. Furthermore, amongst the higher echelons of the Solidarity leadership, Wałęsa's abilities and his suitability for the office he held were increasingly questioned by those who were either personally disappointed in him, or by those who had never been admirers of Wałęsa's mercurial and unpredictable style of leadership.

At the First Congress, Wałęsa's candidacy for the union's presidency was subsequently challenged by three other candidates. He ultimately retained his leadership position on the basis of 55 percent of the vote, a relatively low percentage given his former status. According to Touraine, "many delegates . . . wanted to give a lesson in democracy to the leader who sometimes abused his position as the movement's symbol."[138] In general, both during and after the Congress, Wałęsa had to struggle to maintain his prestige and standing in the eyes of rank and file union members.

Such struggles are typical of the unstable and fickle nature of the relationship between a charismatic leader and his followers. According to Weber:

> by its very nature, the existence of charismatic authority is specifically unstable. The holder may forego his charisma; he may feel "forsaken by his God," as Jesus did on the cross; he may prove to his followers that "virtue is gone out of him." It is then that his mission is extinguished, and hope waits and searches for a new holder of charisma. The charismatic holder is deserted by his following, however, [only] because pure charisma does not know any legitimacy other than that flowing from personal strength, that is, one which is constantly being proved.[139]

Herein lies the negative aspect of Wałęsa's charisma. Because it coexisted with the value-rational conviction people felt for the principles of the natural rights doctrine, the instability associated with charismatic leadership ultimately undermined the strength of the doctrine as well. Whereas, at first, the close association of Wałęsa with Solidarity and the principles animating Solidarity strengthened the attachment people felt to the movement, that attachment was increasingly questioned as Wałęsa's personal authority diminished.

In short, the charismatic communities of the movement invalidated the authority of the Party by releasing people from their fears and elevating them from the subordinate position they had been forced to occupy in the Leninist state. Moreover, by putting the doctrine into practice, the communities made available a new identity of citizenship and a new model of civic conduct based on democratic rules and procedures. These achievements served as the "charge of powder" that spelled the beginning of the end of Leninist rule in Poland. In this context, the "destructive" capacity of Solidarity, to recall Ernest Barker's assessment of the impact of natural rights on the American Revolution, is manifestly evident.

Solidarity's "constructive" capacity to serve "as a foundation for the building of new constitutions"[140] and new institutions is, on the other hand, more problematic because Solidarity did not succeed in making absolutely binding the identity and mode of conduct mandated by the natural rights doctrine. Although a civic understanding of citizenship and democratic proceduralism was central to the Solidarity experience, it was not decisive in the transformatory process. Unfortunately, the negative features of the charismatic communities resulted in the failure to actualize fully critical aspects of the doctrine. As a result of this development, the movement was riddled with conflicts that ultimately led different constituencies to adopt different interpretations of the doctrine, while other groups simply broke with the doctrine altogether. Consequently, even before Solidarity was in a position to establish the institutional domains appropriate to the doctrine, the doctrine itself was fragmented under the impact of the charismatic communities. It was therefore unable to remain an uncontested and cohesive foundation for determining consciousness and conduct within the movement.

Three critical points of tension between the doctrine and the reality of the communities paved the way for conflicting viewpoints within the movement. First, as we have seen, by retaining divisions and distinctions between social groups, the communities left unresolved in practice *who* has the right to exercise citizenship by participating in the movement's decision-making process. For example, suspicion of advisors meant that their participation was periodically subject to curtailment efforts. The standard set by the doctrine's emphasis on the universal unconditional rights of citizenship and participation was not met. Meanwhile, the groundwork was again established for workers and intellectuals to develop separate positions and perspectives.

Second, the question of *how* decision-making was to be exercised was not satisfactorily resolved. The effort to centralize and unify Solidarity's decision-making structures, while understandable in terms of tactical considerations, did appear to many to violate the principles of self-government, autonomy and democracy embedded in the doctrine. Again, the stage was set for enduring conflicts over organizational form and content in the absence of an uncontested sovereign source of political authority. That these conflicts were kept in check is largely due to Wałęsa's mediating leadership.

As Touraine notes, "Lech Wałęsa is not only the charismatic hero of Gdańsk, the star surrounded by journalists. He is above all, the central figure of Solidarity, the man who brings together its different elements and symbolizes its unity."[141] Yet reliance on Wałęsa to symbolize and maintain the movement's unity came at a price. In addition to the inherent instability of charismatic leadership, the existence of such a leader ran counter to the doctrine's emphasis on the responsibility of individuals to determine and exercise their own consciences. The abdication of personal conscience and consciousness in the fervor of devotion to a charismatic leader became, therefore, increasingly suspect—and even dangerous—in the eyes of those

Solidarity members unimpressed by Wałęsa. This third point of tension between doctrine and reality was subsequently expressed in conflicts over Wałęsa's leadership as those who, for personal or ideological reasons, felt that his presence undermined the movement's integrity mobilized to present their views.

The frustrations and conflicts generated by an unchanging external environment also added to the problems faced by Solidarity; the question of how and on what basis to confront the Party in order to guarantee the implementation of reforms inevitably divided the movement. At the time of the First Congress, the split between the advocates of negotiation and the advocates of radical action was becoming increasingly evident. There was, according to Touraine:

> [a] growing gap between the supporters of limited action, negotiated step by step and progressively forcing the adversary to retreat rather than seeking to overthrow him, and, on the other hand, those who, because of the worsening economic crisis, because they felt the strength of the movement, and because in any case they hardly believed any more that it was possible to negotiate with this regime, wanted to see a tougher attitude which might lead to acts of rupture.[142]

What rendered all of these conflicts and differences of opinion acute was the growing tendency to consider those holding different positions insufficiently democratic. Due to the problematic conception of citizenship put into practice by the movement, each internal conflict became more than a simple difference of interests or opinions. Instead, a more fundamental issue could immediately be brought into play—namely, which group or constituency substantively represented the better citizens. Each group subsequently claimed to be the only valid interpreters and representatives of Solidarity's ethos. In the absence of a common enemy, the inevitable outcome of such a zero-sum conceptualization of conflict would have been fragmentation on the basis of irreconcilable differences. Given the existence of the Party, however, an atmosphere of continuous tension was created as external conditions and pressures fueled conflicts in the movement, while simultaneously forcing the disparate elements of the movement to remain united.

In addition, given Solidarity's commitment to non-violence and peaceful transformation from below, tensions were created as the movement was unable to take direct autonomous action to bring external realities into line with Solidarity's internal principles and mode of conduct. As Touraine notes, "faced with a totally undemocratic system, it lived within itself the democracy which it wanted for the whole of society."[143] Unlike the American and French cases, where revolutionaries could take independent action to make their principles binding for the rest of society, Solidarity was, ultimately, dependent on the scope of action allowed by the Party. Living democracy only within the movement in a hostile environment with no immediate prospects for extending or safeguarding that democracy, required the continuous exercise of self-discipline and vigilance. Both on an individual level and on an organizational level, constant discipline and alertness can generally only be sustained for a short period of time before anxieties, fears and exhaustion set in.

During the course of 1981, fears and anxieties did begin to take their toll as faith in the charismatic leadership of Wałęsa, and in Solidarity, began to wane. In an atmosphere characterized by the simultaneous decline of faith and the rise of fear, the transformatory power of Solidarity was attenuated as people turned to behaviors and identities that promised a greater degree of personal security. In the search for greater security, one could either reduce one's commitment to Solidarity or turn to alternative identities, such as those offered by nationalism and populism. Indeed, the attractiveness of such alternatives was on the rise by the time of the First Congress. As Touraine recalls, the democratic component of Solidarity "was weakened by an upsurge combining nationalism with the discourse of workers' power, having fundamentalist tendencies, and representing a populist appeal to both national and class identity."[144]

Solidarity's ability to effect an uncontested transformation of identity based on its civic definition of citizenship was thereby further reduced as competing identities emerged. While some groups, mainly, albeit not exclusively, comprised of intellectuals, maintained a value-rational commitment to the civic definition of citizenship, others, mainly workers and peasants, embraced a more affectual devotion to Wałęsa or to the community of workers or to the community of "true Poles." In these groups, citizenship was cast in particularistic rather than universalistic terms. However, since these latter groups still claimed to be acting on the basis of values inherent in the ethos, the appropriate interpretation of the ethos itself became contested ground.

Taken together, the tensions faced by Solidarity, in conjunction with the problematic conception of citizenship and political authority generated by the charismatic communities, weakened the movement's ability to fulfill a "constructive" role. Unable to effect a transformation of the external environment, and increasingly unable to effect an internal transformation of people's consciousness and conduct, the movement fell prey to instability, irreconcilable conflicts and undemocratic identities. However, with the imposition of martial law in December 1981, these tendencies and their potentially negative effects were temporarily put on hold.[145] Although the problems would arise again after 1989, the immediate task of sustaining Solidarity underground restored a sense of unity and purpose to those activists willing and able to continue their work on behalf of the movement. Since many movement members, however, were unable or unwilling to participate in the underground structures, emigration and a retreat into non-political activities left only the most committed Solidarity members active. For such members, a common purpose was relatively easy to establish. In addition, the restoration of unity and purpose was, ironically, facilitated when the authorities placed Wałęsa under house arrest.

In the absence of charismatic leadership, commitment to the values and principles represented by the cause, rather than personal devotion to a leader, became paramount. A relatively cohesive and committed group of activists was therefore able to sustain underground Solidarity for over seven years in the face of government reprisals, and in the face of growing competition as a quasi-underground civil society began to flourish in the mid-1980s. Subsequently, in 1988, when growing labor unrest forced the government to reconsider negotiations with Solidarity, the Party faced a unified and committed Solidarity leadership that was able to negotiate successfully the first transition from communist rule in Eastern Europe, on the basis of democratic practices and procedures, and a commitment to the protection of each citizen's natural rights.

However, in the wake of the 1989 elections and the establishment of the first post-communist government in Eastern Europe, Solidarity's unity began to unravel as internal dynamics and external pressures again combined to produce differing interpretations of Solidarity's ethos, as well as undermining popular support for Solidarity. As in the 1980–81 period, Solidarity again proved more capable of destroying the authority of the Party than of generating a sustained and widespread commitment to a single interpretation of the values and conduct mandated by its ethos. In this context, the martial law years had not improved Solidarity's capacity to create a binding identity for critical social groups. While a committed minority of Solidarity activists had remained true to the cause, the majority of Poles had returned to the security of prior behaviors and identities. Not surprisingly, therefore, the 1989 elections have been analyzed as a vote against communism, rather than as a vote for Solidarity.

Given this history of strength and fragility, of unity and disunity, of "destructive" power and "constructive" weakness, Solidarity is clearly a complex phenomenon. Yet in terms of assessing the potential institutional consequences of this phenomenon, the essential questions are quite simple: To what extent is Solidarity, in all of its complexity, conducive to liberal democratic outcomes? Moreover, to what extent is Solidarity conducive to capitalist development? A comparative analysis relating Solidarity's charismatic presentation of natural rights to the American and French cases, followed by a detailed examination of the events since 1989, should provide us with an answer.

7 Solidarity and liberal capitalism

At first glance, it would appear that institutional development in Poland since 1989 has little to do with either the ethos or the experience of Solidarity. The goals advocated by the movement such as self-government and workers' self-management seem outdated and irrelevant in the context of competitive party politics and privatization. Solidarity itself has split into a trade union that is only a pale reflection of the original organization, and into numerous political parties that to varying degrees have distanced themselves from the movement in program, if not in personnel. Given this state of affairs, analysts have struggled to come to terms with the apparent irrelevance of Solidarity in the aftermath of the collapse of communist rule. While no one has yet attempted an explicit analytical linkage of the two phases of Solidarity's legal existence (1980–81 and post-1989), three approaches can be discerned in the literature dealing, at least indirectly, with the question of Solidarity's relationship to the current reform processes. Most analysts continue to affirm Solidarity's importance in setting the stage for a successful transition to democracy. Michael Bernhard, for example, sees Solidarity as the vehicle for the "self-liberation of civil society" in Poland.[1] Seen from this perspective, Solidarity might be less relevant now, but only because it has been so successful in placing Poland on the path to liberal democracy. Having given birth to civil society, Solidarity today can be viewed as simply another component of that society.

Another approach is represented by observers who see the Solidarity experience in a negative light. In their opinion, the movement has promoted attitudes antithetical to the degree of political and economic competition required by liberal capitalism. Schöpflin, for example, points to the "homogeneity and oversimplification" inherent in the Solidarity program of 1981: "Attitudes were essentially structured by a very strong sense of good and evil, with society cast in the role of the former, and 'them,' the party-state, in the role of the latter."[2] Based on similar reasoning, Jan Gross observes that, during the first few years of post-communist government, "the political legacies of Solidarity and of the Communist Party reinforced each other in this respect: both were inimical to institutionalization of political competition."[3] Instead of having a positive impact on post-1989 developments,

Solidarity has left behind a negative legacy that needs to be overcome, just as Leninist legacies need to be overcome. A third approach maintains that while the movement may successfully have undermined the communist regime, it has imparted no lasting legacy and is, therefore, of little significance, either in a positive or in a negative sense, for the transformations under way in post-communist Poland. In this vein, Jan Kubik concludes that:

> The Solidarity class/movement, united by a common cultural–political vision developed throughout the late 1970s, was remarkably monolithic for only a brief moment—in the late summer and fall of 1980. The cracks in this monolith had already appeared by early 1981. By 1992 it had disappeared almost without a trace.[4]

The reality of Solidarity's relationship to the current reform processes is far more complex, however, than these approaches postulate. Solidarity does not represent an unqualified guarantee that liberal capitalism will be institutionalized in Poland, nor is it a barrier to success, nor is it entirely irrelevant to the transition. Yet, all of these views contain an element of truth. Consequently, the three approaches need to be combined in a different analytical framework in order to examine and explain Solidarity's impact on liberal capitalist development.

Such a synthesis can best be accomplished by explicitly linking Solidarity's past to Solidarity's present. By placing the strengths and weaknesses of Solidarity's charismatic presentation of natural rights in a comparative context, it is possible to analyze the connections between the 1980–81 period and the post-1989 period. Solidarity *is* of limited significance to the contemporary process of institution-building, as Kubik suggests, since this process is informed by institutional domains that have not been derived from the movement's original natural rights articulation. As we shall see, Solidarity was not able autonomously to generate the authoritative parameters for post-communist development in Poland. However, the movement continues to have an impact on the informal behavior and on the attitudes of both public and private actors. In the realm of informal conduct, therefore, Solidarity does have significant influence—at times subverting the reform processes, as Schöpflin indicates, and at times supporting them when formal institutional development aligns with informal norms. In other words, although the "formal, codified belief system"[5] represented by Solidarity's natural rights doctrine has not had a meaningful impact on post-1989 institution-building, the norms and practices developed by social groups participating in the movement continue to structure the informal responses of these groups to the new institutional arrangements.

Yet, why was Solidarity unable to provide the institutional domains for post-Leninist reconstruction? Solidarity's weaknesses in regard to the task of determining the formal institutional basis of a new order can best be illuminated by juxtaposing Solidarity's ethos and charismatic communities to the

American and French cases. When analyzed from a comparative perspective, it is evident that, although Solidarity's ethos does represent a value-rational articulation of a natural rights doctrine similar to the American and French cases, the charismatic communities of the movement ultimately failed to transform fully the consciousness and conduct of participants in a manner consistent with the doctrine. Furthermore, the doctrine itself proved to be contradictory in crucial ways. As a result of these weaknesses, Solidarity's leaders were unable, and at times even unwilling, to determine the essential authoritative parameters of political life from the behavior sanctioned by the communities and legitimated by the ethos.

On the other hand, comparative analysis also allows us to examine the strengths of the movement. As a result of Solidarity, a substantive natural rights doctrine *was* articulated and put into practice, no matter how imperfectly. Participation in the movement represents a formative experience of considerable significance for critical groups in Polish society, especially skilled workers and intellectuals. Consequently, these groups will tend to evaluate contemporary democratization and marketization in light of the only past experience they have had with democratic principles and conduct. Solidarity, while not having a direct influence on formal institution-building, does have an indirect influence on the way in which these institutions are judged since it provides the standard against which to measure progress.

It is still relevant, therefore, to analyze the extent to which Solidarity provides a value-rational foundation for liberal capitalist development in Poland. Indeed, such an analysis is crucial since Poland is the only post-Leninist country that faces a dual legacy. Whereas all post-Leninist countries are experiencing conflicts as the instrumentally imported domains of liberal capitalism are challenged by the social interests and attitudes structured by Leninism, Poland is unique in that a value-rational natural rights articulation has also left its imprint on society. Accordingly, we need to assess the degree to which this articulation resists or resonates with liberal capitalism. If the degree of resonance outweighs the degree of resistance, then the ethos of Solidarity may well provide a value-rational basis of legitimacy for the newly imported domains. This would make Poland the only post-Leninist country that has an indigenous basis of legitimation for liberal capitalism, rooted in normative commitment as well as instrumental compliance. On the other hand, if resistance outweighs resonance, then the Polish polity is likely to be more fragile and less stable than that of its neighbors.

In the course of examining Solidarity in comparative context, it should become clear that Solidarity, in crucial ways, resembles the French Revolution in all of its positive and problematic contours. Given these similarities, one can predict that institutional development in Poland will continue to be volatile as the country copes with its dual legacy: the legacy of the ancien régime and the legacy of Solidarity. The extent to which this legacy will set Poland apart from its neighbors in East Central Europe, and the implications of this legacy for a latecomer to liberal capitalism, will be assessed in the final, concluding chapter. Before examining Solidarity's indirect influence on post-1989 developments, the following section will address the question of why Solidarity was not able directly to influence post-communist institution-building.

SOLIDARITY'S WEAKNESSES: THE FAILURE TO CONSTRUCT INSTITUTIONAL DOMAINS

Shortly after the first non-communist government was constituted in 1989 under the leadership of Prime Minister Mazowiecki, himself a Solidarity activist, it became clear to observers that Solidarity's direct programmatic influence on the new government was minimal. Neither the trade union nor the parliamentary club associated with Solidarity called for a representative summit—a constitutional convention of sorts—to elaborate publicly a reform agenda consistent with the principles, goals and values of the movement. Accordingly, Wesołowski noted in 1990 that:

> Solidarity 'guides' the government mostly by its general vision of change or an 'ethos' which includes such values as national independence, democracy, rule of law, and human solidarity. Solidarity did not provide the cabinet with any definitive program; the cabinet itself had to determine a program.[6]

A closer examination of the program reveals the extent to which Solidarity's ethos provided only very loose guidance, if any. Essentially, the new leadership chose to articulate a reform agenda that simply imported Western, specifically American, conceptions of citizenship (understood in terms of formal rights and individualism), representative government, proceduralism and the self-regulating free market as the constituent elements of the new political and economic order.

The embodiment of this reform agenda is, of course, the Balcerowicz Plan, which went into effect in January 1990. While this plan is best known as "a radical strategy for the rapid transformation of Poland to a market economy,"[7] it assumes an interconnectedness between the political, legal and economic realms. Both Balcerowicz and Sachs, his American advisor, maintain that economic reforms are best undertaken in the context of a democratic government adhering to procedural norms in its bureaucracy and in its legal system. Consequently, when Sachs states that the "main idea" of shock therapy was "to create institutions of the kind already in existence, and with proven merit, in Western Europe,"[8] both political and economic institutions are implied. Also evident in this statement is the intention of importing Western institutional domains as the appropriate parameters for institutional transformation. Balcerowicz, himself, declared in 1989: "We are too poor to experiment. If the rich countries want to experiment, let them. For us, it is better to take proven models."[9] These "proven models" are based on individualistic, independent, entrepreneurial citizens endowed with formal rights, regularly delegating political responsibility to representatives, regularly pursuing their interests by associating in civically inclined voluntary associations, and consistently abiding by impersonal procedural laws. It is increasingly evident, however, that the creation of a market economy and this type of citizen represents an experiment of enormous proportions given the structural and attitudinal legacies of Leninism. The experimental nature of these "proven models" is further augmented by the fact that they represent a considerable departure from the institutional domains that would have followed logically from the natural rights doctrine embodied by Solidarity in 1980–81.

Although Solidarity's substantive natural rights ethos did mandate the domains of citizenship, democratic government and proceduralism, these domains were conceptualized in ways that are not consistent with the adaptation of formalized Western models. The domain of citizenship, for example, is clearly a central attribute of Solidarity's ethos but, as we have seen, it is understood more in terms of collective rights than of individual freedoms. As Marcin Król indicates, a specific kind of citizenship was created in the movement:

> It seems that it was only with the arrival of Solidarity that the Poles developed a full awareness as citizens . . . and even then only of the type that was possible in Poland, which means that this awareness also remained paradoxical.[10]

For Król, the lack of individualism in Solidarity represents a crucial element of this paradoxical civic awareness. Throughout Polish history, "The place of individual nonconformism was taken by social nonconformism of the group, which no longer required from the individual the courage of his convictions, but often did require personal courage."[11] In particular, he believes that the freedom of the individual is missing in the Polish political tradition. During the drafting of the Solidarity Program in 1981, Król criticized the prevailing tendency in the movement to equate justice with individual dignity as this overlooked the more fundamental value of individual freedom. Only by protecting individual freedom could abuses committed in the name of equality and human dignity be prevented. Similarly, only by recognizing and promoting the conflict of individual interests could the romanticism of "moral unity" be superseded by "the democratic unity that is the unity evolving out of conflicts." Accordingly, Król concluded that the freedom of the individual should be "in the forefront of values."[12]

Not surprisingly, given Solidarity's concern with social equality and collective well-being as crucial manifestations of man's dignity, the value of individual freedom was not included in the final version of Solidarity's program. Therefore, the conception of citizenship that emerges from the Solidarity experience is not explicitly linked to individual rights and interests. Instead, Solidarity's vision of citizenship was based on the primacy of the natural right of all human beings to live in both spiritual and physical dignity. Almost the totality of the human condition was thereby captured. Citizenship was not just a political category of membership, it had a social and spiritual dimension as well; to be a citizen was to be a member of a social, political and spiritual community based on mutual respect and solidarity.

While freedom was not neglected in this vision, it was placed in the context of a collective freedom from oppression. Interests, as well, were seen as needing collective representation rather than individual articulation. In a 1980 speech, Kuroń concluded that one of the greatest problems with the communist system was that the interests of workers and consumers were not being represented by the existing unions. Accordingly, Solidarity had to be "a union which reflects the agreement of workers to defend their interests."[13] Central to this defense was the protection of substantive rights, such as the right to work and the right to a dignified standard of living. In this regard, regulating economic exchanges was considered an appropriate means of ensuring these rights. Solidarity itself was in favor of implementing an extensive rationing program in 1981 in order to provide for an equitable distribution of goods throughout Polish society.[14]

Beyond the collective representation of interests, the ultimate goal of the union was the creation of a self-governing republic in which workers could manage their own enterprises and citizens could participate actively in political decision-making. The "will of society" was to be institutionalized in a form of direct democracy allowing for the full expression of citizens' needs and interests. The all-encompassing nature of citizenship was thus complemented by an all-encompassing form of community-based self-government in which a plurality of different organizations and groupings can participate. Given the high level of activism demanded by such a polity, simply following democratic procedures, regulations and laws would not be enough to ensure the appropriate standard of public conduct. Public conduct would have to be self-sacrificing and heroic, as well as being oriented toward proceduralism. Both in the movement and in the ethos, public virtue was conceived in terms of personal courage and loyalty to the cause of solidarity, as well as in terms of procedural fairness.

Clearly, the domains that follow from Solidarity's substantive natural rights ethos are not readily reconcilable with the institutional framework imported from the West and incorporated into the Balcerowicz Plan. Whereas, the Plan was predicated on individual citizens pursuing their material interests, the ethos mandated citizens pursuing their material and spiritual needs on a collective basis. Whereas, the Plan proceeded on the assumption of interest aggregation in the form of political parties that represent clearly defined constituencies in a representative form of government, the ethos mandated a community-based constellation of civic groups participating directly in political decision-making. Whereas, the Plan operated on the assumption of procedurally mediated conflicts of interest and the rule of law, the ethos mandated a procedurally maintained harmony of interests as conflicts are to be overcome by self-sacrificing public actors. Whereas, the Plan was designed to bring about a self-regulating market economy, operating independently of the social and political realms and based on private property, the ethos mandated regulatory intervention in the economy on behalf of social rights and interests. Although Solidarity did not directly address the concept of private property, one can infer from the substantive natural rights doctrine that the right to property cannot be considered absolute if the unrestricted accumulation of property prevents others from maintaining a decent standard of living.

What we see here is a vivid contrast between formal and substantive, between individualistic and collectivistic interpretations of the domains associated with liberal capitalism. In 1989, however, the core elite of Solidarity did not even appear to recognize the contrast, much less generate a debate over the possible reconciliation of formal and substantive rights. Instead, they completely rejected Solidarity's substantive interpretation of natural rights as a basis for constitutional and institutional reform in favor of adopting the Plan. As Jan Gross remarked in a 1992 essay:

> What is the essential point of reference, the shorthand designation, the symbol associated today with the Polish revolution? It is not a Solidarity logo, or one or another of Wałęsa's irreverent bon mots. Rather it is a certain blueprint for economic reform—the Balcerowicz Plan.[15]

Yet what specifically did the rejection of Solidarity's doctrine and the implementation of the Plan entail for the way in which institutional domains were conceptualized by the new leadership? To begin with, citizenship, as in the American case, was treated largely in terms of formal civil and political rights, with only reluctant attention given to substantive social rights. According to Morawski, the reform leadership believes that

> the realization of social rights threatens not only the economic reform (the social umbrella supposedly violates the principles of rational calculation) but also the realization of individual freedom, for it strengthens the state as an institution, which by realizing these rights automatically increases its powers. According to this argument the rights of the citizen can be reduced to civil rights: equality in the face of the law, freedom of speech, religion, etc., in short—to the model of the liberal "minimal state."[16]

This reduction of rights to basic liberties is all the more surprising since the newly elected representatives associated with Solidarity still manifested a concern with citizens' rights as natural rights:

> The need for fundamental civil liberties which constitute an inherent part of the constitutional democracy was taken for granted by the post-communist leaders and legislators. Indeed, they were the whole point of

> political reforms. But in their debates, senators were more concerned with the most basic human rights, perceived as *natural rights* of all human beings, sometimes linked explicitly to Christian values. Concerns with human rights in general, and more specifically, rights to dignity, autonomy and subjectivity of the individual were expressed with some frequency in the Senate deliberations.[17]

However, these perceptions of rights were not considered in the reform process undertaken by Mazowiecki's government. Having rejected Solidarity's conception of natural rights, the leadership also rejected a wide-scale constitutional reform that would have anchored a broader understanding of citizens' rights. For as Maria Los points out: "Such a uniquely balanced liberal–natural law—if at all possible—could be attempted only in a single act of a replacement of the old legal system by a totally new one."[18] Even a new constitution would have represented, at least, "a symbolic break with the legal past."[19] Instead, the existing communist constitution was simply amended and augmented to reflect the new realities. In this context, the only crucial change, apart from deleting references to the leading role of the Party, was represented by the decision to delete all of the references to social justice from the existing constitution.[20] Consequently, even though the amended constitution left intact the "vast array of social and economic rights" typical of a communist constitution, a signal was sent that citizenship was now to be understood in terms of formal rights.

Over all, however, the new leadership opted for legal continuity over the creation of a "comprehensive, new philosophy of a constitutional order, radically divorced from the past."[21] As one Senator explained: "The state must function in an uninterrupted fashion."[22] Accordingly, the formal legality of communist laws had to be respected "even if they were totally unfair and contradicted some other laws within the same legal system."[23] In this context, it is significant to note that the old constitution was not even rewritten until it was thought to pose a threat to the implementation of the Balcerowicz Plan by giving opponents constitutional grounds to invalidate the government's efforts.[24] Maintaining a stable constitutional and legal infrastructure to facilitate the implementation of the Plan was clearly given preference over creating a new system of law that would make the citizenship rights mandated by Solidarity integral to the new polity.

Moreover, in the interests of implementing the Plan effectively and with a minimum of social resistance, Solidarity's conceptions of participatory democracy were abandoned in favor of institutionalizing representative government. As Świderski notes, "it would seem that a considerable divergence exists between the constitutional laws serving representative democracy, which have emerged since the victory of Solidarity in 1989 . . . and the demands expressed by the union's people in 1980."[25] According to Świderski, one can identify three specific ways in which "direct democracy" was carried out by Solidarity in the 1980–81 period: support for citizens' initiatives, organizing of referenda within the union, and efforts to circulate petitions recalling leading political figures.[26]

Such measures, designed to enhance civic participation and control over political representatives, were for the most part rejected in favor of a form of government that demobilizes social activism by fostering the delegation of political power to responsible politicians, thereby giving elites a freer hand in the reform process. Already during the Round Table talks, a pattern was established whereby Solidarity's elites purposefully removed themselves from popular pressure in order to better "represent" social interests vis-à-vis the Party.[27] For example, unlike the shipyard negotiations of August 1980, the Round Table negotiations were held in confidential meetings with no public access other than controlled press conferences and plenary meetings. Active civic participation was further discouraged after the June 1989 elections when Wałęsa and the National Committee of Solidarity curtailed the influence of the Citizens' Committees that had sprung up to organize Solidarity's electoral campaign throughout Poland. The National Committee decided to disband the committees on the provincial level, and to withdraw the name "Solidarity" and financial support from the remaining municipal and communal committees.[28] According to Geremek, this decision did take a large number of able, talented people out of public life and discouraged them from participation in political organizations especially in small localities.[29] While this was a cause of regret for Geremek, there is no doubt that the Solidarity leadership as a whole supported representative, rather than direct, democracy as the most stable and efficient form of government for a citizenry actively engaged in private pursuits in the home and in the market place.

Obviously, the main goal of the Balcerowicz Plan was to facilitate private economic pursuits in order to enhance the productive capacity of the newly emerging economic order. Consequently, the Plan took radical steps to promote the private ownership and entrepreneurship typical of American capitalist development. In this process, as well, the Solidarity program was rejected. In particular, Employee Stock Ownership Plans that would have been consistent with "the traditions and expectations of the Solidarity movement" were rejected early in 1990 as being incompatible with the economic rationale of the Balcerowicz Plan.[30] Given that, in capitalism, "property rights are lodged in the hands of private individuals who exercise them for self-regarding purposes,"[31] employee ownership plans represented a return to the more communally based property rights of socialism, and could, therefore, be considered regressive. Moreover, Western advisors were quick to point out the disadvantages of employee ownership. Sachs is typical in this respect when he notes that:

> Significantly less than 2 percent of the industrial work force in the United States is employed in enterprises where workers own even 20 percent of the shares of the firm, and almost no major industrial firm is majority owned by the workers.[32]

In short, the Balcerowicz Plan "came as a real shock, a decisive break in continuity,"[33] as it contravened every aspect of Solidarity's ethos from self-government in the polity to self-management in the economy. Three possible explanations for this radical break can be derived from the existing literature. For example, it has been argued that such a shock was indeed therapeutic since a break in continuity was precisely what was needed to overcome the democratic shortcomings of both communism and Solidarity. It has also been claimed that the necessity of shock therapy is best explained by the exigencies of the economic crisis Poland faced in 1989. Finally, the discontinuity has been explained by the inherent problems faced by a new political elite as it moves from protest to politics. A brief review of these explanations will make their inadequacies clear.

If Solidarity and communism are inseparably linked, as some observers claim, then the radical departure from Solidarity's ethos can be explained as a justified break with the past. Kurczewski, for example, maintains that "the liberalizing effects of Solidarność were possible only insofar as it coexisted with the Communist Party and its State in its more and more antiquated form."[34] Thus, Solidarity represents a vehicle of "total involvement" which, just like the Party, leaves little room for the autonomous expression of individual interests. Seen from this perspective, removing the Party from political life necessitates doing away with Solidarity as well.

This explanation of why Solidarity's own core elite marginalized the principles and the experience of the movement cannot, however, explain why the "Western" elements of the ethos were also violated. For even if many of Solidarity's attributes can be rejected as the products of "real socialism," or as the products of romantic Polish nationalism, why reject the more positive contributions of the movement? In particular, Solidarity's original emphasis on proceduralism and pluralism was consistently undermined by the new political leadership. Immediately after the June 1989 elections, Solidarity consented to a change in the electoral law that would allow the Communists to elect the thirty-three coalition seats they were allotted as part of the Round Table accords in a second electoral round. Public opinion understandably reacted negatively to this procedural violation of the electoral process. Geremek, for example, recalls a press conference where he faced specific criticism for having "changed the rules in the course of the game."[35] A month later, Jaruzelski was elected president by the Sejm in an obviously doctored process as several Solidarity deputies invalidated their own ballots in order to elect him. In both cases, Solidarity leaders maintain that they violated procedural principles to save the process of democratization. Yet as Jan Gross points out, "it mattered that in the process [of building a *Rechtsstaat*] the successor political camp overtly manipulated the elections, the most important legitimizing procedure of the new polity."[36] It mattered not just by establishing a bad precedent, but also by clearly violating the sense of procedural fairness that had been such a strong part of the Solidarity tradition. Solidarity, in 1980–81, and KOR before it, had never allowed threatening circumstances to undermine proceduralism.

A poor precedent was also established in regard to the plurality of political organizations envisioned in the Solidarity ethos and maintained to some degree in Western democracies. After the 1989 elections, monopolistic tendencies became increasingly evident as Solidarity, the trade union under Wałęsa's leadership, attempted to prevent any competition in the public realm. Accordingly, the Citizens' Committees were undermined with the explicit intention of forcing activists to return to Solidarity, and of preventing the founding of an independent political party which "would have had the spirit of Solidarity as its ideological basis and committees across Poland"[37] as its organizational basis. The union's efforts to control and monopolize political processes came as a complete surprise, not just to the Committees, but to other Solidarity leaders as well. Geremek, for example, states that he was completely taken aback by the initial decision to curtail the Committees in June 1989:

> It was completely surprising to me, not just because there was no earlier discussion about it in the committees, but also because the decision completely went against the tradition and ethos of Solidarity. After all, never had Solidarity feared competition, nor had it pursued a monopoly over the opposition.[38]

In addition, the union's relations with the newly elected Solidarity deputies in the Sejm and Senate were distanced from the very beginning as, contrary to Geremek's expectations, the Citizens' Parliamentary Club received no financial aid from the union, nor was the union willing to allow the club the use of the name "Solidarity."[39] Relations between the faction and the union were increasingly strained as Wałęsa himself monopolized the negotiations leading to the establishment of the first non-communist government. According to Geremek, who was for a time conducting parallel negotiations as head of the parliamentary faction, such "political games should take place in parliament, and not outside of it."[40]

On the whole, Wałęsa's political maneuvering during the period between the June 1989 elections and his own election to the presidency in November 1990 created problems for the establishment of a stable political system based on the representation of a plurality of interests and opinions. Operating outside the procedural norms of the parliamentary system, as he held no elected or appointed political position, Wałęsa nonetheless attempted to exert political influence. As one journalist commented to Wałęsa in June 1990: "You may pass the ball, but by not being on the playing field you do not play by the rules."[41] Wałęsa's most detrimental "pass" at the time was the declaration of a "war at the top" against the "intellectual eggheads" ensconced in the most prominent of the Citizens' Committees, in the Citizens' Parliamentary Club and in Mazowiecki's government.[42] While Wałęsa's stated intention was to prevent a monopolization of power by these former Solidarity leaders, his real intention appears to have been the desire to control and marginalize any competitors in the political arena. The outcome of Wałęsa's "war at the top," whether intended or unintended, was the polarization and personalization of Polish politics, rather than its pluralization. The choosing of sides during the presidential campaign between Mazowiecki and Wałęsa did lead to the formation of numerous post-Solidarity parties and groupings. However, given the hostility, invective and stubbornness that accompanied these divisions, the public perception was that these new parties were based more on personal loyalties and antipathies than on real programmatic differences. In short, these departures from proceduralism and pluralism undermined not just Solidarity, but potentially threatened the entire project of democratization as well. Given these counterproductive effects, one cannot explain the complete departure from the ethos of Solidarity in terms of a general desire to facilitate the construction of a new democratic order by leaving the past behind.

An explanation based on the exigencies of the economic situation the new leadership faced in 1989 suffers from a similar weakness in that the construction of a new economic order was also impeded, rather than assisted, by the complete rejection of Solidarity's ethos. As its first order of business, Mazowiecki's government had to come to grips with a deteriorating economy and rapidly rising hyperinflation. Indeed, from the days of the Round Table negotiations on, economics assumed a primary importance in the thinking of Solidarity's core elite, given that the negotiations came about due to an economic crisis the Communist regime could not solve without the participation of Solidarity. Having assumed full responsibility for the country in the wake of the elections, Solidarity's leaders also assumed the full burden of economic reform, a burden that necessitated Western assistance and foreign debt reductions. With Western advisors pushing for the Balcerowicz Plan, and promising aid on the basis of the Plan, it seems natural that the new leadership would gravitate toward the Western blueprint for institutional reform.

However, while economic conditions are not insignificant determinants of political behavior during this period, these conditions alone cannot explain the radical nature of the break with the ethos and experience of Solidarity. For example, economic reforms could have been articulated with greater attention given to the needs and fears of average Poles. Again, the positive aspects of Solidarity's legacy, such as a respect for popular opinion, were overlooked, even when maintaining the lines of communication between elected representatives and their social constituencies would have strengthened popular support for the reforms. As Zbigniew Bujak, a former Solidarity leader, points out: "in a democratic system, whether one wants to or not, it is necessary to convince people of the best, brightest and most ingenious moves of the government."[43] By not lobbying for social support, Mazowiecki's government faced more voter hostility than might otherwise have been the case. This hostility manifested itself during Mazowiecki's presidential campaign when voters rejected him, in part due to the hardships of the reform, but in part also due to the perceived elitism of his government. Bujak reports a typical explanation as to why people decided not to vote for Mazowiecki: "Because he doesn't speak to me, he doesn't talk with me, he doesn't say what he is doing and why. So, what reason do I have to vote for him?"[44] In addition, by not lobbying for social support, the economic reforms themselves may have been weakened. Sachs, for example, is now calling on "reformers, politicians, and international advisors" to concentrate their efforts on "improved public understanding . . . in order to undo the continuing adverse fiscal legacy of the ancien régime."[45]

Since discarding the "positive" aspects of Solidarity's legacy, as well as the negative ones, might actually have impeded the desired political and economic transformations, it does not seem likely that the wholesale rejection of Solidarity can be entirely explained on the basis of either a desire to transcend the symbiosis of Leninism and Solidarity via "true" democracy or a desire to overcome the economic crisis with Western assistance. Another approach is needed to explain fully why such a "decisive break in continuity" took place. In this regard, the approach offered by analysts who point to the difficulties experienced by the elites of the former opposition, as they struggled to adapt to new forms of political life, appears promising. Staniszkis, for example, writes of an "identity crisis" that permeated the former opposition leaders as they took on new tasks and new roles after the June 1989 elections:

> An essential element of the present identity crisis in the opposition is the problem of continuity. A clear break has taken place from the formula of Solidarity as a social movement. This formula closely linked trade union activity per se with a peculiar understanding of politics and contained a moment of mass mobilization, with clear accents of a cultural revolution. Today we are observing a clear separation of trade union work from political activity, which is now understood differently and is engaged in by professional politicians.[46]

After fighting against the regime for the "recognition of the universal rights of the individual," the opposition now found itself "a participant of the official political process with its rules of the game and rhetoric."[47] Gross elaborates on the nature of this change by pointing to the structural limitations faced by the new political elites as they moved from the protest world of boundless unstructured opportunity in which "anybody could launch a new initiative" to the political world of "confined" power embodied in a "small number of well-defined positions, for which there is bound to be competition."[48] As a result of this narrowing of the boundaries of political activity, competitive careerism focused on government positions began to supplant the more dynamic activism of the protest period. Naturally, this process has led frustrated activists, such as Bujak, to conclude that many former opposition figures "have shown themselves to be greater careerists than idealists engaged, above all, in the realization of the great idea of Solidarity."[49]

Yet, why did this identity crisis lead to the complete rejection of "the great idea of Solidarity?" Careerism can, after all, be linked to the institutional fulfillment of the revolutionary objectives that bring a new elite to power. Indeed, this linkage characterized the American and French Revolutions. Consequently, the change in circumstances as an elite moves from protest to politics, while no doubt unsettling for those involved, cannot in and of itself explain why the institutional domains derived from the doctrine of Solidarity were disregarded in the institution-building process. Staniszkis herself points to an additional process at work in the transition period that can more fully explain this disregard and the attendant symbolic, as opposed to programmatic, usage of Solidarity. In her analysis of the first non-communist government, she discerns "clear inclinations toward the role of a Leninist avant-garde" on the part of the ex-opposition.[50] Specifically, she mentions their hostile attitudes toward the new non-parliamentary opposition, and their efforts to implement a top-down reform agenda with no clear social base of support.[51] Accordingly, just as the Bolsheviks created the proletariat that was to support their regime, the Mazowiecki government began to create the middle class that would support its vision of liberal capitalism. Gross, as well, points to the prevalence of Marxist thinking in Poland:

> Having parted with communism and the vocabulary of Marxist analysis, it [Poland] was captured by the fundamentals of Marxism. In the first place, economics revealed itself with a vengeance to be the key determinant of the political realm. To be sure, Marxist principles were reversed and private ownership appeared as an indispensable foundation for well-ordered politics, for a stable, normalized, if you wish, natural, condition of society. But the framework remains unchanged; circumstances of material life, indeed *property relations*, are posited as the foundation of politics.[52]

Together, the Marxist intellectual inheritance, combined with the influence of Smithian principles imported via foreign experts, would appear to have decisively undermined the salience of Solidarity's doctrine for institutional reform in post-communist Poland. What was considered "natural" after June 1989 was the free market and the social and political conditions derived from such a market—not the natural right of human beings to live in dignity. Unfortunately, Solidarity's core elite was vulnerable to this recasting of what constitutes the "natural condition of society" because of the weaknesses inherent in the doctrine and in the charismatic communities that had determined the struggle against the communist regime. Solidarity's past must, therefore, be related to the post-1989 period in order to gain a complete understanding of how such a "decisive break in continuity" between the ethos and experience of Solidarity and the post-communist institution-building process could take place.

In particular, Solidarity's substantive natural rights doctrine proved to be inadequate for the task of determining an appropriate role for the state in the shaping of a new political and economic order. Whereas the American and French doctrines allow for a consistent conceptualization of the state and its relationship to the desired polity, the Polish doctrine generates contradictory images of the state. These contradictions made it difficult for Solidarity's core elite to relate the 1980–81 doctrine to post-1989 realities. Finding themselves responsible for the state, they could derive few guidelines for their new positions from the ethos that had sustained their past struggles. As a consequence of this ideological void, the new leadership became susceptible to imported visions of the state and its role under liberal capitalism.

As has often been noted, Solidarity in 1980–81 represented an explosion of political activism in the realm of civil society.[53] This activism was mandated by an ethos that oriented participants toward the creation of autonomous and self-governing organizations that would emerge from within society to serve the needs and interests of the Polish population. These organizations were, of course, to be independent of the communist party-state. At the same time, however, protecting the needs and interests of the population meant that such organizations could not be completely autonomous of the state. Since the party-state dominated political and economic life, it automatically became the main focus of Solidarity's efforts to represent the interests of society. These efforts required both an antagonistic attitude toward the state and a qualified acceptance of the role of the state in maintaining the redistributive practices to which people had become accustomed. The nomenklatura privileges protected by the state had to be met with hostility as they violated the principle of equality, while the social and economic services provided by the state had to be preserved on the same grounds. The state as it existed was thereby simultaneously despised for its corruption and needed for its services. Eventually, of course, the realization of a self-governing republic was to overcome this contradiction. Once social organizations gained complete control over the desired distributive functions of the party-state, the despised state itself would be rendered meaningless. Civil society, as it were, would then both govern and represent the population.

The centrality of society in the doctrine of Solidarity is further strengthened by the perception that natural rights are best guaranteed by society, acting collectively, and not by the state. This elevation of society is, of course, an outgrowth of Polish political traditions. Given that the state in Polish history has been "hostile territory for the last two centuries,"[54] Polish society has become the embodiment of the nation. Accordingly, it is society, understood as an organic whole, as "a community of spirits,"[55] that has had the task of preserving the nation. Solidarity's ethos continued this tradition of social solidarity and collective self-preservation, while adding the task of defending the natural rights of citizens to the list of society's responsibilities. On a symbolic level, this conception of society's collective attributes and its defensive role is reflected in the very names "Solidarity" and "KOR" ("Workers' Defense Committee" later renamed the "Committee for Social Self-Defense").[56] On a concrete programmatic level, Solidarity's commitment to society as the fountainhead of democracy is evident in the October 1981 program:

> Democracy must not be rule exercised by groups placing themselves above society and claiming the right to determine the needs and to represent the interests of society. Society must be able to speak with its full voice, to express various social and political opinions; it must be able to organize in such a way as to guarantee a fair share in the material and spiritual achievements of the nation for all, as well as to liberate all the nation's possibilities and creative forces.[57]

Society therefore represents the ultimate embodiment of democratic popular sovereignty. The responsibility for protecting the rights and interests of Polish citizens can only be delegated to social organizations, not to the institutions of the state. In this context, the state serves a purely utilitarian function as the provider of employment and resources, and is otherwise devoid of greater significance or legitimacy.

The antagonistic relationship between state and society envisioned in Solidarity's doctrine is consistent with Polish political traditions, and with the interests of social groups dependent on the party-state for their livelihood, yet resentful of the omnipotence and corruption of that state. However, the doctrine provides neither a consistent nor a positive image of the role of the state in a non-antagonistic setting. In such a setting, should the state immediately be superseded by social authority according to the ideal of the self-governing republic? Or should it remain as a utilitarian necessity, albeit circumscribed by independent, self-governing organizations? Or should a democratic state and its elected representatives be considered a constituent element of society, rather than its remote and hostile overseer? All of these options represent possible derivations from the doctrine, with very little indication as to which option is the most consistent with the ideals and principles of Solidarity.

In all of the derivations, however, the state is treated with great ambivalence, as a set of institutions that needs to be augmented, circumvented or even transcended by social initiatives. For the most part, the state is a necessary evil at best with no autonomous merit or legitimacy. Not surprisingly, given this ambivalence, public virtue in Polish political traditions and in Solidarity's doctrine is not seen in terms of "public service in the political sphere."[58] Instead, open struggle against the state and self-sacrificing heroism have, over the centuries, become the ideal characteristics of the virtuous public servant.

The contrast with the American and French conceptions of the state, as derived from their respective natural rights doctrines, is evident. In the American case, a positive, albeit limited, role for the state follows logically from the formal natural rights doctrine. The paramount need to protect formal rights mandated the creation of a minimal "umpire" state that would best guarantee rights by allowing the greatest scope for individual freedoms. To further guard these rights and liberties, the Constitution was established as the ultimate source of political authority, to which even the state had to defer. In the French substantive natural rights articulation as well, the state is seen in a positive light as the guarantor and provider of the social, economic and political rights to which citizens are entitled. Accordingly, the French state with its extensive interventionary capabilities has become the ultimate source of authority in the polity.

While the scope of state prerogatives is different in each case, there is very little ambivalence or contradiction in either doctrine as to the type of state, limited or interventionary, that would best preserve and guarantee revolutionary goals and accomplishments. Consequently, the doctrines provided clear parameters for post-revolutionary state-building. Although these parameters did not prevent struggles over specific institutional arrangements within the state, they did establish the basic boundaries within which these struggles took place. Stanley Katz, for example, notes that in the American case, in spite of considerable differences in the new political leadership, there was an "universal agreement that all government was to be feared as inevitably self-aggrandizing and hostile to individual liberties and that, consequently, government needed to be somehow limited in the exercise of power."[59] In France, as we have seen, a similar consensus existed as to the role of the state in preserving, protecting and promoting the rights and welfare of French citizens. These new post-revolutionary states were subsequently legitimated as they both embodied and protected the ideals of the natural rights doctrines. Given the positive role played by the state, service to the state was validated as a desirable manifestation of public virtue. American and French revolutionary elites could therefore take on new roles and tasks within the structures of the state in the conviction that both their material and ideal interests would be fulfilled. In other words, the transition from revolutionary protest to routine politics—from struggles against the state to struggles within the state—could take place with relative ease as this transition did not necessitate a reappraisal of revolutionary ideals and commitments. Careerism and idealism could be pursued simultaneously by public actors.

In the case of post-revolutionary Poland, however, Solidarity's doctrine did not provide a positive, uncontested vision of the state's relationship to democratic principles and practices. Consequently, former Solidarity activists, now holding public office after the June 1989 elections, did not have an ideological foundation that would validate both their new roles within the state and the state itself. A turn toward stark political realism and statist thinking soon began to fill this void, as Kamiński indicates:

> Without getting into particulars, I would claim that despite their former anti-statist positions, at least an important part of the present elite has turned statist. More and more often one hears about the "matters of state" which cannot be grasped by an unprepared person, about the "reason of state," etc.[60]

Naturally, other Solidarity activists, generally not holding public office, interpreted this kind of thinking as elitist, being more concerned with the implementation of reforms and with the protection of new privileges, than with the needs and interests of "unprepared" average citizens. The criticisms of Bujak are typical in this respect. For him, the new elites simply perpetuated the "us versus them" gap between the government and the population instead of overcoming it by reaching out to all citizens as Solidarity had once done. Accordingly, he goes so far as to apologize publicly for what Solidarity has become now that it represents the state and a narrow elite rather than society as a whole: "This situation is killing the spirit of Solidarity, is depriving us of the ability to act effectively, is pushing away many able people, and is even killing hope. Therefore, I apologize for Solidarity."[61]

Consequently, Solidarity's core elite was initially divided between those operating within the structures of the state and those outside of the state. Whereas the latter group attempted to hold on to Solidarity's legacy, the former group increasingly attempted to justify their new positions and policies with reference to imported models of state-society relations. In this conflict, the effort to sustain Solidarity's ethos in the post-1989 period was severely weakened as different interpretations of the ethos were supported by different parties and factions. As Skąpska points out:

> as it has been very quickly realized, formal and negative rights and liberties, linked with such open-ended idioms as human dignity, do not provide transformational processes with clear-cut measures and principles. Once enabling the broadest social cooperation, the meanings of the concepts of fundamental rights [have] currently become [the] subject of bitter struggles.[62]

Bujak, for example, represents a continuation of the substantive natural rights orientation that dominated Solidarity in the 1980–81 period. In order to support this orientation, he briefly formed his own party in 1991. Yet, there was also a formal natural rights component to the doctrine. The rights of the individual *were* recognized as important, albeit not to the extent advocated by Król and others. After June 1989, the proponents of individual rights mobilized as well, in order to push for greater recognition of this aspect of Solidarity's legacy. Wiktor Osiatynski, for example, notes that by simply amending the old constitution, the new leadership did not go far enough in guaranteeing citizenship rights: "it is the realm of the protection of rights, which had always been one of the most cherished values of the anti-Communist opposition, that has changed the least under the new allegedly democratic regime."[63] With logic similar to Bujak's, he concludes that "the interest of the political class in individual rights has been vanishing," as this class prefers "to take care of their [*sic*] own business."[64] Given this state of affairs, the Polish Helsinki Committee for Human Rights decided in 1989 to "suspend the membership of anyone who had taken a political post"[65] in order to pursue the cause of protecting individual rights in Poland more effectively.

Still another direction was pursued by Wałęsa during the period before his election to the presidency. Without advocating a consistent ideological line, he attempted to maintain the authority of his charismatic, as opposed to elected, leadership. It seems that for Wałęsa, Solidarity's legacy and democratization itself could best be safeguarded by his continued political presence, however he might choose to exert his influence. Accordingly, he stated in 1990 that "I will build democracy—democratically, semidemocratically, and even undemocratically."[66] While this statement was severely criticized for its "ends justify the means" philosophy, it is just as indicative of the centrality that Wałęsa accorded to himself in the political process. Not "we will build democracy," but "I" will build it—singlehandedly, if necessary. Given this self-image, Wałęsa surrounded himself, after the June 1989 elections, with new supporters and advisors who were committed to the sole aim of furthering his position in the polity.[67]

The fragmentation of Solidarity's legacy into three different interpretations—substantive rights, formal rights and charismatic—represented as they were by separate, and often hostile, factions undermined the overall standing and strength of those advocating a return to Solidarity's principles. Consequently, those members of the core elite who found themselves in elected and appointed positions were in a stronger position to advocate a radical departure from Solidarity's past, beginning with a new conception of the state. Since Solidarity's doctrine offered no guidance in this respect, both French and American models were considered. Kamiński, for example, notes that along with its statist tendencies, the new elite advocated "the French model as the pattern to be followed in solving our own institutional problems."[68] At the same time, the American concept of the limited state also appeared attractive from an economic standpoint, as this concept would justify a contraction of the state's social welfare expenditures.[69] Although clear differences exist between France's centralized interventionist state and America's decentralized limited state, Mazowiecki's government and its supporters attempted to adopt both models simultaneously. In order to fulfill the reform agenda, a state along the French model was considered necessary, while the reforms themselves were intended to result in a limited state along the American model. Means derived from the French model were thereby meant to serve ends derived from the American model. This logic is rather reminiscent of Marxist thinking in which the interventionist state, mandated by the "dictatorship of the proletariat," is ultimately supposed to "wither away" once the task of transformation has been completed.

In sum, while the portion of Solidarity's core elite located outside of the state fragmented and was incapable of mounting a united effort in support of the doctrine articulated in 1980–81, the part of the core elite taking responsibility for the state was susceptible to imported images of the democratic state in particular, and of liberal capitalism in general, since Solidarity's doctrine provided no clear guidance for their new roles and responsibilities. These imported images were subsequently synthesized more in terms of the Marxist intellectual heritage, than in terms of the intellectual framework bequeathed by Solidarity. The "primacy of economics" and the type of state advocated by the first post-Communist government in 1989 are, ironically, more consistent with Marxist thinking, than with the principles and practices embodied by Solidarity in 1980–81. Both the fragmentation of the Solidarity leadership outside of government, and the vulnerability of those inside the government to a combination of Smithian and Marxist principles, can be explained more fully by the weaknesses of Solidarity's original charismatic communities. These communities, ultimately, did not provide a strong enough foundation for a transformation of conduct and consciousness that would have resulted in a more unified core elite wholly committed to a single interpretation of the doctrine. In other words, even if Solidarity's doctrine had contained a consistent view of the state, it is likely, given the problematic nature of the communities, that the core elite would have fragmented anyway.

As we noted in the preceding chapter, the transformatory capacity of the communities during the 1980–81 period was adversely affected by both external and internal factors. Externally, the Party still dominated public life, narrowing the scope and boundaries of what could be changed. Internally, the movement was increasingly conflict ridden over definitions of membership, over the exercise of authority and, ultimately, over the nature of the doctrine itself. According to Jerzy Holzer these factors were related as external "paralysis" contributed to growing internal "aggressiveness":

> Solidarity's paralysis was apparent from summer 1981, and the reaction to this was growing aggressiveness. This was expressed in two, equally unproductive, directions. The first was growing controversies within Solidarity itself. . . . Wałęsa and his advisors were accused of being too conciliatory, yet positive solutions were not that easy to find, and were hardly convincing. There were also accusations of a more personal character: Wałęsa was accused of leading in a non-democratic way and some of his advisors of acting underhandedly. More dangerous was the stirring up of mass hatred. The emerging anti-intelligentsia tendencies can easily be linked with a populist demagogy (often provoked by other members of the intelligentsia, who tried to use them against Wałęsa's advisors). Nationalist demagogy went even further: rivals were accused of lacking

> patriotic feelings, and these accusations were often accompanied by recalling real or supposed sins from the past, for example of collaboration with the Communists. Hidden behind all of this one could find anti-Semitic feelings which, directed against several members of the former KOR, or Wałęsa's advisors with Jewish origins, tried to discredit both groups. The nearer the December catastrophe of the introduction of martial law came, the more one could witness antagonisms, even absurd ones, within Solidarity.[70]

However, these internal suspicions, accusations and ideological departures from Solidarity's doctrine were not just related to external "paralysis." After June 1989, when opportunities for decisive reform presented themselves, when the time of paralysis ended, all of the internal divisions and faultlines came to the fore again—in spite of the change in external circumstances. Consequently, the cause of Solidarity's internal fragility and lack of ideological cohesion is related to the nature of the charismatic communities themselves.

Solidarity's communities were unable fully to put into practice the universal collective understanding of citizenship mandated by the doctrine. The communities of 1980–81 were largely based on previously existing networks of social interaction, and, therefore, provided only limited opportunities for sustained interactions between various social groups. Yet precisely these interactions are crucial for effecting a diminishment of status and class distinctions that citizenship requires, and for paving the way for future associational participatory politics. In order for all members of a polity to be regarded as fully equal citizens endowed with rights, including the right to organize and to participate in government, the rights and interests of average people need to be recognized as legitimate by virtue of a natural rights doctrine. In addition, these rights and interests also need to be *experienced* as legitimate within the communities. In other words, individuals must learn to accord one another equal recognition as citizens, and must act on the principle of "equal recognition through representation in government"[71] already within the context of the communities. As we have seen in the American and French cases, disparate individuals from different socioeconomic backgrounds first began to associate with one another on a regular and voluntary basis in the charismatic communities of the revolutions. A pattern of associative conduct was thereby established as the counterpart to the civic consciousness mandated by the natural rights doctrine.

Solidarity, as well, attempted to create the basis for associational conduct that would correspond to its civic definition of citizenship and that would, by virtue of a social leveling process, fill the gap in Polish social and political life between membership in small groups and membership in the nation. As numerous sociologists have pointed out, Polish society was not just divided by class and status distinctions, it was also segmented by the prevalence of exclusive, personalized, generally class-based networks of small groups that enabled people to cope with the system through informal means.[72] In this context, Janine Wedel notes that:

> Solidarity propagated an ideology of "help each other" and in its rhetoric encouraged people to think beyond the interests of their families and środowiska [small groups]. The organization offered help in solving problems with the state bureaucracy and provided some legal and material assistance; it encouraged relationships beyond the środowisko and broke down class barriers. Solidarity's open atmosphere created the conditions for an explosion of neighborhood and local self-government activities.[73]

Wedel concludes, however, that martial law forced Solidarity itself to turn into "a tangle of loosely organized, clandestine networks in which activity could be organized and recourse sought only through informal means."[74] And, one might add, familiarity with one's fellow activists. Doubtlessly, martial law contributed greatly to Solidarity's failure to replace informal personal networks with formal impersonal associations. However, the foundation for such associations was already impaired by the fact that the original strike communities were based on the previously existing, enclosed worlds of the Leninist industrial plants in which outsiders, such as intellectual advisors, were at a permanent disadvantage vis-à-vis the already constituted informal networks of workers. According to Sergiusz Kowalski, this disadvantage was heightened by the anti-intellectualism he perceives in the movement:

> Already in the days of the first Solidarity . . . the union of 10 million members intended to reduce the role of white collars, and of intellectuals in particular, to that of technical "advisors" or "experts" who should speak up (to the point at that) only when asked to, and shut up when the workers would not wish them to speak.[75]

Solidarity, therefore, from the very beginning, never fully overcame the personalized networks of interaction based largely on class membership. In this context, Tymowski states that:

> Social movement activity (both intelligentsia opposition groups and workers' strikes) depended on an intricate network of micro-structures comprised of środowiska. Even in the most intense "conspiratorial" conditions of martial law, individuals did not "join" groups through formal procedures such as trial memberships, adopting pseudonyms, limited acquaintance with the rest of the organization, and so forth, on the model of the Communist cells or partisan/Home Army organization. Opposition and Solidarity activity was overwhelmingly conducted with people one already knew—from school, church-related activities, a workplace or professional grouping—often in a pattern of interlocking środowiska.[76]

Accordingly, contrary to Wedel's assessment, these networks already operated within the first legal period of Solidarity's existence and had a negative impact on the extent to which associational conduct could be brought into line with civic consciousness. Most significantly, attitudes of distrust and suspicion toward non-members were maintained within the networks, even if these non-members were now a part of the same overall organization. Solidarity was, subsequently, fragmented from within as hostilities between workers and intellectuals, between "true" Poles and dubious Poles, between various oppositional groupings, could not be overcome since they were organizationally sustained by the different środowiska. The ability of Solidarity's charismatic communities to transcend status and class differences was impaired by personalized, substantive criteria of membership that undermined the universal understanding of citizenship articulated in the doctrine.[77]

As a result of this inadequate social leveling, the right of *all* citizens to participate in government on the basis of equal representation was not fully acknowledged nor acted upon in Solidarity's original communities. Consequently, the type of citizen a Pole can be, the type of political activities a Pole can undertake are both still linked to class and status conditions. In the post-1989 environment, for example, the stigma of working-class origins has again become a deterrent to active political participation. The criticisms Wałęsa has undergone, especially since his election to the presidency, are a case in point:

> Wałęsa gets many critical comments from a wide range of people of various backgrounds and sensibilities. . . . Almost every Pole would probably like to be Wałęsa. But on the other side of the coin, just as anyone can imagine himself to be Wałęsa, then anyone can criticize and castigate him without the least embarrassment ("after all, he's just a common peasant and an unmannered yokel"). This is why national criticism of Wałęsa is often aggressive and far too severe when set against his transgressions.[78]

Ironically, given Solidarity's working-class membership, Wałęsa's original charisma has now disappeared completely, in large part because of his own working-class origins. While Wałęsa may still have faith in his charismatic abilities, unquestioning popular faith in his leadership has been replaced with widespread skepticism over his lack of polish and his inability to represent the Polish nation in a properly distinguished fashion.

In short, Solidarity's communities failed to translate the abstract rights of citizenship into appropriate forms of conduct, characterized by the associational participation of all citizens in public life. Instead, the communities fragmented partially along class lines, and partially along ideological lines as the different środowiska provided organizational support for different understandings of both the appropriate interpretation of the doctrine and of which group or class represented the "better" citizens. A unified core elite, dedicated to a single interpretation of Solidarity's doctrine, could not and did not emerge from this setting. The conflicts Solidarity was undergoing in 1981, consequently reemerged in 1989 to impair the ability of the doctrine to generate the institutional domains for post-communist reconstruction.

In this regard, Solidarity's experience is similar to the French Revolution in which the complete transformation of consciousness and conduct was also impaired. While the degree of social leveling that did take place within the French communities was greater than in the Polish case, given the absence of środowiska and the presence of the state as a generally accepted locus of political authority, the conflicts between the communities ultimately minimized the extent to which status and class distinctions could be overcome. Accordingly, the causes and consequences of the weaknesses of the charismatic communities are similar in both cases.

The type of natural law articulated by Solidarity, in its substantive and collective attributes, is obviously similar to the natural rights doctrine that animated the French revolutionaries. In both cases, the individual citizen is directly linked to the greater collectivity of the nation, and, in both cases, the "general will" of the collective citizenry matters more than the freedom of the individual to oppose this majority. A similar emphasis on the substantive, as opposed to formal, interpretation of natural rights is also evident. Rights were not just intended to preserve the citizen's realm of choice and action, but were also intended to preserve a certain basic equality of condition for all citizens. Babeuf and the sans-culottes would well have understood Solidarity's intention to provide all citizens with "the social minimum" to which they were entitled.

Because of these similar visions of citizenship, the charismatic communities were also similarly flawed. Paradoxically, a collective understanding of citizenship leads inevitably to conflicts over who—which group—can best represent the collectivity. These conflicts, in turn, serve to sustain rather than diminish status and/or class distinctions. Consequently, in both the French and Polish cases the social leveling within the communities was not as extensive as in the American Revolution. In the American case, the individualistic conception of citizenship facilitated a diminishment of status distinctions as people were judged on the basis of individual abilities and interests rather than on the basis of collective membership. The result, according to Gordon Wood, "was a society of plain, ordinary people all busy pursuing their own private interests. All thought they had equal rights, all were in equal competition with one another."[79] And, all were engaged in seeking "equal recognition through representation in government." As Daniel Webster noted, "Our system begins with the individual man."[80]

The charismatic communities of the French Revolution were, however, not able to provide such a direct foundation for associative, representative politics, as they could not effect a wholesale diminishment of status distinctions. The exclusionary nature of these communities, as membership was based on demonstrated virtue, combined with each community's claim to be the sole representative of the "general will," severely limited the experience of citizenship as a common identity cutting across all status barriers. The stage was thereby set for conflicts and fragmentation. As Keith Michael Baker points out in regard to the deputies of the 1789 National Assembly:

> it was a condition of the generality of the general will, in Rousseau's conception, that it be neither alienated nor represented. How then could the deputies avoid profound contradiction when they found themselves compelled to combine the theory of the general will with the practice of representation unavoidable in a large state? Nothing was to prove more problematic for the revolutionaries—or more volatile in its implications—than this notion of representing the general will, which opened up the constant risk that the will represented might be the particular will of the representative body rather than the general will of the nation.[81]

In other words, while citizenship was legitimated by the natural rights doctrine, it was only incompletely experienced in the communities struggling over the appropriate definition and embodiment of the general will. A change in conduct never fully matched the change in consciousness. As a result, a great deal of suspicion and hostility divided the revolutionary groups from one another, divisions that ultimately culminated in the Terror.

The unstable character of revolutionary leadership represents another similarity between the French and Polish communities. In both cases, particular leaders were heralded as embodying the collectivity, while leadership in general was equated with demonstrated virtue, with heroic self-sacrifice rather than with formally delegated authority. Once such leaders failed to meet the expectations of their followers, their standing was immeasurably diminished. In this context, both past and present hostility directed toward the former Solidarity leadership in general, and toward Wałęsa in particular, is comparable with the hostility directed against many leaders of the French Revolution as they fell from grace. This contrasts sharply with the respect accorded to America's "founding fathers," whose reputation was based more on how well they carried out delegated authority, rather than on how charismatic they were. Overall, the unstable nature of charismatic leadership in both the Polish and French cases contributed to the failure to establish routinized avenues for political participation for all citizens, regardless of class, status or virtue.

Clearly, a collective conception of citizenship does cause specific problems for the charismatic communities attempting to enact this conception. Conflicts emerge over which community best embodies the collective, while leadership tends to become personalized, with charisma adhering more to particular leaders, than to the values animating the struggle. As a consequence, the communities are weakened, and are unable directly to effect post-revolutionary institution-building. The process of deriving institutional domains from the natural rights doctrine is, therefore, more complicated in the French and Polish cases than in the case of the American Revolution and its aftermath.

In the case of France, only the fact that the identity of citizenship continued to be supported by critical social groups, who were willing to mobilize to protect their rights and interests, enabled the domain of citizenship to be sustained throughout the country's turbulent post-revolutionary history. This domain, in conjunction with the universal acceptance of the French state as the ultimate source of political authority, eventually allowed for a consolidated liberal capitalist democracy to emerge in France.

The following section will examine the likelihood of a similar outcome in Poland by assessing the strengths of Solidarity. In spite of Solidarity's weaknesses, and the resulting inability of Solidarity's elite to derive the domains of post-communist institution-building from the doctrine, Solidarity did effect considerable changes in the lives of average Poles. According to Erik Allardt:

> When one adopts a revolutionary ideology one gets a new reality. . . . A revolutionary ideology in itself does not bring about a change in the existing power relations or in the existing institutions. On the other hand, it seems reasonable to say that a revolutionary ideology certainly implies a reinterpretation of existing power relations and existing institutions.[82]

The "new reality" represented by Solidarity was unable to change existing institutions in 1980–81, but it did reinterpret them in ways that ultimately led to their downfall. The same is likely to be true in the post-1989 period. Solidarity may not have a direct effect on existing power relations and on the newly constituted institutional arrangements, but it still provides a basis upon which people can judge, evaluate and interpret the new institutions. Should the imported institutional domains, especially citizenship, be evaluated positively when judged according to the standards established by Solidarity, then the legitimacy of the post-communist changes will be substantially enhanced.

SOLIDARITY'S STRENGTHS: THE IMPACT ON THE DOMAINS OF LIBERAL CAPITALISM

Citizenship

It is not immediately clear that the domain of citizenship and the rights associated with it have any analytical relevance for the study of contemporary Poland. According to Kolankiewicz, the "withdrawal of extensive welfare provision or social rights in return for social safety nets simultaneously undercut the impact of political and civil rights."[83] Consequently, citizenship rights, their meaning, definition and protection in the new polity, have not played a significant role in public debates or concerns. Instead, concrete issues connected with social welfare and economic survival have taken on greater meaning and resonance since the Balcerowicz Plan went into effect. Indeed, Polish sociologists have noted a marked instrumentalization of democracy given that values such as "individual freedoms and rights, freedom of speech, rule of law, self-government and individual ownership" are "only recognized if they can be effective as instruments for the realization of economic and social values."[84] Koralewicz and Ziółkowski, therefore, conclude that the political and ethical content of democracy has been downgraded, leading to a "specific axiological void" and the prevalence of instrumental pragmatism.[85] As a reflection of these new values, "the ethos of reliable, productive and satisfying work has given way to the ideal of pragmatic, instrumental efficiency, frequently understood as the ruthless struggle for individual advantage according to the principle 'the ends justify the means.' "[86] Whether defending or promoting their socioeconomic well-being, average Poles are perceived as being more interested in the "bottom line" than in exercising and protecting the rights and freedoms of citizenship. Even the new class of private entrepreneurs, the much hoped for and much heralded middle class, has been polled as supporting authoritarian political solutions in order to "do away with strikes disturbing productivity" and to ensure market stability.[87]

This landscape of growing "economic Darwinism" is complemented by socio-political analyses that present:

> [A] negative picture of society gradually falling into apathy and indifference, where the majority of individuals take a negative stance toward reforms, and where only 40% of the voters participated in the election (the lowest percentage in Europe); a picture of a society of sleeping demons (woken up in the city of Mława, where riots against the Gypsy community took place and in Józefów, where riots against a settlement of AIDS victims took place).[88]

In this vein, Miszalska writes about a "lack of trust in the democratic election process among Poles."[89] Poles are not exercising their most basic right, the right to vote, as they see "no relation between participation in the election process and the exercise of political influence."[90] As a result, "citizen privatism," namely, a "retreat from political participation and a burdening of the state authorities with the responsibility for public issues," appears to be increasing.[91] Unfortunately, the "society of engaged, free and trustworthy individuals"[92] promoted by Solidarity has given way to a demoralized, apathetic society on the one hand, and an isolated, arrogant political elite on the other.

In contrast to these negative assessments, other sociologists offer more positive images. Rychard, for example, maintains that "low participation in formal 'macro' politics does not mean passivity. On the contrary, there are many signs of new forms of social activity."[93] Such activities can be documented in the growing numbers of private businesses and of non-governmental organizations. Already, in 1993, 60 percent of the population was employed in the private sector, while in 1996 some 45,000 non-governmental organizations were registered.[94] While the number of NGOs is inexact, it is likely to be the highest number in the region, employing an estimated 70,000 people, with about two million actively involved on a voluntary basis.[95] In addition, confidence and participation in the institutions of local government appears to be increasing. According to CBOS data, approval ratings for local government have continuously been ranked at or over the 50 percent mark since January 1993, which is consistently higher than the approval ratings for the national government.[96] In the light of these patterns, Rychard concludes that a new socioeconomic order "from below" may be taking shape, one that will result in "the real emergence of a civil society in Poland."[97] Kolankiewicz echoes this conclusion by stating that "the so-called macrosystemic rules, based on economic programs largely imported and imposed from above, now function alongside new microrationalities driven by grass-roots interests."[98] Accordingly, Poles are seen as beginning to represent their interests primarily on the level of local communities—a process which should eventually spread upward to the level of national parliamentary politics.

While these assessments reach different conclusions regarding the way in which Poles are adapting to life after Balcerowicz, they are based on similar assumptions regarding the relationship of rights and interests. In both cases, citizenship rights, especially the imported formalized version of these rights, are deemed irrelevant to the emerging pursuit of socioeconomic interests. Even the value-rational legitimacy provided by Solidarity's conception of natural rights, being "insufficiently grounded in material interests"[99] in the post-1989 period, has not been able to provide a coherent civic identity within which interests could be pursued. Consequently, interests are developing on purely instrumental grounds without an ethical or principled justification. For some sociologists, this is a cause for concern as, in their opinion, the naked pursuit of wealth is unlikely to provide a firm foundation for citizenship rights or for democracy. For others, the pursuit of self-interest can and will provide a solid basis for associative politics and the eventual development of civic consciousness. In the first case, interests lead to social apathy and political extremism; in the second case, interests lead to social activism and political participation at a grass-roots level. In neither case, does the Solidarity experience have any bearing on the processes or the outcomes.

On closer examination of post-1989 realities, however, it is not clear that Solidarity's legacy can or should be dismissed so readily. Both the social apathy and the social activism observed by Polish sociologists can be explained by the impact of Solidarity on the major social groups that participated in the movement. Essentially, intellectuals and workers are responding differently to the reforms, based on different interpretations of the Solidarity experience. While intellectuals are, by and large, supportive of the new institutional domains, workers have been resistant to the imported version of liberal capitalism. These different responses have, of course, been analyzed according to the different opportunity structures faced by elites and masses in a newly democratizing and marketizing environment. As Kolarska-Bobińska notes:

> In 1988, the "pro-reformist alliance," which included professionals, technicians, and some skilled workers, was already breaking down. . . . In 1990 the gap between professionals and workers grew. With the advent of the market economy, the interests of both groups diverged. The same was apparent when occupational aspirations and the sense of injustice were discussed.[100]

Yet socioeconomic interests alone cannot determine the form and content of collective and individual responses to formal institutions. According to Suzanne Berger, although socioeconomic structures can and do shape interests by providing "points of opportunity around which groups may organize" and mobilize, these structures do not provide "an unequivocal answer to an individual's (or group's) problem of identity."[101] Identity, in this sense, provides the standards according to which one defines one's interests, and the criteria by which one judges what is the correct or appropriate course of action to represent these interests.

As we have seen, Solidarity in 1980–81 provided a new civic identity for Poles based on a unique articulation of the natural rights doctrine. However, given the fragmented nature of Solidarity's charismatic communities, different interpretations of that doctrine were made possible. Consequently, in addition to the inadequate social leveling produced by these communities, class-based understandings of rights have emerged. In the post-1989 setting, it has become increasingly evident that the formal rights supported by intellectuals are at odds with the substantive rights advocated by workers. Not just different interests are at stake, but also different interpretations of civic identity and natural rights. Workers are determining and representing their interests with reference to Solidarity's primary emphasis on collective and substantive citizenship, just as intellectuals are attempting to fuse the secondary formal and individualistic aspects of Solidarity's doctrine with imported conceptions of liberalism. As a result, although Solidarity was unable to generate new institutional domains, it appears to have generated two conflicting means of legitimation for the domains of liberal capitalism, borne by the two social groups that originally supported the movement. For example, social apathy and economic frustrations are most immediately felt by unskilled and skilled workers employed in the large industrial complexes typical of Leninist development. As is well known, these workers played a considerable role in Solidarity. Their resistance to the reforms initiated after 1989 is, however, not simply due to their disadvantaged material position vis-à-vis marketization. The imported domains of liberal capitalism also violated their understanding of the substantive rights embodied in Solidarity's ethos. Sociological research documents the extent to which workers in general, and skilled workers in particular, still retain a vision of democracy that is based on an equality of condition, as well as on an equality of opportunity.[102] Social and economic rights are, therefore, perceived as being inherent to citizenship. In their absence, civil and political rights become devoid of content and meaning—simply a reflection of empty legal formalism.

Furthermore, the collective sense of citizenship articulated by Solidarity was, from the perspective of workers, consistently violated by the post-communist governments as they espoused the creed of individual responsibility and entrepreneurship while visibly preferring some groups over others. The intellectuals associated with Solidarity, now in charge of the government after June 1989, decided that workers as a class would be hostile to the implementation of the Balcerowicz Plan, and that they had to be treated accordingly. The following assessment made in September 1989 by a prominent Solidarity advisor is typical:

> Heavy-industry workers are thus a group dominated neither by creative, entrepreneurial attitudes nor, above all, by responsibility for one's decisions and acceptance of the rules of the game in accordance with which one can not only win but can also lose. This is combined with the great drama of the collapse of the work ethic. I am afraid that in many people irreversible changes of mentality have occurred, so that demands have become disassociated from a sense of responsibility for one's work.[103]

Workers thus received contradictory signals. On the one hand, citizenship was now to be understood in terms of individual initiative and responsibility, yet, on the other hand, they, as a group, were deemed incapable of such attributes. Moreover, as Skąpska points out, the privatization processes under way seemed directly to violate the principles of individual rights and formal equality by privileging some groups over others in the name of economic efficiency.[104] Accordingly, the workers were well aware that the so-called "nomenklatura privatization" represented a divergence from the norms and principles they were being held to. Not surprisingly, the new individualistic conception of civic rights and responsibilities did not meet with much approval under these circumstances.

This contradiction between the imported domain of formal, individualistic citizenship and Solidarity's understanding of citizenship in largely substantive and collective terms has, for the workers, resulted in a mixture of apathy and actively organized resistance. While the majority of Polish workers have subsided into passivity, a vocal and contentious minority have organized themselves to resist what they perceive to be unjust and untenable violations of *both* their rights and interests. Comparative research conducted by Kubik and Ekiert indicate that between 1989 and 1993, "Poland had the highest incidence of protest among the East Central European countries" studied (including Hungary, Slovakia, East Germany).[105] They go on to define protest actions ranging "from single isolated strikes to nationwide protest campaigns involving hundreds of schools, hospitals, and enterprises as well as thousands of workers and public sector employees."[106] Correspondingly, Poland also has the most numerous and competitive trade unions in East Central Europe. Aside from Solidarity and Solidarity 80 (which initiated the great majority of protest actions), there are almost 200 nationwide trade union organizations. The fact that the collective protests organized by these trade unions "emerged as the most important form of participation in public life"[107] can be directly linked to the ethical and organizational legacies of Solidarity. Not only do workers have first-hand knowledge of how to organize such activities, strikes and other disruptive protests are considered legitimate and appropriate forms of participation. As Kubik and Ekiert conclude:

> The high level of acceptance of disruptive protest, and especially strikes, can be linked to legacies of the Solidarity movement, which symbolically elevated a strike to the most noble form of resistance against the unjust authorities and made it a part of a routinized repertoire of political action. These results make Poland one of the most contentious nations in the world.[108]

Poland may be contentious, but, as the authors point out, the protest actions have remained "decidedly nonviolent."[109] This can be seen as another legacy of the Solidarity movement. It also appears that the protesters view their actions in a civic context, "based on an acceptance of the existing order, intending only to *correct* the governmental—mostly economic—policies" on behalf of society as a whole.[110] While divisive, nationalistic rhetoric is not unknown, the majority of activist workers have couched their demands in terms reminiscent of original Solidarity.[111] This corresponds to Koralewicz's findings that the workers associated with Solidarity in 1980–81 are less prone to favor authoritarian rhetoric or leaders due to the broadening of their "cognitive perspective":

> Let us stress once again the special role that membership in Solidarity played for respondents with less education. The broadening of the cognitive perspective of this category of people (for the most part composed of unskilled and skilled workers) has come about under the influence of experiences resulting from the assumption of a new social role in the independent, self-governing trade union. . . . The performance of a new role, demanding participation in decision making, sharing of the responsibility for definite actions often requiring courage and initiative, and the use of new information, in which inter-human contacts and broadening of the system of ties within the organization were doubtlessly intensified, enlarged the cognitive perspective of and reduced authoritarianism among persons with only lower education.[112]

It would appear that the workers influenced by their membership in Solidarity still possess the capacity for rational, responsible thought that they discovered, or rather uncovered, during the 1980–81 period. In this context, the following exchange, which took place during the August strikes, is paradigmatic: "WAŁĘSA: [I]n sum, I am a worker and therefore I speak of how I feel in the way that I am capable of. WÓJCIK: Yes, but a worker is also capable of thinking. WAŁĘSA: Of course."[113]

In short, the conception of citizenship articulated and put into effect by Solidarity continues to structure the way in which workers' interests have been shaped in the post-1989 period. Both the organizational form and the ethical content of their resistance have been significantly determined by their experiences in the movement. Most importantly, however, the very fact that workers have been mobilized to such an extent in Poland alone is a consequence not only of material threats (which, after all, are faced by workers throughout the region), but also of the threat to their identity as citizens. They have been attempting to hold the post-communist governments accountable to the standard established by the substantive and collective form of citizenship developed within Solidarity.

In this effort, the "contentious" pattern of collective action established by Polish workers bears significant similarities to the French history of class-based protest politics.[114] In France, as well, the extra-parliamentary forms of protest that first emerged during the Revolution have long been considered both legitimate and appropriate means for citizens, especially lower-class citizens, to communicate their interests and frustrations to the state. Accordingly, one can argue that the tradition of collective action established during the 1980–81 period in Poland will have a similarly enduring impact on the polity.[115]

At the same time, the intellectuals who participated in Solidarity have, by and large, accepted the formal rights-based, individualistic form of citizenship imported via the Balcerowicz Plan as consistent with their interpretation of the Solidarity experience. Along with providing the major electoral base of support for the two political parties most directly associated with liberal capitalist reform (the Democratic Union and the Liberal Democratic Congress, now joined into the Freedom Union), Polish intellectuals remain active in the protection of civil, as opposed to social and political, rights. Furthermore, rather than engaging in collective action directed at the state, this social group has been instrumental in the promotion of associative, self-help oriented, non-governmental organizations that promote causes such as environmental protection, minority rights, women's rights, and charities on a community level. Research also shows that former Solidarity intellectuals are active in local government, a realm of participatory opportunity that has until recently been unique to Poland.[116] In 1990, Poland became the first post-communist country to engage in a democratic reform of local government, allowing for substantial autonomy and decentralization.[117] This reform as well is a direct legacy of Solidarity's concern with self-government, and has been quite successful in stimulating and supporting a multitude of community initiatives. Kuroń even concludes that on the level of non-governmental social services, these community initiatives compare very favorably to those in the West.[118] As in the case of worker activism, these associative and participatory endeavors are not just reflections of material interests; rather they are a reflection of the civic identity developed and experienced before and during the Solidarity movement. Unlike workers, however, intellectuals have drawn on the formal, individualistic aspects of Solidarity's ethos. According to Koralewicz, intellectuals are translating their individual sense of responsibility into collective actions designed to change certain realities for the better.[119] Needless to say, these efforts support the conception of citizenship imported by Mazowiecki's government. Within this social group we see citizens valuing and utilizing the formal civil and political rights implicitly envisioned in the Balcerowicz Plan. Economic entrepreneurship is thereby accompanied by civic entrepreneurship.

In sum, the perceptions of citizenship developed during the 1980–81 period continue to shape the pursuit of interests in the post-1989 era by providing certain standards for the way in which interests are evaluated and represented. Although a large portion of Polish society may be politically apathetic and withdrawn, viewing democracy only in instrumental terms, a significant minority exists, comprised of both skilled workers and intellectuals, that continues to see citizenship in active, as opposed to passive, terms.[120] Guided by different understandings of citizenship, both these social groups nonetheless use the rights of citizenship to legitimate the promotion of their interests. Citizenship has consequently emerged as the dominant category of political membership in Poland, successfully marginalizing other categories of membership based, for example, on ethnicity. The Solidarity experience has, in this regard, provided ample grounds for the legitimation of the domain of citizenship. The problem is that the grounds are too ample, encompassing both formal and substantive interpretations of rights.

Clearly, the middle-class coalition of skilled workers and intellectuals that provided the social base for Solidarity's emergence in 1980–81 has broken apart. Different interpretations of citizenship and different modes of civic organization have been the result. In the midst of the apathy of the majority, a vocal minority of Poles has been divided between formal and substantive conceptions of natural rights. Different, class-based, worlds have thereby been forming between those who resist the transformations on the basis of substantive rights and those who support the imported liberal capitalist domains. As Jedlicki recently pointed out: "We are facing a possible split in which the effect would be the existence of two distinctly differing worlds alongside one another. At the moment that is only a danger, but a very real one."[121]

Such class-based polarization is likely to lead Poland back to the prewar era of a "gentry democracy" restricted to the privileged classes, while the rest of society remains marginalized—but not necessarily passive. If current trends continue, Poland will be more volatile than its East Central European neighbors as groups threatened with marginalization use the ethical and organizational "repertoire" they have inherited from Solidarity to protest their material and social conditions.

There are, however, indications that a reconciliation is possible between the two interpretations of citizenship—between the skilled workers and intellectuals. Here Jedlicki, as a member of the intelligentsia, appears to offer an olive branch:

> It might well be that it is more important that the other half of society be protected against rapid degradation and a sense of not belonging. I am not thinking of some kind of a disaster. Rather of the need for a basic redefining of the whole strategy of transformation. It is already clear that economic growth is no cure for unemployment by itself. It may very well be that we shall have to restate just what our final goals really are.[122]

In this vein, the proposed Bill of Rights prepared between 1990 and 1993 offers another indication that formal and substantive rights can be reconciled as a potential restatement of "final goals." The bill makes a neat distinction between the formal (civil and political) rights of citizenship that the state is bound to guarantee and the substantive (social and economic) rights that the state pledges itself to attempt to attain. The right to work, for example, is not guaranteed, but the state does pledge itself to maintain policies conducive to the creation of new workplaces.[123] While, as James Madison pointed out, all constitutions and bills of rights are ultimately simply "parchment barriers," the legitimacy and the efficacy of any given constitution will depend on the degree to which critical social groups see their rights and interests reflected in it.

In post-Solidarity Poland, this level of acceptance cannot be accomplished by a constitution that is solely based on formal rights, or a constitution that is solely based on substantive rights. In other words, both upper and lower echelons of the middle class need to reach an agreement over the definition of rights and citizenship.

Representative government

The domain of representative government established after 1989 has met with a similar pattern of acceptance on the part of intellectuals and resistance on the part of workers. Whereas, by and large, intellectuals associated with Solidarity believe that representative government is the most appropriate and effective means for implementing far-reaching reforms, workers consider this form of government to be a violation of the more direct forms of participatory and consultative government developed within Solidarity.[124] As we have seen, the first post-communist governments and elected officials acted in ways that distanced them from the population at large and even from other Solidarity members outside of government. The concept of representation prevalent among the new political elites was clearly a Burkean one in which elected officials felt themselves bound to represent the national interest as they understood it, rather than the interests of any immediate or specific constituency.[125] Consequently, the Balcerowicz Plan was implemented without much popular consultation or broad levels of participation—even on a symbolic level, such as Clinton-style town hall meetings, which would have been in keeping with the Solidarity traditions. Instead, Mazowiecki's government in particular withdrew into the narrow circles of trusted former opposition intellectuals, many of whom had known one another since high school.[126]

This replication of the środowiska that had dominated the opposition period, while perhaps understandable given the pressures faced by the new leadership, ultimately led people to believe that one clique had simply replaced the other at the top, with very little changed for those below. In this context, the efforts of Solidarity governments to establish a functioning representative government, characterized by a separation of powers, freely held elections and competitive party politics, did not resonate with the broader population. As late as 1992, only 9 percent of those polled believed that "democracy has replaced the communist dictatorship," while 16 percent believed that a "new Solidarity dictatorship" had simply replaced the old one, and 27 percent were uncertain over how the new leadership would develop.[127] The reduction of representative government to closed door "salon" politics and Burkean elitism clearly represented a violation of what people expected from a democratic government. According to Koralewicz and Ziółkowski, people expected, at the very least, to be consulted:

> More important than the democratic procedures of appointment and supervision of power was the consideration on the part of power of the genuine interests and needs of members of society. The consultative model of power has a very strong element of morality–equality–dignity. The point is to reduce the distance between power and society, to acquire information feedback, to enhance the influence and self-estimation of the ruled, and also for those in power to take society's needs into account and to satisfy them as far as possible.[128]

When these needs were not met, voter turnout dropped to the lowest levels in Europe, disapproval ratings soared and, eventually, the post-Solidarity elites were removed from power.[129]

While the return of the ex-communists to power (in the September 1993 parliamentary elections) was not novel to Poland, the type of protest voting and the degree to which representative government has been contested are. For example, no other country of the region produced a Stan Tymiński, a candidate for presidency with no political biography and a shady past spent largely abroad, yet who appeared to support post-communist social and economic change. Ultimately, he received 25 percent of the votes cast in the second round of the 1990 presidential election. Some analysts have tended to explain Tymiński's success in terms of "homo sovieticus," namely the political immaturity of a population conditioned by communism.[130] Research indicates, however, that the vote for Tymiński was largely a vote against Solidarity. Voters were frustrated with the elitism of Mazowiecki's government, the disintegration of the Solidarity camp, and Wałęsa's "war at the top."[131] Seen from this perspective, Tymiński's success was more reminiscent of French popular support for the "man-on-horseback"—for a national figure above politics who might restore post-revolutionary law and order and transcend growing class conflicts.

Significantly, Tymiński indicated in rather vague terms that he wanted to restore law and order by consolidating the post-1989 gains rather than by rolling back the clock in counter-revolutionary fashion. He promised to make everyone a millionaire within the new system, presenting himself as an example of a capitalist rags-to-riches story. His candidacy did not, therefore, represent a traditional authoritarian solution to the problems of the day. His electoral success, consequently, must be understood as a powerful reaction to the *way* change was being pursued by the Solidarity leadership, not necessarily as a protest against change itself. As Grabowska notes:

> The presidential campaign of 1990 revealed, possibly for the last time in so clear a way, the subjective and affranchised aspirations of the Polish society. The promises of L. Wałęsa to "refresh Warsaw" and quickly privatize the state economy and the promises of Stan Tymiński, that under his rules "everyone will grow rich," awoke hopes for more genuine participation in power and a greater likelihood of individual economic activity, which were to be supported by the process of privatization and the plans of Tymiński. Democracy was to be, at last, not just abstract power upon the people and for the people, but also by the people.[132]

The intensity of this type of protest is unique to Poland, as the Solidarity experience generated a standard of democratic governance according to which the new political elites could be judged and, ironically, found wanting.

Also unique to Poland, and another manifestation of the degree of protest prevalent in Polish society, is the strength of leftist political orientations. While ex-communist parties have been successful throughout the region in pursuing a pragmatic social democratic course, Poland was the first country to establish a non-communist left-wing party as well—the Union of Labor—which was founded, in large part, by former Solidarity activists.[133] Along with a social democratic economic agenda, the party favors a more participatory style of government and appears more ideologically committed to the 1980–81 ideals of a self-governing republic than any other political group. Although the Union of Labor received only 7.3 percent of the vote in the September 1993 elections, this is still a remarkable achievement for a small party with almost no organizational base. Again, the electoral success of both the post-communist and the post-Solidarity Left has been explained with reference to the "homo sovieticus" phenomenon, and/or with reference to the economic interests of threatened social groups such as workers, pensioners and state sector employees.[134] Granted, these are significant explanatory variables, yet they might not tell the whole story. Resistance to the post-1989 violation of the type of democracy put into practice by Solidarity in 1980–81 may also play a role in ensuring the electoral success of the Left. Accordingly, the political impact of the Left in Poland may well be more substantial and durable than elsewhere in East Central Europe as their constituency is voting on the basis of normatively grounded protest against the imported domain of representative government, as well as on the basis of economic interests.

In addition to the leftist critiques of representative government, right-wing conservative political groups and the Catholic Church itself have also, directly and indirectly, contested this form of government.[135] For these critics, the issue is less one of improving levels of popular participation than of improving the type of representation that is being offered by the post-communist governments; they argue that Polish nationalist, Catholic interests and values should be represented, rather than liberal, cosmopolitan, secular ones. Although these parties are not represented in the current parliament, one-third of the electorate did vote for the Right in September 1993. While not all of these voters had been associated with the Solidarity movement of 1980–81, a considerable number were. For the less educated, rural members of the movement the religious symbolism of Solidarity was important and meaningful. In the eyes of these Poles, the secularization and materialism of capitalism in general, and the moral inadequacies of representative government in particular, are poor substitutes for the moral high ground once occupied by the movement.

Overall, one can see a growing split between clerical and anticlerical tendencies in Poland as the Church attempts to promote its agenda of anchoring Christian values both constitutionally and institutionally in the new polity. In these attempts, the Church has resisted the secularism of all post-1989 governments, be they post-Solidarity or ex-communist. Opponents of the Church are increasingly fearful that the separation of church and state, a fundamental prerequisite for a liberal democratic government, will be jeopardized if the Church continues to dictate policies in the cultural, educational and medical realms.[136] Interestingly, the point of departure for this conflict would appear to lie with the first post-communist government. In keeping with the formal, individualistic understanding of rights advocated by the Mazowiecki government, Kulerski, a Solidarity activist and secretary of state in the Ministry of Education from 1989 to 1991, promoted the teaching of values based on the Universal Declaration of the Rights of Man. According to a conversation Kulerski had with a representative of the Church, the Church resisted this proposal on the grounds that the Universal Declaration was based on the Declaration of the Rights of Man and Citizen articulated during the French Revolution. Because the French Church had suffered enormous losses during the Revolution, the Polish Church could not agree to the Universal Declaration in spite of its humanistic and Christian elements.[137] With direct reference to French history, similar post-revolutionary faultlines would appear to be opening up in Poland as the Church struggles to avoid the loss of influence it would suffer if a secularized, Western understanding of rights prevails.

Finally, the weak and fragmented nature of the political party system is another indication that the institutionalization of a truly representative government is problematic, even for the intellectual elites. As Wesołowksi indicates:

> some unrealistic beliefs were nurtured by several prominent Solidarity intellectuals and politicians. They believed that the post-Solidarity parties would keep cooperating in spite of divergences. They did not foresee that once internal disputes flared up, they would acquire a dynamic of their own which would explode the unity and create divisions hard to overcome.[138]

In part, this dynamic of dissolution was carried forward by the opposition tradition of operating and organizing in small groups and informal networks. Once the overarching unity of the Solidarity movement eroded after the June 1989 elections, it is not surprising that these środowiska began to develop in divergent, often hostile, directions. As a result of this development, parties remain small, anchored in personality rather than program, and weakly organized at a grass-roots level. Rather than appealing to a new popular constituency, post-Solidarity parties have tended to function on the basis of old elite networks. Not surprisingly, polls indicate widespread dissatisfaction with party politics. According to one 1993 study, "over half the respondents (53 percent) accepted the statement that 'nobody needs political parties except their leaders and activists.' "[139]

In short, representative government, as it has been implemented in Poland, has faced considerable opposition. What sets Poland apart from other post-Communist states, in this context, is the extent to which the opposition on both the Left and the Right can mobilize the population, mainly the working class, by referring, either directly or indirectly, to the ideal standards of political life achieved within the Solidarity movement. In particular, the idea of participatory unity as opposed to divisive, cliquish party politics remains a potent rallying call. As late as September 1994, 42 percent of the Poles "supported the idea of recreating the unified Solidarity movement" although "only 28 percent believed such unification was possible."[140] Consequently, political groupings and parties seek to represent the "common good" in an abstract fashion, rather than particular interests represented in a parliamentary system. According to Wesołowski this tendency has resulted in the instability of parliamentary government, and in the rise of "dual thinking" on the part of average citizens. On the one hand, democracy is still valued but, on the other hand, "democratic mechanisms" are viewed with increasing hostility.[141] In effect, Solidarity's legacy has weakened the domain of representative government by investing alternative visions of government with greater normative legitimacy.

Given this degree of resistance to representative government, what will the likely outcomes be for Poland? What kind of democratic government will be institutionalized in the wake of the Solidarity experience? Corporatism has already been mentioned by several analysts as a possible outcome of the current tensions between the dual legacies of communism and Solidarity on the one hand, and the imported domain of representative government on the other. Indeed, Bialecki and Heyns find that corporatism, on a de facto basis, is already operating in Poland:

> Corporatism is common in Poland today not because it is necessarily the most efficient way of exercising power and control, nor simply because it has been imposed from above. It seems doubtful, in fact, that this particular style of ruling was even the conscious choice of elites. In a country that routinely managed many diverse aspects of life through social networks, such a system seems natural.[142]

In other words, the tradition of środowiska maintained under communism and within Solidarity, as well, is antithetical to the development of a representative government based on the unfettered interplay of interests.

Other analysts, however, see precisely the opposite; namely, the need for a mixture of representative and participatory styles of government as the only institutionalized outcome consistent with Solidarity's legacies. Kurczewski, for example, concludes that:

> The classroom opposition between representative and participatory democracy takes a different shape in practice. In a developed modern democracy, representatives, the executive power, the judiciary, and political parties are of importance. Americans may complain about low participation in elections and low interest in local government, but in American life there are still thousands of active associations. . . . The political class needs to be under the direct pressure and control of the various associations that represent the specific interests and values of various social categories and groups.[143]

Based on Kurczewksi's analysis of Solidarity in 1980–81 such "direct pressure and control" was a constituent element of the movement and, consequently, has deep roots in Polish political culture.

A third outcome is, however, more likely based on an extrapolation of current trends. Polish political life might well fluctuate for quite some time between elite-based corporatism operating behind the façade of representative government, and periods of active social mobilization on behalf of participatory politics advocated either in the name of social democracy or conservative Christianity. Whereas the development of such façade democratic governments is the probable fate of many post-communist states,

Solidarity has generated an ideal standard of popular government that will continue to cause special political and social tensions if elitist deviations depart too far from accepted standards. One can therefore predict a rather stormy future as Poles struggle to invest the domain of representative government with greater legitimacy, or abandon the task in favor of some alternative form of government.

Proceduralism

In contrast, it appears as if the legitimacy of rules, laws and procedures as the primary basis for adjudicating conflicting interests is relatively well established in post-communist Poland. Indeed, democratic proceduralism was one of the major factors given in public opinion surveys that justified obedience to the new authorities.[144] Proceduralism has also been promoted consistently by the media as journalists have been quick to criticize political actors for violating rules and procedures. In general, the law-abiding nature of Polish citizens has been established by cross-national surveys. For example, Skąpska's work indicates that "in Poland, civic legalism is strongly linked with the ultimate value of citizens' rights, therefore it has more substantial, and less formal characteristics."[145] She attributes this respect for civic rights as an ultimate value to Polish traditions, including the most recent experience of Solidarity. In addition, Poles manifest a "high level of declared legality."[146] In other words, they declare an unwillingness to break laws even if they are unfair, or if it is in their interest to do so. While, in reality, Poles may not always live up to this ideal, the "ideal of a well ordered society" is clearly present. Skąpska goes on to indicate that this ideal is missed by Poles in the current circumstances.[147] The ensuing gap between the ideal and the real may well be due to the conflicts that emerged in the post-1989 period regarding which type of law—positive or natural—should constitute the foundation of a new judicial system.

The newly elected officials of Mazowiecki's government, and Solidarity intellectuals overall, decided early on to operate on the principle of legal positivism. Existing laws would be maintained and honored, even if they had been formulated by the communists to uphold an entirely different system. As Maria Los indicates, "arguments in favor of the recognition of legal continuity referred often to the principle that legal outcomes of the formerly binding laws had to be respected in order to conform to the venerable dictum that the law must not act retrospectively (*lex retro non agit*)."[148]

There were, however, also more pragmatic grounds for choosing legal continuity:

> To be consistent, they would have to rule the whole inherited legal system as null and void, thereby creating a situation of total chaos and lawlessness in the period following the end of the communist rule and until a

> new system of law were put into place. Moreover, all legal decisions of the communist period would have to be invalidated, releasing a flood of retroactive claims and counter-claims in all possible areas of social, political and economic life, not to mention the necessity of immediate opening of all prison gates, dismissing of the entire criminal justice system's personnel, and canceling of all law degrees granted by communist universities (including those held by many parliamentarians!).[149]

Paradoxically, the choice of legal continuity over a natural-law-based reform of the system came to be embodied by Mazowiecki's 1989 declaration of a "thick line" between the communist past and the democratic present. While the declaration was meant only to make a distinction between the communist system, which should be condemned, and the people associated with it, who should be forgiven if they broke no existing laws, the declaration's ultimate effect was to undermine public faith in the rule of law. It seemed as if laws were still being manipulated to protect the guilty. In addition, legal continuity

> did not provide a symbolic break with the communist normative order, which would signal the birth of a new system of law that can be trusted and treated as a guide and facilitator, no longer perceived as an oppressive, alien and corruption-prone tool of the monopolistic party.[150]

In this case as well, the Solidarity intellectuals and elected representatives took positions that were removed from those of the other social groups that had participated in the movement. While proceduralism is valued by these groups, it derives its legitimacy and meaning from its connection with substantive justice, as opposed to formal legality. According to Skąpska, nearly 60 percent of Poles justify obedience to the law with reference to the concept of social justice. Expectations of social justice therefore underlie people's acceptance of formal procedures.[151] If justice is denied or circumvented, proceduralism loses its significance.

By neglecting natural law principles and foreclosing even a symbolic retribution for past sins on the part of the communists, Mazowiecki's government alienated the majority of Poles. For example, although research indicates that most Poles were not in favor of individually based lustration policies, almost 50 percent of those polled in 1990 were in favor of banning the communist party as an organization from political life. According to Rychard, "it is possible to conclude that for one-quarter of those who advocate eliminating the communist party as a political power, this is because they think that the communists are still in power."[152] Given the policies of the first post-communist government, this was not an illogical conclusion to reach at the time.

Even though the ex-communists were subsequently returned to power in 1993, this should not obscure the damage done to the concept of the rule of law by the strict adherence to legal positivism. Indeed, "legal nihilism" rather than a respect for the law seems to be the outcome of such policies, especially when seen in conjunction with Poland's laborious post-communist constitution-writing process. What greater meaning can constitutional laws have when they are so clearly the product of particular interests and parties operating within the parliament? Why should average Poles obey the law when public authorities are perceived as having violated the principle, if not the letter, of the law? The initial faith in the validity of democratic procedures would appear to be eroding rather rapidly. In the wake of popular disappointments regarding the rule of law, there is a general sense that proceduralism and the legal system have failed to live up to their promise to adjudicate interests in a fair and impartial manner.

While the spread of "legal nihilism" is not unique to Poland, widespread frustration over the conduct of public officials is a rather specific Polish trait. Impersonalism, the efficient discharging of duties and responsibilities and the effective representation of interests, has never been an adequate standard for the evaluation of public servants. Instead, as we have seen, Polish history in general and Solidarity in particular have established the heroic selfless servant of the "common good" as the appropriate embodiment of public virtue. Obviously, this standard is almost impossible to maintain in routinized political life where compromises, selfish interests and rampant egotism play their roles. The fact that Solidarity's elected representatives after June 1989 were unable to live up to the heroic standard had a negative impact on the legitimacy of democracy itself. According to Miszalska:

> The disenchantment with democracy may be viewed through the normative model of the politician/parliamentarian, present in common consciousness. The model focuses, first, on moral attitudes (honesty, loyalty, adherence to ideals, incorruptibility) and next on intellectual qualifications and competence, and the style of policy making. Significantly less importance is attributed to political programs and options. The normative vision of Parliament encompasses its composition by individuals of an unblemished reputation and outstandingly competent, one could say "the best of the best." The peculiar feature of the ideal politician/parliamentarian is, paradoxically, his lack of involvement in political issues, impartiality with regard to political and ideological options or group interests. Thus, policy making is not seen as a "stirring" of different interests, but as implementing the rather obscure "common good."[153]

Not living up to this "normative model" cost Solidarity politicians dearly in terms of popularity and support, especially during the Mazowiecki era. Not only did public opinion turn against them, but so too did unelected Solidarity leaders such as Wałęsa and Bujak, who claimed that particular interests were being served by the government and that the ideals of Solidarity were being betrayed.

Ultimately, the Solidarity camp split under conditions that led people to believe that selfish, egotistic interests were being pursued at the general expense of the population. The reputation of public actors supposedly implementing democratic reforms was thereby irrevocably tarnished and, by association, democratic government itself suffered. Elsewhere in the region, people may feel a lack of trust or a lack of enthusiasm for their public officials, but a sense of betrayal that is specifically linked to high expectations of moral conduct on the part of public officials is uniquely Polish. The very fact that Poles do have a sense that public service is a valid and, indeed, almost sacred calling is significant in this regard. In other post-communist states, "public service is not understood as an ideal" nor seen as a particularly legitimate calling.[154] Unfortunately, the Polish perception of ideal public service has not resulted in greater stability. Instead, the behavior of public officials in particular and existing circumstances in general have been subjected to regular scrutiny and contestation.

In short, while no society prefers corrupt and immoral or amoral public servants, Solidarity, in 1980–81, represented an organized expression of resistance to these traits, as well as embodying a higher moral standard. The corruption of Gierek's party ultimately fueled the sense of injustice that mobilized such widespread participation in the movement. Consequently, Poles have both an ethical and an organizational base for resisting behaviors deemed inappropriate in the public realm. For example, unlike the spontaneous demonstrations against mafia crimes in Russia and Lithuania, the businesses of an entire neighborhood (Warsaw's Old Town) organized a three-day strike in order to demand an end to police corruption, the inattention of public officials and the paying of protection money to the mafia.[155] Based on the Solidarity model, organized resistance in the form of strikes has, by and large, become the standard response in Poland to perceived violations of norms and expectations.

While, in the long run, such resistance may result in a less corrupt polity, in the short run, holding officials accountable to an heroic concept of public virtue has had debilitating effects on public perceptions of both proceduralism and the entire reform process. High expectations of the Solidarity leadership led Poles to support a program of transformation that was "more radical and unrealistic than that pursued elsewhere in the region."[156] Inevitable disappointments in that leadership have subsequently led to more bitterness and confusion over the reforms and their ultimate outcomes. As Bialecki and Heyns conclude:

> Many Poles have realized by now that the final destination point on the road of change is by no means as certain as originally thought; neither when it can be achieved, nor where exactly Poland might land are clear.[157]

All in all, the rollercoaster of high expectations and bitter awakenings both in regard to democratic leaders and the rule of law has undermined the support of most social groups for proceduralism as a critical component of the reform process. While, by and large, intellectuals still support the rule of law, working-class Poles see proceduralism as a cover for the pursuit of particular interests or as a poor substitute for heroic, virtuous leadership. Proceduralism, as an institutional domain establishing the parameters of public conduct, is therefore only weakly legitimated. As a result, noncompliance with the law is a prevalent fact of life, especially in the economic realm where tax evasion and the abuse of unemployment benefits are common.

The free mar ket

Although these economic "evasions" might eventually reach critical proportions, the greatest concern among analysts is the extent to which certain socioeconomic interests might impede the process of marketization and privatization. In this context, the workers who supported Solidarity originally are perceived to be structurally disadvantaged by their employment in the large, obsolete industrial complexes. Consequently, it has been assumed that these workers are almost inherently hostile to the market and to private enterprise. This was certainly the conclusion reached by Solidarity intellectuals as they began to encounter social resistance to their implementation of the Balcerowicz Plan. Even Kuroń became critical of the socialist "myth" of the primacy of the working class which perpetuated the self-importance of this group and fueled their resistance to reforms.[158] Yet, a closer reading of the available evidence reveals that while workers object to the concept of the free market imported under the Plan, they are not opposed to marketization per se.

Specifically, the free market goal of an economy entirely based on private ownership has been resisted in favor of a limited version of privatization and continued state ownership of necessary social services (such as health, education and transportation) and large industries. Adamski, for example, finds that the skilled workers and technical specialists, the groups "most active during the social protest of the 1980s," are "conspicuous by their relatively strong support for the privatization of large factories" when compared to other social groups.[159] "It should be mentioned, however, that this support is mainly for a limited form of privatization."[160] Even 50 percent of the workers in the large enterprises support some version of privatization. In general, survey research conducted from 1990 onwards demonstrates that a mixed economy model "which would preserve some social control over privatized property" is consistently preferred by workers, while intellectuals are more likely to support a complete privatization of the economy.[161]

In other words, these social groups maintain different views of what a market economy should entail. Among workers, there is a general acceptance of the need for economic rationalization, private property and a competitive economy—even if one's own job in the state sector may be lost in the process. Solidarity, the trade union, did after all fully support the implementation of the Balcerowicz Plan. Even when economic conditions worsened for the workers, the union consistently attempted to find compromise solutions by negotiating with the government. However, workers maintain the conviction that certain critical economic sectors and the protection of the weakest members of society should continue to be under state control. This conviction is in keeping with Solidarity's original 1981 program which stipulated that: "The union recognizes the need for restoring market equilibrium within the framework of a reliable anti-crisis program, which would be in line with the principle of protecting the weakest members of the population."[162] While the market, understood as a "decentralized competitive economy," was supported in 1981, it was to be embedded in a larger social context. Almost fifteen years later, this contingent support for market principles is still prevalent among workers. These views conflict, however, with those of the intellectuals who, by and large, support the more radical economic transformation envisioned in the Plan, i.e. the complete liberation of the economy from political and social controls. An exception, here, might well be the more critical attitudes of Catholic intellectuals who, like Turowicz, are more in favor of government intervention "to protect people harmed by capitalism."[163]

Significantly, the workers would appear to be more representative of society at large. According to Kolarska-Bobińska, the overwhelming majority of Polish society "prefers both a welfare state and a tame market, a market without extreme social consequences."[164] Overall, the market alone is not seen as a fair mechanism for the distribution of rights, resources and privileges in society. There is a generalized belief that "the allocation of privileges should be based on social, rather than political or economic criteria."[165] "Social perceptions of justice" should, consequently, be taken into consideration in the reform process according to most Poles. Accordingly, the majority of Poles believe that the policies of the Third Republic violate these principles by undermining the weak and supporting the strong and rich. Unrestricted privatization thus becomes a mechanism through which the strong can steal from the weak, namely the workers. The fact that some 50 percent of new owners have actually emerged from the old nomenklatura substantiates popular perceptions of the unjust nature of the reforms.[166] In this context, government policies are seen as a betrayal of social justice, not simply as misguided, unbalanced or inefficient.

Clearly, at issue here are the conceptions of rights and justice that were developed during the Solidarity movement. Workers, in particular, believe that they have the right to be consulted in the privatization process and that employee ownership is more just than any other form of ownership. Again this is a legacy of Solidarity's original insistence on worker self-management. It is not surprising, therefore, that workers resist private ownership, in part, because of "the uncertain legal status of Polish trade unions in the private sector."[167] Since eliminating workers' self-management councils was a precondition for privatization, workers subsequently concluded that their rights and interests would be unprotected in the private sector. There is a widespread concern, therefore, not just with employment and economic survival, but also with the status and dignity acquired through Solidarity's promotion of self-management. Consequently, many workers (and Poles in general) would prefer to begin their own businesses rather than accept employment with private firms. In the fall of 1990, for example, 33 percent of those employed outside of agriculture "declared the wish to work for themselves."[168] Furthermore, more than half of these respondents preferred self-employment for the "greater chance of autonomy and self-fulfillment" it offered, rather than the financial opportunities involved.[169] Accordingly, such businesses are "frequently small and not very profitable,"[170] but they do allow Poles to regain the sense of autonomy and personal efficacy experienced within the context of the movement.

Given the ethical legacy of Solidarity, it is also not surprising that both workers who are winning and those who are losing in the process of marketization maintain the same principles of social justice. In other words, economic differentiation has not led to a differentiation of values and norms. Free market principles are increasingly rejected as they conflict with ideals such as equality and social cooperation, regardless of whether the respondents are doing well or poorly on a personal level.[171]

While analysts have concluded that such rejections are linked to the communist past and to the presence of "peasant and Roman Catholic traditions in Poland,"[172] the impact of Solidarity on average Poles cannot be overlooked as an explanatory variable. Indeed, the simultaneous rejection of market principles *and* the acceptance of individual entrepreneurship is directly related to the Solidarity experience. For example, the standard of dignity upheld within the movement has facilitated individual initiative and risk-taking by imbuing ordinary people with a sense of self-confidence and self-respect. Furthermore, the practice of self-management, which became a "symbol of freedom and autonomy" during the 1980–81 period, has come to legitimate individual entrepreneurship. If self-management is no longer possible on an enterprise level, then at least it can be achieved on a personal level by becoming one's own boss or by fighting for greater employee rights. In this context, Kolarska-Bobińska is correct when she observes that:

> In the nineties we appear to be witnessing the adjustment of institutions initially shaped in the centrally planned economy to a new socio-political order. In the new socio-economic order self-management is being used to secure the influence and autonomy of employees rather than to serve the interests of firms. Self-management is also a symbol of freedom and autonomy, the same values that many identify with the market.[173]

In the same vein, Kuroń notes that the "widespread capacity for self-organization, as developed in the Solidarity movement, contributed to the fact that the introduction of the market enabled many people and social groups to initiate a true transformation."[174] At the same time, however, these standards and practices delegitimate the imported domain of the free market as many other people are no longer able to live in dignity, and the rights and opportunities associated with enterprise self-management have been rendered meaningless.

This interplay of individuals taking advantage of business opportunities within the new market, while rejecting free market principles, again sets Poland apart from its neighbors. In large part as a result of Solidarity, many Poles have supported marketization on a behavioral level by taking advantage of the freedom and autonomy it can provide. Yet, on the level of principles, they also have a clear sense that the free, self-regulated market is inconsistent with their beliefs and expectations. A "tame market" along the lines of France's semi-regulated market would certainly be more in keeping with the substantive natural rights doctrine originally articulated by Solidarity. However, the development of such a market has been and continues to be resisted by the intellectual elites who supported the imported domain of the free market. In their eyes, such "corrective" measures as market regulations, state-funded welfare policies, tariff barriers and limited privatization all represent backsliding into the communist past. For many former opposition intellectuals, the Balcerowicz Plan has become an absolute standard according to which progress should be measured, especially in the economic realm. Unfortunately, as Kolankiewicz points out, this is a standard without any legitimacy for the population at large, which perceives the free market mainly in terms of "economic instrumentalism."[175]

It would appear, then, that the central problem of marketization in Poland is not the inability of society to behave in ways consistent with the market, nor is it a legitimacy deficit; rather it is a problem of two conflicting types of legitimacy. On the one hand, intellectuals believe in the legitimacy of the free market as exemplified by its Anglo-American manifestation. On the other hand, workers, and most average Poles, believe in the legitimacy of a semi-regulated market as the only appropriate embodiment of the ideals of social justice developed in the past. Even though natural rights are not explicitly referred to in either vision, there is a clear conflict here between formal and substantive interpretations of economic rights. Whereas Polish neo-liberals express themselves in terms reminiscent of Adam Smith, Polish society is acting and thinking in ways that resemble the French case. From the preference given to being one's own boss, to the expected role of the state in providing for the social welfare of the collective, the similarities are apparent.

To date, these competing legitimacies do not appear to have undermined the reform process. Instead, Polish sociologists note that there is a general acceptance of the "idea of the market economy" which has "created a permanent framework within which new compromises could be made."[176] In other words, formal and substantive interpretations of the market have together determined the range of options available for debate and implementation. Opposition to marketization itself has, therefore, not been able to emerge in any significant organized way.[177]

Nor is wide-scale opposition likely, as long as average citizens can access the opportunities of the market by opening their own businesses, thereby becoming small property owners with a vested interest in the existence of some kind of market economy. While an economy comprised of small entrepreneurs may not fit the model of advanced capitalism, it was, as we have seen, a crucial component of French and early American development. In Poland, as well, such entrepreneurship can eventually play a constructive role by generating social support for a synthesis between the freedom and autonomy of the market and the freedom and autonomy represented by the domain of citizenship. Indeed, to the extent that both workers and intellectuals engage in small businesses, the growth of small property ownership might well provide an occupational basis for the restoration of a social coalition between these upper and lower echelons of the middle class. Ultimately, just as in the case of citizenship, the avoidance of class-based polarization will be critical in determining whether or not the formal and substantive images of the market can be reconciled institutionally.

Overall, however, one can conclude that, although tensions exist between formal and substantive, between individualistic and collectivistic understandings of rights, the domains of citizenship and the free market are generally accepted and considered legitimate in Poland. Based on the principles and behaviors experienced within the Solidarity movement, critical social groups are supportive of these institutional transformations in regard to both attitudes and actions. Debates have emerged over the type of citizenship and market that is desired, but not over the domains themselves. In contrast, the domains of representative government and proceduralism are more contested as alternative conceptions of government and public virtue have been contrasted to existing realities. Here, the standards set by Solidarity have not been met, nor do individual Poles feel they can do much to rectify the situation. Unlike the realms of citizenship and the market, where the scope for personal action is greater, the government, the legal system and the realm of public officialdom are perceived as being beyond the scope of average people. These institutions belong to "them," to those in power, not to the citizenry at large. True to Polish traditions, the state is viewed with hostility and suspicion—even if it is now supposed to be a liberal democratic state.

The state, therefore, is unlikely to become an accepted arena for the representation of interests and for the reconciliation of formal and substantive interpretations of citizenship and the market. In addition, the development of bureaucratic efficiency and administrative stability have been hampered by the lack of faith in public servants and impersonal proceduralism. Consequently, the legacy of Solidarity would appear to be mixed. On the one hand, citizenship and the market have been legitimated, albeit according to two different interpretations of the Solidarity experience, while representative government and rule by law have met with considerable informal resistance. In the short run, this legacy is likely to render the Polish polity more volatile than the other Central European countries as the competing value-rational principles of democratic legitimacy continue to structure the responses of critical social groups to formal institutions in different ways. If, in this context, economic and social polarization becomes too great, while the state becomes too corrupt and particularized, the existing value-rational commitment to democracy, citizenship and the market will be difficult to sustain, both by workers and intellectuals. The inequalities of condition would be too great to overcome in the pursuit of a common civic identity. Poland would then be likely to follow the course of "poor capitalist" development, wherein elite privileges are contested sporadically by populist-Peronist demagogues. In this case, the Solidarity experience would ultimately be proven to be either detrimental in promoting social polarization based on different interpretations of rights, or meaningless as the processes of dependent development take hold. Poland would simply become another case of a failed democratic transition.

If, on the other hand, the coalition between upper and lower ranks of the middle class can be restored on the basis of equal access to market opportunities and a redefinition of citizenship rights to accommodate some balance of formal and substantive rights, the value-rational basis of legitimacy for liberal capitalist institutions generated by the ethos and experience of Solidarity will have had an enduringly positive impact on Poland. As in the case of France, the attainment of a stable form of representative government might take many years and numerous constitutions, but eventually the legitimacy of and compliance with the domains of citizenship and the market will prove strong enough to assure a comparable outcome. In this event, Kuroń will be proven correct when he states that, although all post-communist countries are plagued by particularism, nationalism and religious fundamentalism, only Poland has Solidarity: "The other countries lack the experiences and accomplishments of Solidarity, and so they will have greater difficulties in overcoming these conflicts."[178] Accordingly, Solidarity will have provided both a unique source of legitimacy for liberal capitalism and a lasting barrier against alternative identities and institutional arrangements.

Given these two possible scenarios for the future, the long-term significance of Solidarity for Polish democracy, and for stable capitalist development, would appear to be just as ambivalent as the movement's current legacy. What does appear clear, however, is the vulnerable and contingent nature of Solidarity's achievements. Solidarity has provided a value-rational basis of legitimacy for two of the domains of liberal capitalism. Yet the strength of this legitimacy, both in attitudinal and behavioral terms, is dependent on the restoration of a social coalition between intellectuals and workers. In the wake of marketization, such a coalition would obviously not replicate the middle class that emerged under Leninism to support Solidarity, but would instead resemble the "common-man"-based social and political coalitions that characterized French and American development. Whereas, in general, the existence of a broad middle class does not guarantee support for democracy, in Poland a reconciliation between the upper and lower ranks of the newly emerging middle class would represent a continuation of the social foundation that promoted and supported Solidarity's articulation of natural rights. It is reasonable to assume, therefore, that a Polish middle class would support institutional development based on a compromise between formal and substantive rights. The question is, can such social, ideological and institutional compromises be attained, given that the particular problems of being a latecomer to liberal capitalism will have to be overcome as well? This is the question that the epilogue will address.

Epilogue

The Polish Revolution in comparative context

The difficulties posed by the post-Leninist environment for liberal capitalist development have been well mapped out in recent years.[1] On the one hand, the experience of really-existing socialism destroyed essential attributes of liberal capitalism such as associative behavior based on civic trust, private property rights, the rule of law, and faith in political party organization. On the other hand, Leninism, unintentionally of course, bolstered the strength of alternative identities and institutions based on nationalism and ethnicity. Indeed, in many parts of the former Soviet Union a symbiotic relationship has developed between the old *nomenklatura apparat* and the ideals and aims of nationalism. Staying in power even after the formal collapse of the Communist Party has, therefore, been legitimated through nationalist appeals and rhetoric. Unlike the ancien régime that gave way to the eighteenth-century era of democratic revolutions, Leninist regimes would appear to have generated few positive institutional and cultural legacies that could support or constitute the building blocks of a new order. The age of Enlightened Absolutism, and feudalism before it, had after all left relatively stable state boundaries, increasingly efficient bureaucracies, a Roman Law legal foundation, and a tradition of representative "constituted bodies" in their wake.[2] When combined with Catholic humanism and Protestant individualism, these elements of the old order provided the Enlightenment and the natural-rights-based democratic revolutions with fertile ground upon which to build. In contrast, Leninism has left behind weak and contested states, a corrupt bureaucratic infrastructure and growing "legal nihilism." However, perhaps the most debilitating legacy is a widespread culture of socioeconomic entitlement which was rooted institutionally in the Leninist economic system; a system that was geared less toward the production and sale of expanding goods and services, and more toward the redistribution of limited goods and services along political and social criteria. The Leninist state and factory may not have provided much, but they did come to be seen as collective providers, rather than as facilitators for individual achievement.

In addition to these particular legacies, post-Leninist states also face the general problems of being latecomers to liberal capitalist development. On a political level, these problems have been analyzed with reference to the craftsmanship needed by political elites as they seek to cope with the simultaneous transformations of the political, economic and social realms.[3] Unlike the first democratic states, which were able to "sequence" their development in stages, latecomers must attempt to address all realms at once. Generally, whether in the post-Leninist context or in post-authoritarian Latin America, this simultaneity entails nothing less than promoting political democratization, economic liberalization and a dynamic civil society concurrently.

Although much has been written about the positive or negative effects of attempting political democratization and economic liberalization at the same time, not much effort has been made to differentiate between the different social bases of resistance to these reforms.[4] Clearly, social resistance has emerged when certain community standards are violated by liberal capitalist initiatives. Yet, just as these standards are not uniform, neither is social opposition to the new institutional arrangements. Instead, community standards can be established according to three different sets of evaluative criteria: those based on a traditional "moral economy,"[5] those based on a social rights agenda and those based on religious grounds. If anti-reform movements and generalized resistance are based predominantly on moral economy conceptions of the appropriate relationship between the social, economic and political realms, nationalist-populist opposition is likely to dominate. If, on the other hand, the effort to retain social rights such as the right to work is preeminent, socialist-oriented opposition will prove the most resistant to the full implementation of liberal capitalist reforms. Finally, religiously derived hostility toward reforms can generate movements demanding the complete subordination of society, government and the economy to a given theocracy.

In most cases of latecomer development, however, these responses to liberal capitalism will all tend to be present simultaneously. The simultaneous necessity of social, political and economic reforms is thereby matched by the simultaneous emergence of traditional, socialist and religious manifestations of social resistance. In this context, it is not surprising that reform-oriented elites tend to isolate themselves from society, believing that only state-led, as opposed to society-driven, dictates and initiatives will have the desired transformatory effects. This entrenchment in, and reliance on, the state is further strengthened by the economic imperatives of late development. As Alexander Gerschenkron points out in his seminal article, "Economic backwardness in historical perspective," the role of the state in fostering economic modernization, especially in terms of capital accumulation and investment, will tend to be greater in backward countries.[6] However, once entrenched in an increasingly dominant state, and socially isolated, there is growing incentive for instrumentally oriented elites to divert state resources to themselves while maintaining the façade of a reform agenda. Motivated both by the need to buy off vocal opponents by giving them a piece of the pie, and the desire to maintain a certain standard of living, governing elites begin, in Weber's words, to "live off of politics" rather than "for politics."[7] Left unchecked, the processes set in motion by liberal capitalist reforms in latecomer societies tend to result in bloated states, redistribution-oriented economies and corrupt elites.[8] Consequently, importing liberal capitalist institutions without a social base of support beyond a narrow reform elite leaves the reform effort itself vulnerable to contestation and eventual cooptation.

Yet, how can a social base of support for reforms be attained in an inherently difficult and often hostile environment? Here, the history of how liberal capitalist institutions were originally diffused or successfully exported beyond the borders of the countries that initially experienced modern democracy via revolution is of considerable significance. As we have seen, the French and American Revolutions resulted in liberal capitalist democracies that were legitimated by a natural rights doctrine and supported by the same social groups—the upper and lower middle orders—that participated in the charismatic communities of the revolutions. Under the joint influence of the doctrine and the communities, a change of consciousness and conduct took place that ultimately replaced monarchical authority with the authority derived from free and equal citizens. But what of the other European nations that did not experience an indigenous democratic revolution, yet still evolved into stable liberal capitalist countries?

Essentially, liberal capitalist domains were introduced slowly into these countries on the basis of social compromises that incorporated and thereby deflected potentially hostile social constituencies. In the late eighteenth and nineteenth centuries, the Scandinavian countries, in particular, were very successful in overcoming urban–rural and worker–capitalist divisions by giving all major social groups a representative stake in the newly emerging forms of political and economic life.[9] Germany and Japan replicated this achievement in the post-World War II era as the interests of industrialists, farmers and workers were brought into balance. In this process of bargaining and compromise, no single group achieved all of its goals, but neither did any one group come away empty handed.

These successful efforts to create a social support base for liberal capitalism can, of course, be explained by the existence of an expanding resource base generated by highly productive economies. Certainly, the availability of such resources facilitated the defusing of social discontent. However, the ultimate success of social compromise policies was also due to the recognition that traditional, religious and social-rights-based criticisms of liberal capitalism needed to be accommodated, and that these institutions must accordingly be adapted to specific national conditions. In other words, the willingness of political elites to pursue compromise is predicated on a philosophical distancing from the strict tenets of liberal capitalism, just as much as it is based on the availability of economic resources. The different forms of consensual democracy developed in Scandinavia and Japan, the famous German social market economy, and the cultural conservatism of

Ireland are all examples of how the imported domains of liberal capitalism can be reconciled with national traditions that are not, at first glance, consistent with modern development. Paradoxically, by retaining certain principles and practices that might be antithetical to the pure form of liberal capitalism, the legitimacy of liberal capitalism has itself been enhanced in these countries.

In short, in the absence of a revolutionary value-rational basis of legitimacy for liberal capitalism, the modernizing elites of these countries produced, by a mixture of accident and design, a different basis of legitimacy for liberal capitalist domains. By incorporating the social bases of discontent, *and* by acknowledging the community standards that produced this discontent, a synthesis was achieved between modern institutions and culturally specific forms of traditional legitimation. This synthesis, built as it was on elite-social interaction, prevented the emergence of bloated and corrupt states. In particular, traditionally embedded concepts of reciprocity between rulers and ruled prevented elites from becoming isolated and self-serving.[10] Clearly, such syntheses are not universally replicable, based as they are on the existence of particular national traits and privileged economic positions. However, this type of legitimation is analytically instructive as it points out the weaknesses of diffusing liberal capitalist institutions on the basis of instrumental rationality alone. Elites attempting to import liberal capitalist domains solely on instrumental grounds, without adequate social support and without a principled basis for compliance with the new order, will not be able to withstand the pressures toward isolation and entrenchment in the state. In an environment of limited economic resources, these pressures will be even more pronounced. Social and economic polarization, rather than socioeconomic transformation, is likely to be the ultimate outcome of such policies. In those cases where instrumental acceptance of democratic and capitalist rules of the game have been successful, most notably in Greece, Portugal and southern Italy, membership in the European Union provided additional resources in order to prevent polarization from becoming too great. Yet even these resources could not deter the growth of the state in the case of Greece, and increasingly debilitating levels of corruption in Italy. In contrast, where traditional authority relations and norms of reciprocity served to maintain linkages between elites and social groups, a principled legitimation for liberal capitalism was made possible—even if no indigenous democratic revolution took place.

Consequently, in addition to the American and French value-rational legitimations of liberal capitalism, two other modes of legitimation have characterized efforts to diffuse the institutions brought to life by the eighteenth-century revolutions. Whereas the success of instrumental justifications for liberal capitalism appears to be highly contingent on favorable economic and political alliances, the success of traditional legitimations would appear to be less dependent on external factors and more deeply rooted in domestic conditions. Here, too, a contingency exists, but it is one based on the possible affinities of national political cultures and liberal capitalist institutions.[11]

Most successful are, of course, the cases of liberal capitalist development that emerged on a revolutionary basis. As we have seen, a natural rights articulation combined with the transformation of consciousness and conduct achieved in the charismatic communities of the revolutions generated a value-rational commitment to liberalism powerful enough to create completely new forms of political, social and economic life. Based on equality not hierarchy, on rights not privileges, on actual not symbolic representation, these new forms of life transformed not just France and the United States but the world at large. Yet, even in these cases, a contingency exists. Liberal capitalist institutions are considered legitimate to the extent that they fulfill the ideals of the revolutions. In France, the gap between governing institutions and ideals based on substantive rights resulted in a long period of contestation over representative government. In the United States, as well, Huntington points to the "creedal passion periods" that erupt without fail when the gap between institutions and ideals becomes too great.[12] Accordingly, even though the United States experienced a less conflictual institutionalization of liberal capitalist domains, given the preponderance of a formal natural rights articulation, the revolutionary period established certain standards and evaluative criteria that governing institutions must live up to or face organized popular discontent.

When placed in this comparative context, it is clear that post-Leninist Poland faces a similar challenge of bringing new institutions into line with the ideals and expectations generated by Solidarity. However, it is also evident that Polish elites are behaving in ways that resemble the isolationist dynamic of instrumentally motivated reformers attempting to import liberal capitalist domains. Consequently, Poland is experiencing the tensions between formal and substantive interpretations of natural rights just as France did, while simultaneously experiencing the problems of latecomer development. The successful legitimation of liberal capitalism in Poland will, therefore, be contingent on two conditions: favorable external circumstances, such as eventual European Union membership, and overcoming the ideals versus institution gap. Both conditions would appear to be necessary in order to restore the social coalition needed to support liberal capitalist reforms. Additional resources provided by the European Union are likely to prevent the growing threat of socioeconomic polarization, but they alone will not minimize people's opposition to institutions that violate their sense of what is just. Likewise, not even the most perfect balance between ideals and institutions will result automatically in economic prosperity. Without foreign markets, credits and investments to help overcome the structural deficiencies of backwardness, social tensions and income disparities are still likely to increase.

In short, without favorable external circumstances and a concerted effort to make institutional realities reflect widely held ideals and principles,

Poland will not be able to avoid the problematic outcomes of latecomer development. Elsewhere in East Central Europe, the former condition alone or combined with a possible synthesis between national traditions and liberal capitalist institutions would appear to be sufficient for the institutionalization of stable liberal democracies. It is even possible that the Czech Republic and Hungary would be able to succeed largely on the basis of such a synthesis. The Czech Republic, in particular, appears to be reestablishing the controlled, semi-corporatist version of democracy maintained during the interwar period.[13] In Poland, however, the experience of Solidarity has set different terms for the institutionalization and legitimation of liberal capitalism.

Without a comparatively grounded appreciation of the origins of modern democracy, it would be impossible to ascertain the differences between indigenous democratic revolutions and democracy by diffusion, and between early and latecomers to liberal capitalism. It would also be easy to overlook the specific attributes of the Polish case. Poland is not just another post-Leninist state, nor is it just another semi-peripheral, backward East European country facing the daunting task of liberal capitalist development. Instead, Poland is one of the few nations that has experienced an indigenous democratic revolution which renders it comparable to the American and French cases. Yet, even within this exclusive grouping, there are considerable variations, as this comparative work has attempted to demonstrate.

In many respects, the Polish and French cases are very similar, beginning with the shared emphases on substantive natural rights, and collective understandings of citizenship, and ending with similar difficulties in regard to the domain of representative government. In other respects, however, the Polish articulation of natural rights and the nature of Solidarity's charismatic communities manifest unique characteristics such as the humanistic philosophical foundation for the rights of man, and the limited experience of social leveling. The latter characteristic in particular, acting in conjunction with the socially polarizing effects of marketization, has proven to be among Solidarity's most consequential weaknesses. Taken together, these weaknesses have rendered Poland perhaps even more vulnerable to the problems and pitfalls of post-communist latecomer development than its immediate neighbors.

Clearly, Poland lacks the structural advantages France had in overcoming its turbulent post-revolutionary history. The difficulties are, therefore, that much greater for Poland. In the long run, however, the similarities between the democratic revolutions of France and Poland may well outweigh the differences. Given generous leadership in the European Union and reconciliatory leadership in Poland, Solidarity's strengths would undoubtedly prove to be of lasting benefit in providing a value-rational basis of legitimacy for liberal capitalism that is supported by both upper and lower echelons of the middle class. If such a positive outcome were indeed to transpire, this entire comparative analysis could be concluded with the following, remarkably similar, assessments of the French and Polish national characters:

> when I consider this nation in itself, I find it . . . indocile by temperament, more readily accommodating itself to the arbitrary and even violent empire of a prince than to the free and regular government of its principal citizens; today the declared enemy of all obedience, but tomorrow subservient with a sort of passion that even those nations most made for servitude cannot muster; easily led by the leash so long as no one resists, yet ungovernable as soon as the example of resistance is somewhere given; always fooling its masters who either fear it too much or too little; never so free that the prospect of enslaving it is hopeless, yet never so enslaved that it might not break its yoke.[14]
>
> (De Tocqueville)

> [Poles are] an astonishingly vital people who sink easily into moronic apathy and who show their virtues only in circumstances which would crush and destroy any other human group; a refinement of taste, which produced lyrical poetry comparable to that of Elizabethan England, combined with irony and brilliance but always threatened by drunken torpor and parochial mumblings; habits of religious and political tolerance, acquired in the multidenominational and multinational Respublica headed by an elected king, which gave way, as a result of collective misfortunes, to a wounded, morbid nationalism. . . . This chaos of elements seemingly so disparate, yet interrelated by a logic of their own, may contain some lessons of universal portent.[15]
>
> (Miłosz)

One can only hope that the future of Miłosz's "devils and angels"[16] will resemble the recent past of de Tocqueville's indocile nation.

Notes

PREFACE

1 The relationship between Solidarity and democracy is one of the most debated and contested aspects of the post-1989 transition in Poland itself. For an overview of the various positions taken, as the recent experience of Solidarity has been placed in the long-standing Polish tradition "of arguments over failed heroic uprisings, over loyalty and irredentism, over the choice between realism and honor," see Michał Cichy (1996: 133–156) "Requiem for the moderate revolutionist" and Andrzej Tymowski (1996: 157–160) "Ethos reconsidered."

2 See, for example: Timothy Garton Ash (1985) *The Polish Revolution: Solidarity*; Lawrence Weschler (1984) *The Passion of Poland*; Andrew Arato (1981: 23–47) "Civil society against the state: Poland 1980–81"; David Ost (1990) *Solidarity and the Politics of Anti-Politics*; Michael H. Bernhard (1993) *The Origins of Democratization in Poland*; Jan Kubik (1994) *The Power of Symbols Against the Symbols of Power: The Rise of Solidarity and the Fall of State Socialism in Poland*; Michael Kennedy (1991) *Professionals, Power and Solidarity in Poland*; Jerzy Holzer (1984) *"Solidarność," 1980–1981: Geneza i Historia.*

3 Philippe Schmitter and Terry Karl, "What democracy is . . . and is not," in *Journal of Democracy*, vol. 2, no. 3 (Summer 1991), pp. 75–88.

4 Adam Przeworski, *Democracy and the Market: Political and Economic Reforms in Eastern Europe and Latin America*, Cambridge: Cambridge University Press, 1991, p. 73.

5 See, for example, Ghassan Salame (ed.), *Democracy Without Democrats: The Renewal of Politics in the Muslim World*, London: I. B. Tauris, 1994.

6 Max Weber, *Economy and Society*, Berkeley: University of California Press, 1978, p. 867.

7 Staughton Lynd, *Intellectual Origins of American Radicalism*, New York: Pantheon Books, 1968, p. 161.

8 "Yankee" declaration in 1765 quoted in Richard L. Bushman, *From Puritan to Yankee: Character and the Social Order in Connecticut, 1690–1765*, New York: W. W. Norton, 1970, p. 286.

INTRODUCTION: REVOLUTION, DEMOCRACY AND SOLIDARITY

1 Czesław Miłosz, "Why," in Czesław Miłosz, *Facing the River*, translated by the author and Robert Hass, Hopewell, NJ: Ecco Press, 1995, pp. 7–8.

2 The following overview of the various interpretations of the events of 1989 is indebted to Krishan Kumar, "The revolutions of 1989 in East-Central Europe

and the idea of revolution," in Richard Kilminster and Ian Varcoe (eds.), *Culture, Modernity and Revolution: Essays in Honor of Zygmunt Bauman*, New York: Routledge, 1996, pp. 127–153.
3 Daniel Chirot cited in Kumar, *ibid.*, p. 127.
4 Kumar, *ibid.*, p. 140.
5 *Ibid.*, p. 148.
6 Zygmunt Bauman, *Intimations of Postmodernity*, London: Routledge,1992, p. 179.
7 *Ibid.*, p. 156.
8 *Ibid.*
9 *Ibid.*, p. 171.
10 *Ibid.*
11 Charles Tilly, *European Revolutions 1492–1992*, Oxford: Blackwell Publishers, 1995, p. 234.
12 Miłosz, *op. cit.*, pp. 7–8.
13 S. N. Eisenstadt cited in Kumar, *op. cit.*, p. 24.
14 Timothy Garton Ash, *The Magic Lantern*, New York: Vintage Books, 1993, p. 14.
15 *Ibid.*
16 Tilly, *op. cit.*, p. 234.
17 *Ibid.*, p. 235.
18 *Ibid.*, p. 184.
19 *Ibid.*, p. 235.
20 Charles Tilly, *From Mobilization to Revolution*, New York: McGraw-Hill, 1978, p. 191.
21 Kenneth Jowitt, *New World Disorder: The Leninist Extinction*, Berkeley: University of California Press, 1992, p. 254.
22 Tilly, *From Mobilization to Revolution*, *op. cit.*, p. 192.
23 *Ibid.*, p. 200.
24 *Ibid.*, p. 192.
25 *Ibid.*, p. 193.
26 Michael Walzer, "A theory of revolution," in *Marxist Perspectives*, no. 5 (Spring 1979), p. 30.
27 *Ibid.*, p. 31.
28 *Ibid.*, p. 30.
29 For an analysis of the middle class in Poland that gave rise to Solidarity see: Jacek Kurczewski, *The Resurrection of Rights in Poland*, Oxford: Clarendon Press, 1993.
30 Walzer, *op. cit.*, p. 31.
31 *Ibid.*, p. 32.
32 *Ibid.*
33 On the Polish opposition's stated intention to live as if they were in a free country see: Jan J. Lipski, *KOR: the History of the Workers' Defense Committee in Poland 1976–1981*, Berkeley: University of California Press, 1985. See also Timothy Garton Ash, *The Polish Revolution: Solidarity*, New York: Vintage Books, 1985. On the dissimulation prevalent in Leninist regimes, see Kenneth Jowitt, *op.cit.*
34 Theda Skocpol, *States and Social Revolutions: A Comparative Analysis of France, Russia, and China*, Cambridge: Cambridge University Press, 1979, p. 4.
35 See, for example, Roman Laba, *The Roots of Solidarity*, Princeton: Princeton University Press, 1991.
36 For such an interpretation of the role of miners in the Bolivian Revolution of

1952, see Theda Skocpol, *Social Revolutions in the Modern World*, Cambridge: Cambridge University Press, 1994, pp. 313–315.

37 Skocpol, *States and Social Revolutions*, *op. cit.*, pp. 4–5.
38 *Ibid.*, p. 4.
39 *Ibid.*, p. 232.
40 For a critical interpretation of Solidarity along these lines see: Sergiusz Kowalski, *Krytyka Solidarnośćiowego Rozumu*, Warsaw: PEN, 1990.
41 Hannah Arendt, *On Revolution*, New York: Penguin Books, 1977, p. 34.
42 *Ibid.*
43 Elbaki Hermassi cited in Skocpol, *States and Social Revolutions*, *op. cit.*, p. 4.
44 Skocpol, *Social Revolutions*, *op. cit.*, p. 336.
45 *Ibid.*, p. 315.
46 *Ibid.*, p. 336.
47 *Ibid.*, p. 200.
48 Tilly, *From Mobilization to Revolution*, *op. cit.*, p. 50.
49 *Ibid.*
50 *Ibid.*, p. 228.
51 *Ibid.*, p. 229.
52 *Ibid.*, pp. 228–229.
53 *Ibid.*, p. 50.
54 *Ibid.*, p. 200.
55 *Ibid.*, p. 204.
56 Peter Calvert, *Revolution and Counter-Revolution*, Minneapolis: University of Minnesota Press, 1990, p. 77.
57 William H. Sewell, Jr., "Ideologies and social revolutions: reflections on the French case," in T. C. W. Blanning (ed.), *The Rise and Fall of the French Revolution*, Chicago: University of Chicago Press, 1996, p. 309.
58 *Ibid.*, p. 289.
59 Theda Skocpol, "Cultural idioms and political ideologies in the revolutionary reconstruction of state power: a rejoinder to Sewell," in T. C. W. Blanning (ed.), *op. cit.*, p. 319.
60 Skocpol, *Social Revolutions*, *op. cit.*, p. 336.
61 Walzer, *op. cit.*, p. 30.
62 Michael Walzer, *The Revolution of the Saints: A Study in the Origins of Radical Politics*, Cambridge: Harvard University Press, 1965, p. 17.
63 *Ibid.*, p. 19.
64 Tilly, *From Mobilization to Revolution*, *op. cit.*, p. 37.
65 *Ibid.*
66 *Ibid.*, p. 203.
67 *Ibid.*
68 Anthony Arblaster, *Democracy*, Minneapolis: University of Minnesota Press, 1987, p. 6.
69 Skocpol, *States and Social Revolutions*, *op. cit.*, p. 170.
70 *Ibid.*
71 *Ibid.*
72 Max Weber, *Economy and Society*, Berkeley: University of California Press, 1978, p. 953.
73 *Ibid.*, p. 31.
74 *Ibid.*, p. 36.
75 See, for example, Wolfgang Mommsen, *Max Weber and German Politics 1890–1920*, Chicago: University of Chicago Press, 1984; Wolfgang Schluchter, *The Rise of Western Rationalism: Max Weber's Developmental History*, Berkeley: University of California Press, 1981.

76 Max Weber, *op.cit.*, p. 867.
77 *Ibid.*, p. 215.
78 *Ibid.*, p. 1117.
79 *Ibid.*, p. 48.
80 Max Weber, *The Protestant Ethic and the Spirit of Capitalism*, New York: Charles Scribner's Sons, 1958, p. 197.
81 As Weber points out, "according to the kind of legitimacy which is claimed, the type of obedience, the kind of administrative staff developed to guarantee it, and the mode of exercising authority, will all differ fundamentally." Weber, *Economy and Society*, *op. cit.*, p. 213.
82 *Ibid.*, p. 1209.
83 *Ibid.*
84 *Ibid.*
85 For an analysis of the significance Weber ascribes to natural law, see Arista Maria Cirtautas, "Max Weber and the legitimation of German democracy," in Kurt-Jürgen Maass (ed.), *From Two to One: US Scholars Witness the First Year of German Unification*, Bonn: Alexander von Humboldt Foundation, 1992.
86 Weber, *Economy and Society*, *op. cit.*, p. 870.
87 *Ibid.*
88 Michael Freeden, *Rights*, Minneapolis: University of Minnesota Press, 1991, p. 55.
89 *Ibid.*, p. 52.
90 *Ibid.*, p. 55.
91 *Ibid.*
92 Weber, *op.cit.*, p. 4.
93 *Ibid.*, p. 19.
94 *Ibid.*, p. 21.
95 Weber illustrates the relationship between formal natural law and the capitalist economic order in the section "The formal qualities of revolutionary law – natural law," in *Economy and Society*, *Op. cit.*, pp. 865–880.

1 THE CHARISMATIC PRESENTATION OF NATURAL RIGHTS: A WEBERIAN THEORY OF DEMOCRACY

1 David Held, *Models of Democracy*, Stanford: Stanford University Press, 1987, p. 1.
2 Max Weber, *The Protestant Ethic and the Spirit of Capitalism*, New York: Charles Scribner's Sons, 1958, p. 47.
3 *Ibid.*, p. 48.
4 *Thomas Paine Reader*, edited and with an Introduction by Michael Foot and Isaac Kramnick, London: Penguin Books, 1987, p. 14.
5 *Ibid.*, p. 32.
6 *Ibid.*, p. 33.
7 This is a paraphrasing of Weber's definition of capitalism as the "rational capitalistic organization of (formally) free labour," *The Protestant Ethic*, *op. cit.*, p. 21.
8 Thomas Paine, *The Rights of Man*, New York: Anchor Books, 1989, pp. 305–306.
9 *Ibid.*, pp. 303–304.
10 *Ibid.*, p. 306.
11 *Ibid.*
12 *Ibid.*, p. 307.

13 *Ibid.*, p. 331.
14 *Ibid.*, p. 415.
15 *Ibid.*, p. 410.
16 *Ibid.*, p. 411.
17 *Ibid.*
18 *Ibid.*, p. 418.
19 *Ibid.*, p. 419.
20 *Ibid.*
21 *Ibid.*, pp. 419–420.
22 *Ibid.*, p. 434.
23 *Ibid.*
24 *Ibid.*, p. 422.
25 *Ibid.*, p. 444.
26 Max Weber, *Economy and Society*, Berkeley: University of California Press, 1978, p. 26.
27 Max Weber, *The Protestant Ethic*, p. 27.
28 Thomas Paine, *op. cit.*, p. 353.
29 Max Weber, *Economy and Society*, p. 25.
30 *Ibid.*
31 *Ibid.*, p. 26.
32 Thomas Paine, *op. cit.*, p. 398.
33 *Ibid.*, p. 400.
34 Max Weber, *Economy and Society*, p. 26.
35 Samuel P. Huntington, *The Third Wave: Democratization in the Late Twentieth Century*, Norman and London: University of Oklahoma Press, 1991, p. 7.
36 *Ibid.*
37 *Ibid.*
38 *Ibid.*, p. 11.
39 H. Gerth and C. Wright Mills (eds.), *From Max Weber: Essays in Sociology*, New York: Oxford University Press, 1946, p. 280.
40 Quoted in Thomas Paine, *op. cit.*, p. 282.
41 Max Weber, *Gesammelte Politische Schriften*, Tübingen: J. C. B. Mohr Verlag, 1988, pp. 63–64.
42 In writing this segment on natural law, I have drawn on numerous sources. For example: Karl-Heinz Ilting, "Naturrecht," in *Geschichtliche Grundbegriffe*, vol. 4, Stuttgart: Ernst Klett Verlag, 1978, pp. 245–313; Wolfgang Schieder, "Brüderlichkeit," in *Geschichtliche Grundbegriffe*, vol. 1, Stuttgart: Ernst Klett Verlag, 1975, pp. 552–581; Georg Jellinek, "Die Erklärung der Menschen-und Bürgerrechte," in *Zur Geschichte der Erklärung der Menschenrechte*, edited by Roman Schnur, Darmstadt: Wissenschaftliche Buchgesellschaft, 1964, pp. 1–128; Winfried Brugger, *Menschenrechtsethos und Verantwortungspolitik: Max Webers Beitrag zur Analyze und Begründung der Menschenrechte*, Freiburg: Verlag Karl Alber, 1980; Stefan Breuer, *Sozialgeschichte des Naturrechts*, Opladen: Westdeutscher Verlag, 1983.
43 *The Merriam–Webster Dictionary*, 1974.
44 Thomas Paine, *op. cit.*, p. 304.
45 Max Weber, *Economy and Society*, p. 85.
46 As Weber indicates, "the concept of 'substantive rationality,' on the other hand, is full of ambiguities. It conveys only one element common to all 'substantive' analyses: namely, that they do not restrict themselves to note the purely formal and (relatively) unambiguous fact that action is based on 'goal oriented' rational calculation with the technically most adequate available methods, but

apply certain criteria of ultimate ends, whether they be ethical, political, utilitarian, hedonistic, feudal (ständisch), egalitarian, or whatever" (*ibid.*).

47 Peter Gay, *The Enlightenment: The Science of Freedom*, New York: W. W. Norton, 1977, p. 457.

48 A. L. Morton quoted in Anthony Arblaster, *Democracy*, Minneapolis: University of Minnesota Press, 1987, p. 30. As an example of Leveller attitudes, Christopher Hill quotes the following passage from the Declaration of 14 June 1647:

> We were not a mere mercenary Army, hired to serve any arbitrary power of a state, but called forth and conjured by the several declarations of Parliament, to the defence of our own and the people's just rights and liberties. And so we took up arms in judgement and conscience . . . and are resolved . . . to assert and vindicate the just power and rights of this kingdom in Parliament, for those common ends premised, against all arbitrary power, violence and oppression.

Quoted in Christopher Hill, *The Century of Revolution 1603–1714*, New York: W. W. Norton, 1980, p. 110.

49 Christopher Hill, *The Collected Essays of Christopher Hill. Vol. 2: Religion and Politics in Seventeenth Century England*, Amherst: University of Massachusetts Press, 1986, p. 335.

50 Max Weber, *Economy and Society*, *op. cit.*, p. 865.

51 *Ibid.*, p. 866.

52 *Ibid.*, p. 1117.

53 Gerth and Mills, *From Max Weber, op. cit.*, p. 280.

54 Max Weber, *Economy and Society*, pp. 1209–1210.

55 Max Weber, *The Protestant Ethic*, p. 197.

56 Max Weber, *Economy and Society*, p. 242.

57 *Ibid.*, p. 245.

58 *Ibid.*, pp. 266–267.

59 *Ibid.*, p. 299.

60 Christopher Hill, *The Collected Essays*, *op. cit.*, p. 329.

61 Max Weber, *Economy and Society*, p. 267.

62 See Max Weber, *On Charisma and Institution Building*, Selected Papers, edited and with an Introduction by S. N. Eisenstadt, Chicago: University of Chicago Press, 1968.

In addition, the formulation of these definitions owes a great deal to my colleagues Kenneth Jowitt and Stephen Hanson.

63 *Ibid.*, pp. xxxvii–xxxviii.

64 *Ibid.*, p. xxxix.

65 Douglass C. North, *Institutions, Institutional Change and Economic Performance*, Cambridge: Cambridge University Press, 1990, p. 3.

66 *Ibid.*, p. 4.

67 Max Weber, *On Charisma and Institution Building*, *op. cit.*, p. xl.

68 *Ibid.*

69 *Ibid.*, p. xxxix.

70 Mary Douglas, *How Institutions Think*, London: Routledge & Kegan Paul, 1987, p. 46.

71 *Ibid.*, pp. 46–47.

72 For a similar but much more detailed comparative historical overview of these institutional changes, see Reinhard Bendix, *Nation-Building and Citizenship*, Berkeley: University of California Press, 1977.

73 Gail Bossenga, "From corps to citizenship: the bureaux des finances before the

French Revolution," in *Journal of Modern History*, vol. 58, no. 3 (September 1986), p. 632.

74 On the institutional legacies of the old order, such as the existence of constituent bodies like the Estates General, see R. R. Palmer, *The Age of Democratic Revolution: A Political History of Europe and America, 1760–1800*, vols. 1 and 2, Princeton: Princeton University Press, 1964.

75 Definition taken from *The Random House Dictionary*, New York: Ballantine Books, 1980.

76 Simon Schama, *Citizens: A Chronicle of the French Revolution*, New York: Alfred A. Knopf, 1989, p. 858.

77 Michael J. Lacey and Knud Haakonssen, "History, historicism, and the culture of rights," in Lacey and Haakonssen (eds.), *A Culture of Rights: The Bill of Rights in Philosophy, Politics and Law 1791–1991*, Cambridge: Cambridge University Press, 1991, p. 3.

78 The representation of citizens' interests has, of course, taken various forms ranging from pluralism to neo-corporatism. See, for example, Suzanne D. Berger (ed.), *Organizing Interests in Western Europe: Pluralism, Corporatism and the Transformation of Politics*, Cambridge: Cambridge University Press, 1981.

79 Alexander Hamilton, James Madison and John Jay, *The Federalist Papers*, New York: Bantam Books, 1982, p. 264.

80 *Ibid.*, pp. 263–264.

81 Hanna Pitkin, *The Concept of Representation*, Berkeley: University of California Press, 1967, p. 196.

82 Thomas Paine, *op. cit.*, pp. 419–420.

83 Liah Greenfeld, *Nationalism: Five Roads to Modernity*, Cambridge: Harvard University Press, 1992; R. R. Palmer, *The Age of Democratic Revolution*, *op. cit.* See also Rogers Brubaker, *Citizenship and Nationhood in France and Germany*, Cambridge: Harvard University Press, 1992.

84 Greenfeld, *op. cit.*, p. 10.

85 *Ibid.*, p. 16.

2 FORMAL NATURAL RIGHTS AND THE AMERICAN REVOLUTION

1 Alexander Hamilton, James Madison and John Jay, *The Federalist Papers*, New York: Bantam Books, 1982, p. 265.

2 Quoted in Gordon S. Wood, *The Radicalism of the American Revolution*, New York: Alfred A. Knopf, 1992, p. 169. To a large extent, the following account draws on Wood's work.

3 The concept of "lower" orders at the time did not include servants or wage laborers who were considered incapable of independent thought and action, given their dependent economic status. "Lower" orders in this case refers to the lower echelons of small independent producers and/or property owners.

4 The works of Forrest McDonald (*We the People: The Economic Origins of the Constitution*, Chicago: University of Chicago Press, 1958 and *E Pluribus Unum: The Formation of the American Republic, 1776–1790*, Boston: Houghton Mifflin, 1979) represent an example of socioeconomic history, while Bernard Bailyn, *The Ideological Origins of the American Revolution*, Cambridge: Harvard University Press, 1967 and Morton White: *The Philosophy of the American Revolution*, New York: Oxford University Press, 1978 are examples of intellectual history.

For a similar effort to integrate the two approaches, albeit from a different analytical perspective, see Forrest McDonald, *Novus Ordo Seclorum: The Intellectual Origins of the Constitution*, Lawrence: University of Kansas Press, 1985.

For case studies that seek to integrate ideas and social context see T. H. Breen, *Tobacco Culture: The Mentality of the Great Tidewater Planters on the Eve of Revolution*, Princeton: Princeton University Press, 1985 and T. H. Breen, *Puritans and Adventurers: Change and Persistence in Early America*, Oxford: Oxford University Press, 1980.

5 Wood, *op. cit.*, p. 172.

6 *Ibid.*

7 *Ibid.*, p. 190. For all too brief a period, the potential for social mobility was apparently color blind to a considerable extent. According to Breen and Innes, it is only at the "end of the seventeenth century that there was an inexorable hardening of racial lines" (p. 5). On the situation of Virginia's free black planters see T. H. Breen and Stephen Innes, *"Myne Owne Ground": Race and Freedom on Virginia's Eastern Shore, 1640–1676*, Oxford: Oxford University Press, 1980.

8 On the susceptibility of Virginia planters to conspiracy theories as a result of their increasing indebtedness to British merchants, and their subsequent receptivity to "abstractions about liberty and rights, independence and virtue" (pp. 158–159), see T. H. Breen, *Tobacco Culture*, *op. cit.*

9 Wood, *op. cit.*, p. 87.

10 *Ibid.*, pp. 244–245.

11 Quoted in Charles S. Olton, *Artisans for Independence: Philadelphia Mechanics and the American Revolution*, Syracuse: Syracuse University Press, 1975, p. 37.

12 Sean Wilentz, *Chants Democratic: New York City and the Rise of the American Working Class, 1788–1850*, Oxford: Oxford University Press, 1984, p. 87. Later, of course, as the Federalists became associated with increasing elitism, the artisans withdrew their support from the party, but not from the Constitution.

13 There is a revisionist school of thought which maintains that Lockean liberalism and the natural rights doctrine were less significant than Republican ideology in the minds of the "founding fathers." For an analysis of this revisionist debate and a compelling, well-documented defense of the "liberal tradition" in American historiography, see Steven M. Dworetz, *The Unvarnished Doctrine: Locke, Liberalism and the American Revolution*, Durham, NC: Duke University Press, 1990.

14 McDonald, *Novus Ordo Seclorum*, *op. cit.*, p. viii.

15 Ernest Barker, *Traditions of Civility*, Cambridge: Cambridge University Press, 1948, p. 310. The following discussion of the impact of the natural rights doctrine owes much to Sir Ernest Barker's interpretation.

16 Carl Becker, *The Declaration of Independence*, New York: Vintage Books, 1958, p. 78.

17 Quoted in T. H. Breen, *The Character of the Good Ruler: A Study of Puritan Political Ideas in New England, 1630–1730*, New Haven: Yale University Press, 1970, pp. 274–275.

18 Quoted in Richard L. Bushman, *From Puritan to Yankee: Character and the Social Order in Connecticut, 1690–1765*, New York: W. W. Norton, 1970, pp. 283–284.

19 *Ibid.*, p. 282.

20 Quoted in Breen, *The Character of the Good Ruler*, *op. cit.*, p. 273.

21 Quoted in Garry Wills, *Inventing America: Jefferson's Declaration of Independence*, New York: Vintage Books, 1979, p. 191.

22 R. R. Palmer, *The Age of Democratic Revolution: A Political History of Europe and America, 1760–1800,* Princeton: Princeton University Press, 1964, vol. 1, p. 234.
23 Quoted in Bernard Bailyn, *Pamphlets of the American Revolution*, vol. 1, Cambridge: Harvard University Press, 1965, p. 108.
24 *Ibid.*
25 Quoted in Richard Walsh, *Charleston's Sons of Liberty: A Study of the Artisans 1763–1789*, Columbia: University of South Carolina Press, 1959, p. 98.
26 Quoted in Becker, *op. cit.*, p. 8.
27 For accounts of this new egalitarian society and the political movements that supported it, see the works of Gordon Wood (*The Radicalism of the American Revolution, The Creation of the American Republic, 1776–1787*) and, of course, the classic work of Alexis de Tocqueville, *Democracy in America*, edited and abridged by Richard D. Heffner, New York: Mentor Books, 1956, 1984.
28 Wilentz, *op. cit.*, p. 93.
29 *Ibid.*, p. 102.
30 *Ibid.*, p. 93.
31 Quoted in G. B. Nash, *Race and Revolution*, Madison: Madison House, 1990, p. 59.
32 *Ibid.*
33 Charles S. Hyneman and Donald S. Lutz (eds.), *American Political Writing During the Founding Era 1760–1805*, vol. II, Indianapolis: Liberty Press, 1983, p. 860.
34 Nash, *op. cit.*, p. 81.
35 For Noah Webster's critique of natural rights, see Hyneman and Lutz (eds.), *op. cit.*, pp. 1220–1240.
36 Nash, *op. cit.*, pp. 81–82.
37 Quoted in Bailyn, *op. cit.*, p. 50.
38 For an analysis of how the ideals of the revolutionary era have continued to animate successive waves of American protest movements, see Samuel P. Huntington, *American Politics: The Promise of Disharmony*, Cambridge: Harvard University Press, 1981.

See also Staughton Lynd, *Intellectual Origins of American Radicalism*, New York: Pantheon Books, 1968, in which Lynd traces the tradition of American radicalism back to the natural rights doctrine of the Revolution.

39 Quoted in R. R. Palmer, *op. cit.*, vol. 1, p. 235.
40 Simon Schama, *Citizens: A Chronicle of the French Revolution*, New York: Alfred A. Knopf, 1989. p. 181.
41 Max Weber, *Economy and Society*, Berkeley: University of California Press, 1978, p. 245.
42 *Ibid.*, p. 866.
43 Quoted in Walsh, *op. cit.*, p. ix.
44 *Ibid.*
45 See especially Gordon S. Wood, *op. cit.*
46 Barker, *op. cit.*, p. 270.
47 George F. Scheer and Hugh F. Rankin, *Rebels and Redcoats: The American Revolution Through the Eyes of Those Who Fought and Lived It*, New York: Da Capo Press, 1957, p. 18.
48 *Ibid.*
49 *Ibid.*
50 Quoted in Olton, *op. cit.*, p. 52. Olton also provides evidence of the moderation of the revolutionary activities. See, for example, p. 89.
51 Barker, *op. cit.*, p. 276.

52 Quoted in Barker, *ibid.*, p. 274. For a detailed elaboration of Wise's contribution to colonial thought, see Breen, *The Character of the Good Ruler*, *op. cit.*, pp. 251–261.
53 On the colonial militias, see T. H. Breen, *Puritans and Adventurers: Change and Persistence in Early America*, Oxford: Oxford University Press, 1980, pp. 24–45.
54 Weber, *Economy and Society*, *op. cit.*, p. 1209. For a detailed case study of the role of religion, specifically the Great Awakening, in changing public attitudes toward authority in pre-revolutionary Connecticut, see Bushman, *op. cit.*
55 De Tocqueville, *op. cit.*, pp. 95–96.
56 *Ibid.*, p. 157.
57 *Ibid.*, pp. 157–158.
58 *Ibid.*, p. 156.
59 Quoted in Bernard Schwartz, *The Bill of Rights: A Documentary History*, vol. 1, New York: Chelsea House Publishers, 1971, p. 200.
60 *Ibid.*, p. 202.
61 *Ibid.*, p. 234.
62 *Ibid.*
63 Quoted in Becker, *op. cit.*, p. 8.
64 Alfred H. Kelly and Winfred A. Harbison, *The American Constitution: Its Origins and Development*, 5th edition, New York: W. W. Norton, 1976, p. 85.
65 Quoted in Knud Haakonssen, "From natural law to the rights of man," in Lacey and Haakonssen (eds.), *op. cit.*, p. 34.
66 Quoted in Bernard Schwartz, *op. cit.*, p. 212.
67 Quoted in Haakonssen, *op. cit.*, p. 51.
68 Bernard Bailyn, *Faces of Revolution: Personalities and Themes in the Struggle for American Independence*, New York: Vintage Books, 1992, p. 103.
69 Quoted in *ibid.*
70 William Manning, *The Key of Liberty*, edited and with an Introduction by Michael Merrill and Sean Wilentz, Cambridge: Harvard University Press, 1993, p. 52.
71 *Ibid.*, p. 58.
72 *Ibid.*, p. 75. Manning was not alone both in his adherence to the rule of law and in his advocacy of "democratic societies." Wilentz, for example, describes how the artisans of New York City formed a Democratic Society at the end of the eighteenth century. According to Wilentz, the "public stance" of this society "cannot be understood as 'radical,' let alone 'revolutionary' ; in the truest test of its faith, during the Whiskey Rebellion, the society condemned government repression and the excise tax system, but also stoutly disapproved of the rebels' armed resistance to 'the execution of constitutional law.'" Wilentz, *op. cit.*, p. 68.
73 Forrest McDonald, *The Presidency of George Washington*, Lawrence: University of Kansas Press, 1974, p. 25. While McDonald is doubtlessly correct that only Washington "could inspire the trust that was crucial to the radical experiment in federal government" (*ibid.*), it is also true that trust in a single leader proved to be a transient state of affairs for Americans who have since tended to put greater faith in laws and in the Constitution.
74 See Jack N. Rakove, "Parchment barriers and the politics of rights," in Lacey and Haakonssen, *op. cit.*, pp. 98–143, for an illuminating account of Madison's position on rights and representation.
75 See *ibid.*, p. 133 and Madison himself in *Federalist 10* (Alexander Hamilton, James Madison and John Jay, *The Federalist Papers*, New York: Bantam Books, 1982).
76 On factions, see Madison's *Federalist 37*, *ibid.*

77 On the extent to which the economic interests of artisans, merchants and other social groups resonated with the Federalist vision, see Cathy D. Matson and Peter S. Onuf, *A Union of Interests. Political and Economic Thought in Revolutionary America*, Lawrence: University of Kansas Press, 1990.
78 Manning, *op. cit.*, p. 28.
79 *Ibid.*, p. 16.
80 De Tocqueville, *op. cit.*, pp. 107–108.
81 Iwona Jakubowska-Branicka, "Expectations regarding law and the emerging concept of legality in the process of democratic transformation," paper delivered at the Law and Society Congress, held in Glasgow, Scotland, July 10–13, 1996. Jakubowska-Branicka defines "legal rigourism" as the belief that it is necessary to obey a law even if it is considered unjust. She goes on to note (p. 14) that:

> It is evident that within the populations studied [US, France, Spain, Poland, Hungary, Bulgaria], the Americans stood apart as a society characterized by the highest legal rigourism both with regard to the individual and to the state, a society for which social advantage of the law was the most important and the opinion of the majority mattered the least.

As an explanation for this tendency, Jakubowska-Branicka supports de Tocqueville's analysis that Americans feel themselves bound by the law because they themselves have created it. Accordingly, unjust laws must be changed, not disregarded or ignored.
82 De Tocqueville, *op. cit.*, p. 107.
83 The mobilizing role of pamphlets during the Revolution is, of course, well known. Even before the Revolution, religious and political controversies were brought to the attention of the general public through publications that departed from the standard mode of "presenting politics as high-level deliberations of wise and dispassionate men" and initiated a new style of public discourse designed, for example, to "mobilize public opinion in a legislative controversy, using specific facts and accusations to impugn the motives of an acknowledged ruler" (Bushman, *op. cit.*, p. 249).
84 With the possible exception of the Netherlands, which experienced a formal natural rights articulation and is, therefore, more similar to the American case. On the democratic revolution in the Netherlands, see R. R. Palmer, *op. cit.*, and Simon Schama, *Patriots and Liberators: Revolution in the Netherlands 1780–1813*, New York: Vintage Books, 1977.
85 The expulsion of the loyalists was not, however, an insignificant event. R. R. Palmer points out that more people were expelled and more property was confiscated in the American Revolution than in the French Revolution. Moreover, these American "émigrés" did not return, thereby adding to the stability of the post-revolutionary political order. See Palmer, *op. cit.*, vol. 1, pp. 188–189.
86 As Michael Rogin pointed out to me, American conflicts over rights can, however, be viewed in another light—one that pits the Madisonian tradition of individualism against the Painite tradition of a more "collective individualism," which shows greater sensitivity to community needs and to maintaining an equality of opportunity for all Americans regardless of wealth and position. Whereas the former tradition is supportive of capitalist entrepreneurship, the latter tradition has consistently attempted to ameliorate and/or regulate the worst effects of capitalist development (Rogin, personal communication).

Clearly, both traditions have coexisted in American history, sometimes quite uneasily indeed, but what is noteworthy from a comparative standpoint is the extent to which even in the Painite tradition it is still the individual who is vested with rights and responsibilities. The tension between the traditions is over which individual—the average American or the successful American—should be taken as the standard for political life and public policy.

3 SUBSTANTIVE NATURAL RIGHTS AND THE FRENCH REVOLUTION

1 Maurice Agulhon, *The French Republic 1879–1992*, Oxford: Blackwell Publishers, 1993, p. 2.
2 François Furet, *Revolutionary France 1770–1880*, Oxford: Blackwell Publishers, 1992, p. 73.
3 *Ibid.*
4 *Ibid.* Furet does appear to give implicit weight to the individualism of the revolutionary philosophy as a factor contributing to the turbulence of the period following 1789. In his assessment, the individualism expressed, for example, in the Declaration of the Rights of Man led to considerable intellectual opposition which ultimately accompanied counter-revolutionary mobilization. While agreeing with Furet that the nature of the revolutionary ideals needs to be considered, I maintain that it is the pervasive collectivism embedded in these ideals, rather than the attenuated individualism, that contributed to the post-revolutionary problems.
5 Georges Lefebvre, *The Coming of the French Revolution*, Princeton: Princeton University Press, 1989, p. 50.
6 Quoted in Simon Schama, *Citizens: A Chronicle of the French Revolution*, New York: Alfred A. Knopf, 1989, p. 301.
7 Quoted in *ibid.*, p. 331.
8 *Ibid.*, p. 574.
9 R. R. Palmer and Joel Colton, *A History of the Modern World*, 7th edition, New York: McGraw-Hill, 1992, p. 363.
10 See Robert Darnton, *The Literary Underground of the Old Regime*, Cambridge: Harvard University Press, 1982, for an account of the mixed social composition of the Enlightenment literary and cultural world in pre-revolutionary France.
11 On England's different trajectory, see Michael Walzer, *The Revolution of the Saints: A Study in the Origins of Radical Politics*, Cambridge: Harvard University Press, 1965, especially pp. 232–267, where Walzer discusses upper-class receptiveness to the Puritan values that ultimately transformed that class and facilitated its "adjustment to modern politics and society" (p. 236).
12 Liah Greenfeld, *Nationalism: Five Roads to Modernity*, Cambridge: Harvard University Press, 1992, pp. 152–153.
13 See Palmer and Colton, *op. cit.*, p. 365.
14 On the status anxiety of this social group and its consequences for the French Revolution, see Greenfeld, *op. cit.*, pp. 89–188.
15 The frustrated ambition of educated members of the middle orders is well documented by Darnton, *op. cit.*
16 See Albert Soboul's classic work, *The Parisian Sans-Culottes and the French Revolution 1793–1794*, Oxford: Clarendon Press, 1964.
17 Schama, *op. cit.*, p. 131.
18 *Ibid.*
19 *Ibid.*, p. 137.
20 *Ibid.*, p. 181.
21 Quoted in *ibid.*, p. 110.

22 Crane Brinton, *The Jacobins*, New York: Russell & Russell, 1961, p. 72.
23 Palmer and Colton, *op. cit.*, pp. 318–319.
24 Quoted in Steven Lukes, *Individualism*, London: Basil Blackwell, 1973, p. 77.
25 Robert Darnton, *The Great Cat Massacre and Other Episodes in French Cultural History*, New York: Vintage Books, 1985, p. 249.
26 *Ibid.*, p. 237.
27 Darnton, *The Literary Underground*, p. 68.
28 Rousseau, "Discourse on inequality," in Alan Ritter and Julia Conaway Bondanella (eds.), *Rousseau's Political Writings*, New York: W. W. Norton, 1988, pp. 6–7.
29 Rousseau, *On Social Contract or Principles of Political Right*, in *ibid.*, pp. 85–86.
30 *Ibid.*, p. 93.
31 *Ibid.*, p. 103.
32 *Ibid.*, p. 98.
33 *Ibid.*
34 *Ibid.*, p. 104.
35 Quoted in Lukes, *op. cit.*, p. 49.
36 Palmer and Colton, *op. cit.*, p. 324.
37 See Schama's chapter on "The Cultural Construction of a Citizen" in *Citizens*, *op. cit.*, pp. 123–182.
38 See the writings of Edouard Lefebvre such as *Considérations politiques et morales sur la France constituée en république*, 1897, quoted in Isser Woloch, *The Jacobin Legacy: The Democratic Movement Under the Directory*, Princeton: Princeton University Press, 1970, p. 153.
39 Quoted in Brinton, *op. cit.*, p. 216.
40 Quoted in Yehoshua Arieli, *Individualism and Nationalism in American Ideology*, Cambridge: Harvard University Press, 1964, p. 146.
41 Quoted in Georges Lefebvre, *op. cit.*, pp. 219–220.
42 Quoted in Brinton, *op. cit.*, p. 216.
43 *Ibid.*, p. 204.
44 *Ibid.*
45 Soboul, *op. cit.*, p. 109.
46 *Ibid.*
47 See Soboul and Brinton for accounts of the self-governing tendencies of the sans-culottes and Jacobin communities.
48 Quoted in Schama, *Citizens*, p. 578.
49 Brinton, *op. cit.*, p. 218.
50 *Ibid.*, p. 181.
51 Quoted in Woloch, *op. cit.*, p. 226.
52 Brinton, *op. cit.*, p. 149.
53 Quoted in Eric Hobsbawm, "The making of a bourgeois revolution," in Ferenc Fehér (ed.), *The French Revolution and the Birth of Modernity*, Berkeley: University of California Press, 1990, p. 40.
54 Quoted in Georges Lefebvre, *op. cit.*, p. 221.
55 Quoted in *ibid.*
56 Quoted in *ibid.*, pp. 221–222.
57 Quoted in *ibid.*, p. 222.
58 Arieli, *op. cit.*, p. 96.
59 Quoted in Georges Lefebvre, *op. cit.*, p. 221.
60 Quoted in Soboul, *op. cit.*, p. 57.
61 Quoted in *ibid.*, p. 60.
62 Woloch, *op. cit.*, p. 153.

63 Quoted in Furet, *op. cit.*, p. 370.
64 *Ibid.*, p. 310.
65 *Ibid.*, p. 313.
66 *Ibid.*, p. 343.
67 *Ibid.*, p. 296.
68 *Ibid.*, p. 297.
69 *Ibid.*, p. 343.
70 *Ibid.*
71 *Ibid.*, p. 344.
72 *Ibid.*, p. 343.
73 Patrice Higonnet, "Cultural upheaval and class formation during the French Revolution," in Fehér, *op. cit.*, p. 96.
74 Furet, *op. cit.*, p. 341.
75 Michelet quoted in *ibid.*, p. 322.
76 Quoted in *ibid.*, p. 325.
77 *Ibid.*, p. 387.
78 *Ibid.*, p. 361. On the restricted nature of representation envisioned already in the works of Abbé Sieyes, see William H. Sewell, Jr., *A Rhetoric of Bourgeois Revolution: The Abbé Sieyes and "What is the Third Estate?,"* Durham and London: Duke University Press, 1994.
79 Higonnet, *op. cit.*, p. 96.
80 Quoted in *ibid.*, p. 95.
81 Palmer and Colton, *op. cit.*, p. 608. The following account of post-revolutionary French history is based largely on Palmer and Colton.
82 Furet, *op. cit.*, p. 535.
83 Palmer and Colton, *op. cit.*, p. 891.
84 Bossenga, *op. cit.*, p. 631.
85 *Ibid.*, p. 635.
86 *Ibid.*, p. 634.
87 *Ibid.*, p. 635.
88 See, for example, Palmer and Colton, *op. cit.*, p. 609.
89 Quoted in Georges Lefebvre, *op. cit.*, p. 219.
90 Higonnet, *op. cit.*, p. 76.
91 For an excellent overview of Napoleon's policies, see Louis Bergeron, *France Under Napoleon*, Princeton: Princeton University Press, 1981.

4 NATURAL RIGHTS AND LIBERAL CAPITALIST DEVELOPMENT: AN OVERVIEW

1 The question of how, under what conditions, liberal democracy has been diffused successfully into countries that did not experience an indigenous democratic revolution will be discussed in the epilogue.
2 Eric Hobsbawm, "The making of a bourgeois revolution," in Ferenc Fehér (ed.), *The French Revolution and the Birth of Modernity*, Berkeley: University of California Press, 1990, p. 39.
3 *Ibid.*, p. 41.
4 Georges Lefebvre, *The Coming of the French Revolution*, Princeton: Princeton University Press, 1989, p. 50.
5 François Furet, "Europe after utopianism," in *Journal of Democracy*, vol. 6, no. 1 (January 1995), p. 84.
6 Thomas Paine, *The Rights of Man*, New York: Anchor Books, 1989, p. 418.
7 *Ibid.*, p. 307.

8 Quoted in Albert O. Hirschman, *The Passions and the Interests: Political Arguments for Capitalism Before Its Triumph*, Princeton: Princeton University Press, 1977, p. 103.
9 Max Weber, *The Protestant Ethic and the Spirit of Capitalism*, New York: Charles Scribner's Sons, 1958, pp. 17–18.
10 *Ibid.*, p. 21.
11 *Ibid.*, p. 22.
12 Karl Polanyi, *The Great Transformation*, Boston: Beacon Press, 1957, p. 68.
13 Weber, *op. cit.*, p. 21.
14 Alan Macfarlane, *The Culture of Capitalism*, Oxford: Basil Blackwell, 1989, p. 226.
15 Polanyi, *op. cit.*, p. 71.
16 *Ibid.*, p. 68.
17 Specifically, Sachs notes the benefits of "global economic integration" as countries are increasingly linked "not merely by international trade, but also through networks of production, finance, and shared economic institutions. Almost no country in the world dares to stand aloof from these trends." Jeffrey Sachs, "Shock Therapy in Poland: Perspectives of Five Years," Tanner Lecture, 6 October 1994, p. 3. Sachs goes on to state that "Poland took to a market economy like the proverbial fish to water" (p. 13). This simile is representative of the general mindset in which free market activities are assumed to be inherent in human nature.
18 *Political Writings of John Locke*, edited and with an Introduction by David Wootton, New York: Mentor, 1993, p. 262.

Overall, this analysis of Locke has been guided by C. B. Macpherson, *The Political Theory of Possessive Individualism*, Oxford: Clarendon Press, 1962.
19 *Ibid.*, p. 351.
20 *Ibid.*, p. 324.
21 *Ibid.*, p. 325.
22 *Ibid.*, p. 278.
23 *Ibid.*, p. 274.
24 *Ibid.*, p. 277.
25 *Ibid.*, p. 274.
26 *Ibid.*, p. 303.
27 *Ibid.*, p. 263.
28 On Locke's acceptance of the unequal distribution of wealth, see Macpherson, *op. cit.*, pp. 194–221.
29 *Political Writings of John Locke*, *op. cit.*, p. 276.
30 *Ibid.*, p. 285.
31 See Macpherson, *op. cit.*, p. 209.
32 *Political Writings of John Locke*, *op. cit.*, p. 304.
33 For Locke's assessment of the conditions of wage-labor, see Macpherson, *op. cit.*, pp. 216–218.
34 *Political Writings of John Locke*, *op. cit.*, p. 273.
35 *Ibid.*, p. 447.
36 Quoted in Macpherson, *op. cit.*, p. 206.
37 *Ibid.*, p. 221.
38 *Ibid.*
39 Adam Smith, *The Wealth of Nations*, Oxford: Oxford University Press, 1993, p. 120.
40 *Ibid.*
41 *Ibid.*, p. 230.
42 *Ibid.*, p. 354.

43 *Ibid.*, p. 391.
44 *Ibid.*, p. 292.
45 *Ibid.*, p. 391.
46 *Ibid.*, p. 354.
47 *Ibid.*, p. 330.
48 Kathryn Sunderland, "Introduction," in *ibid.*, p. xix.
49 *Ibid.*, p. xvii.
50 *Ibid.*, p. 268.
51 *Ibid.*, p. xxi.
52 D. D. Raphael and A. L. Macfie, "Introduction," to Adam Smith, *The Theory of Moral Sentiments*, Oxford: Oxford University Press, 1979, p. 7.
53 *Ibid.*
54 For an elaboration of the importance Smith placed on self-command and frugality, see Raphael and Macfie, *op. cit.*
55 Michael Walzer, *The Revolution of the Saints: A Study in the Origins of Radical Politics*, New York: Atheneum, 1973, pp. 305–306.
56 *Ibid.*, p. 303.
57 Weber, *op. cit.*, pp. 211–212.
58 *Ibid.*, p. 256.
59 *Ibid.*, p. 114.
60 *Ibid.*, p. 249.
61 *Ibid.*
62 *Ibid.*, p. 109.
63 Walzer, *op. cit.*, p. 304.
64 *Ibid.*, p. 303.
65 Max Weber, *Economy and Society*, Berkeley: University of California Press, 1978, p. 868.
66 *Ibid.*, p. 867.
67 *Ibid.*, p. 868.
68 *Ibid.*, p. 869.
69 *Ibid.*, p. 873.
70 *Ibid.*, p. 869.
71 *Ibid.*, p. 870.
72 Quoted in Arthur M. Schlesinger, Jr., *The Politics of Upheaval: The Age of Roosevelt*, Boston: Houghton Mifflin Company, 1960, p. 480.
73 Quoted in James W. Ceaser *et al.*, *American Government. Origins, Institutions and Public Policy*, Dubuque, IA: Kendall/Hunt Publishing, 1992, p. 88.
74 Davis Newton Lott, *The Presidents Speak: The Inaugural Addresses*, New York: Holt, Rinehart & Winston, 1969, p. 232.
75 Quoted in Schlesinger, *op. cit.*, p. 459.
76 *Ibid.*
77 Samuel P. Huntington, *American Politics: The Promise of Disharmony*, Cambridge: Harvard University Press, 1981, p. 38.
78 Quoted in Schlesinger, *op. cit.*, p. 481.
79 Weber, *Economy and Society*, p. 873.
80 *Ibid.*, p. 870.
81 *Ibid.*, p. 871.
82 *Ibid.*, p. 872.
83 *Ibid.*, p. 874.
84 Polanyi, *op. cit.*, p. 72.
85 Text of the Declaration contained in Georges Lefebvre, *op. cit.*, pp. 221–225.
86 For example, see Tony A. Freyer, *Producers versus Capitalists: Constitutional Conflict in Antebellum America*, Charlottesville: University Press of Virginia,

1994, for an excellent account of how small producers used the Constitution to protect themselves.

87 For an account of the failure of German liberals to forge an alliance with the lower middle orders, see Jonathan Sperber, *Rhineland Radicals: The Democratic Movement and the Revolution of 1848–1849*, Princeton: Princeton University Press, 1991.

88 Gordon Wright, *France in Modern Times*, New York: W. W. Norton, 1987, p. 270.

89 *Ibid.*, p. 268.

90 *Ibid.*, p. 269.

91 *Ibid.*, p. 359.

92 *Ibid.*, p. 372.

93 Polanyi, *op. cit.*, p. 71.

94 *Ibid.*

95 Wright, *op. cit.*, p. 404.

96 *Ibid.*, p. 409.

97 R. R. Palmer and Joel Colton, *A History of the Modern World*, 7th edition, New York: McGraw-Hill, 1992, p. 886.

98 Wright, *op. cit.*, p. 272.

99 François Crouzet, quoted in *ibid.*, p. 273.

100 Weber, *Economy and Society*, p. 1209.

101 *Ibid.*, p. 874.

102 *Ibid.*, p. 875.

103 Max Weber, *Gesammelte Politische Schriften*, Tübingen: J. C. B. Mohr Verlag, 1988, pp. 63–64.

104 *Ibid.*

105 Weber, *The Protestant Ethic*, p. 181.

106 Weber, *Gesammelte Politische Schriften*, *op. cit.*, p. 64.

107 *Ibid.*

108 *Ibid.*, p. 65.

109 Weber, *The Protestant Ethic*, p. 182.

110 Wright, *op. cit.*, p. 269. On the extent to which the English working class in general, and the Chartists in particular, demanded the right to political participation in the existing system, rather than a complete transformation of the system, see E. P. Thompson, *The Making of the English Working Class*, New York: Vintage, 1963, and Dorothy Thompson, *The Chartists*, New York: Pantheon Books, 1984.

111 It would appear that T. H. Marshall's conclusions regarding the evolution of citizenship in the original liberal states are more accurate than Weber's; see T. H. Marshall, *Citizenship and Social Class*, Cambridge: Cambridge University Press, 1950.

112 For an overview of the relationship between capitalism and democracy as it has been analyzed in the social sciences, see Dietrich Rueschemeyer *et al.*, *Capitalist Development and Democracy*, Chicago: University of Chicago Press, 1992, pp. 12–39.

113 Such bureaucratic structures can be weak or strong depending on the state in question. For example, the German Second Reich and Japan after the Meiji Restoration were characterized by efficient, centralized bureaucracies. Many post-colonial states, on the other hand, especially in Africa, are characterized by ineffective, corrupt, self-serving bureaucracies. What all of these states have in common, however, are: regulatory as opposed to participatory governing structures; top-down, command-driven policy making as opposed to bottom-up, input-oriented policy making; and hierarchical, executive-oriented

leadership as opposed to the associational leadership embodied in an active legislature and a representative party system. In short, while these bureaucracies may embody a degree of proceduralism and impersonalism, and pursue a program of capitalist development, they do not coexist with the institutional domains of citizenship and representative government.

114 Seymour Martin Lipset, *Political Man: The Social Bases of Politics*, Baltimore: Johns Hopkins University Press, 1994, p. 31.

115 Michael Mandelbaum, "Introduction," in *Making Markets: Economic Transformation in Eastern Europe and the Post-Soviet States*, edited by Shafiqul Islam and Michael Mandelbaum, New York: Council on Foreign Relations Press, 1993, p. 13.

116 Socioeconomic, political, historical and ideological factors may, however, combine to produce two other outcomes, aside from liberal capitalism and capitalism without liberalism. The Asian NICs, for example, appear to be moving from a pattern of authoritarian, development-oriented rule to limited representative government. The socioeconomic processes underlying this evolution can be seen in the reduction of social polarization (due to the income equalization policies pursued by the regimes in question), and the growth of an educated, articulate middle class. In these cases, an ethic of social responsibility may well act as a "functional equivalent" for the natural rights doctrine in promoting the domains of representative government and citizenship.

Another outcome can be seen in Europe where liberal democratic institutions were established in countries that did not directly experience a charismatic manifestation of the natural rights doctrine. In these cases, the domains of liberal capitalism were either infused with a different source of legitimacy other than the natural rights doctrine, or they exist on an instrumental basis alone. The Scandinavian countries provide an example of the former tendency wherein liberal capitalism has been legitimated by customs and traditions upholding a participatory style of government and an ethos of social equality. For an analysis of how these traditions have been institutionalized over time in Norway, see Harry Eckstein, *Division and Cohesion in Democracy: A Study of Norway*, Princeton: Princeton University Press, 1966. The latter tendency is exemplified by countries such as Austria and Greece where competitive party systems exist, along with adequate resources to maintain an acceptable standard of living for the population at large, thereby minimizing social divisions and antagonisms. However, neither a traditional nor a natural rights basis exists for a value rational commitment to liberalism. Political elites support liberal capitalist institutions instrumentally to the extent that such support is rewarded by the liberal capitalist core, or more specifically, the European Union. While instrumental acquiescence may eventually turn into more affectively oriented legitimacy as institutions provide benefits over time, the different bases of compliance have consequences for the institutional development of liberal capitalism. These consequences will be examined briefly in the epilogue.

5 THE MARXIST–LENINIST RESPONSE TO NATURAL RIGHTS AND LIBERAL CAPITALISM

1 For more on Babeuf and his contribution to socialism, see Edmund Wilson, *To the Finland Station: A Study in the Writing and Acting of History*, New York: Farrar, Straus & Giroux, 1972, pp. 83–93.

2 Quoted in Andrzej Walicki, *Marxism and the Leap to the Kingdom of Freedom:*

The Rise and Fall of the Communist Utopia, Stanford: Stanford University Press, 1995, p. 20.

3 James O'Rourke quoted in *ibid.*, p. 19.

4 *Ibid.*

5 Philip Selznick, *The Organizational Weapon*, New York: McGraw-Hill, 1952.

6 Kenneth Jowitt, *New World Disorder The Leninist Extinction*, Berkeley: University of California Press, 1992, p. 254.

7 Karl Marx and Frederick Engels, *Collected Works*, New York: International Publishers, 1975, vol. 3, p. 155.

8 *Ibid.*, p. 152.

9 See Ernst Bloch, *Natural Law and Human Dignity*, Cambridge: MIT Press, 1986, for a systematic effort to reconcile Marxism to the natural law tradition. While criticizing the "illusions in bourgeois natural law" from a Marxist perspective, Bloch still maintains that: "It needs to be made clear that, precisely with respect to the humiliated and degraded, Marxism inherits some of this wealth of natural law, and that in places it finds some unsatisfied demands in it" (p. 188). See also Walicki, *op. cit.*, for an analysis of Marx's interpretation of rights that is similar to that developed in this chapter.

10 Walicki, *op. cit.*, p. 17.

11 *Ibid.*, p. 12.

12 Marx and Engels, *op. cit.*, vol. 3, p. 149.

13 *Ibid.*, p. 79.

14 *Ibid.*, p. 174.

15 *Ibid.*

16 *Ibid.*, p. 167.

17 *Ibid.*, p. 160.

18 *Ibid.*, p. 162.

19 *Ibid.*, p. 159.

20 *Ibid.*, p. 162.

21 *Ibid.*, pp. 162–163.

22 *Ibid.*, p. 164.

23 *Ibid.*

24 *Ibid.*, p. 167.

25 *Ibid.*, p. 168.

26 *Ibid.*

27 *Ibid.*, p. 154.

28 *Ibid.*, p. 153.

29 *Ibid.*, p. 154.

30 *Ibid.*, p. 156.

31 See Walicki, *op. cit.*, p. 29.

32 *Ibid.*

33 Marx and Engels, *op. cit.*, vol. 24, p. 87.

34 *Ibid.*, p. 86.

35 *Ibid.*, p. 87.

36 *Ibid.*, vol. 5, pp. 31–32.

37 *Ibid.*, p. 37.

38 *Ibid.* It is worth noting here that this brief overview of Marx's views cannot do justice to the complexity of his intellectual engagement with Hegel. For a nuanced discussion, see Shlomo Avineri, *The Social and Political Thought of Karl Marx*, Cambridge: Cambridge University Press, 1968.

See also Stephen E. Hanson, *Time and Revolution: Marxism and the Design of Soviet Institutions*, Chapel Hill, NC: University of North Carolina Press, 1996, for an analysis of Engels' efforts to systematize Marx's "dialectical method" into "a universal explanation of all scientific phenomena, social and natural" (p. 56). See also, Walicki, *op. cit.*, pp. 111–207, for his chapter on "Engels and 'Scientific Socialism.' "

39 *Ibid.*, p. 49.
40 *Ibid.*, p. 52.
41 *Ibid.*, p. 87.
42 *Ibid.*, p. 53.
43 Quoted in A. J. Polan, *Leninism and the End of Politics*, Berkeley: University of California Press, 1984, p. 80.
44 Max Weber, *The Protestant Ethic and the Spirit of Capitalism*, New York: Charles Scribner's Sons, 1958, p. 197.
45 V. I. Lenin, *What is to be Done?*, Moscow: Foreign Languages Publishing House, 1950, p. 218.
46 *Ibid.*, p. 247.
47 *Ibid.*, pp. 292–293.
48 Polan, *op. cit.*, p. 120.
49 Quoted in *ibid.*, p. 126.
50 *Ibid.*, p. 80.
51 Quoted in Kenneth Jowitt, *The Leninist Response to National Dependency*, Berkeley, CA: Institute of International Studies, UCB, 1978, p. 39. Overall, this line of analysis is based on Jowitt's work. See especially pp. 34–39.
52 Max Weber, *op. cit.*
53 Teresa Toranska, *"Them": Stalin's Polish Puppets*, New York: Harper & Row, 1988, pp. 135–136.
54 Kenneth Jowitt, *op. cit.*, p. 34.
55 Walicki, *op. cit.*, p. 19.
56 This analysis owes a great deal to Kenneth Jowitt, "Political culture in Leninist regimes," in Jowitt, *New World Disorder*, pp. 50–87.
57 Quoted in Jowitt, *New World Disorder*, p. 66.
58 Polan, *op. cit.*, p. 129.
59 Teresa Toranska, *op. cit.*, p. 44.
60 Quoted in Bartlomiej Kamiński, *The Collapse of State Socialism: The Case of Poland*, Princeton: Princeton University Press, 1991, p. 21.
61 Kenneth Jowitt, *Leninist Response*, p. 34.
62 *Ibid.*, p. 36.
63 *Ibid.*, p. 39.
64 *Ibid.*, p. 42.
65 Teresa Toranska, *op. cit.*, p. 94.
66 This analysis is based on the work of Kenneth Jowitt, see *New World Disorder*, *op. cit.*
67 *Ibid.*, pp. 250–251.
68 This term was coined by Jowitt. On corruption in Leninist regimes, see Jowitt, "Neotraditionalism," in *ibid.*, pp. 121–158.
69 *Ibid.*, p. 252.
70 The following survey of postwar Polish history draws heavily from R. F. Leslie (ed.), *The History of Poland Since 1863*, Cambridge: Cambridge University Press, 1980, and from Keith John Lepak, *Prelude to Solidarity: Poland and the Politics of the Gierek Regime*, New York: Columbia University Press, 1988.

    On Bierut's death see, for example, Peter Raina, *Political Opposition in Poland 1954–1977*, London: Poets and Painters Press, 1978, p. 34.
71 Z. A. Pelczynski, "The October turning point," in Leslie (ed.), *op. cit.*, p. 346.
72 Teresa Toranska, *op. cit.*, p. 121.
73 See, for example, Z. A. Pelczynski, *op. cit.*, pp. 344–367.

74 Keith John Lepak, *op. cit.*, p. 67.
75 Z. A. Pelczynski, *op. cit.*, p. 338.
76 Keith John Lepak, *op. cit.*, p. 120.
77 See, for example, Z. A. Pelczynski, *op. cit.*, pp. 341–343.
78 Teresa Toranska, *op. cit.*, p. 153.
79 Z. A. Pelczynski, *op. cit.*, p. 342.
80 Teresa Toranska, *op. cit.*, p. 141.
81 *Ibid.*, p. 134.
82 Z. A. Pelczynski, *op. cit.*, p. 326.
83 *Ibid.*, p. 341.
84 Quoted in Kenneth Jowitt, *New World Disorder*, p. 225.
85 Quoted in Keith John Lepak, *op. cit.*, pp. 40–41.
86 See the introduction in Adam Michnik, *Letters from Prison and Other Essays*, Berkeley: University of California Press, 1985, pp. xvii–xlii, and Lech Wałęsa, *A Way of Hope*, New York: Henry Holt, 1987.
87 Tadeusz Nowak, *Zanim powstała Solidarność*, Lublin: Norbertinum, 1990, p. 49.

Later Nowak recalls that Wałęsa elaborated further on his activities in a conversation with a troublemaking skeptic:

> I am an activist for Free Trade Unions. . . . in which we protect the rights guaranteed to us by various laws. We protest the groundless firing of people from work, we organize self-defense groups. . . . We conduct cheap lessons in the shape of discussions. Our main goal is the defense of the worker, guaranteed by the Sejm and the Constitution of the People's Republic.
>
> (pp. 58–59)

88 See Jacek Kurczewski, *The Resurrection of Rights in Poland*, Oxford: Clarendon Press, 1993, pp. 100–126, for an elaboration of this new class in Polish society.
89 *Ibid.*, p. 118.
90 *Ibid.*, pp. 117–118.
91 *Ibid.*, p. 100.
92 Eric Hobsbawm, "The making of a bourgeois revolution," in Ferenc Fehér (ed.), *The French Revolution and the Birth of Modernity*, Berkeley: University of California Press, 1990, p. 41.
93 Z. A. Pelczynski, *op. cit.*, pp. 446–447.
94 *Ibid.*, p. 330.
95 Kurczewski, *op. cit.*, p. 400.
96 *Ibid.*
97 Quoted in Peter Raina, *op. cit.*, p. 33.
98 Michnik, *op. cit.*, p. xxvi.
99 For contrasting analyses of the role of the Church in post-war Poland, see Maryjane Osa, "Resistance, persistence and change: the transformation of the Catholic Church in Poland," in *East European Politics and Societies*, vol. 3, no. 2 (Spring 1989), pp. 268–299; and Ewa Morawska, "The Polish Roman Catholic Church unbound: change of face or change of context?" in Stephen E. Hanson and Willfried Spohn (eds.), *Can Europe Work? Germany and the Reconstruction of Postcommunist Societies*, Seattle: University of Washington Press, 1995, pp. 47–78.

While Osa highlights the organizational flexibility of the Polish Church in responding to new social and political realities, a line of analysis that is consistent with the interpretation developed in these pages, Morawska maintains that the Church did not transform itself either organizationally or doctrinally. Instead, it retained its conservative traditional worldview throughout the communist era. Opposition figures like Michnik simply made the mistake of reading too much "liberalization" into Church pronouncements.

100 Kurczewski, *op. cit.*, p. 400.
101 Keith John Lepak, *op. cit.*, p. 38.
102 *Ibid.*, p. 39.
103 *Ibid.*, p. 150.
104 *Ibid.*, p. 149.
105 Peter Raina, *Independent Social Movements in Poland*, London: Orbis Books, 1981, p. 605.
106 For an elaboration of the events of 1976, see Jan Kubik, *The Power of Symbols Against the Symbols of Power: The Rise of Solidarity and the Fall of State Socialism in Poland*, University Park, PA: Pennsylvania State University Press, 1994.

Indeed, most analyses of Solidarity begin with the protest demonstrations of 1976 and the subsequent formation of KOR. However, this approach begs the question of what gave rise to 1976? Consequently, a broader analysis is needed that emphasizes the structural variables (the rise of a new class, the weakness of the Party and the post-1956 strength of opposition organizations) that provided the antecedent conditions for 1976 *and* for 1980.

107 Stefan Nowak, "Values and attitudes of the Polish people," in *Scientific American*, vol. 245, no. 1 (July 1981), p. 53.
108 See Michnik, *op. cit.*, pp. 135–149.
109 Nowak, *op. cit.*, p. 53.
110 *Ibid.*, p. 52.
111 On the evolution of these protest efforts see, for example, Peter Raina, *Independent Social Movements, op. cit.*
112 Nowak, *op. cit.*, p. 51.
113 *Ibid.*
114 Keith John Lepak, *op. cit.*, p. 188.
115 I owe this insight to my colleague Stephen Hanson.
116 Peter Raina, *op. cit.*, p. 371.
117 Quoted in *ibid.*, pp. 372–373.
118 Most of the recent work published on Solidarity emphasizes the social composition of the movement as a critical analytical variable. See, for example, Michael H. Bernhard, *The Origins of Democratization in Poland*, New York: Columbia University Press, 1993; Jerome Karabel, "Polish intellectuals and the origins of Solidarity: the making of an oppositional alliance," in *Communist and Post-Communist Studies*, vol. 26, no. 1 (March 1993), pp. 25–46; Roman Laba, *The Roots of Solidarity*, Princeton: Princeton University Press, 1991; Michael Kennedy, *Professionals, Power and Solidarity in Poland*, Cambridge: Cambridge University Press, 1991.
119 See Gordon H. Skilling, *Czechoslovakia's Interrupted Revolution*, Princeton: Princeton University Press, 1976.
120 Without subscribing to the official Soviet view that the 1956 uprising in Hungary consisted only of reactionary "feudalists and lumpen elements" bound on lynching every Communist Party official in sight, it is true, however, that "the old (prewar) parties promptly reappeared and squabbled over how to divide the ministerial posts after the Communists were gone." Thomas W. Simons, Jr., *Eastern Europe in the Postwar World*, New York: St. Martin's Press, 1991, p. 98. Although they cannot be described as "feudalists," conservative traditionalists clearly competed with more progressive reformers during the uprising, and at times threatened to become the dominant ideological force of the revolution. See also: Charles Gati, *Hungary and the Soviet Bloc*, Durham,

NC: Duke University Press, 1986; and Ferenc Fehér and Agnes Heller, *Hungary 1956 Revisited*, London: Allen & Unwin, 1983.

121 Quoted in Peter Raina, *op. cit.*, p. 447.

6 SOLIDARITY'S ARTICULATION OF NATURAL RIGHTS

1 For an overview of the different opposition groups beginning to use the language of rights, see Peter Raina, *Independent Social Movements in Poland*, London: Orbis Books, 1981.

2 Adam Michnik, *The Church and the Left*, Chicago: University of Chicago Press, 1993, p. 203.

3 On Renaissance humanism and its relationship to the Enlightenment, see Peter Gay, *The Enlightenment: The Rise of Modern Paganism*, New York: W. W. Norton, 1977, pp. 261–279.

4 Russell Kirk, introduction to Giovanni Pico della Mirandola, *Oration on the Dignity of Man*, Chicago: Regnery Gateway, 1956, pp. xvii–xviii.

5 Peter Gay, *op. cit.*, p. 270.

6 *Ibid.*

7 On the critique of natural rights, see Jeremy Waldron (ed.),*"Nonsense upon Stilts," Bentham, Burke and Marx on the Rights of Man*, London: Methuen, 1987.

8 Solidarity Information Bulletin, Issue No. 1, October 1981, p. 1.

9 Adam Michnik, "Towards a civil society: hopes for Polish democracy," in *TLS*, 19–25 February 1988, p. 198.

10 Joel Feinberg, *Rights, Justice, and the Bounds of Liberty: Essays in Social Philosophy*, Princeton: Princeton University Press, 1980, p. 151.

11 Adam Michnik, *Letters From Prison and Other Essays*, Berkeley: University of California Press, 1985, p. 148. Translation augmented with the Polish original, Adam Michnik, "Nowy Ewolucjonizm," in *Aneks*, London, 1978, reprinted in Adam Michnik, *Szanse polskiej demokracji*, London: Aneks, 1984, p. 87.

The line of analysis developed here, comparing the parallel thinking of Michnik and Tischner, has recently been validated—at least indirectly—by the publication of an extensive joint interview; see Adam Michnik, Józef Tischner and Jacek Żakowski, *Między Panem a Plebanem*, Kraków: Znak, 1995. For example, both men have the same memories of Solidarity:

> [AM]: That was my Poland, with which I easily identified. In the fall of 1980, for the first time in my life I identified not with the ideal Poland, a product of a certain intellectual–sentimental project, a result of reading and reflection, but with the really existing Poland which actually surrounded me. I went to work and to union meetings and I loved these people. It was extraordinary.
>
> [JT]: I felt the same [p. 320].

12 Russell Kirk, *op. cit.*, p. xvii.

13 Leszek Kolakowski, *Toward a Marxist Humanism*, New York: Grove Press, 1968, p. 141.

14 *Ibid.*, p. 209.

15 *Ibid.*, p. 129.

16 *Ibid.*, p. 140.

17 Adam Michnik, interview in *Gazeta Wyborcza*, 25–26 April, 1992, p. 8.

18 Adam Michnik, "The moral and spiritual origins of Solidarity," in William Brinton and Alan Rinzler (eds.), *Without Force or Lies: Voices from the*

Revolution in Central Europe in 1989–90, San Francisco: Mercury House Books, 1990, p. 248.

19 Adam Michnik, *Letters From Prison*, p. 5.
20 *Ibid.*, p. 6.
21 Adam Michnik, "The moral and spiritual origins," p. 241.
22 Adam Michnik, *Letters From Prison*, p. 317.
23 *Ibid.*
24 *Ibid.*, p. 316.
25 *Ibid.*, p. 317.
26 *Ibid.*, p. 145.
27 *Ibid.*, p. 144.
28 *Ibid.*
29 *Ibid.*
30 *Ibid.*, p. 147.
31 Adam Michnik, "The moral and spiritual origins," p. 241.
32 *Ibid*, p. 243.
33 *Ibid.*
34 *Ibid.*
35 *Ibid.*, p. 242.
36 Adam Michnik, *Letters From Prison*, p. 145.
37 *Ibid.*
38 *Ibid.*, p. 94.
39 Adam Michnik, *The Church and the Left*, p. xiii.
40 *Ibid.*, p. 257.
41 *Ibid.*
42 *Ibid.*, p. xiii.
43 Adam Michnik, "The moral and spiritual origins," p. 246.
44 Adam Michnik, *Letters From Prison*, p. 126.
45 Józef Tischner, *The Spirit of Solidarity*, San Francisco: Harper & Row, 1984, p. 88.
46 *Ibid.*, p. 42.
47 *Ibid.*, p. 4.
48 *Ibid.*, pp. 2–3.
49 *Ibid.*, p. 6.
50 *Ibid.*
51 *Ibid.*
52 *Ibid.*, p. 81.
53 *Ibid.*, p. 24.
54 *Ibid.*, p. 81.
55 *Ibid.*, p. 88.
56 *Ibid.*, p. 24.
57 *Ibid.*.
58 *Ibid.*, p. 102.
59 *Ibid.*, p. 43.
60 *Ibid.*
61 *Ibid.*, p. 42.
62 *Ibid.*
63 *Ibid.*, p. 41.
64 *Ibid.*, p. 43.
65 *Ibid.*
66 *Ibid.*, p. 24.
67 *Ibid.*, p. 49.
68 *Ibid.*, p. 90.

69 Adam Michnik, *Letters From Prison*, p. 168.
70 *Ibid.*, p. 163.
71 *Ibid.*
72 *Ibid.*, pp. 167–168.
73 Peter Raina, *Independent Social Movements in Poland*, p. 439.
74 *Ibid.*, p. 475.
75 *Ibid.*, p. 478.
76 Quoted in Neal Ascherson, *The Polish August*, London: Penguin Books, 1981, p. 283.
77 Peter Raina, *Independent Social Movements in Poland*, p. 610.
78 *Ibid.*
79 Peter Raina (ed.), *Poland 1981: Towards Social Renewal*, London: George Allen & Unwin, 1985, p. 173.
80 *Ibid.*, p. 174.
81 Peter Raina, *Independent Social Movements in Poland*, p. 439.
82 Peter Raina, *Poland 1981*, p. 194.
83 Peter Raina, *Independent Social Movements in Poland*, p. 614.
84 Peter Raina, *Poland 1981*, p. 173.
85 *Ibid.*, pp. 188–189.

For a recent analysis that corresponds, up to a point, to the one developed in these pages, see Jerzy Szacki, *Liberalism After Communism*, Budapest/New York: Central European University Press, 1994, pp. 82–89. Szacki, as well, emphasizes the "collective individualism" of the dissident movement. Accordingly, he states that while "the dissident movement is probably the most serious manifestation of individualism in the political . . . thought of Eastern Europe" (p. 83), "as a rule the manifestation of the autonomy of the individual in relation to the state turned out to be inseparable from the desire to participate in a community" (p. 85). Szacki goes on, however, to state that "the idea of the autonomy of the individual, which underpinned the dissident movement, simply disappeared" in Solidarity (p. 112). Although "elements of liberal thought . . . were not completely eliminated" (p.112), Solidarity's collectivism completely overshadowed all other elements (see pp. 114–117). In my opinion, this is too extreme a view, and too rooted in elitest conceptions of all the bad things that can happen when good ideas become "disseminated among the masses" (p. 117).

86 *Ibid.*, p. 174.
87 *Ibid.*, p. 185.
88 *Ibid.*, p. 187.
89 *Ibid.*, p. 174.
90 *Ibid.*, p. 327.
91 *Ibid.*, p. 347.
92 *Ibid.*
93 *Ibid.*, p. 346.
94 *Ibid.*, p. 349.
95 Jósef Tischner, *The Spirit of Solidarity*, p. 81.
96 Bogdan Borusewicz, "Chcieli mieć demokrację i głosowali na demokrację," in Rzeczpospolita, *Co zrobiliśmy z naszą wolnością*, Warsaw: Presspublica, 1995, p. 178.
97 Peter Raina, *Poland 1981*, p. 173.
98 Czesław Miłosz, *The History of Polish Literature*, Berkeley: University of California Press, 1983, pp. 27–28.
99 John C. Olin (ed.), *Christian Humanism and the Reformation: Selected Writings of Erasmus*, New York: Fordham University Press, 1987, pp. 34–35.

100 Erasmus, "Letter to Martin Dorp," in *ibid*., p. 94.
101 Erasmus, "Letter to Paul Voltz," in *ibid*., p. 128.
102 Andrzej Walicki, *Philosophy and Romantic Nationalism: The Case of Poland*, Oxford: Clarendon Press, 1982, p. 19.
103 For an elaboration of Poland's historical experience with liberalism, see Szacki, *op. cit*., pp. 43–72.
104 Adam Michnik, Józef Tischner and Jacek Żakowski, *op. cit*., pp. 318–321.
105 Walicki, *op. cit*., p. 47.
106 *Ibid*., p. 50.
107 Arista Maria Cirtautas and Edmund Mokrzycki, "The articulation and institutionalization of democracy in Poland," in *Social Research*, vol. 60, no. 4 (Winter 1993), pp. 787–820.
108 Peter Raina, *Poland 1981*, p. 191.
109 J. Szyłak, "My reminiscences of August 1980," in *Sisyphus Sociological Studies*, vol. III, Warsaw: PWN, 1982, pp. 295–296.
110 J. Gajda, "August 1980 as I saw it," in *ibid*., p. 241.
111 *Ibid*., pp. 238–239.
112 *Ibid*., p. 251.
113 Adam Michnik, "Towards a civil society," in *op. cit*., p. 198.
114 *Ibid*.
115 Quoted in Timothy Garton Ash, *The Polish Revolution: Solidarity*, New York: Vintage Books, 1985, p. 279.
116 Quoted in *ibid*., pp. 279–280.
117 J. Kuczma, "August 1980 as I remember it," in *Sisyphus Sociological Studies*, *op. cit*., p. 271.
118 *Ibid*., pp. 261–262.
119 W. Pawełec, "Seventeen hot days," in *ibid*., p. 275.
120 G. Kaszuba, "The strike in the Ustka shipyard in August 1980," in *ibid*., p. 281.
121 *Ibid*., p. 285.
122 J. Szyłak, *op. cit*., p. 305.
123 *Ibid*., p. 307.
124 J. Kuczma, *op. cit*., pp. 263–264.
125 J. Szyłak, *op. cit*., p. 301.
126 J. Gajda, *op. cit*., p. 237.
127 J. Kuczma, *op. cit*., p. 254.
128 J. Szyłak, *op. cit*., pp. 293–294.
129 See the account by J. Kuczma, *op. cit*., p. 267.
130 J. Szyłak, *op. cit*., p. 308.
131 Alain Touraine, *Solidarity: Poland 1980–81*, Cambridge: Cambridge University Press, 1983, pp. 141–142.
132 M. Szuta, "The strike in the northern shipyard in Gdańsk," in *Sisyphus Sociological Studies*, *op. cit*., p. 231.
133 For an account of this incident, see Timothy Garton Ash, *op. cit*., pp. 214–215. See also George Sanford (ed.), *The Solidarity Congress, 1981*, New York: St. Martin's Press, 1990.
134 J. Gajda, *op. cit*., p. 250.
135 Quoted in Grzegorz Fortuna, "Be great, Mr. Wałęsa," in *The Book of Lech Wałęsa: A Collective Portrait by Solidarity Members and Friends*, New York: Simon & Schuster, 1982, pp. 153–160.
136 *Ibid*., p. 155.
137 Quoted in *ibid*.
138 Alain Touraine, *op. cit*., p. 150.

139 H. Gerth and C. Wright Mills (eds.), *From Max Weber: Essays in Sociology*, New York: Oxford University Press, 1946, p. 248.

140 Ernest Barker, *Traditions of Civility*, Cambridge: Cambridge University Press, 1948, p. 310.

141 Alain Touraine, *op. cit.*, p. 149.

142 *Ibid.*, p. 143.

143 *Ibid.*, p. 182.

144 *Ibid.*, p. 145. Indeed, in retrospect, Solidarity has been analyzed as a coalition comprised uneasily of Catholic nationalists, worker populists and intellectual liberal democrats. This coalition was viable, the argument continues, only under communism, and after its collapse in 1989, the coalition naturally split apart into its component elements. These elements, now organized into various political groupings and parties, and driven by different interests and agendas, are engaged in ongoing debates and conflicts over the future of Poland. Specifically, contested issues include: the role of the Catholic Church in a democratic country; the role of trade unions in a liberal capitalist country; and, most importantly perhaps, whether the state should be based on civic or ethnic conceptions of membership and citizenship.

While this is a compelling interpretation, one must keep in mind that the Solidarity movement, just like the American and French Revolutions, represents much more than an instrumentally determined coalition of latently antagonistic forces. Within the context of the movement, a natural rights doctrine was articulated which did reorient people's attitudes and behaviors. That this reorientation was incomplete is due more to the external conditions in which the movement operated, and to its specific sociological characteristics, than to its "coalitional" composition.

145 Unfortunately, a more detailed examination of Solidarity's underground years is beyond the scope of this work. These years do, however, represent an important, and as yet insufficiently studied, period of the movement's history. Among the few works on this subject are: Maciej Łopiński, Marcin Moskit and Mariusz Wilk, *Konspira: Solidarity Underground*, Berkeley: University of California Press, 1990; and Steven G. Stoltenberg, "An underground society: the evolution of Poland's Solidarity, 1982–1989," unpublished dissertation, University of California, Berkeley, 1993.

7 SOLIDARITY AND LIBERAL CAPITALISM

1 Michael H. Bernhard, *The Origins of Democratization in Poland*, New York: Columbia University Press, 1993, pp. 10–13.

2 George Schöpflin, "Culture and identity in post-Communist Europe," in Stephen White, Judy Batt and Paul G. Lewis (eds.), *Developments in East European Politics*, Durham, NC: Duke University Press, 1993, p. 23.

3 Jan T. Gross, "Poland: from civil society to political nation," in Ivo Banac (ed.), *Eastern Europe in Revolution*, Ithaca: Cornell University Press, 1992, p. 70.

4 Jan Kubik, *The Power of Symbols Against the Symbols of Power: The Rise of Solidarity and the Fall of State Socialism in Poland*, University Park, PA: Pennsylvania State University Press, 1994, p. 269.

For a similar assessment of Solidarity's current relevance see: Jerzy Szacki, *Liberalism After Communism*, Budapest/New York: Central European Press, 1994. For example, on p. 113 Szacki states that "Solidarity was of little importance for the development of liberalism in Poland, to which it made at most an indirect contribution by introducing a 'revaluation of values' to politics and society at large."

5 Stephen Hanson, "The Leninist legacy and institutional change," in *Comparative Political Studies*, vol. 28, no. 2 (July 1995), p. 312.

In his work Andrzej Tymowski makes a similar distinction between social norms embedded in political culture and the formal pattern of liberal capitalist institutionalization. In his opinion, social resistance to the post-1989 reforms can be explained by the enduring norms of egalitarianism, paternalism and societal solidarism which Solidarity embodied in 1980–81; see Andrzej Tymowski, "The roots of counter-reform: Homo Sovieticus or moral economy?," paper delivered at the 5th World Congress of Central and East European Studies, August 1995. However, by focussing exclusively on the traditional aspects of Solidarity's ethos, this approach overlooks the positive reinforcement that Solidarity's non-traditional norms might lend to the current reform processes.

6 Wlodzimierz Wesołowski, "Transition to democracy: the role of social and political pluralism," in *Sisyphus Sociological Studies*, vol. 7, 1991, p. 93.

7 Jeffrey Sachs, "Shock therapy in Poland: perspectives of five years," Tanner Lecture, 6 October 1994, p. 1. For a full elaboration of the Balcerowicz Plan, see Jeffrey Sachs, *Poland's Jump to the Market Economy*, Cambridge: MIT Press, 1993.

8 *Ibid.*, p. 5.

9 Quoted in *ibid.*

10 Marcin Król, "The Polish syndrome of incompleteness," in Stanislaw Gomulka and Antony Polonsky (eds.), *Polish Paradoxes*, London: Routledge, 1990, p. 74.

For an assessment of Solidarity's articulation of individual rights, see also Wiktor Osiatynski, "Constitutionalism and rights in the history of Poland," in Louis Henkin and Albert J. Rosenthal (eds.), *Constitutionalism and Rights: The Influence of the US Constitution Abroad*, New York: Columbia University Press, 1990.

11 *Ibid.*, p. 72.

12 Quoted in Jacek Kurczewski, *The Resurrection of Rights in Poland*, Oxford: Clarendon Press, 1993, p. 207.

13 Jacek Kuroń, *Politika i odpowiedzialność*, London: Aneks, 1984, p. 173.

14 On Solidarity's rationing program, see Kurczewski, *op. cit.*, pp. 295–334.

15 Gross, *op. cit.*, p. 68.

16 Witold Morawski, "Institution and citizenship building in the former socialist countries," paper delivered at the conference "In Transition," held at Indiana University, September 1993, p. 6.

17 Maria Los, "Legislating the post-totalitarian transition," in *The Polish Sociological Bulletin*, no. 3/4, 1992, p. 354.

18 *Ibid.*, p. 347.

19 *Ibid.*, p. 349.

20 For a first-hand account of the "renovation" of the Communist Constitution see: Bronisław Geremek and Jacek Żakowski, *Rok 1989. Bronisław Geremek opowiada Jacek Żakowski pyta*, Warsaw: Plejada, 1990, pp. 371–381.

21 Los, *op. cit.*, p. 349.

22 Quoted in *ibid.*

23 Quoted in *ibid.*

24 Geremek and Żakowski, *op. cit.*

25 Bronisław Świderski, *Gdańsk i Ateny: O demokracji bezpośredniej w Polsce*, Warsaw: Widawnictwo IFiS PAN, 1996, p. 217.

See also Świderski, "Gdańsk i Ateny," in *Przegląd Polityczny*, no. 30 (Spring 1996), pp. 13–16 in which the author calls for a reanimation of Polish traditions of direct democracy linked both to Solidarity and the "szlachta" democracy of the seventeenth and eighteenth centuries: "It would seem to be an interesting effort today to use the old direct democracy in such a way as to bestow the equality of the nobility upon every Pole" (p. 15).

In the same issue of *Przegląd Polityczny*, (pp. 5–11), Paweł Śpiewak also concludes that greater levels of civic participation are necessary to counteract "elitist tendencies." In this context, he describes a "republican" school of democratic thinkers in contemporary Poland who "believe that democracy requires openness to all groups of people, that it requires, above all, participation and a shared sense of responsibility and that without these attributes neither prudence nor freedom will find their place" (p. 11).

26 *Ibid.*, pp. 217–218. For further elaboration of the Athenian nature of Solidarity's form of democracy, see also pp. 177–182.

27 This pattern was foreshadowed during the martial law years when the Solidarity leadership was often critical of spontaneous popular expressions of discontent. During the initial outbreak of strikes in 1988, for example, Wałęsa was extremely hesitant to commit himself and Solidarity to the support of a younger generation of strikers who appeared more radical and more violent than their predecessors in 1980. On the 1988 strikes, see Paweł Smołeński and Wojciech Giełżyński, *Robotnicy 88*, London: Aneks, 1989. For an account of the Round Table negotiations, see Krzysztof Dubiński, *Magdalenka Transakcja Epoki*, Warsaw: Sylwa, 1990.

28 For an analysis of the conflict over the Citizens' Committees, see Jadwiga Staniszkis, *The Dynamics of the Breakthrough in Eastern Europe: The Polish Experience*, Berkeley: University of California Press, 1991, pp. 147–152. For an analysis of the subsequent evolution of the Committees, see Tomasz Grabowksi, "From a civic movement to political parties: the rise and fall of the Solidarity Committees in Poland, 1989–1991," paper presented at the Annual Meeting of the American Political Science Association, Chicago, 31 August–3 September 1995.

29 Geremek and Żakowski, *op. cit.*, p. 201.

30 Andrzej Tymowski, "The unwanted social revolution: Poland in 1989," in *East European Politics and Societies*, vol. 7, no. 2 (Spring 1993), pp. 187–188.

31 Ellen Comisso, "Property rights, liberalism and the transition from 'actually existing' socialism," in *East European Politics and Societies*, vol. 5, no. 1 (Winter 1991), p. 167.

32 Sachs, *Poland's Jump*, *op. cit.*, p. 83.

33 Tymowski, "Unwanted social revolution," *op. cit.*, p. 188.

34 Jacek Kurczewski, "The resurrection of rights in Poland," in *The Polish Sociological Bulletin*, no. 2, 1991, p. 112. While Kurczewski offers a largely positive assessment of the Solidarity experience, the implications of his argument can place Solidarity in a more negative light. Indeed, during the mid- to late 1980s, critical analyses of Solidarity began to emerge in Poland which maintained that the failings of both Solidarity and communism needed to be overcome by political rationality (i.e. cooperation with the communist government as opposed to romantic opposition) and market rationality (i.e. implementation of capitalist economic reforms). Among the critics were numerous economists, such as Leszek Balcerowicz, and former Solidarity members who would go on to form the Liberal Democratic Congress (Kongres Liberalno-Demokratyczny). For a scholarly assessment of these market oriented liberal trends and their impact, see Szacki, *op. cit.*; see also Andrzej Walicki, "Liberalism in Poland," in *Critical Review*, vol. 2, no. 1, 1988. For a recent assessment of the "symmetrical relationship" between Polish communism and Solidarity, see Świderski, *op. cit.*, pp. 192–193.

35 Geremek and Żakowski, *op. cit.*, p. 200.
36 Gross, *op. cit.*, p. 63.
37 Jaroslaw Kurski, *Lech Wałęsa: Democrat or Dictator?*, Boulder: Westview Press, 1993, p. 42.
38 Geremek and Żakowski, *op. cit.*, p. 201.
39 *Ibid.*, pp. 208–209.
40 *Ibid*, p. 236.
41 Quoted in Kurski, *op. cit.*, p. 87.
42 For more on Wałęsa's conflicts with his former friends and advisors see Kurski, *ibid.*
43 Zbigniew Bujak and Janusz Rolicki, *Przepraszam za Solidarność*, Warsaw: BGW, 1991, p. 145.

In this context, it is worth noting that, with the benefit of hindsight, even such avowed supporters of marketization such as Donald Tusk (a founding member of the Liberal Democratic Congress) admit that the hubris of the first post-communist governments led to their decline in popularity and effectiveness: "to this day, the decisions ruining the popularity of our governments, while reasonable from the point of view of the interests of the state, are the result of the pride of our ministers and prime ministers" (p. 2). Donald Tusk, "Krajobraz po bitwie," in *Przegląd Polityczny*, no. 30 (Spring 1996), pp. 2–3.

44 *Ibid.* See also Stanislaw Gebethner and Krzysztof Jasiewicz, (eds.), *Dlaczego Tak Głosowano: Wybory prezydenckie 90*, Warsaw: PAN, 1993, for a complete analysis of the 1990 presidential election.
45 Jeffrey Sachs, "Post-communist parties and the politics of entitlements," unpublished manuscript, 1994.
46 Staniszkis, *op. cit.*, pp. 142–143.

Another perspective on the "identity crisis" faced by Solidarity activists as they took on public positions of authority can be derived from Walzer's work. Historically, according to Walzer, humanism did not result in the disciplined and systematic pursuit of politics characteristic of the modern era:

> There did emerge, among Florentine humanists for example, a new and striking sense of the virtues of political life and the civic duty of citizens. But in practice the intense antagonisms of classes and families among the Italians culminated in conspiracy, assassination, riot, and internal coup, rather than in systematic organization, sustained activity or revolution. Civic virtue never triumphed over familial loyalty; the idea of shared citizenship never overcame an extraordinary concern with hierarchical status . . . the new consciousness thus produced only an intensely personal, faction-ridden politics.
>
> (Walzer, *The Revolution of the Saints*, *op. cit.*, p. 8)

While one cannot take such historical analogies too far, it does appear as if the above description bears some similarity to the contemporary state of Polish politics (minus, of course, the more radical manifestations of "assassination, riot and internal coup"). It might well be, therefore, that the humanistic attributes of Solidarity's ethos are matched by the "purely personal ambitions" (p. 12) typical of Renaissance humanists.

47 Walzer, *ibid.*, p. 75.
48 Gross, *op. cit.*, p. 70.
49 Bujak and Rolicki, *op. cit.*, p. 150.
50 Staniszkis, *op. cit.*, p. 146.
51 One example of the new government's hostility toward the post-1989 non-parliamentary opposition can be seen in its treatment of workers who went on

strike in 1990. Mazowiecki's cabinet refused to initiate negotiations with the workers, preferring Thatcherite policies to Solidarity ones. In the end, Wałęsa had to defuse the strikes, an accomplishment for which he received no acknowledgement from the government (see Kurski, *op. cit.*, pp. 93–95).

52 Gross, *op. cit.*, p. 66. It is worth clarifying here that the Solidarity leadership was clearly not Marxist or Leninist in a formal ideological sense given its adherence to democratic norms, principles and practices. Nonetheless, Marxism in a more diffuse sense does appear to have—unconsciously, no doubt—informed the intellectual frame of reference of the new elites.

53 Bernhard's book, *op. cit.*, represents the most recent application of the civil society framework to the study of KOR and Solidarity. However, the best effort in this tradition remains Andrew Arato, "Civil society against the state: Poland, 1980–81," in *Telos*, 47, 1981, pp. 23–47.

54 Tymowski, "Unwanted social revolution," *op. cit.*, p. 198.

See also Szacki, *op. cit.*, pp. 93–97, for an analysis of the "nation without a state" tradition in Poland.

55 Andrzej Walicki, "The three traditions in Polish patriotism," in Gomulka and Polonsky (eds.), *op. cit.*, p. 31.

56 Tymowski, "Unwanted social revolution," *op. cit.*, p. 196.

57 Peter Raina, *Poland 1981: Towards Social Renewal*, London: George Allen & Unwin, 1985, p. 327.

58 Walicki, "Polish patriotism," *op. cit.*, p. 32. According to Walicki:

> In the stateless conditions of existence in Poland, it was difficult for Polish patriots, deeply imbued as they were with the knightly traditions of the gentry, to find a legal outlet for patriotic public activity. The ethos of public service in the political sphere, characteristic of the ancient democracy of the gentry, became transformed, very one-sidedly, into the ethos of an open struggle on the battlefield, in accordance with the gospel of heroism preached by the great romantic poets.

59 Stanley N. Katz, *Constitutionalism in East Central Europe: Some Negative Lessons from the American Experience*, Providence: Berghahn Books, 1994, p. 11.

60 Antoni Z. Kamiński, "Prospects for democracy in Poland," in *Sisyphus Sociological Studies*, vol. 7, 1991, p. 122.

On this turn to the state, see also Jerzy Szacki, "Republika Obywateli," in *Przegląd Polityczny*, no. 30 (Spring 1996), pp. 70–73. According to Szacki, "it is characteristic that at times people (for example, Mazowiecki) who earlier spoke of civil society, now speak of the civil state, which doesn't make much theoretical sense, but illustrates well the turn which was impossible to avoid" (p. 72).

61 Bujak and Rolicki, *op. cit.*, p. 159.

62 Grażyna Skąpska, "From rights to myths: transformation in postcommunist Europe," unpublished manuscript, 1994, pp. 12–13.

63 Wiktor Osiatynski, "A Bill of Rights for Poland," in *East European Constitutional Review*, vol. 1, no. 3 (Fall 1992), p. 29.

64 *Ibid.*, p. 30.

65 *Ibid.*

66 Quoted in Kurski, *op. cit.*, p. vi.

67 Given that these supporters and advisors often had their own political agendas, and that Wałęsa is notoriously mercurial in his attitudes toward his co-workers, the faces around Wałęsa have changed continuously over the past four years (see Kurski, *op. cit.*).

68 Kamiński, *op. cit.*, p. 122.

69 Balcerowicz, for example, justifies privatization as an essential element of democratization given that privatization limits the role of the state, as well as enhancing economic growth and stability. In his address to the 5th World Congress of Central and East European Studies, held in Warsaw, August 1995, Balcerowicz clearly equated democracy with a limited state. In 1991, however, as Deputy Prime Minister and Minister of Finance, Balcerowicz stated that: "Under the circumstances the state is responsible for the construction of a new economic system" (quoted in Lena Kolarska-Bobińska, *Aspirations, Values and Interests: Poland 1989–94*, Warsaw: IFIS Publishers, 1994, p. 85). Consequently, even in Balcerowicz's thinking, the means of state intervention can and should be used to facilitate the end of a limited state. For further analysis of this contradictory logic, and the role of the state during the transition period, see Kolarska-Bobińska, *op. cit.*, pp. 83–103.

70 Jerzy Holzer, "Solidarity's Adventures in Wonderland," in Gomulka and Polonsky (eds.), *op. cit.*, p. 108.

71 Gordon S. Wood, *The Radicalism of the American Revolution*, New York: Alfred A. Knopf, 1992, p. 245.

72 Walicki, "Polish patriotism," *op. cit.*, p. 33. Following the work of Stefan Nowak, Walicki states that:

> Thus, an average Pole does not belong to a large-scale institutionalized civil society; he belongs to different primary groups and, secondly, he belongs to his nation; not a nation as a system of political and economic institutions, but a nation as national tradition, national culture, the sphere of uniting symbols, of subliminated, lofty, patriotic feelings.

73 Janine Wedel, "The ties that bind in Polish society," in Gomulka and Polonsky (eds.), *op. cit.*, p. 250.

74 *Ibid.*

75 Sergiusz Kowalski, "The 'Wise Guys' and their after-life in a free Poland," paper delivered at the 5th World Congress of Central and East European Studies, August 1995, p. 11; see also Sergiusz Kowalski, *Krytyka Solidarnościowego Rozumu*, Warsaw: PEN, 1990. In this latter work, Kowalski notes that in the minds of non-intellectual Solidarity members:

> Rights and duties are determined by the functional division of labor within the sphere of a community aiming towards an organic form. From this perspective, the participation of intellectuals in the decision-making structures of the union is seen as an anomaly, a disturbance of the natural order of things. In an ideal situation, an intellectual should be an expert who never goes beyond his prescribed competencies. If he tries to play a double role, he is condemned for leaving the position given to him within the division of labor, prompted by personal ambitions or a non-social interest [p. 118].

76 Tymowski, "Unwanted social revolution," *op. cit.*, pp. 195–196.

77 Clearly, informal personal networks exist everywhere, including established Western democracies. The question is when and how do these networks prove to be a barrier to the associative, impersonal public life characteristic of modern polities. In terms of developing a universalistic understanding of citizenship that allows all members of the polity to participate on a formally equal basis, personal networks, such as środowiska and patron–client relations, can represent competing definitions of political membership and competing ways of interest articulation. In other words, rather than articulating my interests as a citizen by associating with other like-minded citizens, I turn to my personal relationships with friends, colleagues or patrons to accomplish my desired

objectives. Apart from the negative consequences for the creation of civic identities, interests articulated through personal relationships are not readily amenable to public scrutiny and democratic mechanisms of accountability.

78 Kurski, *op. cit.*, p. 52.

79 Wood, *op. cit.*, pp. 358–359.

80 Quoted in *ibid.*, p. 359.

81 Keith Michael Baker, "The idea of a Declaration of Rights," in Dale Van Kley (ed.), *The French Idea of Freedom: The Old Regime and the Declaration of Rights of 1789*, Stanford: Stanford University Press, 1994, p. 195.

82 Erik Allardt, "Culture, structure and revolutionary ideologies," in *International Journal of Comparative Sociology*, vol. XII (1971), p. 30.

83 George Kolankiewicz, "Elites in search of a political formula," in *Daedalus*, vol. 123, no. 3 (Summer 1994), p. 155.

84 Jadwiga Koralewicz and Marek Ziółkowski, "Changing value systems," in *Sisyphus. Social Studies*, vol. 1 (IX), 1993, p. 136.

85 *Ibid.*, p. 135.

86 Marek Ziółkowski, "The pragmatic shift in Polish social consciousness: with or against the tide of rising materialism?" in Edmund Wnuk-Lipiński (ed.), *After Communism: A Multidisciplinary Approach to Radical Social Change*, Warsaw: IFIS Publishers, 1995, p. 172.

87 Kolarska-Bobińska, *op. cit.*, p. 80.

88 T. Szawiel quoted in Mirosława Grabowska, "Civil society after 1989: rebirth or decease?" in Wnuk-Lipiński (ed.), *op. cit.*, p. 192.

89 Anita Miszalska, "On political alienation of Poles," in *Sisyphus. Social Studies*, vol. 1 (IX), 1993, p. 147.

90 *Ibid.*

91 *Ibid.*, p. 144.

92 T. Szawiel quoted in Grabowska, *op. cit.*, p. 192.

93 Andrzej Rychard, *Reforms, Adaptation, and Breakthrough*, Warsaw: IFIS Publishers, 1993, p. 149.

94 Kolankiewicz, *op. cit.*, p. 154; Koralewicz, data presented at the 5th World Congress of Central and East European Studies, Warsaw, August 1995.

95 Data provided by *Informator o organizacjach Pozarządowych w Polsce*, Jawor 94/95, vols I and II, Warsaw, 1995. Updated data provided by a Jawor representative.

96 Kolarska-Bobińska, *op. cit.*, p. 137.

97 Rychard, *op. cit.*, p. 152.

98 Kolankiewicz, *op. cit.*, p. 156.

99 *Ibid.*, p. 155.

100 Kolarska-Bobińska, *op. cit.*, p. 39.

101 Suzanne Berger, "Introduction," in S. Berger (ed.), *Organizing Interests in Western Europe: Pluralism, Corporatism and Transformation of Politics*, Cambridge: Cambridge University Press, 1981, p. 12.

102 See, for example, Koralewicz and Ziółkowski, *op. cit.*

103 Quoted in Kolarska-Bobińska, *op. cit.*, p. 136.

Even Adam Michnik, in a 1991 article, expressed concerns about the fundamentalist populism and extreme demands for egalitarianism that might emerge in the wake of reforms; see Adam Michnik, "Three fundamentalisms," in Michael Bernhard and Henryk Szlajfer (eds.), *From the Polish Underground: Selections from Krytyka, 1978–1993*, University Park, PA: Pennsylvania State University Press, 1995, pp. 231–238.

104 Skąpksa, *op. cit.*, pp. 16–17.

105 Jan Kubik and Grzegorz Ekiert, "Rebellious civil society and the consolidation

of democracy in Poland, 1989–1993," paper presented at the 5th World Congress of Central and East European Studies, Warsaw, August 1995, p. 24.

Since this data was presented, levels of popular protest in Poland have fluctuated, decreasing in 1994–95 and rising slightly again in 1996. Although it is too early to tell what the pattern of protest will ultimately look like, it does seem clear that Solidarity has established a "repertoire" of protest that Poles will continue to use.

106 *Ibid.*

107 *Ibid.*

108 *Ibid.*, p. 23.

109 *Ibid.*, p. 27.

110 *Ibid.*, p. 29. Other analyses support this conclusion; see, for example, Carrie Timko, "The 1992–93 Strike Wave and the Disorganization of Worker Interests in Poland," paper presented at the 1996 Annual Meeting of the American Political Science Association. As Timko indicates, "it was more common in this period for strikers to frame their demands around statements that they were in favor of reform and restructuring, but that they wanted these programs to be implemented more quickly, more efficiently or with less corruption" (p. 17).

111 In recent years, several branches of the trade union Solidarity have become associated with neo-fascist tendencies. The Ursus branch in particular has been active in promoting a radical populist and anti-Semitic agenda. However, from the perspective of the Kubik and Ekiert study, and from ongoing research on shop-floor activism, it would appear that these negative tendencies are limited in scope, representing only a minority of active workers.

112 Jadwiga Koralewicz, "Authoritarianism and confidence in political leaders and institutions," in Władysław W. Adamski (ed.), *Societal Conflict and Systemic Change: The Case of Poland 1980–1992*, Warsaw: IFIS Publishers, 1993, p. 179. While Koralewicz's conclusions are based on data from the mid-1980s, they are apparently still relevant to the present situation.

113 Quoted in Świderski, *op. cit.*, p. 182.

It is worth repeating here that not all Polish workers, and not all Poles who have been marginalized by the post-1989 socioeconomic changes, have expressed their dissatisfaction in keeping with the traditions of Solidarity. Many of those marginalized have remained apathetic, or have expressed their disapproval in protest voting (for the ex-communists and for candidates such as Tymiński). My point here is that those citizens who have chosen to be active in public life (many of whom originally participated in the movement), whether in trade union activity or in NGOs, have acted in ways that are consistent with their experiences in Solidarity.

114 The similarities with France are noted in passing by Kubik and Ekiert in a more recent version of their paper, "Collective Protest and Democratic Consolidation in Poland, 1989–1993," unpublished manuscript, May 1996, pp. 39 and 48.

115 On the history of movements and the legacies they leave, see Sidney Tarrow, *Power in Movement: Social Movements, Collective Action, and Politics*, Cambridge: Cambridge University Press, 1994.

116 Research data presented by Jadwiga Koralewicz at the 5th World Congress of Central and East European Studies, August 1995.

117 On the reform of local government, see Arista Maria Cirtautas, "The post-Leninist state: a conceptual and empirical examination," in *Communist and Post-Communist Studies*, vol. 28, no. 4 (December 1995), pp. 379–392; and Tomasz Grabowski, *op. cit.*

118 Jacek Kuroń, "Soziale Gerechtigkeit als soziale Bewegung," in *Transit. Europäische Revue*, Heft 6 (Fall 1993), p. 10.

119 Koralewicz, data presented at the 5th World Congress of Central and East European Studies, Warsaw, August 1995.

120 On active versus passive citizenship, see Bryan S. Turner, "Outline of a theory of citizenship," in *Sociology*, vol. 24, no. 2, 1990, pp. 189–217.

121 Jerzy Jedlicki quoted in *The Warsaw Voice*, 6 August 1995, p. S1.

While other cleavages certainly exist in Polish society—an urban–rural split, for example—this cleavage within the "middle class" that supported Solidarity is the most significant for the type of citizenship, universal or restricted, that will develop in Poland.

122 *Ibid.*

123 On the proposed Bill of Rights see W. Osiatynski, *op. cit.*, and Andrzej Rzepliński, "The Polish Bill of Rights and Freedoms: a case study of constitution-making in Poland," in *East European Constitutional Review*, vol. 2, no. 3 (Summer 1993), pp. 26–29.

124 See Koralewicz and Ziółkowski, *op. cit.*, and Miszalska, *op. cit.*, for an elaboration of the type of democracy envisioned by average, working-class Poles.

125 For studies of the attitudes of the first post-Communist representatives, see Jacek Wasilewski, "The contract-based diet and elite formation in Poland," in *The Polish Sociological Bulletin*, no. 1, 1993, pp. 41–57; and Ireneusz Bialecki and Bogdan W. Mach, "The social and economic orientations of Polish legislators against a background of the views of Polish society," in *The Polish Sociological Bulletin*, no. 2, 1992, pp. 167–186.

126 Ireneusz Bialecki and Barbara Heyns, "Democracy, interests and corporatism in Poland," in W. W. Adamski (ed.), *op. cit.*, p. 258.

127 Kolarska-Bobińska, *op. cit.*, p. 65.

128 Koralewicz and Ziółkowski, *op. cit.*, p. 131.

129 Voter turnout in 1991 was only 42 per cent. Since then turnout has returned to more normal levels in the 1993 and 1995 elections.

130 The term "homo sovieticus" is most widely associated with Józef Tischner; see, for example, Tischner, *Etyka Solidarnośći oraz Homo Sovieticus*, Warsaw: Wydawnictwo Znak, 1992.

131 For an analysis of the 1990 presidential elections, see Krzysztof Jasiewicz, "Polish elections of 1990: beyond the Pospolite Ruszenie," in W. Conner and P. Płoszajski (eds.), *Escape from Socialism: The Polish Route*, Warsaw: IFIS Publishers, 1992, pp. 181–198.

132 Grabowksa, *op. cit.*, p. 196.

133 Recently, of course, the Czech social democratic party has done quite well in the 1996 parliamentary elections. It now appears as if the Union of Labor will not fare well in the upcoming parliamentary elections which are to be held in the fall of 1997. However, even if this party departs the political stage, general support for the Left in Poland is unlikely to diminish in the near future.

134 See, for example, Edmund Mokrzycki, "The legacy of real socialism, group interests, and the search for a new utopia," in Connor and Płoszajski (eds.), *op. cit.*, pp. 269–283.

135 On the linkages between religiosity and political behavior in Poland, see Tadeusz Szawiel, "Social and political attitudes of the Polish Catholics," in *Sisyphus. Social Studies*, vol. 1 (IX), 1993, pp. 177–196.

136 In a recent collection of *Rzeczpospolita* interviews, for example, many of those interviewed expressed their concerns about church–state relations, from both points of view; see: Rzeczpospolita, *Co zrobiliśmy z naszą wolnością*, Warsaw: Presspublica, 1995, which contains a compilation of these articles.

The current debate over the public role of religious principles in general and the Catholic Church in particular can also be seen as an important determinant of the type of citizenship Poland will institutionalize—either Catholic/nationalist or secular/civic. It is likely, however, that the new Constitution—if accepted in the May 1997 popular referendum—will settle the debate in favor of a more secular and civic identity. Consequently, the problems for citizenship arising from class-based polarization (as discussed above) are likely to be more durable and of longer significance.

137 Wiktor Kulerski, "W którym miejscu jest bumerang?" in *ibid.*, pp. 90–91.

138 Wlodzimierz Wesołowski, "Formation of political parties in post-communist Poland," in *Sisyphus. Social Studies*, vol. 1 (IX), 1993, p. 12.

139 *Ibid.*, p. 25

140 CBOS poll quoted in T. Grabowski, *op. cit.*, p. 22.

141 Wesołowski, *op. cit.*, p. 12.

142 Bialecki and Heyns, *op. cit.*, p. 258.

For an analysis of Solidarity in which corporatism is seen as the likely outcome, see also David Ost, *Solidarity and the Politics of Anti-Politics*, Philadelphia: Temple University Press, 1990.

143 Jacek Kurczewski, *The Resurrection of Rights in Poland*, Oxford: Clarendon Press, 1993, pp. 450–451.

144 See Andrzej Rychard, "Old and new institutions of public life," in W. W. Adamski (ed.), *op. cit.*, p. 221.

145 Grażyna Skąpska, "Popular legitimation of legal state in Spain and Poland," paper prepared for the 1996 Congress of the American Law and Society Association and the Research Committee of the Sociology of Law, ISA, held in Glasgow, Scotland, July 1996, p. 12.

146 *Ibid.*, p. 14.

147 *Ibid.*

148 Los, "Legislating the post-totalitarian transition," *op. cit.*, p. 348.

149 *Ibid.*

150 *Ibid.*

151 Skąpska, "Popular legitimation," *op. cit.*, p. 15.

152 Rychard, "Old and new institutions," *op. cit.*, p. 214.

153 Miszalska, *op. cit.*, p. 147.

154 George Schöpflin, "Postcommunism: the problems of democratic construction," in *Daedalus*, vol. 123, no. 3 (Summer 1994), p. 132.

155 This strike took place in the summer of 1994, and was accompanied by a public letter of protest to President Wałęsa.

156 Bialecki and Heyns, *op. cit.*, p. 263.

157 *Ibid.*

158 See, for example, Jacek Kuroń, "Soziale Gerechtigkeit," *op. cit.*

159 W. W. Adamski, "Privatization and group interests," in W. W. Adamski (ed.), *op. cit.*, p. 230.

160 *Ibid.*

161 *Ibid.*, p. 226.

162 Peter Raina (ed.), *Poland 1981: Towards Social Renewal*, London: Allen & Unwin, 1981, p. 334.

For an interesting analysis of the post-1989 reforms in light of Solidarity's original program, see Maurice Glasman, "The great deformation: Polanyi, Poland and the terrors of planned spontaneity," in Christopher G. A. Bryant and Edmund Mokrzycki (eds.), *The New Great Transformation? Change and Continuity in East-Central Europe*, London: Routledge, 1994, pp. 191–217.

163 Jerzy Turowicz, "Nie zrobiliśmy dobrego użytku," in Rzeczpospolita, *op. cit.*, p. 129.

164 Kolarska-Bobińska, *op. cit.*, p. 41.

165 *Ibid.*, p. 121.
166 Edmund Wnuk-Lipiński and Jacek Wasilewski, "How much communism is left with us?" in *Politicus, Bulletin of the Institute of Political Studies,* Polish Academy of Sciences, special issue, August 1995, p. 43.
167 Kolarska-Bobińska, *op. cit.*, p. 112.
168 *Ibid.*, p. 110.
169 *Ibid.*
170 *Ibid.*, p. 125.
171 *Ibid.*, p. 123.
172 *Ibid.*, p. 41.
173 *Ibid.*, p. 40.
174 Kuroń, "Soziale Gerechtigkeit," *op. cit.*, p. 10.
175 Kolankiewicz, *op. cit.*, p. 154.
176 Kolarska-Bobińska, *op. cit.*, p. 11.
Indeed, Szacki goes so far as to state that economic liberalism has become dominant in Poland, in contrast to political liberalism which has not been as successful in the post-1989 period (see Szacki, *Liberalism After Communism, op. cit.*, pp. 207–213).
177 This is not to say that opposition has not taken shape at all. The extreme radicalism of the Ursus workers and the farmers' association "Samoobrona" demonstrate that both the tame market and the free market have been contested. Yet these organizations have remained on the margins of Polish political life.
178 Kuroń, "Soziale Gerechtigkeit," *op. cit.*, p. 21.

EPILOGUE: THE POLISH REVOLUTION IN COMPARATIVE CONTEXT

1 See, for example, Kenneth Jowitt, *The New World Disorder The Leninist Extinction*, Berkeley: University of California Press, 1992; George Schöpflin, *Politics in Eastern Europe*, Oxford: Blackwell, 1993; Vladimir Tismaneanu, *Reinventing Politics: Eastern Europe from Stalin to Havel*, New York: Free Press, 1992.
2 On the positive vestiges of the ancien régime, see R. R. Palmer, *The Age of Democratic Revolution: A Political History of Europe and America, 1760–1800*, Princeton: Princeton University Press, 1959–64, 2 volumes; see also Dale Van Kley (ed.), *The French Idea of Freedom: The Old Regime and the Declaration of Rights of 1789*, Stanford: Stanford University Press, 1994.
3 G. DiPalma, *To Craft Democracies*, Berkeley: University of California Press, 1991.
4 See, for example, a recent volume of *Journal of Democracy* which is devoted to the issue of "Economic Reform and Democracy," vol. 5, no. 4, October 1994.
5 On the moral economy, see James C. Scott, *The Moral Economy of the Peasant: Rebellion and Subsistence in Southeast Asia*, New Haven: Yale University Press, 1976.
6 The article appears in Alexander Gerschenkron, *Economic Backwardness in Historical Perspective*, Cambridge: Harvard University Press, 1966.
7 See Max Weber, "Parliament and government in a reconstructed Germany," contained in Max Weber, *Economy and Society*, Berkeley: University of California Press, 1978, pp. 1381–1469.
8 With the exception of Czechoslovakia, this was certainly the mode of development for inter-war Eastern Europe; see Andrew Janos, *The Politics of*

Backwardness in Hungary 1825–1945, Princeton: Princeton University Press, 1982.

9 See H. Arnold Barton, *Scandinavia in the Revolutionary Era, 1760–1815*, Minneapolis: University of Minnesota Press, 1986. According to Barton:

> [T]he Scandinavian nobility lost almost entirely such special status as it possessed between 1760 and 1815, not through the abolition of its existing privileges but through the granting of similar privileges to the other social orders. Opportunities for advancement and social standing were opened up to burghers, clergy, lower officials, and in Sweden and Finland, to those numerous "nonnoble persons of quality" who did not fit into any of the old Estates but who constituted an increasing proportion of the emerging, amalgamated middle classes.
>
> (p. 370)

In regard to the peasantry, Barton points out that, "The basic similarity of the Nordic peasantries by 1815 was secured not only through emancipations from old restrictions, but in the Danish monarchy by protection of the peasant from the free play of economic forces" (p. 371).

10 Bendix, following Weber, distinguishes between "social relations that are maintained by the reciprocity of expectations, and others that are maintained through orientation toward an exercise of authority. The latter orientation typically involves a belief in the existence of a legitimate order" (Reinhard Bendix, *Nation-Building and Citizenship*, 2nd edition, Berkeley: University of California Press, 1977, p. 19). Although these two relationships are analytically distinct, in any given case they may overlap empirically.

11 For an analysis of Japanese society that reveals certain affinities between traditional social behaviors and post-World War II development, see Chie Nakane, *Japanese Society*, Berkeley: University of California Press, 1970. For example, according to Nakane (p. 144):

> What the Japanese mean by "democracy" is a system that should take the side of, or give consideration to, the weaker or lower; in practice, any decision should be made on the basis of a consensus which includes those located lower in the hierarchy. Such a consensus—reached by what might be termed maximum consultation—might seem a by-product of the post-war "democratic" age; yet it is not at all new to the Japanese, representing as it does, a very basic style of the traditional group operation.

12 Samuel P. Huntington, *American Politics: The Promise of Disharmony*, Cambridge: Harvard University Press, 1981.

13 On inter-war Czech democracy, see Joseph Rothschild, *East Central Europe Between the Two World Wars*, Seattle: University of Washington Press, 1974, pp. 73–136.

14 De Tocqueville, quoted in Dale Van Kley, "Introduction," in Dale Van Kley (ed.), *The French Idea of Freedom*, *op.cit.*, p. 20.

15 Czesław Miłosz quoting from his *History of Polish Literature*, in "Polish Contrasts," the Inaugural Lecture of the 25th annual summer school of Polish language and culture at the Jagiellonian University, delivered by Czesław Miłosz, Kraków, July 1994, p. 27.

16 *Ibid.*, p. 28.

Bibliography

Adamski, Władysław W., "Privatization and group interests," in Władysław W. Adamski (ed.), *Societal Conflict and Systemic Change: The Case of Poland 1980–1992*, Warsaw: IFIS Publishers, 1993.

Agulhon, Maurice, *The French Republic 1879–1992*, Oxford: Blackwell Publishers, 1993.

Allardt, Erik, "Culture, structure and revolutionary ideologies," *International Journal of Comparative Sociology,* XII (1971), pp. 24–40.

Arato, Andrew, "Civil society against the state: Poland, 1980–81," *Telos, 47* (Spring 1981), pp. 23–47.

Arblaster, Anthony, *Democracy*, Minneapolis: University of Minnesota Press, 1987.

Arendt, Hannah, *On Revolution*, New York: Penguin Books, 1977.

Arieli, Yehoshua, *Individualism and Nationalism in American Ideology*, Cambridge: Harvard University Press, 1964.

Ascherson, Neal, *The Polish August*, London: Penguin Books, 1981.

Ash, Timothy Garton, *The Polish Revolution: Solidarity*, New York: Vintage Books, 1985.

—— *The Magic Lantern*, New York: Vintage Books, 1993.

Avineri, Shlomo, *The Social and Political Thought of Karl Marx*, Cambridge: Cambridge University Press, 1968.

Bailyn, Bernard, *Pamphlets of the American Revolution*, vol. 1, Cambridge: Harvard University Press, 1965.

—— *The Ideological Origins of the American Revolution*, Cambridge: Harvard University Press, 1967.

—— *Faces of Revolution: Personalities and Themes in the Struggle for American Independence*, New York: Vintage Books, 1992.

Baker, Keith Michael, "The idea of a Declaration of Rights," in Dale Van Kley (ed.), *The French Idea of Freedom: The Old Regime and the Declaration of Rights of 1789*, Stanford: Stanford University Press, 1994.

Barker, Ernest, *Traditions of Civility*, Cambridge: Cambridge University Press, 1948.

Barton, H. Arnold, *Scandinavia in the Revolutionary Era, 1760–1815*, Minneapolis: University of Minnesota Press, 1986.

Bauman, Zygmunt, *Intimations of Postmodernity*, London: Routledge, 1992.

Becker, Carl, *The Declaration of Independence*, New York: Vintage Books, 1958.

Bendix, Reinhard, *Nation-Building and Citizenship*, 2nd edition, Berkeley: University of California Press, 1977.

Berger, Suzanne (ed.), *Organizing Interests in Western Europe: Pluralism, Corporatism and the Transformation of Politics*, Cambridge: Cambridge University Press, 1981.

Bergeron, Louis, *France Under Napoleon*, Princeton: Princeton University Press, 1981.

Bernhard, Michael H., *The Origins of Democratization in Poland*, New York: Columbia University Press, 1993.

Bernhard, Michael and Szlajfer, Henryk (eds.), *From the Polish Underground: Selections from Krytyka 1978–1993*, University Park, Penn: Pennsylvania State University Press, 1995.

Bialecki, Ireneusz and Heyns, Barbara, "Democracy, interests and corporatism in Poland," in Władysław W. Adamski (ed.), *Societal Conflict and Systemic Change: The Case of Poland 1980–1992*, Warsaw: IFIS Publishers, 1993.

Bialecki, Ireneusz and Mach, Bogdan W., "The social and economic orientations of Polish legislators against a background of the views of Polish society," in *The Polish Sociological Bulletin*, no. 2, 1992, pp. 167–186.

Bielasiak, Jack and Hicks, Barbara, "Solidarity's self-organization: the crisis of rationality and legitimacy in Poland, 1980–81," in *East European Politics and Societies*, vol. 4, no. 3 (Fall 1990), pp. 489–512.

Bloch, Ernst, *Natural Law and Human Dignity*, Cambridge: MIT Press, 1986.

The Book of Lech Wałęsa: A Collective Portrait by Solidarity Members and Friends, New York: Simon & Schuster, 1982.

Borusewicz, Bogdan, "Chcieli mieć demokrację i głosowali na demokrację," in Rzeczpospolita, *Co zrobiliśmy z naszą wolnością*, Warsaw: Presspublica, 1995.

Bossenga, Gail, "From corps to citizenship: the Bureaux des finances before the French Revolution," in *Journal of Modern History*, vol. 58, no. 3 (Sept. 1986), pp. 610–642.

Breen, T. H., *The Character of the Good Ruler: A Study of Puritan Political Ideas in New England, 1630–1730*, New Haven: Yale University Press, 1970.

—— *Puritans and Adventurers: Change and Persistence in Early America*, Oxford: Oxford University Press, 1980.

—— *Tobacco Culture: The Mentality of the Great Tidewater Planters on the Eve of Revolution*, Princeton: Princeton University Press, 1985.

Breen, T. H. and Innes, Stephen, *"Myne Owne Ground": Race and Freedom on Virginia's Eastern Shore, 1640–1676*, Oxford: Oxford University Press, 1980.

Breuer, Stefan, *Sozialgeschichte des Naturrechts*, Opladen: Westdeutscher Verlag, 1983.

Brinton, Crane, *The Jacobins*, New York: Russell & Russell, 1961.

Brubaker, Rogers, *Citizenship and Nationhood in France and Germany*, Cambridge: Harvard University Press, 1992.

Brugger, Winfried, *Menschenrechtsethos und Verantwortungspolitik: Max Webers Beitrag zur Analyze und Begrundung der Menschenrechte*, Freiburg: Verlag Karl Alber, 1980.

Bujak, Zbigniew and Rolicki, Janusz, *Przepraszam za Solidarność*, Warsaw: BGW, 1991.

Bunce, Valerie and Csanadi, Maria, "Uncertainty in the transition: post-communism in Hungary," in *East European Politics and Societies*, vol. 7, no. 2 (Spring 1993), pp. 240–275.

Bushman, Richard L., *From Puritan to Yankee: Character and the Social Order in Connecticut, 1690–1765*, New York: W. W. Norton, 1970.

Calvert, Peter, *Revolution and Counter-Revolution*, Minneapolis: University of Minnesota Press, 1990.

Ceaser, James W., O'Toole, L. J., Bessełte, J. M. and Thurow, G., *American Government: Origins, Institutions and Public Policy*, Dubuque, IA: Kendall/Hunt Publishing, 1992.

Cichy, Michał, "Requiem for the moderate revolutionist," in *East European Politics and Societies*, vol. 10, no. 1 (Winter 1996), pp. 133–156.

Cirtautas, Arista Maria, "Max Weber and the legitimation of German democracy," in Kurt-Jürgen Maass (ed.), *From Two to One: US Scholars Witness the First Year of German Unification*, Bonn: Alexander von Humboldt Foundation, 1992.

—— "The post-Leninist state: a conceptual and empirical examination," in *Communist and Post-Communist Studies*, vol. 28, no. 4 (December 1995), pp. 379–392.

Cirtautas, Arista Maria and Mokrzycki, Edmund, "The articulation and institutionalization of democracy in Poland," in *Social Research*, vol. 60, no. 4 (Winter 1993), pp. 787–820.

Comisso, Ellen, "Property rights, liberalism and the transition from 'actually existing' socialism," in *East European Politics and Societies*, vol.5, no. 1 (Winter 1991), pp. 162–188.

Conner, W. and Płoszajski, P. (eds.), *Escape from Socialism: The Polish Route*, Warsaw: IFIS Publishers, 1992.

Darnton, Robert, *The Literary Underground of the Old Regime*, Cambridge: Harvard University Press, 1982.

—— *The Great Cat Massacre and Other Episodes in French Cultural History*, New York: Vintage Books, 1985.

DiPalma, Guiseppe, *To Craft Democracies*, Berkeley: University of California Press, 1991.

Douglas, Mary, *How Institutions Think*, London: Routledge & Kegan Paul, 1987.

Doyle, William, *Origins of the French Revolution*, 2nd edition, New York: Oxford University Press, 1989.

Dubiński, Krzysztof, *Magdalenka Transakcja Epoki*, Warsaw: Sylwa, 1990.

Dworetz, Steven M., *The Unvarnished Doctrine: Locke, Liberalism and the American Revolution*, Durham, NC: Duke University Press, 1990.

Eckstein, Harry, *Division and Cohesion in Democracy: A Study of Norway*, Princeton: Princeton University Press, 1966.

Elster, Jon, "The possibility of rational politics," in David Held (ed.), *Political Theory Today*, Stanford: Stanford University Press, 1991.

Fehér, Michael (ed.), *The French Revolution and the Birth of Modernity*, Berkeley: University of California Press, 1990.

Fehér, Ferenc and Heller, Agnes, *Hungary 1956 Revisited*, London: Allen & Unwin, 1983.

Feinberg, Joel, *Rights, Justice and the Bounds of Liberty: Essays in Social Philosophy*, Princeton: Princeton University Press, 1980.

Foot, Michael and Krammick, Isaac (eds.), *Thomas Paine Reader*, London: Penguin Books, 1987.

Fortuna, Grzegorz, "Be great, Mr. Wałęsa," in *The Book of Lech Wałęsa: A Collective Portrait by Solidarity Members and Friends*, New York: Simon & Schuster, 1982.

Freeden, Michael, *Rights*, Minneapolis: University of Minnesota Press, 1991.

Freyer, Tony A., *Producers versus Capitalists: Constitutional Conflict in Antebellum America*, Charlottesville: University Press of Virginia, 1994.

Furet, François, *Revolutionary France 1770–1880*, Oxford: Blackwell Publishers, 1992.

—— "Europe after utopianism," in *Journal of Democracy*, vol. 6, no. 1 (January 1995), pp. 79–89.

Gajda, Jan, "August 1980 as I saw it," in *Sisyphus Sociological Studies*, vol. III, Warsaw: PWN, 1982, pp. 236–251.

Gati, Charles, *Hungary and the Soviet Bloc*, Durham, NC: Duke University Press, 1986.

Gauchet, Marcel, *Die Erklärung der Menschenrechte: Die Debatte um die bürgerliche Freiheiten 1789*, Reinbeck: Rowohlt Taschenbuch Verlag, 1991.

Gay, Peter, *The Enlightenment: The Rise of Modern Paganism*, New York: W. W. Norton, 1977.

—— *The Enlightenment: The Science of Freedom*, New York: W. W. Norton, 1977.

Gebethner, Stanisław and Jasiewicz, Krzysztof (eds.), *Dlaczego Tak Głosowano: Wybory prezydenckie 90*, Warsaw: PAN, 1993.

Geremek, Bronisław and Żakowski, Jacek, *Rok 1989. Bronisław Geremek opowiada Jacek Żakowski pyta*, Warsaw: Plejada, 1990.

Gerschenkron, Alexander, *Economic Backwardness in Historical Perspective*, Cambridge: Harvard University Press, 1966.

Gerth, Hans and Mills, C. Wright (eds.), *From Max Weber: Essays in Sociology*, New York: Oxford University Press, 1946.

Glasman, Maurice, "The great deformation: Polanyi, Poland and the terrors of planned spontaneity," in Christopher G. A. Bryant and Edmund Mokrzycki (eds.), *The New Great Transformation? Change and Continuity in East-Central Europe*, London: Routledge, 1994.

Goodwyn, Lawrence, *Breaking the Barrier: The Rise of Solidarity in Poland*, Oxford: Oxford University Press, 1991.

Grabowska, Mirosława, "Civil society after 1989: rebirth or decease?" in Edmund Wnuk-Lipiński (ed.), *After Communism: A Multidisciplinary Approach to Radical Social Change*, Warsaw: IFIS Publishers, 1995.

Grabowski, Tomasz, "From a civic movement to political parties: the rise and fall of the Solidarity Committees in Poland, 1989–1991," paper presented at the annual meeting of the American Political Science Association, Chicago, 31 August–3 September 1995.

Greenfeld, Liah, *Nationalism: Five Roads to Modernity*, Cambridge: Harvard University Press, 1992.

Gross, Jan T., "Poland: from civil society to political nation," in Ivo Banac (ed.), *Eastern Europe in Revolution*, Ithaca: Cornell University Press, 1992.

Haakonssen, Knud, 'From natural law to the rights of man," in Michael J. Lacey and Knud Haakonssen (eds.), *A Culture of Rights: The Bill of Rights in Philosophy, Politics and Law 1791–1991*, Cambridge: Cambridge University Press, 1991.

Hamilton, Alexander, Madison, James and Jay, John, *The Federalist Papers*, New York: Bantam Books, 1982.

Hanson, Stephen E., "The Leninist legacy and institutional change," in *Comparative Political Studies*, vol. 28, no. 2 (July 1995), pp. 306–314.

—— *Time and Revolution: Marxism and the Design of Soviet Institutions*, Chapel Hill, NC: University of North Carolina Press, 1996.

Held, David, *Models of Democracy*, Stanford: Stanford University Press, 1987.

Higonnet, Patrice, "Cultural upheaval and class formation during the French Revolution," in Ferenc Fehér (ed.), *The French Revolution and the Birth of Modernity*, Berkeley: University of California Press, 1990.

Hill, Christopher, *The Century of Revolution 1603–1714*, New York: W. W. Norton, 1980.

—— *The Collected Essays of Christopher Hill. Vol. 2: Religion and Politics in Seventeenth Century England*, Amherst: University of Massachusetts Press, 1986.

Hirschman, Albert O., *The Passions and the Interests: Political Arguments for Capitalism Before Its Triumph*, Princeton: Princeton University Press, 1977.

Hobsbawm, Eric, "The making of a bourgeois revolution," in Ferenc Fehér (ed.),

The French Revolution and the Birth of Modernity, Berkeley: University of California Press, 1990.

Holzer, Jerzy, *"Solidarność," 1980–1981: Geneza i Historia*, Paris: Instytut Literacki, 1984.

—— "Solidarity's Adventures in Wonderland," in Stanislaw Gomulka and Antony Polonsky (eds.), *Polish Paradoxes*, London: Routledge, 1990.

Huntington, Samuel P., *American Politics: The Promise of Disharmony*, Cambridge: Harvard University Press, 1981.

—— *The Third Wave: Democratization in the Late Twentieth Century*, Norman and London: University of Oklahoma Press, 1991.

Hyneman, Charles S. and Lutz, Donald S. (eds.), *American Political Writing During the Founding Era 1760–1805*, vol. II, Indianapolis: Liberty Press, 1983.

Ilting, Karl-Heinz, "Naturrecht," in *Geschichtliche Grundbegriffe*, vol. 4, Stuttgart: Ernst Klett Verlag, 1978.

Islam, Shafiqul and Mandelbaum, Michael (eds.), *Making Markets: Economic Transformation in Eastern Europe and the Post-Soviet States*, Introduction by Michael Mandelbaum, New York: Council on Foreign Relations Press, 1993.

Jakubowska-Branicka, Iwona, "Expectations regarding law and the emerging concept of legality in the process of democratic transformation," paper presented at the Law and Society Congress, Glasgow, Scotland, July 1996.

Janos, Andrew, *The Politics of Backwardness in Hungary 1825–1945*, Princeton: Princeton University Press, 1982.

Jasiewicz, Krzysztof, "Polish elections of 1990: beyond the Pospolite Ruszenie," in Walter D. Conner and Piotr Płoszajski (eds.), *Escape from Socialism: The Polish Route*, Warsaw: IFIS Publishers, 1992.

Jellinek, Georg, "Die Erklärung der Menschen-und Bürgerrechte," in Roman Schnur (ed.), *Zur Geschichte der Erklärung der Menschenrechte*, Darmstadt: Wissenschaftliche Buchgesellschaft, 1964.

Jowitt, Kenneth, *The Leninist Response to National Dependency*, Berkeley: Institute of International Studies, University of California, 1978.

—— *New World Disorder: The Leninist Extinction*, Berkeley: University of California Press, 1992.

Kamiński, Antoni Z., "Prospects for democracy in Poland," in *Sisyphus Sociological Studies*, vol. 7, 1991, pp.115–122.

Kamiński, Bartlomiej, *The Collapse of State Socialism: The Case of Poland*, Princeton: Princeton University Press, 1991.

Karabel, Jerome, "Polish intellectuals and the origins of Solidarity: the making of an oppositional alliance," in *Communist and Post-Communist Studies*, vol. 26, no. 1 (March 1993), pp. 25–46.

Kaszuba, Gerard, "The strike in the Ustka shipyard in August 1980," in *Sisyphus Sociological Studies*, vol. III, Warsaw: PWN, 1982, pp. 278–288

Katz, Stanley N., *Constitutionalism in East Central Europe: Some Negative Lessons from the American Experience*, Providence: Berghahn Books, 1994.

Kelly, Alfred H. and Harbison, Winfred A., *The American Constitution: Its Origins and Development*, 5th edition, New York: W. W. Norton, 1976.

Kennedy, Michael, *Professionals, Power and Solidarity in Poland*, Cambridge: Cambridge University Press, 1991.

Kolakowski, Leszek, *Toward a Marxist Humanism*, New York: Grove Press, 1968.

Kolankiewicz, George, "Elites in search of a political formula," in *Daedalus*, vol. 123, no. 3 (Summer 1994), pp. 143–157.

Kolarska-Bobińska, Lena, *Aspirations, Values and Interests: Poland 1989–94*, Warsaw: IFIS Publishers, 1994.

Koralewicz, Jadwiga, "Authoritarianism and confidence in political leaders and institutions," in Władysław W. Adamski (ed.), *Societal Conflict and Systemic Change: The Case of Poland 1980–1992*, Warsaw: IFIS Publishers, 1993.

Koralewicz, Jadwiga and Ziółkowski, Marek, "Changing value systems," in *Sisyphus. Social Studies*, vol. 1 (IX), 1993, pp.123–139.

Kowalski, Sergiusz, *Krytyka Solidarnośćiowego Rozumu*, Warsaw: PEN, 1990.

—— "The 'Wise Guys' and their after-life in a free Poland," paper delivered at the 5th World Congress of Central and East European Studies, Warsaw, August 1995.

Król, Marcin, "The Polish syndrome of incompleteness," in Stanislaw Gomulka and Antony Polonsky (eds.), *Polish Paradoxes*, London: Routledge, 1990.

—— "Poland's longing for paternalism," in *Journal of Democracy*, vol. 5, no. 1 (January 1994), pp. 85–95.

Kubik, Jan, *The Power of Symbols Against the Symbols of Power: The Rise of Solidarity and the Fall of State Socialism in Poland*, University Park, PA: Pennsylvania State University Press, 1994.

Kubik, Jan and Ekiert, Grzegorz, "Rebellious civil society and the consolidation of democracy in Poland, 1989–1993," paper delivered at the 5th World Congress of Central and East European Studies, Warsaw, August 1995.

Kuczma, Jósef, "August 1980 as I remember it," in *Sisyphus Sociological Studies*, vol. III, Warsaw: PWN, 1982, pp. 252–271.

Kulerski, Wiktor, "W którym miejscu jest bumerang?" in Rzeczpospolita, *Co zrobiliśmy z naszą wolnością*, Warsaw: Presspublica, 1995.

Kumar, Krishan, "The revolutions of 1989 in East-Central Europe and the idea of revolution," in Richard Kilminster and Ian Varcoe (eds.), *Culture, Modernity and Revolution: Essays in Honor of Zygmunt Bauman*, New York: Routledge, 1996.

Kurczewski, Jacek, "The resurrection of rights in Poland," in *The Polish Sociological Bulletin*, no. 2, 1991, pp. 102–112.

—— *The Resurrection of Rights in Poland*, Oxford: Clarendon Press, 1993.

Kuroń, Jacek, *Politika i odpowiedzialność*, London: Aneks, 1984.

—— "Soziale Gerechtigkeit als soziale Bewegung," in *Transit. Europäische Revue*, Heft 6 (Fall 1993), pp. 6–24.

Kurski, Jaroslaw, *Lech Wałęsa: Democrat or Dictator?*, Boulder: Westview Press, 1993.

Laba, Roman, *The Roots of Solidarity*, Princeton: Princeton University Press, 1991.

Lacey, Michael J. and Haakonssen, Knud (eds.), *A Culture of Rights: The Bill of Rights in Philosophy, Politics and Law 1791–1991*, Cambridge: Cambridge University Press, 1991.

Lefebvre, Georges, *The Coming of the French Revolution*, Princeton: Princeton University Press, 1989.

Lenin, V. I., *What is to be Done?*, Moscow: Foreign Languages Publishing House, 1950.

Lepak, Keith John, *Prelude to Solidarity: Poland and the Politics of the Gierek Regime*, New York: Columbia University Press, 1988.

Leslie, R. F. (ed.), *The History of Poland Since 1863*, Cambridge: Cambridge University Press, 1980.

Lijphart, Arend, "Constitutional choices for new democracies," in *Journal of Democracy*, vol. 2, no. 1 (Winter 1991), pp. 72–84.

Lipset, Seymour Martin, *Political Man: The Social Bases of Politics*, Baltimore: Johns Hopkins University Press, 1994.

Lipski, Jan J., *KOR: The History of the Workers' Defense Committee in Poland 1976–1981*, Berkeley: University of California Press, 1985.

Locke, John, *The Political Writings of John Locke*, Introduction by David Wootton (ed.), New York: Mentor, 1993.

Łopiński, Maciej, Moskit, Marcin and Wilk, Mariusz, *Konspira: Solidarity Underground*, Berkeley: University of California Press, 1990.
Los, Maria, "Legislating the post-totalitarian transition," in *The Polish Sociological Bulletin*, no. 3/4, 1992, pp. 345–364.
Lott, Davis Newton, *The Presidents Speak: The Inaugural Addresses*, New York: Holt, Rinehart & Winston, 1969.
Lukes, Steven, *Individualism*, London: Basil Blackwell, 1973.
Lynd, Staughton, *Intellectual Origins of American Radicalism*, New York: Pantheon Books, 1968.
Macfarlane, Alan, *The Culture of Capitalism*, Oxford: Basil Blackwell, 1989.
Macpherson, C. B., *The Political Theory of Possessive Individualism*, Oxford: Clarendon Press, 1962.
Manning, William, *The Key of Liberty*, Introduction by Michael Merrill and Sean Wilentz (eds.), Cambridge: Harvard University Press, 1993.
Marody, Mira, "State and Society," paper presented at University of Washington, US–Polish Economic Roundtable, September, 1991.
Marshall, T. H., *Citizenship and Social Class*, Cambridge: Cambridge University Press, 1950.
Marx, Karl and Engels, Frederick, *Collected Works*, New York: International Publishers, 1975.
Matson, Cathy D. and Onuf, Peter S., *A Union of Interests: Political and Economic Thought in Revolutionary America*, Lawrence: University of Kansas Press, 1990.
McDonald, Forrest, *We the People: The Economic Origins of the Constitution*, Chicago: University of Chicago Press, 1958.
—— *The Presidency of George Washington*, Lawrence: University of Kansas Press, 1974.
—— *E Pluribus Unum: The Formation of the American Republic, 1776–1790*, Boston: Houghton Mifflin, 1979.
—— *Novus Ordo Seclorum: The Intellectual Origins of the Constitution*, Lawrence: University of Kansas Press, 1985.
Michnik, Adam, *Szanse polskiej demokracji*, London: Aneks, 1984.
—— *Letters from Prison and Other Essays*, Berkeley: University of California Press, 1985.
—— "Towards a civil society: hopes for Polish democracy," in *TLS*, 19–25 February 1988, pp. 198–199.
—— "The moral and spiritual origins of Solidarity," in William Brinton and Alan Rinzler (eds.), *Without Force or Lies: Voices from the Revolution in Central Europe in 1989–90*, San Francisco: Mercury House Books, 1990.
—— *The Church and the Left*, Chicago: University of Chicago Press, 1993.
—— "Three fundamentalisms," in Michael Bernhard and Henryk Szlajfer (eds.), *From the Polish Underground: Selections from Krytyka, 1978–1993*, University Park, PA: Pennsylvania State University Press, 1995.
Michnik, Adam, Tischner, Józef and Żakowski, Jacek, *Między Panem a Plebanem*, Kraków: Znak, 1995.
Miłosz, Czesław, *The History of Polish Literature*, Berkeley: University of California Press, 1983.
—— "Why," in C. Miłosz and R. Hass (trans.), *Facing the River*, Hopewell, NJ: Ecco Press, 1995.
Miszalska, Anita, "On political alienation of Poles," in *Sisyphus. Social Studies*, vol.1 (IX), 1993, pp. 141–159.
Mokrzycki, Edmund, "The legacy of real socialism, group interests and the search for a new utopia," in Walter D. Conner and Piotr Płoszajski (eds.), *Escape From Socialism: The Polish Route*, Warsaw: IFIS Publishers, 1992.

Mommsen, Wolfgang, *Max Weber and German Politics 1890–1920*, Chicago: University of Chicago Press, 1984.

Morawska, Ewa, "The Polish Roman Catholic Church unbound: change of face or change of context?" in Stephen E. Hanson and Willfried Spohn (eds.), *Can Europe Work? Germany and the Reconstruction of Postcommunist Societies*, Seattle: University of Washington Press, 1995.

Morawski, Witold, "Institution and citizenship building in the former socialist countries," paper delivered at "In Transition" conference, Indiana University, Bloomington, September 1993.

Nakane, Chie, *Japanese Society*, Berkeley: University of California Press, 1970.

Nash, Gary B., *Race and Revolution*, Madison: Madison House, 1990.

North, Douglass C., *Institutions, Institutional Change and Economic Performance*, Cambridge: Cambridge University Press, 1990.

Nowak, Stefan, "Values and attitudes of the Polish people," in *Scientific American*, vol. 245, no. 1 (July 1981), pp. 45–53.

Nowak, Tadeusz, *Zanim powstała Solidarność*, Lublin: Norbertinum, 1990.

O'Donnell, Guillermo, "Delegative democracy," in *Journal of Democracy*, vol. 5, no. 1 (January 1994), pp. 55–69.

Olin, John C. (ed.), *Christian Humanism and the Reformation: Selected Writings of Erasmus*, New York: Fordham University Press, 1987.

Olton, Charles S., *Artisans for Independence: Philadelphia Mechanics and the American Revolution*, Syracuse: Syracuse University Press, 1975.

Osa, Maryjane, "Resistance, persistence and change: the transformation of the Catholic Church in Poland," in *East European Politics and Societies*, vol. 3, no. 2 (Spring 1989), pp. 268–299.

Osiatynski, Wiktor, "Constitutionalism and rights in the history of Poland," in Louis Henkin and Albert J. Rosenthal (eds.), *Constitutionalism and Rights: The Influence of the US Constitution Abroad*, New York: Columbia University Press, 1990.

—— "A Bill of Rights for Poland," in *East European Constitutional Review*, vol. 1, no. 3 (Fall 1992), pp. 29–32.

Ost, David, *Solidarity and the Politics of Anti-Politics*, Philadelphia: Temple University Press, 1990.

Paine, Thomas, *The Rights of Man*, New York: Anchor Books, 1989.

Palmer, R. R., *The Age of Democratic Revolution: A Political History of Europe and America, 1760–1800*, vols. 1 and 2, Princeton: Princeton University Press, 1964.

Palmer, R. R. and Colton, Joel, *A History of the Modern World*, 7th edition, New York: McGraw-Hill, 1992.

Pawełec, Władysław, "Seventeen hot days," in *Sisyphus Sociological Studies*, vol. III, 1982, pp. 272–277.

Pelczynski, Zbigniew A., "The October turning point," in R. F. Leslie (ed.), *A History of Poland Since 1863*, Cambridge: Cambridge University Press, 1980.

—— "Solidarity and the 'Rebirth of Civil Society' in Poland, 1976–81," in John Keane (ed.), *Civil Society and the State*, London: Verso Press, 1988.

Pico della Mirandola, Giovanni, *Oration on the Dignity of Man*, Introduction by Russell Kirk, Chicago: Regnery Gateway, 1956.

Pitkin, Hanna, *The Concept of Representation*, Berkeley: University of California Press, 1967.

Polan, A. J., *Leninism and the End of Politics*, Berkeley: University of California Press, 1984.

Polanyi, Karl, *The Great Transformation*, Boston: Beacon Press, 1957.

Przeworski, Adam, "Some problems in the study of transition to democracy," in Guillermo O'Donnell, Philippe Schmitter and Lawrence Whitehead (eds.),

Transitions from Authoritarian Rule: Comparative Perspectives, Baltimore: Johns Hopkins University Press, 1988.

—— *Democracy and the Market: Political and Economic Reforms in Eastern Europe and Latin America*, Cambridge: Cambridge University Press, 1991.

Raina, Peter, *Political Opposition in Poland 1954–1977*, London: Poets and Painters Press, 1978.

—— *Independent Social Movements in Poland*, London: Orbis Books, 1981.

—— (ed.), *Poland 1981: Towards Social Renewal*, London: Allen & Unwin, 1985.

Rakove, Jack N., "Parchment barriers and the politics of rights," in Michael J. Lacey and Knud Haakonssen (eds.), *A Culture of Rights: The Bill of Rights in Philosophy, Politics and Law 1791–1991*, Cambridge: Cambridge University Press, 1991.

Rothschild, Joseph, *East Central Europe Between the Two World Wars*, Seattle: University of Washington Press, 1974.

—— *Return to Diversity: A Political History of East Central Europe Since World War II*, 2nd edition, New York: Oxford University Press, 1993.

Rousseau, Jean-Jacques, *Rousseau's Political Writings*, Alan Ritter and Julia Conaway Bondanella (eds.), New York: W. W. Norton, 1988.

Rueschemeyer, Dietrich, Stephens, E. H. and Stephens, J. D., *Capitalist Development and Democracy*, Chicago: University of Chicago Press, 1992.

Rychard, Andrzej, "Old and new institutions of public life," in Władysław W. Adamski (ed.), *Societal Conflict and Systemic Change: The Case of Poland 1980–1992*, Warsaw: IFIS Publishers, 1993.

—— *Reforms, Adaptation, and Breakthrough*, Warsaw: IFIS Publishers, 1993.

Rzeczpospolita, *Co zrobiliśmy z naszą wolnością*, Warsaw: Presspublica, 1995.

Rzepliński, Andrzej, "The Polish Bill of Rights and Freedoms: a case study of constitution-making in Poland," in *East European Constitutional Review*, vol. 2, no. 3 (Summer 1993), pp. 26–29.

Sachs, Jeffrey, *Poland's Jump to the Market Economy*, Cambridge: MIT Press, 1993.

—— "Post-communist parties and the politics of entitlements," unpublished manuscript, 1994.

—— "Shock Therapy in Poland: Perspectives of Five Years," Tanner Lecture, 6 October 1994.

Salame, Ghassan (ed.), *Democracy Without Democrats: The Renewal of Politics in the Muslim World*, London: I. B. Tauris, 1994.

Sanford, George (ed.), *The Solidarity Congress, 1981*, New York: St. Martin's Press, 1990.

Schama, Simon, *Patriots and Liberators: Revolution in the Netherlands 1780–1813*, New York: Vintage Books, 1977.

—— *Citizens: A Chronicle of the French Revolution*, New York: Alfred A. Knopf, 1989.

Scheer, George F. and Rankin, Hugh F., *Rebels and Redcoats: The American Revolution Through the Eyes of Those Who Fought and Lived It*, New York: Da Capo Press, 1957.

Schieder, Wolfgang, "Brüderlichkeit," in *Geschichtliche Grundbegriffe*, vol. 1, Stuttgart: Ernst Klett Verlag, 1975.

Schlesinger, Arthur M., Jr., *The Politics of Upheaval: The Age of Roosevelt*, Boston: Houghton Mifflin Company, 1960.

Schluchter, Wolfgang, *The Rise of Western Rationalism: Max Weber's Developmental History*, Berkeley: University of California Press, 1981.

Schmitter, Philippe and Karl, Terry, "What democracy is . . . and is not," in *Journal of Democracy*, vol. 2, no. 3 (Summer 1991), pp. 75–88.

Schöpflin, George, "Culture and identity in post-Communist Europe," in Stephen

White, Judy Batt and Paul G. Lewis (eds.), *Developments in East European Politics*, Durham, NC: Duke University Press, 1993.
—— *Politics in Eastern Europe*, Oxford: Blackwell Publishers, 1993.
—— "Postcommunism: the problems of democratic construction," in *Daedalus*, vol. 123, no. 3 (Summer 1994), pp. 127–141.
Schwartz, Bernard, *The Bill of Rights: A Documentary History*, vol. 1, New York: Chelsea House Publishers, 1971.
Scott, James C., *The Moral Economy of the Peasant: Rebellion and Subsistence in Southeast Asia*, New Haven: Yale University Press, 1976.
Selznick, Philip, *The Organizational Weapon*, New York: McGraw-Hill, 1952.
Sewell, William H., Jr., *A Rhetoric of Bourgeois Revolution: The Abbé Sièyes and "What is the Third Estate?,"* Durham and London: Duke University Press, 1994.
—— "Ideologies and social revolutions: reflections on the French case," in T. C. W. Blanning (ed.), *The Rise and Fall of the French Revolution*, Chicago: University of Chicago Press, 1996.
Simons, Thomas W., Jr., *Eastern Europe in the Postwar World*, New York: St. Martin's Press, 1991.
Skąpska, Grażyna, "From rights to myths: transformation in postcommunist Europe," unpublished manuscript, 1994.
—— "Popular legitimation of legal state in Spain and Poland," paper prepared for the 1996 Congress of the American Law and Society Association and the Research Committee of the Sociology of Law, ISA, held in Glasgow, Scotland, July 1996.
Skilling, Gordon H., *Czechoslovakia's Interrupted Revolution*, Princeton: Princeton University Press, 1976.
Skocpol, Theda, *States and Social Revolutions: A Comparative Analysis of France, Russia, and China*, Cambridge: Cambridge University Press, 1979.
—— *Social Revolutions in the Modern World*, Cambridge: Cambridge University Press, 1994.
—— "Cultural idioms and political ideologies in the revolutionary reconstruction of state power: a rejoinder to Sewell," in T. C. W. Blanning (ed.), *The Rise and Fall of the French Revolution*, Chicago: University of Chicago Press, 1996.
Smith, Adam, *The Theory of Moral Sentiments*, Introduction by D. D. Raphael and A. L. Macfie (eds.), Oxford: Oxford University Press, 1979.
—— *The Wealth of Nations*, Oxford: Oxford University Press, 1993.
Smolar, Alexander, "The dissolution of Solidarity," in *Journal of Democracy*, vol. 5, no. 1 (January 1994), pp. 70–84.
Smołeński, Paweł and Giełżyński, Wojciech, *Robotnicy 88*, London: Aneks, 1989.
Soboul, Albert, *The Parisian Sans-Culottes and the French Revolution 1793–1794*, Oxford: Clarendon Press, 1964.
Sperber, Jonathan, *Rhineland Radicals: The Democratic Movement and the Revolution of 1848–1849*, Princeton: Princeton University Press, 1991.
Spielman, Richard, "The Eighteenth Brumaire of General Wojciech Jaruzelski," in *World Politics*, vol. 37, no. 4 (July 1985), pp. 562–585.
Staniszkis, Jadwiga, *Poland's Self-Limiting Revolution*, Princeton: Princeton University Press, 1984.
—— *The Dynamics of the Breakthrough in Eastern Europe: The Polish Experience*, Berkeley: University of California Press, 1991.
Stoltenberg, Steven G., "An underground society: the evolution of Poland's Solidarity, 1982–1989," unpublished dissertation, University of California, Berkeley, 1993.
Świderski, Bronisław, *Gdańsk i Ateny: O demokracji bezpośredniej w Polsce*, Warsaw: Widawnictwo IFiS PAN, 1996.

—— "Gdańsk i Ateny," *Przegląd Polityczny*, no. 30 (Spring 1996).

Szacki, Jerzy, *Liberalism After Communism*, Budapest/New York: Central European University Press, 1994.

—— "Republika Obywateli," *Przegląd Polityczny*, no. 30 (Spring 1996), pp. 70–73.

Szawiel, Tadeusz, "Social and political attitudes of the Polish Catholics," in *Sisyphus. Social Studies*, vol. 1 (IX), 1993, pp. 177–196.

Szuta, Mieczysław, "The strike in the northern shipyard in Gdańsk," in *Sisyphus Sociological Studies*, vol. III, 1982, pp. 227–235.

Szyłak, Jan, "My reminiscences of August 1980," in *Sisyphus Sociological Studies*, vol. III, 1982, pp. 289–309

Tarrow, Sidney, *Power in Movement: Social Movements, Collective Action, and Politics*, Cambridge: Cambridge University Press, 1994.

Thompson, Dorothy, *The Chartists*, New York: Pantheon Books, 1984.

Thompson, E. P., *The Making of the English Working Class*, New York: Vintage, 1963.

Tilly, Charles, *From Mobilization to Revolution*, New York: McGraw-Hill, 1978.

—— *European Revolutions 1492–1992*, Oxford: Blackwell Publishers, 1995.

Timko, Carrie, "The 1992–93 Strike wave and the disorganization of worker interests in Poland," paper presented at the Annual Meeting of the American Political Science Association, San Francisco, September 1996.

Tischner, Józef, *The Spirit of Solidarity*, San Francisco: Harper & Row, 1984.

—— *Etyka Solidarnośći oraz Homo Sovieticus*, Warsaw: Wydawnictwo Znak, 1992.

Tismaneanu, Vladimir, *Reinventing Politics: Eastern Europe from Stalin to Havel*, New York: Free Press, 1992.

Tocqueville, Alexis de, *The Old Regime and The Revolution*, New York: Harper, 1856.

—— *Democracy in America*, abridged by Richard D. Heffner (ed.), New York: Mentor Books, 1984.

Toranska, Teresa, *"Them": Stalin's Polish Puppets*, New York: Harper & Row, 1988.

Touraine, Alan, *Solidarity: Poland 1980–81*, Cambridge: Cambridge University Press, 1983.

Turner, Bryan S., "Outline of a theory of citizenship," in *Sociology*, vol. 24, no. 2, 1990, pp. 189–217.

Tusk, Donald, "Krajobraz po bitwie," *Przegląd Polityczny*, no. 30 (Spring 1996).

Tymowski, Andrzej, "The unwanted social revolution: Poland in 1989," in *East European Politics and Societies*, vol. 7, no. 2 (Spring 1993), pp. 169–202.

—— "The roots of counter-reform: Homo Sovieticus or moral economy?" paper presented at the 5th World Congress of Central and East European Studies, Warsaw, August 1995.

—— "Ethos reconsidered," in *East European Politics and Societies*, vol. 10, no. 1 (Winter 1996), pp. 157–160.

Van Kley, Dale (ed.), *The French Idea of Freedom: The Old Regime and the Declaration of Rights of 1789*, Stanford: Stanford University Press, 1994.

Waldron, Jeremy (ed.), *"Nonsense upon Stilts," Bentham, Burke and Marx on the Rights of Man*, London: Methuen, 1987.

Wałęsa, Lech, *A Way of Hope*, New York: Henry Holt, 1987.

Walicki, Andrzej, *Philosophy and Romantic Nationalism: The Case of Poland*, Oxford: Clarendon Press, 1982.

—— "Liberalism in Poland," *Critical Inquiry*, vol. 2, no. 1, 1988.

—— "The three traditions in Polish patriotism," in Stanislaw Gomulka and Antony Polonsky (eds.), *Polish Paradoxes*, London: Routledge, 1990.

—— *Marxism and the Leap to the Kingdom of Freedom: The Rise and Fall of the Communist Utopia*, Stanford: Stanford University Press, 1995.

Walsh, Richard, *Charleston's Sons of Liberty: A Study of the Artisans 1763–1789*, Columbia, SC: University of South Carolina Press, 1959.

Walzer, Michael, *The Revolution of the Saints: A Study in the Origins of Radical Politics*, Cambridge: Harvard University Press, 1965.

—— "A theory of revolution," in *Marxist Perspectives*, no. 5 (Spring 1979), pp. 30–44.

Wasilewski, Jacek, "The contract-based diet and elite formation in Poland," in *The Polish Sociological Bulletin*, no. 1, 1993, pp. 41–57.

Weber, Max, *The Protestant Ethic and the Spirit of Capitalism*, New York: Charles Scribner's Sons, 1958.

—— *On Charisma and Institution Building*, Introduction by S. N. Eisenstadt (ed.), Chicago: University of Chicago Press, 1968.

—— *Economy and Society*, Guenther Roth and Claus Wittich (eds.), Berkeley: University of California Press, 1978.

—— *Gesammelte Politische Schriften*, Tübingen: J. C. B. Mohr Verlag, 1988.

Wedel, Janine, "The ties that bind in Polish society," in Stanislaw Gomulka and Antony Polonsky (eds.), *Polish Paradoxes*, London: Routledge, 1990.

Weschler, Lawrence, *The Passion of Poland*, New York: Pantheon Books, 1984.

Wesołowski, Wlodzimierz, "Transition to democracy: the role of social and political pluralism," in *Sisyphus Sociological Studies*, vol. 7, 1991, pp. 79–94.

—— "Formation of political parties in post-communist Poland," in *Sisyphus. Social Studies*, vol. 1 (IX), 1993, pp. 9–32.

White, Morton, *The Philosophy of the American Revolution*, New York: Oxford University Press, 1978.

Wilentz, Sean, *Chants Democratic: New York City and the Rise of the American Working Class, 1788–1850*, Oxford: Oxford University Press, 1984.

Wills, Garry, *Inventing America: Jefferson's Declaration of Independencė*, New York: Vintage Books, 1979.

Wilson, Edmund, *To the Finland Station: A Study in the Writing and Acting of History*, New York: Farrar, Straus & Giroux, 1972.

Wnuk-Lipiński, Edmund (ed.), *After Communism: A Multidisciplinary Approach to Radical Social Change*, Warsaw: IFIS Publishers, 1995.

Wnuk-Lipiński, Edmund and Wasilewski, Jacek, "How much communism is left with us?" in *Politicus, Bulletin of the Institute of Political Studies*, Polish Academy of Sciences, Special Issue, August 1995, pp. 39–44.

Woloch, Isser, *The Jacobin Legacy: The Democratic Movement Under the Directory*, Princeton: Princeton University Press, 1970.

Wood, Gordon S., *The Radicalism of the American Revolution*, New York: Alfred A. Knopf, 1992.

Wright, Gordon, *France in Modern Times*, New York: W. W. Norton, 1987.

Ziółkowski, Marek, "The pragmatic shift in Polish social consciousness: with or against the tide of rising materialism?" in Edmund Wnuk-Lipiński (ed.), *After Communism: A Multidisciplinary Approach to Radical Social Change*, Warsaw: IFIS Publishers, 1995.

Index

abolitionism 61
Abramowski, Edward 172
absolutism 9, 45, 46, 77, 256
Adams, Samuel 56, 62, 69–70; Declaration of Rights (1772) 67, 69
Adamski, Władisław W. 249
agriculture, collectivization of 154, 155
Agulhon, Maurice 75
Allardt, Erik 231
American Civil War (1861–1865) 74
American Constitution (1789) 26, 46, 53, 67, 72–4, 272n; debates on 70–2; Fourteenth Amendment 121–2; ratification of 57
American Declaration of Independence (1776) 53, 59, 60, 67, 68, 75
American democracy, permeability of 72–4
American Revolution (1775) xi, 50, 60, 63, 260; antecedents 55–7; charismatic communities and the 62–7; and formal natural rights 52–74, 107; institutional consequences of the 67–74; institutional domains compared with French Revolution 102; and natural rights doctrine 57–62, 107
Anabaptism 120
ancien régime 78–80, 89–90
Anglican Church 56
Anti-Federalists 57, 71
anti-Semitism 226, 296n
Antraigues, Comte d' 77
Arblaster, Anthony 14
Arendt, Hannah 9
aristocracy, France 75–6
Aristotle 32
asceticism 119
Ash, Timothy Garton 3
Ausgleichsformel 167, 174
Austria 280n
authority: of Leninist Party 145–53; limits to 47–8; political 77
autonomy: defined 33, personal 31–2, 33, 287n; proof of 34–5; *see also* freedom

Babeuf, François-Noël 133, 229
Bailly, Sylvain 77
Baker, Keith Michael 230
balance of power 47–8; France 98–100
Balcerowicz Plan 209–10, 211–14, 217, 232, 235, 237–8, 240, 249–50, 252
Baltic coast strikes 162, 180, 193–4, 198
Barker, Ernest 58, 62, 64, 65, 201
Bauman, Zygmunt 2
Bentham, Jeremy 167
Berger, Suzanne 234
Bernhard, Michael 206
Bialecki, Ireneusz 244, 248
Bierut, Bolesław 153, 154
Bill of Rights (1791) 46, 59, 72
black community 61–2
Blum, Léon 126
Bolsheviks 144, 146, 150, 151
Bonald, Vicomte de 96
Bonapartism 95, 96
Borusewicz, Bogdan 186
Boston Tea Party (1773) 64
bourgeoisie 76, 78–9, 85, 99, 106, 140
Brezhnev, Leonid Ilich 152–3
Brinton, Crane 81, 91
Brissot, Jacques Pierre 83, 92
Bujak, Zbigniew 217–19, 223, 247–8
bureaucracies: compared 279n; French 101–2, 103
bureaucratization 129, 130, 131
Burke, Edmund 23

Burlamaqui, Jean-Jacques 59
Bushman, Richard L. 59
Butler, Justice 122

Calvert, Peter 11–12
capitalism: advanced, Weber on 31, 129–30; and equality of citizenship 131; legitimation by natural law 128–30; and natural law 105–32; Occidental form of (Weber) 110, 111; and Protestant ethic 120; relationship with liberalism 105–32; and the self-regulating market 110–11; the spirit of 21–2, 36, 109–10; Weber's definition 266n
cartels 125, 126
Catholic Church 19, 119: France 75–6; in Poland 153, 154, 156–7, 159–60, 165, 242–3, 283–4n, 297n; as model for KOR 173–4
Catholic University of Lublin 156
Catholicism, synthesis with socialist humanism 166–91, 256
Chałasiński, Józef 159
charisma 63: in conjunction with value-rationality 38–41, 51; and democracy 17, 36–41; in French Revolution 81–2; and natural law 37, 40–1; recognition of 38–9, 41; transformatory power of 38–9; Weber's concept of 16, 19, *see also* routinization of charisma
charismatic communities xi, 38–9, 41, 43, 51; of the American Revolution 54, 62–7; of the French Revolution 76, 77–8, 88–93; Leninist Party and 143–6; as precondition for revolution 107; of Solidarity 192–205, 225–31
charismatic domination 40–1; legitimacy of 13, 15–16
Chartism 131, 279n
Chateaubriand, François Auguste René, vicomte de 98
Chinese Revolution (1911) 7
Chirot, Daniel 1
Christianity 34
Church and the Left, The (Michnik) 173–4
Cicero 32
citizens: the charismatic creation of 50, 53–4; and self-government, France 90
Citizens' Committees, Poland 214, 216
citizens' interests 47–8
Citizen's Parliamentary Club, Poland (Obywatelski Klub Parlamentarny) 216
citizenship xi, 45–6, 51; active or passive 238, 297n; as an institutional domain 45–6, 49, 53, 67, 69, 93; collectivistic understanding in French Revolution 50–1, 77; French 80–1, 97, 103–4; imported American model to Poland 209–10, 211–12; individualistic understanding in American Revolution 50–1, 66–7; legitimation for Polish 238; as a new category of identification 107; in Poland 165–6, 168, 184–6, 203, 254, 297–8n; Solidarity's vision of Polish 192–7, 210–11, 231–9
civil rights 212–13; and natural rights 165; Paine on 23, 24; in Poland 164; versus human rights 138
civil rights movements 61–2, 74
civil service, French 100–1, 102
civil society 257; Polish 206; and political community 137–40
class interests, and capitalism 130–1
class struggle; French Revolution 76, 97; in revolution 6–8, 10; revolutionary Leninist 144–6
Clinton, Bill 122
collective action, value-rationality and charismatic setting 16–17
collective bargaining 9, 124, 126
collective consciousness 5
collective interests 124–7
collective rights: French emphasis on 82–7, 274n; and individual rights 50–1, 94, 166
collegiality 39
colonial society 55–6, 62, 116
Committees of Correspondence, American 54
common good 47–8
communism 9, 133–4, 140, 141–2; end of 1–2, 205; Michnik on 171; in Poland 240–1, 245–6; Polish resistance to ix, 158–60; Solidarity and 215–16
Communist Party, Poland 19, 152–3; corruption in 189–91; legacy of 206–7; *see also* Leninist Party
Condorcet, Marquis de 87
Conference of Workers' Self-Management, Poland 155
Congregationalism 65

conscience, and dignity 175–6, 177
consciousness, transformation of 54, 76–7, 88, 142, 143, 146, 258
consensual democracy 258, 300n
conservatism 50, 51
constitution: formally written 46–7; Leninist 148–9; Paine on forming of a 25, 26; and popular sovereignty 46–7; supreme in America 102, 151, 272n
contract rights 121, 123, 124
cooperatives, Polish 172
core elite 43, 50; of American Revolution 56–8, 62–7; in French Revolution 78, 81–2, 85–7, 88–9; Polish 158–60, 162–4, 165; revolutionary, crystallization of 106; of Solidarity 212, 214–19, 223–31
corporatism, in Poland 244
Critique of the Gotha Program (Marx) 140
"Critique of Hegel's Philosophy of Law" (Marx) 136, 141
Cromwell, Oliver 36, 37
Crooked Circle Club (Klub Krzywego Koła) 155
Czech Republic 261, 297n
Czechoslovakia (1968) 4, 6, 164, 191

Darnton, Robert 82–3
De Gaulle, Charles 97, 98, 100
Décadi 91
Declaration of the Rights of Man, Universal 242–3
Declaration of the Rights of Man (and Citizen 1789) 2, 32, 75, 93–4, 102–3, 125, 242
democracy: and advanced capitalism 129–31; characteristics of modern 22, 45–51; and charisma 17, 36–41; disenchantment of Poles with 247–9; Huntington's definition 29–30; ideal typical representation of modern 19, 21–51; instrumentalization of in Poland 232–9; and natural law 17, 40–1; revolution and Solidarity ix–x, 1–20; the spirit of modern 21–31, 49–51; Weberian theory of 13–14, 15–20, 21–51; and the will of the people 21, *see also* direct democracy; latecomers to democracy; plebiscitary democracy
democratic centralism 147–8
democratic rule, types of 39
democratic socialism, in Poland 165, 169
"democratic societies" 70, 272n
Democratic Union, Poland (Unia Demokratyczna) 237
democratization x, 257, 294n
Descartes, René 170
Dickinson, John 60
dictatorship of the proletariat 147–51
Diderot, Denis 82
dignity: and freedom 210–11; and human rights 174–82; of man as guiding principle of Solidarity 167–70, 174
direct democracy 39, 290–1n
Directoire period (1795–9) 95
divine right, rule by 44, 46
division of powers 39, 71–2
domination: legitimacy of traditional 13, 15–16; Weber's typology of legitimate 15–16
Dorr, Harbottle 69–70
Douglas, Mary, on institutions 44

East Central Europe 208, 261
Eastern Europe, collapse of communism (1989) 1, 205
"Economic backwardness in historical perspective" (Gerschenkron) 257
economic Darwinism, in Poland 232
economic integration, global (Sachs) 277n
economic interests 109; and political rights 123
economic liberalism 257, 299n
economics, populist 131
economy, centrally planned 148
Economy and Society (Weber) 18
égalité 77
égalité de fait, l' 95
Eisenstadt, S.N. 42, 43–4
Ekiert, Grzegorz 235–6
elections 45, 47–8
elites, reform-oriented 257–8; *see also* core elite
emancipation, political and human 135–9
empiricism 119
Employee Stock Ownership Plans, Poland 214
Encyclopédie 82
Engels, Friedrich 141, 143
England, colonial resistance to 55–6, 62

Enlightenment 2, 17, 45, 46, 79, 82, 120, 129, 256; compared with humanism 188; *philosophes* 36, 167
equality 28, 32, 33, 45, 84, 96–7; before God 34; before the law 68; French Revolution 100–1; grounded in natural law 60–1; social 181–3, 189, 210, *see also égalité*; *égalité de fait*
Erasmus, Desiderius 186
Estates General 80–1
ethical democracy (Tischner) 177–8
ethical norms, reason and 27–8
ethos 16; of modern democracy 22; of natural rights 27, 30, 40, *see also* Solidarity, ethos of
European Union 261, 280n; membership of 259, 260
executive, French 98–9, 100

façade democracies 48, 244–5, 257–8
Federalists 57, 71–2, 270n
Feinberg, Joel 168
feudalism 44, 45, 78, 93, 104, 256
Feuillants 92
Fifth Republic, France (1958–) 98, 108
Foot, Michael 22
formal natural law principles 17–18, 35, 51; and capitalist development 121–4
formal natural rights: and the American Revolution 52–74; and substantive rights, in Poland 166, 238–9, 255
Forten, James 62
Fortuna, Grzegorz 200
Fourth Republic, France (1946–58) 99, 127
Fowle, Daniel 59
France: state as guarantor and provider of rights 100–3, 151, 222; substantive natural rights principle 75–104, 125–8
Franklin, Benjamin 22
fraternité 77
free competition, Weber on 124
free market xi, 8; as institutional domain of liberal capitalism 53; and natural law 109–32; origins of the 109–32; in Poland 249–55
Free Trade Unions, Poland 157, 283n
free will 170, 176
freedom 28–9; as collective self-actualization 135–9; and democracy 177–8; experience of 9; Marx on 134; positive and negative definitions 31; the will to 31–5, *see also* autonomy; emancipation; liberty
freedom of competition 121
freedom of contract 121, 123, 124
freedom of information 73, 273n
Freedom Union, Poland (Unia Wolności) 237
French, national character 262
French Constitutent Assembly 75
French constitutions (1789–1958) 25, 98–9
French National Assembly (1789) 77, 81, 88, 230
French Revolution (1789) 2, 7, 23, 260; antecedents 78–82; charismatic communities 76, 77–8, 88–93; charismatic impact of 17, 36, 37; institutional consequences 93–104; institutional domains compared with American Revolution 102; middle strata in 105–6; and natural rights doctrine 76, 82–8; Solidarity compared with 229–31; and substantive natural rights 75–104, 107–8
French Revolution (1848) 99
Furet, François 75, 96, 97, 99, 108

Gadsden, Christopher 63–4
Gajda, Jan 190–1
Gay, Peter 36
Gdańsk Accords (1980) 191, 199
Gdańsk shipyards ix, 181, 197
general will 91, 108, 229–30; (Rousseau) 83–5, 88, 230
Geremek, Bronisław 214, 215, 216
German Ideology, The (Marx) 142
Germany: bureaucracy 279n; East 4, 6; small proprietors in 125–6; social market economy 258
Gerschenkron, Alexander, "Economic backwardness in historical perspective" 257
Gierek, Edward 153, 154, 160–2, 167, 248
Girondins 92
Gomułka, Wladislaw 153, 154, 156
Gorbachev, Mikhail 9
government: Paine on formation of 24, 26; and protection of rights to property 114, *see also* limited government
Grabowska, Mirosława 241

Greece 259, 280n
Greek polis 32
Greenfeld, Liah 51
Gross, Jan T. 206, 212, 215, 218, 219
Grotius, Hugo 118

Hamilton, Alexander 56, 59–60, 70, 74, 123
happiness: collective 188; right to 67; security for the pursuit of 94
Harbison, Winfred A. 68
Hart, Levi 62
Hayek, Friedrich August von 111
Hébert, Jacques-René 92
Hegel, Georg Wilhelm Friedrich 141, 170
Held, David 21
Helsinki Committee for Human Rights, Polish 224
Heltman, Wiktor 188
hereditary rights 53
Hermassi, Elbaki 9–10
Herrschaft see domination
Heyns, Barbara 244, 248
hierarchy 49, 50, 55
Higonnet, Patrice 97, 102–3
Hirschman, Albert O. 157
"historical individuality" 21–2, 50
historical sociology 10
history, Marx's dialectical evolution of 141
History of Polish Literature (Miłosz) 186
Hobsbawm, Eric 106
Holzer, Jerzy 225–6
human rights 9; and dignity 174–82; versus civil rights 138
humanism 166, 292n; Marxist 169–70; Polish 165, 186–8, 261; synthesis with Catholicism 166–91, 256
Hungary (1956) 164, 191, 261, 284n
Huntington, Samuel P. 123, 260; on democracy 29–30

ideal types, Weber's 19
idealism 107
ideas: relationship with actions 54; role of 10, 11–15 (in French Revolution 76)
ideology 12–14
impersonalism 119, 247; charismatic 147, 150–3
inalienable rights 44, 60, 68, 188
Independent Labor Union *see* Solidarity
individual rights 23, 71–2, 76, 121; and collective rights 50–1, 94, 166; in Poland 223–4
individualism 31, 119, 274n; ethical 169–70; in American Revolution 50–1, 67–8, 85, 273n; Marx on origins of 137; Protestant 256
institution building: defined 42, 44; in France 75, 87–8; Solidarity's failure in 230–1
institutional consequences: of the American Revolution 67–74; of the French Revolution 93–104
institutional domains 49–51, 67, 69, 93; defined 43; and differences in institutional development 50, 51; impact of Solidarity on 231–55; of Leninism 146–53; of liberal capitalism 53; of Solidarity 209–31; in USA and Western Europe 44–5
institutionalization 41–51; and formal rights 107–8; of natural rights doctrine 107, 130–1; and substantive rights 108
institutions: definition 42; double aspect of social 42; Douglas on 44; formal or informal 43; gap with ideals 260; North on 42–3; Weberian analysis of 42
instrumental rationality 259; and value-rationality 28–30, 40–1, 50, 72; Weber on 27–8
intellectuals 11; and workers in Poland 197–8, 202, 204, 233–9, 239–45, 294n; opposition to in Solidarity 225–7, 228–31; Polish 20, 154–5, 156, 157–8, 162; and rule of law in Poland 245–9; view of economy in Poland 249–55
interests: relationship with rights 108–9; representation of individual 47–8; role of 10–11, 29–30, 37
interpretative sociology, Weber's 18
"invisible hand" (Adam Smith) 116, 117, 122
"iron cage" (Weber) 129–30

Jackson, Andrew 61
Jacobin clubs xi 81, 85, 86, 88, 89, 91–2, 99
Jacobins 95, 96, 107
Japan 258, 279n; consensual democracy 300n
Jaruzelski, Wojciech 215

Jedlicki, Jerzy 238, 239
Jefferson, Thomas 22, 56, 59, 61, 66, 67, 68–9, 69, 123
John Paul II, Pope 162, 178–9, 187
Jowitt, Ken 5, 134–5, 150, 152, 157
July Monarchy (1830–48) 95–6, 97–8
justice 32, 35, 52, *see also* social justice

Kamiński, Bartlomiej 222–3, 224
Karl, Terry x
Katz, Stanley 222
Kelly, Alfred H. 68
Khrushchev, Nikita Sergeevich, de-Stalinization campaign (1956) 152, 153–4
KIK (Clubs of Catholic Intelligensia) 180–1
Kisielewski, Stefan 173
Kolakowski, Leszek 175, 176; *Toward a Marxist Humanism* 169–70
Kolankiewicz, George 231, 233, 252
Kolarska-Bobińska, Lena 234, 250, 251
KOR (Workers' Defence Committe, later renamed Committee for Social Self-Defence) (Komitat Obrony Robotników) 7, 163–4, 172–4, 180, 197–8, 215–16, 221, 226, 284n; on non-violence 182
Koralewicz, Jadwiga 232, 236, 240
Kowalski, Sergiusz 227
Kramnick, Isaac 22
Król, Marcin 210, 223
Kubik, Jan 207, 235–6
Kulerski, Wiktor 242
Kumar, Krishan 2
Kurczewski, Jacek 158, 159, 215, 244
Kurón, Jacek 169, 211, 237–8, 249, 251–2, 254

labor: Adam Smith on 115–16; commercialization of 110; division of, Marx on 140, 142; free 110; Protestantism and 118–20; right to full product of one's 124, 127–8
Lafayette, Marie-Joseph, Marquis de 31
land enclosures 112, 114
Lassalle, Ferdinand 140
latecomers to democracy x 18, 50–1, 105
latecomers to liberal capitalism 129–30, 208–9, 255, 256–7, 260
laws: in American Revolution 69–73, 273n; Paine on 49, 50
Le Chapelier 92
leadership 77; charismatic 39–41 (Eisenstadt on 43–4; of Lenin 145); French Revolution 90–1, 97
Leclerc 90
Lefebvre, Georges 76, 107
Left, strength in Poland 241–2
legal codes, natural rights and 36–7
legal nihilism 246–7
legal positivism 129, 245–7
legalism, Polish civic 245
legislature, French 98, 99
legitimacy, need for democratic x–xi, 31–2
legitimation: by power of natural law 31–5; modes of 259–60; of social groupings 44
legitimation of democracy 14, 19, 31–5, 40; Weberian alternative 15–20
Lenin, Vladimir Illich 141, 142–3, 167; on control 149; "correct line" 150–2; *What is to be Done?* 144
Lenin Shipyards 157
Leninism 105, 132, 151, 256; corruption in 152–3; institutional domains of 146–53, *see also* Marxism-Leninism
Leninist Party 5, 132, 134–5, 143–53; corruption in 157, 160–2
"Lesson in Dignity, A" (Michnik) 179
Letters from Prison (Michnik) 171
Levellers 36, 268n
lex naturae (Weber) 118–20
liberal capitalism ix, 109, 256; affinities of national political culture with 260–2; criticism of 258–9; institutional domains of 53 (impact of Solidarity on 231–55); legitimation by natural rights doctrine 132; Marxist-Leninist response to 133–64; and Solidarity 206–55, *see also* latecomers to liberal capitalism
liberal capitalist democracy, characteristics of xi
liberal capitalist development: and different institutional bases 280n; and natural rights 105–32
liberal democracy, diffusion of 276n
Liberal Democratic Congress, Poland (Kongres Liberalno-Demokratyczny) 237
liberal democratic countries 48; institutional differences 52
liberal democratic revolution, conditions for 105–9

liberalism 125–6; institutional domains of 93; legitimation by natural law 128–30; relationship with capitalism 105–32
liberté 77
liberty 60–2, 67–9, 84, 94; Adam Smith on 116
Lille Bureau of Finances (1788) 45
limited government 47–8, 67–9, 102, 222, 224, 280n
Lipset, Seymour Martin 131
local government, Polish participation in 233, 237–8
localism, in Poland 161
Locke, John 59, 105, 111–12, 119–20; *Second Treatise of Government* 112–15
Los, Maria 213, 245
Louis Bonaparte 97, 98
Louis XIV 78
Louis XVI 78, 80, 97
Louis-Philippe 98
"lower orders" 54, 269n
Lynd, Staughton xi

McDonald, Forrest 57
Macfie, A.L. 117
Macpherson, C.P. 115
Madison, James 48, 52, 56, 71, 239
man: alienation of (Marx) 137; defining 33; faculty of improvement 66–7; in humanism 166–9; Paine on origins of 23–4, 29, 34; rights as an individual 23
Manning, William 70, 72, 272n
Marivaux, Martin de 81
market, different patterns of development 128
market economy 110
market regulation, France 126–8
Marx, Karl 11, 141–2; *Critique of the Gotha Program* 140; "Critique of Hegel's Philosophy of Law" 136, 141; critique of natural rights 20, 132, 133–4, 135–43; and dictatorship of the proletariat 147; on freedom 134; *On the Jewish Question* 135–6; rejects natural and civil rights linkage 165, 167; *The German Ideology* 142
Marxism 124–5, 169–70, 281n; in Poland 219, 224–5, 293n
Marxism-Leninism, response to natural rights and liberal capitalism 133–64
materialism 31, 141
Mayhew, Jonathan 58
Mazowiecki, Tadeusz 209, 213, 216, 217–18, 219, 224, 238, 240, 241, 242, 245–7, 292–3n; declaration of a "thick line" after communism (1989) 245
meaning, Weber on 18–19
mechanization 130
media, and democratic proceduralism in Poland 245
mercantilism 115, 116
Merrill, Michael 71–2
Michnik, Adam 7, 157, 159, 161, 165, 167, 187, 191; "A Lesson in Dignity" 168, 179; *Letters from Prison* 171; as a secular humanist 169–74; *The Church and the Left* 173–4
middle class: capitalist 8; new Polish 232–3, 255, 261; revolutionary 7–8, *see also* bourgeoisie
"middle strata": French 105–6; Polish 158–64, 188–9
Mignet, F.A. 93
Miłosz, Czesław 1, 3, 187, 262; *History of Polish Literature* 186
minimum standard of living, right to a 124, 127, 183
Minutemen militias 54
Miszalska, Anita 232, 247
mobilization model (Tilly) 11
modernity 2
modernization theory 2
monarchism 9, 44, 45
monarchy 46, 49; absolutist 77, 78; hereditary, Paine on 25
money, role of 113, 115, 123
Monnet, Jean 127
monopolies, power of 123, 125
Moore, Barrington 11
moral authority 19
moral sentiment (Smith) 117
Morawski, Witold 212
Morehead v. Tipaldo 122

Napoleon Bonaparte 77, 88, 97, 98, 103
Nash, Gary 61
nation, concept of the 51
national character 262
national culture, in Poland 165
national economic planning, France 127
national identity, French 92–3

national political culture, affinities with liberal capitalism 260–2
nationalism 256, 257; French 97; Polish 159, 162–3, 204, 215, 254, 294n
natural law 63; and capitalism 105–32; characteristics 32; charisma and democracy 40–1; the charismatic presentation of 36–41; defining 32–3; and free market 109–32; legitimating power of 31–5; and positive law 120–1; as a type of value-rationality 32; Weber's definition xi 15, 120, *see also* ethos of natural rights
natural morality, Protestant concept of 36, 119–20
natural rights 33, 44, 212–13; and the charismatic creation of citizens 53–4; charismatic presentation of 17, 21–51; and civil rights 165; differences in interpretation of 53; and liberal capitalist development 105–32; Marxist-Leninist response to 133–64; Paine on 23, 24; Solidarity's articulation of 165–205
natural rights doctrine: and the American Revolution 57–62; belief in as precondition for democratic revolution 106–7; and French Revolution 76, 82–8; Marx's critique of 20, 132, 133–4, 135–43; and modern democracy xi 17; in Poland 166–91
New Deal 122
new economic order 119–20
nomenklatura 183, 189, 220, 235, 250, 256
non-governmental organizations, in Poland 232–3, 237–8
non-violence 9, 177, 180, 182, 189, 197, 203, 236
North, Douglass C., on institutions 42–3
Nowak, Tadeusz 157, 161–2

Ochab, Edward 149
oligarchy 131
On the Jewish Question (Marx) 135–6
opposition, in Poland 153–64
Osiatynski, Wiktor 223–4

Paine, Thomas: definition of freedom 31; divine origin of man 23–4, 29, 34; on laws 49, 50; on the public good 84–5; on rights and interests 109; *The Rights of Man* 22–9
Palmer, R.R. 51, 59, 78, 82, 85, 127
pamphlets 73, 273n
Paris Commune (1871) 99
participation: and democracy 183–5; French Revolution 90
Patriotic Society 56
patronage 55
peasantry 7, 8, 300n; French 79; Polish 159, 162
Pelczynski, Zbigniew A. 153, 156, 159
People's Councils, Poland 184
Philadelphia mechanics 56, 64–5
Pico della Mirandola 166
plebiscitary democracy 39
pluralism, Poland 184
Po Prostu 155
Polan, A.J. 145, 148
Poland: antecedents to Solidarity 153–64; charismatic communities of Solidarity 192–205; dissatisfaction with party politics 239–45; elections (1989) 4, 205, 214; ex-communists in power (1993) 240–1, 246; and expectations generated by Solidarity 243–5, 260–2; first non-communist government 4, 205; imported model of state 220–5; martial law (1981) 5, 204, 226–7, 291n; natural rights doctrine in 166–91; since 1989 206–55, 296n; Stalinism in 153–7
Polanyi, Karl 110, 111
Poles: national character 262; support for Solidarity 5, 243
Polish Bill of Rights, proposed (1990–3) 239
Polish Constitution: May 1791 187; new (1997 referendum) 239, 247, 297–8n
Polish Revolution: in comparative context 256–62; and French Revolution 261; nature of the 1–10
Polish Students Association 154
Polish United Workers' Party (PUWP) 153
political associations 66
political community 34–5; and civil society 137–40; institutional basis of 45–6
political parties, Polish 206
political processes, leading to revolution 11–12

political rights, and economic interests 123
popular representation *see* representative government
popular sovereignty 12, 51, 84; French Revolution 89–90
popular will *see* will of the people
populism 131, 204
Portugal 259
positive law, and natural law 32–3, 37, 120–1
post-colonial states, bureaucracy in 279n
post-communist governments 292n
postmodernity 2
poverty, Locke on 114–15
power relations 24, 231
privatism, citizen, in Poland 232
privatization, in Poland 232–9, 235, 241, 249–55, 293–4n
privilege 49, 50
procedural fairness 49
proceduralism x-xi, 44, 49, 50; as an institutional domain 44, 45, 49, 53, 67, 69, 93; democracy and 29–30; in France 101–2; in Poland 245–9, 253
profit, and capitalism 109–10
progress, idea of 66–7
Progressives, US 123, 131
proletarian will 134–5
proletariat 142, 143; *see also* dictatorship of the proletariat
property: Adam Smith on 115, 117; Locke on natural rights to 112–15
property rights 67, 121, 125, 214, 219
Protestant Ethic and the Spirit of Capitalism, The (Weber) 21–2, 36, 109–10, 118–20, 129–30
Protestant sects 17, 36, 37, 41, 65
Protestantism 55, 58, 118, 256; and ethical conduct 36
Przeworski, Adam x
public access to government 73
public community, in Greek and Roman times 33–4
public virtue: in American Revolution 69; and charismatic impersonalism of Leninism 147, 150–3; defined 48–9; French Revolution 88–9, 91, 92–3; Polish tradition 211, 221, 253; procedurally defined 45, 48–9 (in France 100–1, 103); and state 222
Pufendorf, Samuel von 59, 65, 118
Puritan Revolution (1640) 13, 14, 36, 118, 120

Quincy, Samuel 58

Radicals, French 99, 131
Ramsay, David 53
Raphael, D.D. 117
rational-legal domination, legitimacy of 13, 15–16
rationalization 129
reason: capacity for 35; charismatic glorification of 17; culture of 45; and ethical norms 27–8; and the institutionalization of rights 41–51
"refolution" 3
reforms, liberal capitalist: resistance to 257–8, 290n; social support base 258–9
Renaissance 166
representation 260; no taxation without 55; Paine on 23, 25; parliamentary 39; principle of popular 45, 47; right to, and right to live in dignity 181–91
representative government xi, 44, 45, 47–8, 50; as an institutional domain 44, 45, 49, 53, 67, 69, 93; in Poland 239–45, 253; Solidarity and 213–14; to protect citizens' rights 109; weak tradition in France 103, 108
republicanism, extra-parliamentary 96
resistance: cultural to French Revolution 78; legitimation of 165; to liberal capitalist reforms, 257–8, 290n
Restoration period, France (1814–30) 95, 98
Revere, Paul 64
revolution: class aspects of 6–8, 10; democracy and Solidarity 1–20; demonstration effect 9–10; "marginal" 4; Walzer's definition 6, 7
"revolution of dignity" 191
Revolution of the Saints, The (Walzer) 12–13
revolutionary class 6–7
revolutionary conditions, for liberal democratic revolution 105–9
revolutionary consciousness 134, 142
revolutionary ideology 231
Rice, David 61
Richir, Marc 98–9
Right, in Poland 242
right to rule 45–6

right to work 124, 176–7, 183, 239
rights: balance between individual and collective 94; institutionalization of, and reason 41–51; relationship with interests 108–9; Rousseau's definition of collectivity of 82
rights of man 24, 59–62, 188; and capitalism and liberalism 128–9
Rights of Man, The (Paine) 22–9
Robespierre, Maximilien de 17, 37, 77, 88, 90–1, 92, 102
Robotnik 163
Roman law 32
Roosevelt, Franklin D. 122
Round Table Talks, Poland (1989) 4, 6, 214, 215, 217
Rousseau, Jean-Jacques 80, 82, 83–6, 90, 230
routinization of charisma 17, 39, 42
rules and procedures, democratic in American Revolution 62–7
Russia: mafia crimes in 248; Tsarist 146–7
Russian Revolution 7, 8, 129, 144, 147
Rychard, Andrzej 232–3, 246

Sachs, Jeffrey 111, 209, 214, 218
Saint-Just, Louis de 90–1
Sakharov, Andrei 174
sans-culottes 85, 92, 95, 127, 133, 229
Scandinavian countries 258, 280n, 300n
Schama, Simon 77, 80, 85
Schmitter, Philippe x
Schöpflin, George 206, 207
scientific socialism 144–6, 148, 151
Second Republic, France (1848–52) 99
Second Treatise of Government (Locke) 112–15
"Sect, Church and Democracy" (Weber) 17
Sejm 184, 215
self-employment, in Poland 250–1, 253
self-government: tradition of community in America 65–6; wish in Poland 183–5
sets of relations 21, 28, 300n
Sewell, William H. 12
Sigismund I 186
Skąpska, Grażyna 223, 235, 245, 246
Skocpol, Theda 7, 8; on ideology 12, 14–15; on structures 10
small property owners: Adam Smith on 117; France 104, 108, 125–6, 127–8
Smith, Adam 105, 109, 111, 119–20, 125, 252; legacy in Poland 219, 225; *The Theory of Moral Sentiments* 117; *Wealth of Nations* 115–18
social coalitions xi, 132, 254–5
social justice 181, 188, 213, 246, 250–1
social leveling: in American Revolution 62–7; French Revolution 88–90, 101; inadequate in Poland 225–31, 261
social mobility: France 78–80; stalling of as a revolutionary precondition 105–6
social order 15
Social Self-Defense Committee, Polish *see* KOR
social welfare: legislation and substantive natural rights principles 125; legislation in USA 121–4; withdrawal of in Poland 231–9
socialism 50, 51, 76, 133, 256, 257; in France 96; open and closed 178; and substantive natural law axioms 124, *see also* scientific socialism
society, as mutual and reciprocal interest 29
Sociology of Law, The (Weber) 36–7, 120–4
"Solidarity 80" 236
Solidarity (Solidarność): antecedent conditions 132–64; articulation of natural rights 108, 165–205; autonomy of 19; Center for Social and Labor Tasks 181; changes since 1989 ix, 206, 289n; charismatic communities of 192–205; compared with French Revolution 229–31; Congress (1981) 196–7, 198, 201, 203; criticisms of 291n; and democracy ix-x, 263n; documents of (1980–1) 180–91; emergence (1980–1) 4–6, 19, 164; established as an independent trade union 155; ethos of x, 6, 19, 188–91, 192–205, 208, 209–12, 287n (departure from 214–30); fragmentation of legacy 224–31, 289n; "identity crisis" in authority 218, 292n; impact on institutional domains of liberal capitalism 231–55; legal existence (1980–1) 192, 206; and Leninist Party 134–5; and liberal capitalism 206–55; membership 185; mixed legacy 253–5; National Committee 214; and "new middle

class" 158; phases of ix–x; Program (1981) 183, 210, 211, 221; revolution and democracy 1–20; a self-limiting movement 4–5; as a social movement 186–91; and society–state opposition 220–3; Statute 181, 182; strengths of 208, 231–55; suppression (Dec 1981) 191; underground resistance 5, 204–5; Ursus branch 296n, 299n; weaknesses of 207–8, 209–31
Sons of Liberty xi, 54, 56, 64, 107
sovereignty: concept in modern democracy 45–6; French conception of 94; multiple 4–6; parliamentary, debated in America 71; of the people 97; pre-American Revolution understanding of 53
Soviet Union 7, 152, 256; *see also* Russia
środowiska 227–8, 240, 243–4, 294n
Stalin, Joseph 149, 152
Stalinism, in Poland 153–7
Stamp Act, US (1765) 56
Staniszkis, Jadwiga 218, 219
Staszewski, Stefan 145–6, 155, 156
state: as embodiment of the general will (France) 84–6, 87; ethos of service to in France 100–3; interventionist role with substantive rights principles 18, 125–8, 220–2; limits to role with formal rights principles 18; and public virtue 222; redistributive role of Polish 188–9; role in establishing parameters of legitimate participation 35; role in fostering economic modernization 257
Stoicism 117, 166, 170
Stone, Justice 123
strike communities, Polish 193–9
strikes 177; incidence in Poland 235–7, 248; Poland (1980) 190–1, 192, 200
student uprising, Poland (1968) 171
substantive natural law principles 17–18, 35, 51; and capitalist development 124–7
substantive rationality, Weber on 267n
substantive rights 95, 96; and formal rights 166; and French Revolution 75–104
Supreme Court, US 122–3
Sutherland, Justice 122–3
Świderski, Bronisław 213–14
Szczepanski, Maciej 161
Szyłak, Jan 190

taxation, not without representation 55
Taylor, A.J.P. 22
Terror, the (1793–4) 78, 87, 95, 230
Theory of Moral Sentiments, The (Smith) 117
Third Estate 76–7, 80, 87
Third Republic, France (1870–1940) 99, 126
Tilly, Charles 3–4, 5, 6, 8, 12; on group interests 10–11; on role of ideas 11–12; on Weber 13
Tischner, Józef 169, 185, 187; Catholic humanist 174–82
Tocqueville, Alexis de 65–6, 72–3, 96, 98, 262
tolerance 178–80, 186–8
Touraine, Alain 196–7, 201, 202–3, 204
Toward a Marxist Humanism (Kolakowski) 169–70
trade unions *see* unions
Turgot, Anne Robert Jacques 82
Turowicz, Jerzy 250
Tymińksi, Stan 240–1
Tymowski, Andrzej 227
tyranny 48, 131

Union of Labor, Polish (Unia Pracy) 241, 297n
unions: competition for Solidarity ix; free Polish 163–4, 180, 236; Polish in private sector 250–1; Russian 144
Universal Declaration of the Rights of Man *see* Declaration of the Rights of Man
urbanization, Polish 7, 158–9
utilitarianism 111

value-rationality 31–2, 76, 130–1, 143; commitment to liberalism 260; of ethos of natural rights 27–8; and individual action 16–17; and instrumental rationality 28–30, 40–1, 50, 72; role in charismatic context 38–41, 51; Weber's definition 27–8; Weber's use of concept 15
Vattel, Emmerich de 59
violence, in French Revolution 81–2
Virginia Declaration (1776) 68

wage-labor contracts 113, 114
Wałęsa, Lech 7, 19, 157, 187, 192, 214, 241, 283n; charisma of 193, 199–205; criticisms of 228, 230; leadership

216–17, 224–31; loss of charisma 228–31, 247–8; under house arrest 205
Walicki, Andrzej 134, 135, 139, 187
Wallerstein, Immanuel 9
Walzer, Michael 8, 118, 120; definition of revolutions 6, 7; on ideology 12–13; *The Revolution of the Saints* 12–13, 14
Warren, Joseph 64
Warsaw, demonstration (1996) ix
Washington, George 70
Wealth of Nations (Smith) 115–18
Weber, Max 258; on advanced capitalism 31; on charismatic authority 201; on civil rights 128–30; on collective action 143; collective definitions 13; definition of capitalism 266n; definition of natural law xi 15, 120; *Economy and Society* 18; on free competition 124; instrumental rationality 27–8; and legitimation of democracy 15–20, 266n; on Protestant sects 65; on scientific socialism 145; "Sect, Church and Democracy" 17; on substantive rationality 267n; *The Protestant Ethic and the Spirit of Capitalism* 21–2, 36, 109–10, 118–20, 129–30; *The Sociology of Law* 36–7, 120–4; on Western capitalism 110, 111
Webster, Daniel 229
Webster, Noah 61–2
Wedel, Janine 227
Werfel, Roman 150–1, 154, 157
Wesolowski, Włodzimierz 209, 243–4
West European democracy, as guardianship 74
What is to be Done? (Lenin) 144
Wiatr, Jerzy 157
Wilentz, Sean 61, 71–2
will of the people 77, 88, 130, 132; and democracy 21
will of society 182, 211
will to freedom 31–5
Wise, John 58, 65
Wojtyła, Cardinal Karol *see* John Paul II, Pope
Wood, Gordon S. 55, 56, 229
work ethic *see* labor
workers 7; and intellectuals in Poland 20, 197–8, 202, 204, 227–31, 233–9, 239–45 (and economy 249–55); suspicion of proceduralism 245–9
workers' councils, autonomous Polish 155, 157, 162, 170
workers' uprising, Poland (1956) 153
working class 50; French 99; Marxism and the 133–4; Polish 172–3
Wright, Gordon 126, 128, 131
Wyszyński, Cardinal 156, 159

Yalta (1945) 189

Zamoyski, Jan 187
Ziółkowski, Marek 232, 240